Eight Outcasts

The publisher and the University of California Press Foundation gratefully acknowledge the generous support of the Sue Tsao Endowment Fund in Chinese Studies.

Eight Outcasts

Social and Political Marginalization in China under Mao

Yang Kuisong

Translated and with an introduction
by Gregor Benton and Ye Zhen

UNIVERSITY OF CALIFORNIA PRESS

University of California Press, one of the most distinguished university presses in the United States, enriches lives around the world by advancing scholarship in the humanities, social sciences, and natural sciences. Its activities are supported by the UC Press Foundation and by philanthropic contributions from individuals and institutions. For more information, visit www.ucpress.edu.

University of California Press
Oakland, California

Originally published as *Bianyuan ren jishi* by Guangdong renmin chuban she, Guangzhou, 2016.

Library of Congress Cataloging-in-Publication Data

Names: Yang, Kuisong, author. | Benton, Gregor, translator, writer of introduction. | Ye, Zhen, 1982- translator, writer of introduction.
Title: Eight outcasts : social and political marginalization in China under Mao / Yang Kuisong ; translated and with an introduction by Gregor Benton and Ye Zhen.
Other titles: "Bian yuan ren" ji shi. English
Description: Oakland, California : University of California Press, [2020] | "Originally published as Bianyuanren jishi by Guangdong renmin chuban she, Guangzhou, 2016." | Includes bibliographical references and index.
Identifiers: LCCN 2019016558 (print) | LCCN 2019019830 (ebook) | ISBN 9780520325272 (cloth : alk. paper) | ISBN 9780520325289 (pbk. : alk. paper) | ISBN 9780520974241 (ebook)
Subjects: LCSH: China—History—1949-1976. | China—History—Cultural Revolution, 1966-1976--Biography.
Classification: LCC DS778.7 .Y38413 2020 (print) | LCC DS778.7 (ebook) | DDC 951.05/60922—dc23
LC record available at https://lccn.loc.gov/2019016558
LC ebook record available at https://lccn.loc.gov/2019019830

Manufactured in the United States of America

29   28   27   26   25   24   23   22   21   20
10   9   8   7   6   5   4   3   2   1

CONTENTS

TRANSLATORS' INTRODUCTION

This book is unusual if not unique in English in that it gives voice to a class of Chinese—social outcasts and counter-revolutionaries—who have rarely or never been allowed to speak freely for and about themselves in public. Even here, they speak through an official filter, that of the minor cadres in the factories, offices, and prisons who recorded their interrogations and in some cases dictated their confessions. So the book is the antithesis of most writing about China and its revolution, which focuses on rulers and leaders and touches on "the masses" at most in the form of high-level generalizations. In this book, the lives of lowly Chinese in trouble with the authorities rise into unaccustomed view. They represent a fairly typical selection of such cases.

All those affected ended in dire straits, sometimes as a result of bad luck, usually because of thought crimes or even real crimes, though of a nature that in other societies and at other times might be classed as minor wrongdoing or no wrongdoing. Chi Weirong, a pleasure-seeker and petty thief whose success as a teacher went to his head, is an example of someone who, as a result (in part) of bad timing, ended up forever ruined. However, Chi was fortunate compared with the old man described in Yang's introduction, who started out picking pockets and ended up before a firing squad as a counter-revolutionary.

The author himself, Yang Kuisong, could easily have ended up in the same plight as the characters his book describes, for he too was arrested and briefly jailed in 1976—for what in China was, and still is, the heinous crime of speaking out publicly against the authorities, in his case by putting up posters criticizing Mao's "Gang of Four" in the last months of their reign. Fortunately for him, by the time of his arrest the political tide had begun to turn; Mao died and the "Gang of Four" soon collapsed. After six months in prison, Yang was released. He not only escaped the fate of a counter-revolutionary but eventually became one of China's best and best-known liberal historians, a voice for its voiceless. In this book, Yang painstakingly pieces together the fate of eight counter-revolutionaries, bad elements, and other "people with problems" between 1949 and the late 1970s, on the basis of a study of their records. Through the detailed accounts found in these files, we become acquainted with how it was to be an object of the constantly twisting and turning political campaigns waged in China after 1949 in the name of revolution.

Most modern revolutions, beginning with the French, started with reigns of terror, the institutionalized application of force to the revolution's real or supposed opponents. Its purpose, in Marx's words, was to shorten "the old society's murderous death throes and the new society's bloody birth throes,"[1] to protect the revolution against its enemies in its vulnerable early years. Violence in the Soviet Union was driven by the Bolsheviks' belief that earlier revolutions in 1789, 1848, and 1871 had failed because their leaders were unprepared for the ferocity of counterrevolution, which as a result consumed them—a mistake the new leaders wanted to avoid repeating. The apprehension in Moscow grew with the rise of Hitler in the West and Japanese militarism in the East. In China, both before and after 1949, extreme measures were justified by pointing to the danger of a restoration of Kuomintang rule aided by U.S. imperialism.

In China, extreme measures were first employed against landlords and rich peasants in the revolutionary turmoil of the mid-1920s, matching the white terror vented on the Communists and their supporters in 1927, when Chiang Kai-shek's Kuomintang turned on and all but destroyed his erstwhile allies. Communist remnants under Mao Zedong and Zhu De fled to the mountains between Hunan and Jiangxi, where they suppressed landlords, "despotic gentry," and supposedly anti-Mao factions in the Communist Party and its Red Army. These campaigns resumed whenever the Communists' red bases became unstable as a result of attacks by Chiang's Nationalists or, starting in the late 1930s, by the Japanese.

However, extreme measures occasioned by military threats alternated with periods of relative stability during which the Communists attempted to build a system based on law. By trying different methods and learning from their mistakes, they gradually switched to more orderly procedures and created a formal legal system. This system placed an ever greater emphasis on reform, especially after the founding of the Chinese Soviet Republic in 1931, when chaotic improvisations were replaced by a trend toward regularization. The trend deepened in 1933, when some basic laws and judicial procedures were enacted, and a system of people's courts was established. This regularization of Chinese Soviet rule resumed and deepened after the arrival of the Long Marchers in 1936 in Yan'an, where Mao and his comrades set up a relatively secure base after a year of frantic, chaotic flight. From Yan'an, the Party revived its united front with the Kuomintang. Class unity was proclaimed and class struggle was suspended, especially its extreme form. The Party's growing maturity and complexity, and its nurturing of a professional cadre, was a factor in this development. This emphasis on reform is seen by many as an essential feature of Mao's revolution, which was built on a rural population, particularly (in the early years) its marginal sectors, which in no way conformed to the proletarian model that theory required and that, in China's case, needed special shaping.

But the trend toward milder treatment was often interrupted during military crises, when formal procedures were again suspended. This happened, for example, during the lead-up to the Long March in late 1934 and in the three following years in the Party's abandoned southern bases, where guerrilla remnants carried out frequent purges in the ruins of the abandoned Chinese Soviet.[2] Even in Yan'an, where the Party refined its mass-line approach during the Anti-Japanese War, it continued, depending on circumstances, to put its enemies, including "national traitors," on mass trial.[3]

The targets of these measures, and of the milder forms of political repression into which they later evolved, can be divided into two main categories, economic and political. Members of classes other than the workers and the poor and middle peasants—the class enemy—were potential counter-revolutionaries on account of their class background, though they could redeem themselves by embracing revolution. People politically hostile to communism were by definition counter-revolutionary, especially if they engaged in active sabotage. Class could heighten or mitigate one's status as a counter-revolutionary; landlords and capitalists were treated more severely than members of lower classes. Good behavior could also mitigate one's treatment. Counter-revolutionaries who surrendered to the Party or cooperated after exposure were often accorded relative leniency. [4]

After 1949, Mao was "selective and strategic in following Stalin's suggestions."[5] The Party retained many methods and techniques from before 1949, and essentially followed a dual model of law. Criminal cases in the early years were usually handled outside the legal system, with much resort to mass trials and extemporary methods during the initial chaos of land reform and in later crises and a renewed emphasis on class-based terminology. Even in later years, the extent of punishment in the case of those found guilty depended on the alleged perpetrator's social class and motivation; while lower-class criminals could expect some leniency, members or former members of reactionary classes would be lucky to get any.

In describing criminal law in China in the early years, Lung-sheng Tao gives an example:

> One authority cites the example of two defendants, both workers, who conspired and attempted to steal some coal from a mine for home use. The first defendant, a forty-year-old worker, was considered a 'corrupt and decadent racketeer,' while the

co-defendant, a sixteen-year-old worker who was 'somewhat influenced by racket-
eers, [was] . . . not a bad element from the vast people's viewpoint.' The first defend-
ant was to be condemned, while the young worker was not criminally liable, because
his act was not an offense in substance.[6]

However, even former reactionaries might be spared death, in line with the Party's belief that no one should be killed "unnecessarily" and the accent should be on
maintaining social stability and neutralizing hostile forces. Even many convicted of
war crimes were spared. After 1949, under Mao, the focus switched back and forth
between published legal codes and high-handed directives and apoplectic circulars
issued by the leading group. Even so, there was a measure of disjuncture between
Chinese and Soviet legal practice in the early 1950s, as illustrated by the observa-
tions of a group of Soviet police specialists sent to China. In their initial response to
Mao's mass campaign against counter-revolutionaries in 1951, they were unable to
hide their reservations, having "not seen such actions" in Russia since the 1920s,
though apparently they were eventually convinced of the campaign's merits.[7]

Even where they copied Russian terror methods, the Chinese imbued them
with their own distinctive style. Reflecting on the different ways in which that
political terror has been applied under communism in different countries, Julia
Strauss argues that the pattern of terror expressed through trials took a different
form in China than in Stalin's Russia. In both countries the trial was conducted as
effective political theater, but whereas in Russia it was staged in the "formal,
enclosed public space of the state's courtroom," in China (and Vietnam) it was
"bottom-up [and] participatory." The show, though similarly stage-managed by
the state at whatever level,

> took place in open public spaces such as stadiums, public parks, and schoolyards, with
> substantial popular participation. Before the show, local cadres carefully coached prese-
> lected witnesses designed to elicit public sympathy, such as the young, the old, the disa-
> bled, and women, to launch highly personalized accusations against the accused. When
> the event went well, it concluded with the public contrition of the accused, the emo-
> tional 'stirring-up' of the crowd, and a crowning culmination of popular support for the
> state's retribution against its enemies, as the accused was led off to the execution ground.
> Public accusation meetings and struggle sessions against counter-revolutionaries and
> landlords were first conducted in the early 1950s against those who were clearly identifi-
> able as having belonged to the 'wrong' classes. But the communicative theatre of public
> accusation continued to provide a repertoire for publicly conducted terror against much
> less obvious targets, such as 'black elements' and 'rightists' later in the 1950s, and for all
> and sundry who were accused of being counter-revolutionaries or capitalist roaders in
> the Cultural Revolution campaigns of 1966–76.[8]

In the early 1950s, shortly after achieving power at national level, the Communists launched a series of major campaigns aimed at eradicating any potential

opposition and remnants of the old regime. The Zhenfan movement (1951–52) targeted "counter-revolutionary elements" (essentially Kuomintang functionaries), while the Sufan movement (1955–56) sought to purge "counter-revolutionary elements" hidden within the Party, the government bureaucracy, and the army. The Three Antis campaign (1951) chiefly targeted corrupt cadres; the Five Antis campaign, remnants of the old capitalist class. Thought reform targeted teachers and intellectuals. Hundreds of thousands were executed, imprisoned, and placed under control in the early 1950s. The experience consolidated the Party's view on the role of suppression in building the new state.

Before the Cultural Revolution broke out in 1966, the Government's "organs of dictatorship" generally classified "people with problems" into one of three categories: counter-revolutionary bad elements, common bad elements, and members of the "counter-revolutionary social base." However, the taxonomy was elastic. It changed over time and could even differ from place to place at any one time. Not everyone "with a problem" was classified as an element. Some of the eight men Yang Kuisong identifies as "marginal people" were described not as elements but as "people with problems." For example, Shang Haowen, in chapter 6, was stigmatized as someone with serious ideological problems. Before 1949, he had been a "backbone member of a reactionary group" who had not "actively engaged in sabotage," but his real problems stemmed from his diary entries, which he disclosed during a campaign. Though never made to wear a bad element or counter-revolutionary "hat," his ideological problems followed him everywhere, and he was frequently targeted for criticism. Some problem people, however, were assigned to the "counter-revolutionary social base."

The idea of people as elements has a long and sorry history in Stalinized forms of Marxism, where the term reflects the reduction of human existence to a "thing among things," a form of "scientific" reification that critical Marxists have sought to discredit. After 1949, as the social and political order evolved, the composition of the class of categories and elements also evolved. In the early days, a three-categories label (landlords, rich peasants, and counter-revolutionaries) was sometimes used, to which bad elements were later added, making four. During the Cultural Revolution, the list came to include other categories—capitalist roaders, reactionary academics, traitors, and spies, whence the nine black. After the Cultural Revolution, the four new labels more or less disappeared, and the rehabilitation around 1979 of most of the rightists brought the five categories back to four.

Before 1949, the definition of a counter-revolutionary was relatively uncomplicated. After 1949, however, the category was divided into active and historical counter-revolutionaries. In 1951, the newly established "Regulations on the Punishment of Counter-revolutionaries" listed the following counter-revolutionary crimes: collusion with imperialism to betray the motherland; instigating, seducing, or bribing public officials, armed forces, or militia units to carry our rebellions; espionage or aiding the enemy; joining counter-revolutionary espionage organizations; using feudal ways and means to carry out counter-revolutionary activities; killing or carrying out acts of sabotage for counter-revolutionary purposes; provoking or inciting behavior for counter-revolutionary purposes; illegally crossing borders for counter-revolutionary purposes; organizing or participating in prison escapes; and harboring or sheltering counter-revolutionary criminals.[9]

As for "historical counter-revolutionaries," a set of "interim measures for the control of counter-revolutionaries" provided guidance on the manner of definition. It stipulated that the following groups be placed under control: counter-revolutionary agents; backbone members of reactionary groups; reactionary leaders; landlords who cling to their reactionary positions; military bureaucrats from the Chiang Kai-shek era who cling to their reactionary positions; and others. According to Deng Ping, a provincial law officer in Hubei in the 1950s, counter-revolutionaries were enemies of the people "that resist the socialist revolution and are hostile to and undermine socialist construction." They were people intent on destroying the Communist Party, or had been so in the past, during the civil war.[10]

The definition of bad elements was rather more arbitrary. According to a document of the State Council, bad elements were political swindlers, traitors, and hooligans—but political swindlers and traitors could also be classified as counter-revolutionaries. According to a semi-official definition, any hooligan, thief, arsonist, murderer, robber, swindler, rapist, or criminal who commits crimes and undermines public order was a bad element, as long as he or she was not a counter-revolutionary. These qualifications suggest that the distinction was unclear and that one's consignment to the worst category, that of counter-revolutionary, could be a matter of bad luck.

Again, Deng Ping described bad elements as law-breaking elements "some [of whom] are involved in problems concerning the enemy and us and should be objects of dictatorship." But not all those who broke laws were bad elements and "no longer [of the] people."[11] There was a difference between ordinary criminals or law-breaking elements among the people and bad elements. Ordinary law-breaking elements among the people, Deng felt, should not all be treated as objects of dictatorship, for their crimes were different in nature: their crimes mostly involved dereliction of duty. They did not commit crimes that upset the social order, unlike bad elements, whose crimes were planned and had a goal: to disrupt the social order. However, bad elements' crimes were often linked to those of counter-revolutionaries and exploited by the latter.

Before 1949, the term "bad element" had been used episodically by the Kuomintang to refer to corrupt and opportunistic groups and individuals. It acquired a narrower meaning under the Communists, signifying an impure person whose actions damage the Party. The concept was formally revived in the early 1950s and during the various movements to suppress counter-revolutionaries, when official documents distinguished between "counter-revolutionaries and other bad elements," while in March 1956 the Party noted that "all counter-revolutionary elements are bad elements."[12] Elements or categories can be further divided into two broad groups, those that offended because of their class background (landlord or rich peasant) and those that did so because of their behavior. The latter group was more complex and socially variegated and could include lower-middle peasants and members of other more plebeian classes. It is therefore evident that assignment to category or element status in China was far from systematic or predictable. Even the terminology was unstable. Both over time and from place to place and case to case, the manner of labeling varied.[13]

In the Mao era, the attitude toward and treatment of counter-revolutionaries, bad elements and other "people with problems" underwent an evolution. The authorities used a range of policies and measures to deal with categories and elements in order to control, monitor, and reform them. Most were not imprisoned but were instead made to wear "hats" and handed over to the "people" (new people with supposedly new minds, attitudes and feelings, collectivist, selfless and devoted to the Party) for control and supervision. These hats symbolized the wearer's political stigma, and removal represented his or her rehabilitation from crime, scandal, or misconduct, though they could be slapped back on again if needed. The wearers were stripped of political rights and restricted to doing manual labor in exchange for meager pay. Their behavior was closely monitored (restrictions were placed on their movements, social contact, and what they could discuss), and they were subjected from time to time to "struggles," i.e., intense sessions of criticism by hostile groups or crowds. The relatives and family of counter-revolutionaries and bad elements often also received labels (as the family of counter-revolutionaries, bad elements, and rightists), and could inherit hats.

Not all bad elements were made to wear hats. For example, Shang Haowen, who was persecuted for writing a diary, underwent an investigation that went on for years but was merely put under administrative watch. However, for those made to wear hats, it was an encumbrance and disgrace short only of jailing or being sent to a labor camp, and a stigma that was hard if not impossible to shake off. Apart from political stigmatization, sanctions employed against categories and elements imposed various forms of discrimination, including less pay (or even a ban on paid work), restrictions on marriage, restrictions on movement, and banishment from one's hometown or village. Some individuals were met with imprisonment and, in extreme cases, execution.

Almost from the start, the Party's policy toward bad elements and counter-revolutionaries stressed reform as well as control and punishment. The origins of the Party's belief in thought reform are usually attributed to its initial reliance after 1927 on "declassed elements," including bandits and local hegemons. Even during the revolutionary years, particularly during the Anti-Japanese War, education and political socialization were seen as essential in prisons run by the Communists. Thought reform was practiced in a drive to remold prisoners' personalities, rectify their faults, and turn them into "new human beings." The prerequisites for such a transformation, apart from education and persuasion, were self-reflection, confession, and repentance, sometimes carried out in small groups. Putting prisoners to work was another way of ensuring and speeding their reform, while at the same time making the prisons economically self-sufficient. But although the ostensible aim of the system was prisoners' spiritual transformation, in reality the bureaucratic mentality of the prison authorities, their military mindset, the conditions of economic scarcity, the lack of a cadre trained in methods of persuasion and reform, and the authorities' customary utilitarianism acted as a brake on any high-minded intentions.

Griffin's comment that "the function, procedures, and infra-structure of the legal system [after 1949] were transferred largely intact from the pre-1949 practices" is an accurate description of the first years of the new regime.[14] The outcome of trials was decided in advance, on the basis of pre-trial findings that resulted from aggressive investigation by police, security organs, and procuratorial authorities. The trial itself merely reviewed those findings and passed sentence on the basis of them. As for the courts, they were firmly under Party control. However, much sentencing was on the basis of informal interrogation and in the form of administrative sanctions, including rehabilitation through labor. Its objects underwent little if any legal procedure, particularly during periods in which the masses were expected to participate in sentencing, and detention could last for an unlimited length of time.

The practice of reform through labor for those "between crime and error" was formally inaugurated in 1957, on the basis of "new life schools" set up in the early 1950s. More than half of those detained for reform were ordinary rather than political offenders. They were mainly from the "dangerous classes" of prostitutes, vagrants, beggars, and the like that fell outside Marx's formal class schema. In 1953, half a million vagrants were interned as objects of reform, and around 400,000 were in detention in 1980, although this figure was soon halved.[15] The intention of the Party was to change them from parasites and disruptors of society into part of the people, imagined as a self-aware collective. However, their detention was in many cases indistinguishable from real imprisonment. In time, the failure of many to reform led to their characterization as a category outside the people, which by 1957 was supposed to have consolidated along lines that conformed to classical Marxist depictions of the popular classes, principally the proletariat.[16]

The designation of individuals and their families as categories and elements created a class of scapegoats that enabled the Party to cow the masses into submission and obedience. Many political movements identify or create enemies as a tool for maintaining order, and against which to pit the majority in a state of sustained hostility. The masses will be more inclined to follow the will of those in power and thus stay safe by shunning the group to which enemy status or erroneous thinking is attributed. This was a particularly useful tool in the early days after 1949, when the government needed to establish control in an era of sometimes violent transition between different social orders.

Some commentators, like Li Ruojian, argue that a main reason campaigns against bad elements and counter-revolutionaries in the early 1950s could win support from the masses was that the Communists succeeded in joining the class of "evil hegemons and local bullies" to that of counter-revolutionaries, thus making the suppression of the latter synonymous with bringing hated bullies to justice.[17] The four categories too were linked to wrong elements in society and demonized, which also led to a meshing of the Party's political goals with the notion of righting social wrongs and the removal of a major threat, historical or actual, to ordinary people's security. Because the definition of categories and elements was in many cases grossly arbitrary, and power of definition was wielded by those claiming to implement directives from on high, the labels often became a weapon that grassroots cadres used to control the masses or assert their own interests.

It is hard to quantify the phenomenon of categories, elements, and counter-revolutionaries, except to say that they comprised a very large number. The composition of the hat-wearer group changed over time, as this book documents in rich detail. The criteria for membership were unclear, the implementation of the rules governing ascription were often interpreted in a highly subjective way, and hat-wearers did not necessarily share the same social characteristics. Official records are said to show that at one point more than 20 million individuals belonged to the four categories.[18] There were said to be between 10 and 15 million landlords and rich peasants in China in 1949,[19] but by 1977, according to census figures, this figure had fallen to around 4.7 million (many had been killed during land reform). One can therefore imagine that the total figure of four categories would indeed have decreased significantly from the earlier 20 million. In the Liaocheng region of Shandong Province alone, the number of four category individuals recorded in 1956 was 102,772, but by 1978 this figure had fallen dramatically to 14,923, less than 15 percent of the 1956 figure.[20]

Thousands of individuals were later found to have been wrongly classified. For example, in 1957 a riot broke out in Guangze in Fujian to protest against a corrupt local cadre. The authorities arrested and tried thirty-nine "rioters"; six were jailed (two died while serving their sentences), two were sentenced to control, and one committed suicide. Their families were also treated as members of the four categories. They were denied private plots, did not receive equal pay for their work, and their children were not allowed go to secondary school or university, join the army, or become public officials. The victims of this case were rehabilitated in 1962.[21]

It is striking that all the main characters in this book are men. Why do women scarcely feature in the story of China's bad elements and counter-revolutionaries?

Because nearly all those so categorized were men. While gathering data from Shanghai on the campaign to suppress counterrevolutionaries, Julia Strauss observed that the vast majority were male.[22] This trend is likely to have been the norm in other campaigns and across the country. In Appendix 4 to the original Chinese edition of this book, Yang Kuisong presents statistics regarding the three "broad categories" of "impure" social classes and strata in a village in June 1960.[23] Of the forty-eight counter-revolutionary bad elements listed, only one was female (a "female bandit leader"); of the nineteen common bad elements, only one was female (a member of the religious sect Yiguandao); and of the "counter-revolutionary social base," only one out of eighty-two was female. Appendix 5, which lists "problem persons" in a municipal clothing factory in 1963, shows that only twelve of the ninety-four employees identified as having "historical problems" were female, and most of their "historical problems" had to do with their class background (landlord)—perhaps family members had been executed by the Chinese Communist Party (CCP) or the women's families had overseas connections.[24]

So women were rarely identified in the ranks of those classed as counter-revolutionaries or bad elements. Rather more women belonged to the "counter-revolutionary social base," but even there they seem to have played little role. The tiny number of women classed as counter-revolutionaries and bad elements can be attributed largely to the fact that women played a far lesser part than men in non-domestic labor and in many places were virtually absent altogether from public life before 1949, except at elite levels. Even after 1949 the presence of women in these two spheres continued to be restricted.

As for landlords and rich peasants, most were classed as counter-revolutionaries less as a result of ideology or bad political or other behavior in the past or under the new regime and more because of their social class. Inevitably, men tended to predominate among them, as holders of land titles and heads of households. It is true that land reform affected households rather than individuals, so the daughters and wives of landlords and rich peasants were assigned to the same categories as their fathers and husbands. Moreover, many fathers and husbands fled at the time of land reform, leaving their womenfolk to face the music. Some such women ended up being classed as part of the "counter-revolutionary social base," but their presence in it has been far less noted than that of men. One class of women far likelier than others to end up as bad elements was prostitutes, included by Mao Zedong in 1926 as part of the lumpen-proletariat that did not conform to the classical categories of class analysis.[25] However, there are no prostitutes in this study, where women figure only marginally—as relatives or girlfriends of the men who had the misfortune to fall foul of the Maoists.

In this book we see China's outcasts and its disenfranchised classes not as a faceless mass but as individuals. We witness the whole process of their experience over years, from arrest to release. This study sets out to right wrongs, by putting them in a critical light, and to humanize groups of people stigmatized by the authorities and whose suffering has generally been disregarded, even after their rehabilitation, full or partial, posthumous or while still alive.

What these individuals have in common are blemished personal histories (e.g., having a bad class background or working for the Kuomintang or the Japanese, though typically at very low levels) or, under the new regime, having been charged with undesirable thoughts or wrongdoing (not necessarily political). Li Lesheng (chapter 2), for example, had worked for several months as a nurse in a Kuomintang-run wartime hospital and had distributed forms at work asking people to join the Kuomintang. He was also a "hooligan," having had sex with men. As a result, he was classified as a bad element and sent to prison.

Beyond blemished personal histories and unsavory words and deeds, bad social connections also got people into trouble. In chapter 7, we see that Che Shaowen's "complex social connections" (both before and after 1949) contributed to his downfall. Before 1949, he had been a rice merchant and had many business ties; during the Japanese occupation he had also worked under the Japanese; and he had joined the Green Gang—which made him a possible traitor. Later, working in a procurement role, he "wheeled and dealed like an old-style merchant" and exchanged small favors, which landed him with the charge of corruption. Luo Guozheng (chapter 8), an "active counter-revolutionary" who was given a hat for saying wrong things, had questionable overseas connections. For years his correspondence with relatives in Japan and Hong Kong was secretly monitored for espionage, but the surveillance failed to yield any evidence. Many of those labeled as counter-revolutionaries or bad elements were victims of bad luck or poor timing—they were in the wrong place at the wrong time. One movement followed another, and the focus shifted. One minute a campaign was targeting the grassroots, the next minute those in local power. Even those carrying out the suppression could, all of a sudden, become its target.

The book illustrates the terrible wastefulness of the system, which destroyed (and continues to destroy) the lives not just of petty offenders but of individuals who in another age could have made a contribution to society—as doctors and administrators or in other capacities. As a result of their stigmatization, their families and even, in some cases, their local communities suffered, sometimes for generations. The loss of knowledge and experience is incalculable. For example, the Chinese medicine doctor Fan Liren (chapter 3) was exposed as a "historical secret-agent element," but because his crimes were deemed to be relatively ordinary and he made a voluntary clean breast, he initially escaped sanctioning. However, not long after the verdict, he got into a fight with the hospital leadership, which landed him back in trouble. Fang was a highly skilled medical practitioner. The reports on him show that he was competent, innovative, and hardworking. His talent was wasted, however, as he spent twelve years in the countryside doing manual labor. When people sought him out for his medical expertise and he tried to help them, he was accused of "violating the brigade's security system," and as a result he was paraded through the streets and publicly denounced.

We also see officialdom and local authorities in a clearer light than usual, and sometimes in a better light. Normally, Western accounts paint lower authorities in China as petty tyrants, void of conscience and human feeling, bent merely on following instructions or pursuing their own selfish and vindictive ends, personal and collective. In most cases the bureaucrats in this book live up to that picture, paying more attention to official circulars and quotas than to individual circumstances. But throughout the book, in most chapters, there are instances of good as well as bad behavior on the part of leaders and officials, though obviously within the limits of the system. Some investigators and inquisitors took their jobs seriously, treated the accused with an unexpected degree of leniency, and let people go where firm evidence was lacking, thus showing touches of integrity and human kindness. On the whole, however, they fulfill one's worst expectations of a faceless, heartless, inaccessible bureaucracy not unlike the nightmarish world encountered by Joseph K. in Kafka's *The Trial* or of the medieval Inquisition.

---

* The English translation is somewhat shorter than the original Chinese text, in order to meet the cap of 130,000 words imposed by the publisher. However, the excisions have not affected the author's conceptual approach, to which the translation is entirely faithful.

The German social psychologist Kurt Lewin coined the term "marginal man" to describe those people who find it hard to adapt to changes in their status or environment and fail to integrate into the social mainstream. In any society, marginalized people stand out from the crowd, so it is not surprising that they feature prominently in creative literature. Historians, however, are more likely to pay attention to "emperors, generals, and ministers." There are few archival studies on marginal people, especially those lacking in eminence or distinction.

What drove me to write this book about people on the edge, and who are considered to have "problems"? The choice was partly inspired by my lifelong study of the history of the Chinese Communist Party and the state it founded. However, I have always felt that historians should pay close attention to human nature, and this was my main spur. All history is, in the end, human history. Human history is infinitely mutable and varied, but we spend only a few decades on this earth, and most of us would, given the choice, opt for a quiet life rather than for chaos. Unfortunately, in the twentieth century, Chinese people experienced political turmoil and social upheavals that followed one another at such speed and so intensely that they were barely able to cope with them.

In 1949, after half a century of civil strife, foreign invasion, revolution, and war, people experienced the social changes brought in by the Communists as earthshaking. The political, economic, ideological, and cultural movements and campaigns that followed not only shocked society but time and again swept ever greater numbers of monsters and demons into the open. These people, together with those who might not qualify as monsters and demons as such but nevertheless had problems and so forfeited the Organization's trust, swelled the ranks of the marginalized.

This book examines eight people with problems, whose lives were not entirely divorced from the sphere of monsters and demons properly understood. At the very least, all were cast onto the margins. One reason for choosing them as study objects was, of course, because the information I gathered about them was relatively concentrated and easy to find. More importantly, their life stories allow us to observe, directly and at close quarters, the rich range of human behavior in the lower reaches of Chinese society in turbulent times.

Based as it is on archives, the study does not include representatives of the rural rich, for whom personal files were not compiled. Most of the objects studied in this book had received an education and had jobs before 1949 and went on after 1949 to work in government administration, industry, mining, the army, education, health, or a service trade. What did they have in common? Apart from all having worked in formally defined units, the main thing they had in common was their problems. A historian is not some private advisor of the sort that knows the tricks of officialdom and the loopholes of the law, someone who helps people write their autobiographies or clean up their personal records, so in explaining their problems and their ups and downs in life, I make no attempt to speak in their defense. All societies have those who do not fit into the mainstream, and because their reasons for not fitting differ from person to person, it is hard to generalize. What this book offers is, in essence, a collection of research materials for a social history. It does not try to reconstruct the entire history of its objects, in all its naked truth. The reader should bear this point in mind.

The writer of a book of biographies should, ideally, supplement the information he or she gains from archives by field work, oral history, and so on. Regrettably, most of the families concerned were reluctant to go into detail about what happened to their relatives, so I achieved only limited success in that regard. What little information I did gain from interviews and field work has been knitted in circumlocutory fashion into the main text rather than explicitly attributed in footnotes. This happened at the insistence of the family members who provided it.

The same goes for the names of the people mentioned in the book, those related to them, and the units and locations where they live and work, in order to protect their privacy.

Yang Kuisong
Shanghai

I no longer remember his name, but he was a little over thirty. His face looked old. He was slightly stooped. His image constantly reappears before my eyes.

I remember when I first saw him he struck me only as short, slight, old, and thin, a wretched-looking man. When the prison guards opened the cell door, he bowed respectfully, his face wreathed in smiles, looking remarkably like a shifty old lag.

I'd just been dragged back to the factory from the detention center in the Beijing Artillery Bureau. I had just had an "active counter-revolutionary" hat slapped onto my head, and after receiving criticism at a general assembly of factory workers and staff, I'd been brought to this new place, I was completely disoriented. Seeing him, I immediately thought of the bad people in revolutionary films. So when the guards slammed the prison door shut behind me, I didn't even want to acknowledge him.

To my surprise, as the guards' footsteps receded into the distance, he sprang up from the bed, put together from a dozen or so rough-hewn semi-circular wooden struts, took from my hands the thin, ragged cotton quilt the prison guards had just given me, and helped me fold it over the bunk. Then he said, "You've only just arrived, you won't be used to the uneven bed boards, I'm used to them, the bit in the middle is a bit flatter, you can sleep there." While doing this, he lowered his voice to tell me that the "government" in the prison—it was a word he often used—set various rules. For example, you must get up when the bell rings in the morning; after getting up, you must fold your quilt on the bed; you must not stand on the bed or at the foot of the bed during the day, but must sit at the end of the bed facing the cell door; you must put the lid back on the plastic toilet bucket after using it; every morning after breakfast someone must slop out the toilet, rinse the bucket, and return it to the cell; twice a week you are let out for half an hour at a time, one cell at a time, and you have to jog to the designated place; having reached it, you must not communicate with prisoners from other cells.

There was another prisoner in the cell. He was slightly younger than I, just eighteen or nineteen. Like me, he had been arrested after the 1976 Tian'anmen Incident. On April 4, at the end of the night shift, he had found himself at a loose end, so he had accompanied his teacher to the Square to see what was going on. He was accidentally arrested during the clearance of the Square. Although he'd only been an onlooker, his teacher had been reading aloud the poems pasted on the Monument, in order to help those writing them down, so he too was carted off, probably because they wanted to check out his teacher's contacts. He'd been interrogated two or three times, but since then he'd been ignored. If you mentioned his teacher and his family, he immediately burst into tears.

When I first arrived in detention, I was taken away almost every day for interrogation, for hours at a time. Each time I went, both of the other prisoners secretly climbed up onto their beds and watched through gaps in the paint on the window, to see in which direction I was taken. Each time I came back, as soon as the prison door slammed shut, the old lag handed me a bowl of cold food and urged me to eat.

The prison food followed a fixed pattern. Every day there was steamed *wotou* made of corn or sorghum (alternating on Sundays with steamed *mantou*) and a bowl of "vegetable soup," actually no more than boiling water with a few small leaves and some drops of oil floating on it. I didn't have much of an appetite in prison, so one *wotou* was enough, but not so for the young apprentice. It turned out that the old lag often gave him half his *wotou*; it seemed to have become a habit.

The old man was a good singer, and used to entertain us with songs. He had a nice voice. He sang *sotto voce* to stop the guards hearing, but he introduced us to all kinds of Chinese and foreign songs, so that even though I was in prison, I felt reasonably relaxed and happy. I learned more than one hundred songs from him.

After I'd been there a few days, I learned something about his life. The young prisoner told me the old man was a thief. Later, the old lag himself told me that he had started stealing as a teenager and been re-educated several times, eventually receiving a prison sentence. As it happened, the day before father and I went to cadre school, the whole family had gone shopping on Dashilan Street at Qianmen, to buy a cotton-padded coat and other things to take down to the countryside. Probably on the bus, father was pickpocketed, and lost all the money we were going to use to buy food and clothes, including the clothing and quilting coupons the entire family had managed to accumulate in the course of the previous year. So there was no shopping and we all went home disappointed. As a result, I bore a big grudge against thieves. I hated them. Whenever I saw an angry crowd beating a thief hauled down from a bus, I thought he deserved it. However, when the old man told me about his life, I could no longer bring myself to hate him.

Strange to say, in the past my impression of thieves had been that they must be from very poor families, children lacking food and clothes. However, the old lag's parents were highly educated scholars, and his mother was even principal of a famous primary school in B municipality. At home there was no need to worry about food and clothing. He even learned the piano. He could read music and had done much light reading. For some reason—he could not say what—one day after receiving a beating he had run away from home for a couple of days. He had gone stealing with an older child and been arrested, thus starting out on the road of crime. The main reason was his strict upbringing. After his arrest, his mother felt humiliated and refused to have him back. With the agreement of the police station, they sent him to a work-study reform school. There, he acquired even more bad friends and became a professional thief.

Naturally, each time he was caught he expressed a determination to reform. However, he told me that once you acquired the thieving habit, getting money was all too easy. It was like smoking opium. Whenever an opportunity arose, his fingers would itch uncontrollably. Finally, at the age of fifteen, he was "struck hard": severe measures were applied, and he was sent to a reform-through-labor camp for several years. When he came out, he had no assured source of income and no home to go to, so he returned to stealing and was again arrested. He was again "struck hard," and, as a repeat offender and no longer a juvenile, sentenced to seven years. By the time he came out, he was nearly thirty. He had no work experience, no work unit to receive him, and nowhere in town to go. He got caught up with the "evacuation in preparation for war." Designated as one of the "four kinds of elements" (landlords, rich peasants, counter-revolutionaries, and bad elements), he was sent directly to a Yanqing mountain village and handed over to the poor and lower-middle peasants to work under their supervision.

2

By that time, I more or less understood the place I was being held. It was Beijing's Number One Detention Center, near Banbu Bridge in Taoranting, also called Banbu Bridge Detention Center. There were two old prisons left behind by the Japanese, one of which looked from the air like a K, so it was called K Block. It had four wings, each consisting of four floors. The other looked from the air like a five-clawed foot, so it was known as the Tortoise Block. It had five corridors, each with two floors. K Block was said to house mainly criminals, the Tortoise Building mainly counter-revolutionaries. This puzzled me. How come the old lag had ended up in a place meant for counter-revolutionaries?

In July 1976, two or three weeks after my imprisonment, we were roused from our sleep at midnight by an earth-shaking noise. The entire prison was in uproar, with prisoners hollering and pounding on their cell doors, in an enormous panic.

However, the cell doors were made of thick, heavy metal-plated wood, with no more than a small window at eye level, through which the guards could monitor the prisoners' activities. This window could only be opened from the outside. The external windows were blacked out by thick paint. As a result, the prisoners had little or no idea of what was going on outside. Everyone knew immediately that something dramatic had happened, but since no one knew where the guards had gone and there was no one in the corridors to respond, the clamor could only grow. However, we were helpless, and resigned to our fate, whatever that might be.

The youngster in our cell was scared to death. First he screamed his head off, then he sat down on his bed and wept. The old lag silently gripped the youngster's shoulder, but at each new wave of commotion he nervously mumbled, "Never mind, never mind," until the wave died down.

That whole day the old lag had seemed unusually relaxed, grinning cheekily to himself or sitting quietly on his bed, his eyes glazed. Each time I tried to talk with him, he absent-mindedly grunted. Only when the lights went out at night did he suddenly lean over and whisper, "Do you miss your family?" I remember I didn't answer. After a while, he let out a long sigh and said: "My mother will be sixty this year."

All night long he kept his head inside his quilt. I heard him quietly sobbing.

Another month or so went by. There were no newspapers or radio broadcasts, so although we noticed the days and nights come and go, no one knew what day it was. Suddenly, a trumpet started playing endless funeral music at a deafening volume, and we knew at once that Chairman Mao had died.

A week later, the youngster was unexpectedly released. That day, the old lag was on tenterhooks. He whispered that according to what he knew of international conventions, the new leaders might be expected to grant an amnesty. However, he seemed worried about his own case. He said: "If there's an amnesty, do you think it should extend to everyone?" I didn't really think it would. The youngster's release seemed to me to be an exception—I'd heard of no further cases along the corridor. But I told him that if there really was an amnesty, a petty crime like his should be covered by it.

Only then did he tell me the truth. It turned out that he had been arrested not for stealing things but as a counter-revolutionary!

A thief had become a counter-revolutionary. It seemed a bit like a fantasy, but it was true.

The reason for the change was simple. Having been sent to the countryside to do supervised labor as one of the four categories, he belonged to an inferior caste, like a leper, and everyone shunned him. Every morning at four o'clock, he and the others were sent out to clean the village streets, and then, after dawn, they were forced to work like beasts of burden until evening, most of the time under direct supervision. They got the fewest work points, they lived in the worst accommodation, and they were constantly hungry. If they left the village, they had to report the fact to the authorities. When others were on holiday, they still had to work. Youngsters who wanted wives stood no chance. After years of this, he and another young four category element concluded that death was better than such a life and decided to escape. Unfortunately, they both lacked experience. They thought they could simply return to the city by heading south along the communication routes. They hadn't realized that the class struggle waged by the revolutionary masses in the towns had intensified, and they were caught and sent back a few days later. Things got a lot worse. They were subjected to one struggle meeting after another and strung up from a roof beam and brutally beaten.

After that, the two of them stayed out of trouble for a while. Then, somehow or other, they heard a wild story about a Free China radio broadcast from Taiwan that had apparently announced that if you wrote a letter to a mailbox in Hong Kong you could get funds to resist oppression. They believed the story. The old lag, styling himself Chief of Staff of the Northern Hebei Detachment, sent a letter to the Hong Kong mailbox. The letter naturally fell into the hands of the public security organs, and the two of them became "active counter-revolutionaries."

After hearing the old lag's story, I fell silent for a while. It seemed unlikely to me that such a person would ever be pardoned. I didn't even know whether I myself would receive an amnesty, and the charges against him were hardly lighter than mine. However, he liked to fantasize. He always maintained that it was never his intention to oppose the Government, and that because it was impossible for a four category element in the rural areas to survive, he had had no choice other than to try to flee. He believed he had done no wrong. He would learn his lesson and the Government would pardon him.

I was moved to another cell a month later, and in January 1977 I was declared innocent. The verdict on the Tian'anmen Incident of April 1976 was overturned and all those who had taken part in it were rehabilitated. It was a long time before I heard again about the old lag.

Just before May 1, 1977, by a curious coincidence, I spotted a court notice pasted on the wall of a Beijing hutong. To my shock, there stood his name, in big letters, crossed out by a red X. Although this was the first time I'd seen the characters for his name, I knew beyond doubt from the description of the crime that it was he. He had secretly conspired with the Kuomintang reactionaries, secretly organized counter-revolutionary armed forces, styled himself Chief of Staff of the Northern Hebei Detachment, and tried to overthrow the Communist Party. He had been "sentenced to death according to law, and the sentence had been immediately implemented."

He had been "struck hard" one final time, and "severely sentenced"—even though this was after the end of the Cultural Revolution.

3

At the time, I was just a worker, as I had been before my arrest. I couldn't judge from a legal point of view whether he had deserved to die. But the fact of his killing left me sad and bewildered.

The few months I shared with this "counter-revolutionary" told me that he was not by nature bad. At the very least, what he had done was hardly in the same league as that of the so-called "heinous counter-revolutionaries" who caused serious damage and instigated extreme ideological confrontation. Even leaving aside his reason for seeking refuge with the Kuomintang in Taiwan, his crime was at most an abortive attempt to perform the counter-revolutionary act of seeking refuge. Since the intention failed, there could naturally be no serious consequences. Yes, he could be convicted for his actions, but given that there were no serious consequences, it stood to reason that he did not need to die.

The tragic fate of this "old lag," just a little over thirty years of age, raised many questions in my mind. How could a child born, like him, of a good family be so easily abandoned? Why was a teenager who had made a mistake punished in such a manner, driving him deeper and deeper into bad ways because of the company he was forced to keep, so that in the end he was unable to extricate himself? What was the point of the four categories label, and why were those designated as such expelled from the cities and sent to the countryside to work under supervision, where they underwent a tragic fate? Why, decades after the founding of New China, was there still no strict legal system, so that at every turn extralegal measures such as "striking hard" were used to punish crime? Why did the Ordinance for the Punishment of Counter-Revolutionaries not distinguish between action and intention, and between completed and aborted action? Is it right to sentence someone to death or indefinite detention merely on the basis of what they say or think, whether or not serious consequences ensue? More important still, I was filled with doubts about the idea, gained from books and films, that all "counter-revolutionaries" are necessarily bad. So I could not but begin to question whether some "counter-revolutionaries" were not perhaps forced by social injustice or some other form of persecution to be as they were. And if a good person, one fundamentally not bad, is nevertheless a "counter-revolutionary," how should we treat him or her?

Since the 1980s, many changes have taken place in society. Members of the four categories have had their hats removed, and even "counter-revolutionaries" are no longer automatically deemed guilty. The notions of humanity and human rights, which in the past were regarded as reactionary, began to appear in official discourse. In other words, had the old lag lived until the 1980s, and especially into the 1990s and beyond, he wouldn't have had to pay with his life for his stupid and impulsive behavior. If he had been born ten or twenty years later, he might not even have been "struck hard" for stealing, or classified as one of the four elements, or sent to work under supervision in the villages, or forced by inhuman treatment to try to flee, thus ending up dead.

But he did end up dead, so we have the duty to ask: why, in those special years, did our society hold human life, human rights, and human dignity in such contempt? Why did we divide people into "revolutionaries" and "counter-revolutionaries," or into grades and ranks, simply on the basis of their different attitudes toward particular classes, parties, ethnicities, nationalities, states, etc., and decide on that basis whether they were lowly or noble, or whether they deserved to live or die?

I was lucky. My tribulations more or less coincided with the overthrow of the Gang of Four and the vindication of the Tian'anmen Incident, so I was not a victim of the political struggle and the so-called class struggle and I was even able to go to university and do non-political academic research. If the Gang of Four had not been overthrown, if the Tian'anmen Incident had not been vindicated, if there had been no reform and opening up, who knows what my fate might have been? Even given my opportunity, how many people have been less fortunate than I, as a result of old stigmas? Many of my brothers and sisters at the cadre school and in the factory were smarter and more able than I and should have enjoyed a better education and received better chances, but they did not. Even after the reforms and the opening up, people were laid off or forced into early retirement and straitened circumstances because they lacked schooling or worked in inefficient industries, and many such people ended up even worse off than before. With that in mind, how can one not deplore the injustices they suffer?

So I am lucky to have had the chance to study modern history, practice my profession, work hard to clarify the innumerable questions that continue to plague me, find answers for all those innocent people whose lives were blighted, and think up ways of avoiding the same mistakes in future, so that everyone can enjoy the same rights and lead a quiet life rather than live in the shadow of fear.

Many scholars might say that this is not the job of a historian. They prefer to live in their ivory towers and devote themselves to the elegant and professional dissection of problems pertaining to their special fields of study. But given the historical and social problems that have accumulated over the decades, I have no time for elegance and professionalism. This is not just a matter of my academic scholarship and self-cultivation but the result of my personal experience, my character, and my sense of urgency, given the limited amount of time left to me on earth. I am unable to divorce myself from social reality, and from the mass of mortal beings that shapes it.

For me, people are at the heart of the study of history. I have never seen history's aim as the propagation of academic learning. In my view, scholars must not be otherworldly. On the contrary, knowledge exists to benefit the progress of human society. Mencius said: "The way is not far from the human being. When human beings try to pursue a course that is far from the common indications of consciousness, that course cannot be considered the way." Johann Gottlieb Fichte said: "Upon the progress of knowledge the whole progress of the human race immediately depends."

If through our study we are unable to persuade each reader of history books that all humans are created equal, that each human life merits respect, rights, and dignity, that attention to the fate of others nurtures a reverence for life, so that we can achieve the goal of improving the human condition and quality; if, instead, our study, because of this or that ideological stance, leads to greater hatred, hostility, and even hurt, I would say it's a kind of knowledge we can do without.

The purpose of learning is humanity and justice. "Kindness is the human mind; righteousness is the human way. How lamentable it is to neglect the way and not pursue it!. . . The great end of learning is none other than to seek the lost mind." Having identified this road, "although tens of thousands oppose me, I will not fear to forge ahead along it."

1

___

Returning to the People's Road

The New Regime's Definition
of Hostile Elements

In New China, "the people" is a familiar political concept. Nearly everything is defined by it. The country is the People's Republic, the government is the People's Government, the army is the People's Liberation Army, and the police are the People's Police. Ultimately, New China's politics advocate implementing People's Democracy, or People's (Democratic) Dictatorship. In a word, "the people are masters of their own affairs."

What is meant by "the people"? On the eve of the founding of New China, when Zhou Enlai was explaining the draft Common Program adopted by the Chinese People's Political Consultative Conference (CPPCC), he stressed its class nature or political nature. He said:

> There is a difference between 'people' and 'citizen.' 'The people' is the working class, the peasantry, the petty bourgeoisie, the national bourgeoisie, and patriotic democratic elements that have consciously crossed over from the reactionary class. After the expropriation of the property of the bureaucratic bourgeoisie and the redistribution of the land of the landlord class, the reactionary activities of the negative elements are to be severely repressed and the more receptive ones among them are to be forced to do manual labor, so that they are transformed into new human beings. Before their transformation, they do not belong to the people, but they are still Chinese citizens, temporarily deprived of people's rights, though bound to carry out their obligations as citizens.[1]

In Old China, it was perhaps enough to be a citizen, but not in New China, where you must at the same time become part of the people. Otherwise, like unreformed bureaucratic bourgeois and landlords, you will be denied political rights and forced to do manual labor in order to become part of the people.

Given this distinction between people and citizens, differentiating politically between members of the nation became not only important but difficult and complex after the founding of New China. This was because after the Revolutionary War the Communists came to believe that a person's class attribution depended not only on his or her position in the relations of production but on his or her ideological and political choices. It was a simple fact that the working class, the peasantry, the petty bourgeoisie, and the national bourgeoisie included many who in the past had chosen to side with the Kuomintang regime of the reactionary bureaucratic bourgeois and the landlords. After the birth of New China, the new regime retained a large number of employees of the old regime, in order to effect a relatively smooth transition. As a result, it had to screen and sift these people.

Such a task is complicated, and naturally took time. The Communists had to launch political campaigns and adopt various measures to carry out this political and ideological screening to root out "alien elements" hidden among "the people," as well as newborn "alien elements." According to Li Ruojian, by the 1960s no less than 0.4 percent had been sifted in this way.[2]

It is not difficult to imagine that those consigned to this "other" register, that of the disreputable, included many who had been reformed by labor and joined the ranks of Zhou Enlai's "new human beings." Typically, they would have been people prominent in the old regime or even war criminals who had fought the Communists on the battlefield. Even people who had helped Emperor Pu Yi in Manchukuo after the Japanese invasion were said to have been reformed, rehabilitated, and returned to the ranks of the people. The question is, among the far larger number of ordinary people originally classified as alien or originally classified as "people" and later identified as aliens, how many underwent transformation and returned to the ranks of "the people"? We seem to lack reliable statistics or research on this.

For some, this transformation was not without effect. Liao Xuechang, of K Municipality in H Province, had occupied a reactionary position in the Kuomintang as a member of a district committee. After the founding of New China, he had initially been accepted as a member of the people and had served as a ranking technical official in the new regime. In 1955, during Sufan, he was found to have concealed some of his past activities and was reclassified as a "counter-revolutionary," but he had committed no crimes and was therefore not required to wear a counter-revolutionary hat. In 1962, when class struggle became the guiding principle, he was, because of his past historical problems and his poor behavior in his new job, put on the "other" register as one of the four categories and was even handed over to a work unit to do manual labor under supervision.

Thereafter, his behavior improved. He did not adopt the resigned attitude of someone who, having erred, would become dispirited and listless, but achieved a model transformation. However, unlike the "heinous" high-ranking war criminals amnestied after 1959, his improved behavior did not save him. Even after the Cultural Revolution, he continued to serve out his sentence under supervision, and was unable to shake off his four categories label. Not until 1978 did he return to the ranks of the people, in a very unexpected fashion.

SLIPPING THROUGH THE NET BY A SHEER STROKE OF LUCK

In October 1949, at the time of the establishment of the People's Republic, Liao Xuechang was still a police officer for the Kuomintang, working for the railway police in W Municipality. A month later, the People's Liberation Army (PLA) occupied W Municipality, and Liao and other members of the railway police were brought under central authority, trained, consolidated, and sent away. Liao took his severance pay and, in early 1950, returned home to K Municipality in H Province. In March 1951, he was introduced by a friend to the K Municipality Construction Bureau, where he worked as an assistant technician, and became a cadre in a construction unit under the new government.

On May 20, 1951, he filled out his "cadre's biography", the first of a countless number of forms given him in the years to come.

In the "family background" column he described himself as "urban poor," and he gave his class origin as "scholar"; in the "schooling" column, he wrote "secondary."

In the "special skills" column, he wrote "surveying."

He described his "family economic situation" as: "no houses, no land, just goods worth 250,000 yuan in old currency, equivalent to 25 yuan in the new currency. A family of six, including a father (65 years old), a wife (27), and three sons (7, 4, and 1). The cost of living is borne by income from father's stall and myself. Monthly income is about 250,000 yuan, a shortfall of around 100,000 yuan."

In the column "participation in political parties and other organizations," he said that he had joined the "fake Kuomintang," but also that he had "already joined the Sino-Soviet Friendship Association."

In the "social relations" column, he cited a couple of people who obviously had good backgrounds: the "former Y County Township Normal School Principal X, a teacher-student relationship" and the person who had introduced him to the job, "Comrade X, engineer currently in the K Municipality People's Government's Construction Bureau, a fellow-student relationship."

In the column "amount of training received," he wrote: "W Municipality liberation officials training course, three months."

For his "biography from the age of eight to the present," he explained: 1923–24, a pupil at an old-style private school in K Municipality; 1925–30, local primary school; 1931–33, local middle school; 1934–36, K Municipality Rural Teachers'

Training School. After 1937, having taught for two years in an elementary school and the rural teachers' training school and joined the evacuation to the southwest because of the war, he attended the police academy for three years, and in September 1940 he was assigned to the G Municipality police as a trainee. He then joined the police departments in W Municipality and F County, and eventually rose to become section chief. In 1945, he was transferred to a railway protection team and a railway police division, where he stayed until Liberation.[3]

What Liao wrote was basically true, but he had failed to mention that he had briefly (between late 1948 and early 1949) served on the Kuomintang's district committee. The new government had publicly decreed that anyone who had served on a committee at or above branch level in the Kuomintang or the Youth Corps should voluntarily surrender to and register with the relevant local authority. After receiving education during Zhenfan, Liao quickly confessed his service on the committee at a group meeting.

Because he confessed of his own accord, and as he was performing well at work, the K Municipality Public Works Construction Bureau continued to view him favorably. Naturally, at the height of the suppression movement, the personnel department, which was particularly alert to the class struggle, still had some doubts about his statements. The department noted in its political review of Liao Xuechang: "(1) The main sources of the record are his personal confession, others' comments, and investigations. (2) His behavior at work is noted in it, but there are relatively few political documents. (3) We hereby declare that the summaries we have made in his case are the result of careful consideration, and that we did not arrive at them hastily."

The personnel department concluded: Liao

> at first concealed his history and failed to say that he had joined the Kuomintang. After the confession [movement], he [admitted] at a group [meeting] that he had been a member of the district committee, but he said that though he joined the Kuomintang, he did not work for it. We analyzed whether, as secretary of the Kuomintang police and a committee member, it would have been possible for him not to work for the Kuomintang. He has already been employed in public affairs for more than six months, carrying out daily external inspections. His performance at work has been average, he has never stepped on anyone's toes.

So the Public Affairs Bureau's personnel department was not happy about Liao's failure to reveal his membership in the Kuomintang committee, in accordance with the government's instruction to repent and register. However, as his subsequent "cadre registration form" showed, he did so out of fear.

On the registration form, Liao had, on one hand, truthfully admitted that while working for the railway he had joined the "fake 60th District Committee"; on the other hand, he had cited many ostensibly positive factors, albeit quite hard to prove, in support of his own "progressive" history. For example, he claimed to have "secretly helped the People's Self-Defense Force on the eve of Liberation to greet Liberation," after the liberation of W Municipality, he had "been in charge of the People's Self-Defense Security Team" and "helped Public Security officers carry out checking and registration," as well as "participating in a four-month training course organized by People's Liberation officers," and so on.

The 1951 Zhenfan movement put the main emphasis on those responsible for "heinous crimes" and did not yet extend to the middle ranks (of cadres) or the inner layer (in the Party). Moreover, Liao had shown himself to be a hard worker and to carry himself with an ease and confidence befitting his position, so the Public Works backbone group had a good impression of him and did not subject his political record to particular scrutiny. It determined that Liao's "general behavior at work is all right, he is neither particularly active nor particularly passive, he does his job and refrains from speaking out," "he complies with the various systems, such as study and activities, and always follows instructions from above." He "takes on heavy responsibilities, he is contracted to a system of payment partly in kind and partly in cash, but he has not allowed pay problems to affect his work." Despite initially concealing his history, he later took the initiative to confess. In any case the initial concealment was probably due to fear of losing his job at the Construction Bureau. The group concluded that it was hard to say whether he was being completely honest, but found that, given his character and current behavior, he "was unlikely to have any big problems dating back to his time with the police."[4]

Cadre investigation required that Liao submit an autobiography. With Zhenfan in full swing and the killing of large numbers underway, Liao tried to portray himself as someone full of loathing for the old society, who had become an enthusiastic supporter of the new society. He talked again and again about his family's straitened circumstances and the barriers that had prevented him from studying. He explained that after the start of the War of Resistance against Japan, he had chosen the police option simply as a way of obtaining tuition fees and a living. He said that at police school he had never paid any attention to politics or current affairs. "Beyond school work, he had no idea of whether any political groups were active in the school." After graduation, he was assigned to G Municipality Police Bureau and then to F County police station, where he dealt with official documents and correspondence, assisted in drafting various documents, and acted as secretary. In 1944, he had been transferred to a railway police team, and had attended to general affairs and judicial and police affairs, still mostly paperwork—after Liberation, the various manuscripts had been filed with the W Municipality Training Course. He said that he had hoped that the Kuomintang would soon collapse, for Kuomintang officials were mercenary and corrupt. After Liberation, he had seen how in the new society everyone joined in the great anti-imperialist and anti-feudal struggle and vigorously served the people. Cadres at all levels "were not worried about basic necessities. Municipal construction moved forward by leaps and bounds, so I admired and respected the Communist Party." As for his joining the Kuomintang police, he explained that he had done so as part of a group and did not understand politics. He "had thought that joining a party was a formality, it had nothing to do with ideology, there was just a bit of discussion of current affairs in the school and I usually smiled and rarely spoke."

When referring to his time on the Kuomintang's district committee, he understated things: "My election as a committee member was because I lived a strict life, played ball games, and played an enthusiastic part in the cooperative and the mess." He was not interested in Party work, so he took a passive stance. "During the six months, all I did was handle documents, attend group meetings, and pay my dues." He made a big thing of his "progressive" activities. He said that on the eve of Liberation, at the invitation of an underground Party member, he had helped organize a number of police officers in a "railway bureau welfare committee" to stay at their posts and greet the arrival of the People's Liberation Army. He had acted as Security Officer and, after the arrival of the People's Liberation Army, had helped the Public Security Bureau to do registration and investigation work. So the Liberation officials had concluded in their review that he belonged among those who "had made a clear confession and were politically aware and, ideologically, relatively advanced."[5]

Kuomintang district committee members belonged, according to the new regime, to the "reactionary core of the Kuomintang and its Youth Corps."[6] During Zhenfan, Liao was let off lightly by his work unit for having concealed his role as a historical counter-revolutionary. He was lucky. He also survived the Three Antis movement in 1952. In the cadre appraisal form he had to fill out at the end of it, he did not even mention having joined the Kuomintang. As well as reaffirming his family's poverty and his lack of complicated social relations, he highlighted his ideological progress, his frugal style of living, his industriousness, and his concern for the hardships suffered by the laboring people. As for his shortcomings, he mainly acknowledged his "insufficient militancy," his "deficient spirit of criticism and self-criticism," his "over-cautiousness in implementing policy," and his "fear of boldly taking responsibility," his focus on technical questions, and his inadequate understanding of the Three Antis movement and its anti-bourgeois significance.

His self-appraisal was passed without comment by the Public Works Appraisal Group, and the Municipal Construction Bureau also signed off.[7]

INESCAPABLE MISFORTUNE

Liao's good luck started running out in 1955. By then, he had been transferred to a district-level Housing Authority. After Zhenfan had screened out current and historical counter-revolutionaries in society, the focus switched to counter-revolutionaries among cadres, and people like Liao whose names had appeared on the lists of backbone elements of the reactionary Party and its Youth Corps became major targets.

Liao had to fill out a new cadre biography. At the time, Sufan had not yet taken off and he had joined a new unit, so he did his best to avoid mentioning his role in the Kuomintang. He said that in 1939 he had joined the fake Kuomintang in C Municipality, and stressed that he "has now cut off relations." Under the rubric "important events and conclusions in the history of the individual," he simply wrote that "historically, during my period of study in W Municipality after Liberation, I confessed everything regarding my responsibility for duties and documents under the reactionary government in the fake-Kuomintang era, and my confession was validated by the organization." He said nothing at all about his time on the Kuomintang district committee.[8] A month later, he would pay dearly for this.

On June 15, 1955, the volume *Materials Relating to the Hu Feng Counter-Revolutionary Clique* was published, with Mao Zedong's Preface. On July 1, the Central Committee issued a directive on Sufan, as a prelude to a rapid extension of the struggle to eliminate counter-revolutionaries across the country.

In the spirit of the directive, organs in the District started putting the spotlight on cadres already under suspicion. The Housing Authority suspended more than a dozen people and brought them together in a warehouse where they were kept in custody and subjected to individual interrogation.

The Housing Authority's special group charged with reviewing Liao's case carried out a meticulous study of his past confessions and decided to carry out an external investigation. It defined the main issues as follows:

1. Had he engaged in any activities during his time at the police academy?
2. What work had he done during his time with the W Municipality police, and why had he not continued working there?
3. During his time as section chief in the F County Police Bureau, including his time as secretary, had he committed any crimes against the people?
4. While working for the railway police, had he joined the Kuomintang's secret-service organization and what bad counter-revolutionary things had he done?
5. In November 1949, after the Liberation of W Municipality, how had he got back to K Municipality? Had he fled for fear of punishment?
6. He had no record of having studied technology, so how come he was so familiar with technology? To resolve these doubts, more information was needed, both from Liao himself, to "provide more leads," and from his associates and people knowledgeable about his circumstances at different times in his career.[9]

Liao was well aware that the review was no trivial matter, so he cooperated actively. At the request of the special group, he provided a written confession, and he did his best to remember and add new things. The group interrogated him four times, and he made six additional submissions on four occasions, August 9, August 26, and September 1 and 3, 1955. In these materials he confessed details he had not mentioned in his previous accounts, but still he said nothing about his time on the Kuomintang district committee.[10]

On the basis of Liao's supplementary confession, on September 14 the special group produced a further twelve pages, covering nearly thirty major doubts. Its main points were as follows:

Liao had confessed that while at Y County senior-middle military training school, his good results in surveying led to his being invited by the commissioner's office to produce a topographic map. The special group asked: "What is a topographic map? Who sent the invitation? Was this the start of his being trusted? Had he joined the Youth Corps? Had he got a job?"

In his confession, Liao admitted that while teaching at the county primary school, he had on two occasions escorted the students' sports team to the county capital and another place for matches, and had once taken a trip to Tianjin. He was asked, "What kind of teaching did he do? Did he and others recruit the students? How many of them were in the Youth Corps? Otherwise, how come a county received funding for playing matches and travelling?"

In his confession, Liao said that Chiang Kai-shek and others had given lectures in person at the school. "Based on those lectures, what had Liao's thinking been at the time? What was the school authorities' attitude to Liao?"

In his confession, Liao admitted that during his teaching practice, the Section Chief had sent him to the training course to teach the fingerprint class. The group asked, "So you were trusted immediately when you started working? Such trust was linked to Liao's behavior at the police school, so wasn't Liao's assertion that he had no choice other than to stay on nonsense? Hadn't he been loyally devoted to the reactionary organization, hadn't he studied and behaved well, and wasn't that why he gained its trust?"

Liao had confessed that he had worked together with the police chief and others at F County train station to investigate a case in which Kuomintang soldiers had committed murder and arson, and that he had captured the perpetrators and taken them to the county government office to be brought to justice. The group asked, "How could that be a crime? Wasn't what happened in the interests of the people? Were the so-called perpetrators really soldiers of the fake Kuomintang? In the final analysis, what kind of perpetrators were they?"

Liao had confessed that after joining the railway police, the traffic police had sent a large number of special agents. He himself had been a member of the verification section and had taken charge of documents relating to the handling of cases, and for the next six months he had served as a railway police instructor. The group said: "You were determined to stay on and cooperate with Dai Li, the agents' boss, and you were trusted to teach them. These things are not straightforward."

Liao had confessed that he had been elected onto the Kuomintang's district committee by a general assembly of its lower-level members. The group asked, "How could such a thing happen? That sort of backbone element is highly likely to be a special agent."

The group concluded: "The confessional materials of September 3 raise a big question: was Liao a special agent or not? We have a letter [informing against Liao] that says that Liao was indeed a special agent. We will pursue the case further on the basis of the leads he has given us."[11]

The group set three directions for its investigation. (1) While chief of the administrative department of F County police and acting secretary, "What work did Liao do, and in what ways did he participate in criminal activities involving the suppression of the people?" (2) During the period in which he worked for the Kuomintang police and the Kuomintang's district committee, "Did he become a secret agent and what bad counter-revolutionary things did he do?" (3) After Liberation, how had he got back to K Municipality, "and had he fled for fear of punishment?"

A few days later, the special group redeployed an official to W Municipality to gather evidence. The official reported as follows.

(1) Together with others in the F County police department, Liao had founded the journal *Jingsheng* ("Siren"), which published police sports news and talked about the benefits of the fake police force, the Youth Corps, and police issues. He had directly commanded an investigation team to investigate cases, and had assigned a detective team to arrest and punish the Trotskyist Wu.

(2) There was no direct evidence that Liao had worked in the intelligence system, but he had merely admitted serving on the Kuomintang district committee and had concealed the fact that he had been its secretary. While working for the police, in August 1948 Liao and others had been jointly responsible for the case of two young men in yellow uniforms. Some said they were deserters, others that there was a suspicion that they were Communists, since they were found to be in possession of tickets to Northeast China [where the Communists were strong]. Liao and others transported them to the fake court in W Municipality.

(3) Liao returned to W Municipality not of his own accord but because he had been demobilized.

The report concluded, first, that publishing *Jingsheng* and the esteem in which Liao was held in the police force confirmed that he had, all along, been loyal to the Kuomintang reactionaries and actively helped them oppress the people; second, that he had served as secretary of the Kuomintang district committee; third, that his arresting of the two young people could be seen as a crime; and, fourth, "that it is very likely that Liao was a special agent, but, from the angle of the current investigation, it is as yet impossible to say for certain and to arrive at a final judgment."[12]

Further investigation showed that, at many points, Liao's confession side-stepped major matters and dwelled on trivia. For example, one of his former police colleagues reported that, in 1941, while working for the police in W Municipality, Liao had served as director of the household registration office, as the trusted subordinate of the head of the inspectorate, and as a special agent. While working for the F County police, Liao had been in charge of administrative affairs and served as secretary and chief of the justice department and in other capacities. While working for the police, he had been in control of all internal and external work. He had set up a special-agent team (of around sixteen people), which handled all cases under the direction of the police bureau and was directly under his control. In January 1946, in the police affairs office, Liao was appointed secretary of the district committee of the police affairs office of the Kuomintang's special railway committee and had joined its executive committee.[13]

The special group again mingled truth and falsehood in their interrogation of Liao, and subjected him to face-to-face interrogation. Liao was extremely nervous, but he was unaware of how things stood, and although he racked his brains for a solution, still he did not dare tell the whole truth about the past. On October 11 and 12, 1955, he confessed new details about the police work he had done, but the group remained highly dissatisfied with Liao's confession, and applied a mixture of hints and pressures.

On October 13, Liao finally had no choice other than to admit to various "crimes" of the sort the group wanted to know about, such as how, while acting as training instructor for the special-agent team in the command headquarters of the G Municipality police department, he had checked for progressive books and magazines at bookshops and arrested some people. While running the police justice course in 1947, he had found gun parts in the possession of a traveler and had determined after interrogation that he was a Communist and transferred him to the W Municipality garrison command for processing; in 1948, he had taken charge of a suspect found loitering in the vicinity of a railway station by the police, and had identified him after interrogation as a Communist suspect and transferred him to W Municipality Garrison Command for disposal;[14] in 1948, near a vegetable market, he had discovered two suspected criminals in military uniform and in possession of Northeastern paper money and had suspected they were Communists and handed them to colleagues for interrogation; in 1949, in the name of the railway police, he had told station staff to look out for "Communist bandits" laying fires and committing destruction, thus spreading malicious slander and propaganda against the Communist Party.[15]

After four days of uninterrupted interrogation, Liao came up with all kinds of things related or unrelated to his case. However, he still did not mention the matter that most concerned the special group, his work as a special agent and his role as secretary of the district committee.

On October 18, Liao was brought before a small-group meeting to be struggled against. The participants said they suspected Liao had been a special agent. Liao immediately admitted that he had talked about the question too simplistically, and needed to add further explanations. However, he insisted that "regarding the question of his joining the secret service, he had investigated it and found that he had never joined."[16] Much the same happened during Liao's interrogations on October 24 and November 4.

Liao's failure during repeated interrogations to confess to serious "counter-revolutionary" crimes, or even to his role on the district committee, was a main reason for the special group's eventual decision to arrest him formally. In mid-November, Liao made a muddled statement about not being able to recall being secretary of the district branch but said that if the Organization knew as a result of its investigations that he had, he had no choice other than to admit it. Liao's attitude was unacceptable to the special group.

On November 20, the group presented its "arrest report." It said:

After Liberation, Liao took part in revolutionary work. Under the Party's and the Organization's long-term guidance, he still failed to speak openly about his historical crimes and persisted in trying to conceal the fact that he had sneaked into our revolutionary ranks. According to our investigations, Liao engaged in the following historical crimes and spying activities. First, in 1946, while working for the railway police, he served on the executive committee of the tenth branch of the Kuomintang's second district committee and was branch secretary. During this period, he re-registered with the Kuomintang and renewed his national identity card. Previously, he had only admitted to being on the branch committee, but as a result of our investigations, meetings, and struggle sessions, he finally admitted having served as branch secretary. Second, while working for the justice division of the police department, in early August 1948, he and two others had captured two young men in yellow uniforms. Some said they were deserters, others suspected they were Communists. They were interrogated and sent for trial. On another occasion, a passenger was caught carrying gun parts. He was thought to be a Communist, and sent for trial. Liao only admitted these crimes after the struggle meeting. Third, our investigation showed Liao to have always been loyal to the Kuomintang reactionaries. He served them in important capacities, and actively helped them repress the people. While secretary to the police chief in F County, he had been in charge of designing rewards and penalties and establishing detailed rules and regulations for checking attendance records. Together with others, he had founded *Siren,* which played up the benefits of the fake police force. He also did some teaching and training to help out. Fourth, he joined the fake police affairs office in 1946, most of whose members were special agents, with whom he got on well. According to a prisoner, Liao was also a special agent, but we believe this charge to be unfair, and that it does not prove conclusively that Liao had become a special agent. This issue requires further investigation.

As suspicions against Liao had not yet been settled and the crime of counter-revolution was not yet enough to warrant his arrest, the report about Liao's arrest was not, in the end, approved by the senior five-person group. A member of the group declared: "Liao's other historical crimes have been confirmed, but a final conclusion has not yet been reached on whether he joined the special service. Our view is, therefore, that he should go into quarantine and engage in introspection, while the investigation continues."[17]

DODGING ANOTHER BULLET

In November 1955, the district authorities and the housing authority formed a joint special investigation team to investigate Liao's case. The special investigation team took into account Liao's background and employment history, as previously established, and reported: "We believe that Liao, from his time at the fake Central Police Academy down to the eve of Liberation, was fully qualified to be a member of the special service. Our preliminary investigation shows that Liao for a long time concealed important historical political crimes and refused to make a frank confession. In 1946, he was secretary of the Kuomintang's police branch in the Railway Bureau and a member of the executive committee, and he has owned up to other crimes. So it is necessary to set up a special investigation team to continue to investigate whether or not Liao was a member of the special service."

New materials then revealed that, in 1938–39, Liao had attended the first and second training courses run under Sino-United States auspices in Xifeng, Guizhou. The report stressed the need for a special investigation team to check whether Liao had joined the special service or one of its peripheral organizations or engaged in criminal activities. However, the report also admitted that there were few new leads on the case, so before the special investigation team embarked on its work, the leadership should get Liao to talk and make new confessions or should produce new witnesses. After that a comprehensive effort should be made to reach out to those who knew him, and to complete the investigation in around three weeks. Finally, "once the leadership has got him to talk, a small group can be set up to interrogate him," after which "a mass meeting can be held to attack him psychologically and fight a battle of wits with him, thus bringing the case to a close."[18]

This new round of investigations could not be executed according to plan. By late November, the higher authorities had asked all units to speed up the first phase of Sufan and to sum up experiences, in order to prepare for the second phase. However, the investigation into Liao across various locations had not come up with any result. In early December, the special investigation team had to start preparing its verdict on him.

In early December, the special investigation team conducted two formal interrogations. This time, the interrogation did not extend to the question of whether or not he was an enemy agent. Moreover, Liao challenged several of the crimes identified by the special investigation team. For example, he did not remember having told the detective team to arrest Wu, the middle-school teacher in F County, or having been involved in the arrest of the two young men in military uniform. However, having seen the prosecution materials, "I had no contrary evidence to put forward, so I had simply accepted the Organization's conclusion based on the materials." As for having served as secretary on the district committee, he argued: "I didn't intend to conceal it, and since I thought that people on committees and at higher levels were anyway backbone members of the Kuomintang," it seemed to him that being secretary made no real difference.[19]

After the interrogation, the special investigation team drafted its final report, which concluded that Liao had admitted all the crimes for which it had evidence. He was asked to sign it. It said:

> After meticulous examination and verification, the facts of the case against Liao have been thoroughly established. Circumstantial evidence has also been obtained. The key issues in Liao's case are as follows. (1) Between 1938 and 1940, while attending the sixth term of section-chief training at the C Municipality fake police school, he joined the Kuomintang and the Chinese Police Academic Research Society. (2) Between September 1942 and March 1944, he worked as administrative chief and secretary for the F County police and, together with others, founded *Siren* magazine. He made a name for himself by leading the police sports section, making propaganda for the Youth Corps, etc. Between 1946 and January 1949, he served on the justice section of the Railway Bureau, worked as an instructor for the Police Training Institute, and served on the executive committee of the tenth branch of the Kuomintang's second district committee, and was its secretary. (4) In August 1948, with others, he seized two men suspected of being deserters or Communists and a passenger carrying gun parts, a Communist suspect. The above interrogation materials show that Liao was a backbone element of the reactionary party. The evidence has, basically, already been identified and no new evidence has been found, so the case should be concluded.[20]

Liao immediately raised some questions about the final draft report. He said he now remembered, regarding the question of the branch secretary, that two general meetings had been held, "as a result of which the Deputy Head served simultaneously as secretary and I and another served simultaneously as committee members. So-and-so paid little attention to his duties, which I and another shared." So it was all right to say that he had done the secretary's work but not that he had served as secretary.

As for the accusation by his former colleague on the detective team that he had ordered the detective team to monitor and arrest people, he denied this charge. He argued: First, the detective team was directly under the command of the Secretary, there was no way he (Liao) could order them about. Second, it was even less true that arresting people, including the monitoring and arrest of teacher Wu, was subject to his command. This was because "organizationally I did not have the authority to supervise or direct the work of the detective team, so I never summoned them to meetings, or confessed to having done so." He also expressed the belief that "the Party has always been pragmatic" and asked the Organization "to continue to study or analyze this matter, in order to clarify it."[21]

Naturally, the special investigation team viewed Liao's defense with disdain. In subsequent reports, it abided by the original verdict. It argued that what the informers had said was sufficient to convict him. However, the special investigation team did not accept all the charges. For example, regarding an informer's claim that Liao was a special agent, and had participated in the Xifeng training class in Guizhou, it declared: "Our investigation of the fake police officials found no evidence that Liao was a special agent, and when, after Liberation, we took possession of the Police Bureau and the inspectorate and the people in charge handed us the list of special agents, Liao's name was not on it. Accordingly, Liao should no longer be suspected of being an enemy spy."

But even though the team did not believe that he was a spy, he still had to be punished. That was because, before Liberation, duties he had undertaken "involved numerous crimes. After Liberation, he had concealed his past and sneaked into the revolutionary ranks, and although during the last few years he had witnessed numerous political campaigns and undergone reviews of his personal history, he had all along concealed his role as branch secretary," which was a bad thing to do. Therefore "we propose that the administration sentences him to re-education through labor."[22]

Because they believed that Liao had deliberately concealed has past, added to which he had challenged the charges leveled against him by the special investigation team on a number of points, this time the leaders were no longer as tolerant as before. The special investigation team proposed re-education through labor, but this was, in the event, replaced by a year's penal surveillance.

On January 16, 1956, the District People's Court issued its verdict, of one year's surveillance and exile to a county in H Province to do agricultural reclamation work. On receiving the sentence, Liao did not initially appeal it. Rather, he quickly wrote a letter accepting it. He also thanked the government for its leniency, and for "giving me the chance to turn over a new leaf." He promised to "raise his proletarian consciousness" and "fight on the production front" during the period of surveillance.

In addition, Liao did not forget to explain why, during Sufan, he had not taken the opportunity to confess his problems. He said that he was forgetful by nature and "a man of few words," so when the movement started, if he remembered things, he would confess them, but otherwise there was nothing he could do. He said he hated the old society, so he wanted to make a complete break with the past and stop thinking about it, and over the years he had forgotten a lot. He said: "I can say from the bottom of my heart that there's nothing I know about that I am concealing." To demonstrate his sincerity, he made a further supplementary confession, and promised that if in future he thought of anything else, he would "immediately confess to the Organization and would no longer conceal things."[23]

Before Liao was sent down to the countryside, he chanced on a copy of *H Province Daily* in which he saw the report by Dong Biwu to the Second Session of the CPPCC, published by the Supreme Court. In it, Dong stressed that the basic spirit of Sufan was to educate the masses, clarify the boundaries between the enemy and ourselves, and punish the most heinous counter-revolutionaries. Because, in his heart of hearts, Liao disagreed with the Organization's sentence, he decided, after some hesitation, to risk an appeal to higher authorities.

Liao wrote:

> Director Dong instructed: 'Those who have a history of general counter-revolutionary problems but are not actively engaged in sabotage may, as long as they make a complete confession, be exempted from punishment or treated leniently.' Since this Sufan movement stipulates the possibility of exemption, I have made a special request for magnanimity, the revocation of criminal sanctions, and their replacement by administrative sanctions. . . . I did not intend to conceal my history, [and] my work for the fake Party was not a specific appointment but a concurrent, part-time post, and in reality I did nothing to harm the interests of the Communist Party. So the post was actually a mere formality. I am not currently engaged in or intend to be engaged in counter-revolutionary activity, which makes me eligible for exemption. Moreover, I had already made frank confessions on several previous occasions of my titular membership of the branch committee and of the fact that I was a backbone member of the Kuomintang, which is why I left out the title 'secretary,' which had entailed no new tasks and did not seem to me to increase the crime.

He also declared that he was not afraid to do reclamation work, but that in view of the fact that

> [I] had received training under the Communist Party as a level-four technician and had more than tens of dollars' worth of engineering books related to housing construction, I am in some senses qualified to serve the people, and if I were allowed to transform myself and improve myself in my old post, I would be even better able to do something for the people. Would it not be a waste of time and brainpower to start again from scratch in another field of work? At the same time, the Party had repeatedly called for special consideration to be shown toward ethnic minorities, so until formal notice has been received, I would request the organization to study how it can best be handled.[24]

Liao's request was forwarded at just the right moment. It turned out that the Central Committee's Sufan "ten-member group" had just issued its "Interim Provisions for Interpreting and Handling Policy Boundaries Regarding Counter-Revolutionaries and Other Bad Elements." The document clearly stipulated a number of criteria to be followed in the re-education through labor of counter-revolutionaries, one of which happened to be germane to Liao's case: "Concealing one's participation in reactionary organizations and in counter-revolutionary crimes is not serious enough to warrant arrest and sentencing, but anyone in the movement who sticks to a reactionary stand and refuses to confess cannot continue to work in an official organization." Although Liao had concealed his role as secretary, he had long ago confessed his membership in the branch committee. His behavior during the movement could not be characterized as "sticking to a reactionary position and refusing to confess," so this stipulation did not apply to him. Considering that Liao belonged to an ethnic minority (he was a Hui Muslim) and the central government had a special policy on ethnic minorities, the district committee decided to treat him in accordance with the stipulation that "wherever there has been long-term concealment of a political problem and a confession has only been made during struggles conducted in the course of the movement, but the confession is found to be true, the appropriate disciplinary action can be taken in the light of specific circumstances,"[25] and therefore revoked Liao's criminal punishment and changed it to an administrative one.

So yet again Liao escaped, and did not have to do land reclamation work.

AN UNEXPECTED DISASTER

The administrative records redefined what Sufan had characterized as being "a backbone element of the reactionary Party and Youth Corps" as a serious mistake, and it had no significant impact on Liao's status as a technical cadre in the housing authority. In 1957, the anti-rightist movement broke out, and Liao was of course honest and reticent. He buried himself in his work. In the second quarter of the year he was named as one of the unit's best workers, and received a bonus of ten yuan.[26] This shows that he was not discriminated against in the unit, and was quite popular.

Because of his repeated good fortune, Liao began to feel confident about his "transformation" and self-renewal.

In 1958, on the eve of the Great Leap Forward, "planting the red flag, pulling out the white flag," "rectifying the entire people," and "cadres going up the mountains and down to the countryside, both red and expert," Liao, already above the age of forty-three, did not actually need to volunteer to go down to the villages and perform manual labor. Nevertheless, adopting the attitude of someone keen to redeem himself by meritorious service, he asked at the start of the year, on his own initiative, to be sent down to an agricultural cooperative near K Municipality, to eat, live, and work alongside the peasants. Most of the cadres sent down were young, but Liao was relatively old and in poor shape. However, he adopted a positive attitude and exerted himself to the utmost. Because farm work relied basically on physical effort, coupled with the fact that there was no Muslim food in the countryside, he couldn't get used to the cooking and often went without, so he found it even harder to keep up with the youngsters. Liao also worried that he might forget some of his technical skills, and therefore wanted to keep up his reading. However, in a collective working environment, you had to hide away if you wanted to read, and he feared he would be criticized for concentrating on non-political academic issues. His life in the village was therefore physically and psychologically painful. Even so, to prove his determination to "reform," he continued to learn from the peasants. He insisted on going down to the fields each day, maintaining a full record of attendance, and working all out. Summing up his performance, he made the following points:

(1) Not long after going to the village, I volunteered to pick up pig manure, in all weathers.
(2) I went down to the fields with five team members to gather grass and I cut my feet and had to stop working, but I bound up the wounds and worked for three days alone, to complete the task.
(3) While paddling in the water, my feet became swollen, but I didn't lose heart, and I hardened myself.
(4) I took the initiative to help team members to build ridges in the paddy fields, in order to stop the water flowing out.
(5) I took the initiative to find someone in the team to find work for me, and when this work was done, to find other work.

The local cadres evaluated Liao's labor rather highly. But they remained skeptical about his political and class stand. They admitted that he was "willing to take the initiative and work hard, had a good relationship with the masses, obeyed the Organization and maintained discipline, ate, lived, and worked with the common people, and actively assisted the team in propaganda and other work." However, in September the "small-team comments" included the following passage: "The said comrade has a historical blemish, and received punishment from the people. . . . He sees going down to the countryside as a gilded opportunity to reform. While baring his heart during the rectification movement, he claimed that he did not resist any review or reprimand during Sufan. The team finds this illogical and not in conformity with the objective facts."[27]

However, during that period the class struggle was at its most relaxed, so political standards were not particularly high. The longer Liao remained working in the village, the more the attitude toward him on the part of others, including the cadres in charge of those sent down, changed.

Six months later, in February 1959, the team's appraisal had changed signifi-cantly from that recorded in September 1958. The new appraisal was generally positive. It said: "This comrade has a historical blemish, having been punished by the people. Ideologically, he is to a certain extent removed from the Organization. He does not usually reveal his thinking. Politically, he is not progressive. After coming down to the countryside, he actively volunteered for labor, and despite his age he was able to bear hardship and to help carry out everyday chores. He was affable and still able to make contact with the masses. He has actively assisted in propaganda work. However, he is unable to reveal his thinking, he does not dare to engage in bold criticism, and he is reserved and lacks enthusiasm."[28]

By October 1959, the team's evaluation was largely positive. Liao

(1) has some understanding of his past mistakes and an urgent desire to reform, he is able to say what's on his mind, and while tempering himself he is always cheerful and in good spirits.
(2) He obeys the dispositions of the Organization, is serious and responsible about his work, and actively reports instances of rightism.
(3) He is a steady and willing worker, serious and responsible, always does his best, and complies with the Organization and the discipline system.
(4) He is able to make contact with the masses, cares about things around him, is able to engage in criticism, and is warm and sincere.
(5) He takes political study seriously, actively participates in social activities, and lives a plain and simple life.

The team only identified a few shortcomings: he was not sufficiently concerned about learning from the leadership; he had a big inferiority complex, and some-times doubted the Organization; he did not deal with problems boldly and inci-sively, and he feared offending people.[29]

However, Liao's efforts to transform himself, together with the more positive evaluation, were not enough to win back the trust of the Organization. His fate went from bad to worse.

After a year and a half doing reclamation work, Liao returned to the housing authority. However, shortly after his return he was, ostensibly because of the tech-nical knowledge he had gained in the countryside, sent out to support rural con-struction. A year later, he returned to the housing authority for real, and was soon afterwards transferred from the district to the lowest level of housing manage-ment.

Even more unexpectedly, his political life, as well as his day-to-day work and his normal life, changed for the worse. His old "historical blemish" had always affected his work, life, and career, and the road grew ever narrower, but his "con-tradiction" was still "among the people," and he had not yet been put in the "other" register (that of the disreputable).

The reason for the change was that, starting in 1960, the economy entered into extreme crisis and the class struggle was once again stepped up. As the campaign spread throughout the lower levels of society, people like Liao with a historical blemish were doomed to become the focus of dealing with the problem. In 1962, the Eighth Plenary Session of the Eighth Central Committee of the Communist Party convened, and Mao Zedong suddenly started to stress class struggle. Activists everywhere began to "crack down hard" on and "strike hard" at landlords, rich peasants, counter-revolutionaries, and bad elements. In the Housing Authority, Liao was the only "backbone reactionary," so he was made to wear the "historical counter-revolutionary" hat, sent for trial, and sentenced to administrative control.[30] His wages, never high, were suspended altogether, and he was given just enough to keep body and soul together.[31]

The sudden blow not only meant that Liao's family members were unable to lift their heads in front of relatives and friends in the neighborhood but affected the children's personal future. Even his younger brother, far away in C Municipality, cut off relations with him. The incident threw Liao into confusion, and put an end to his enthusiasm for "turning over a new leaf."

After his demotion in the Housing Authority, Liao became moody and his attitude toward work became passive. Sometimes he showed signs of impatience. Other staff of good class status and family background would not be punished in this way, but it was different in his case, because of his serious historical problems. The Housing Authority severely criticized him "for not caring about the suffering of the masses, just like the Kuomintang bandits," and for frequently glaring at the masses with "angry, staring eyes." The Authority organized the masses to criticize and denounce him. After being put under surveillance, Liao naturally no longer dared show his impatience, but still he could not get people's forgiveness. In 1963, the Authority issued a written appraisal saying that Liao had not changed. "On the surface he seems to be more honest, and he is very careful in his job and in what he says, but in his heart he is resentful. He refuses to implement what the leadership has decided in relation to his confession, he ignores it and makes no response, and he merely feigns compliance."[32]

In this hostile political atmosphere, Liao received a further four categories hat. In April 1963, he was assigned to an even lower post in the Nimu Cooperative, and forfeited his cadre status.

As one of the controlled four categories who had once been part of "the backbone of the reactionary Party and Youth Corps," Liao stood out even more conspicuously in a low-level cooperative. In the Four Clean-Ups movement that followed shortly afterwards, nearly all the four categories were put under even stricter supervision. Liao's personal file contains many materials pertaining to mass supervision and control. They can only have increased the Organization's ill feeling toward him.

One report said:

At work Liao hoodwinks the masses, sows chaos, and is dissatisfied with the Organization. Why? In the past, he just checked the accounts and said everything is fine; even if there were problems (with some engineering projects) and the funds couldn't be retrieved, it didn't matter. Even more abhorrent, when he went to work he didn't go to the cooperative but worked from home. What was the point of that? As far as I could see, Wu and others, who were working on their own account, often went to Old Liao's house to eat and drink. Old Liao looked after the bills. There was something fishy about it.[33]

Another report said:

Old Liao is one of the four categories. He is not honest. Among the masses, he puts on airs, and at the construction site he's always making indiscreet remarks or criticisms. In addition, he is a very bad man at heart. Once, when he went to the tax office with me about funding for a building project (the project was run by one of those people working on their own account), someone said it should be done with cement, but he got someone to do it using tinplate (tinplate rusts, and after a while has to be replaced). That was a way of getting business for one of the four categories. As a construction official, he was regularly in and out of the artillery school, the airport, and other places where important confidential work was done, it's not acceptable.[34]

Another report said:

The counter-revolutionary Liao has never been honest or dependable at work. He regularly works from home, doing private things and cooking. . . . His work style is divorced from reality and from the masses. He works behind closed doors. He doesn't take responsibility. How can he be a good technician, make cost estimates, and settle accounts? When he makes an estimate, he never puts his cards on the table, so the builders, the suppliers, and the accountants never know what's going on. This results in conflicts between the workers and the team and between the builders and the suppliers and accountants. The workers are in the dark, the builders are in chaos, and the suppliers have no idea how much material to prepare. . . . In the past, we thought the problem lay in his methods of work, that he was too subjective and didn't accept criticism or comments. Now, having participated in the movement and raised our political consciousness, the scales have fallen from our eyes and we realize that it's not a question of his way of working but something he does deliberately.[35]

Another report said: Liao always likes to "make himself important and get the people in charge of enterprises to trust him, regardless of the collective interest or of individual workers losing out"; Liao always has "ulterior motives and tells lies"; he "is often at home, on the excuse that he can work quietly there, but what work is it that he does from home," what's the big secret? Liao's "reactionary character has not changed, he always bawls out the cadres and workers." "Before the Socialist Education movement started, he always said he was too busy to participate in manual labor. But on one occasion, when the Civil Aviation Authority cadres were having a meal and had money to spend, he went."[36]

In 1963, one year after Liao had been placed under surveillance, the Housing Authority's Party branch did some research on whether or not Liao should remain under control, and concluded: "He needs to stay under control, we do not agree that his four categories hat should be removed. Let's wait and see how things turn out."[37] In 1964, during the Four Clean-Ups and the Socialist Education movement, Liao's hat and his surveillance were not on the agenda. In 1965, the class struggle intensified, and it became even less likely that the control order would be lifted.

In July 1965, the Nimu Commune and the Socialist Education work team filled out a "four categories examination and approval form" that divided Liao's problem into four parts:

(1) While a technician with the Nimu Commune, he followed a capitalist manage-ment style. He inflated the cost of labor, by as much as 190 percent. In regard to production, he pays no attention to quality. By inflating the cost of labor and then distributing the profit, he seeks to win over the workers so that they are well disposed toward production, and invites them to eat and drink.
(2) He violates building design regulations, designs his own unauthorized blueprints, and gets others to sign them off, so that as a result they have to be redone, at a cost to the national and collective economy.
(3) While in post, he illegally collaborated in making estimates for private projects with others, and accepted bribes. In addition, he introduced someone to work for the Commune, and accepted half a carton of cigarettes from him.
(4) At work, he was always irresponsible. He slackened off the pace of work, failed to comply with the system, and failed to accept remolding. He usually sat in his office for long periods without going down to the site. He rarely engaged in manual labor, and he kept harping on about 'the noise in the office, that it was not quiet, that it was not easy to work'. . .and used that as an excuse to fool around at home. During the early part of the movement, he had still not corrected his mistakes.[38]

Accordingly, the Commune's Socialist Education work team decided: Liao "has been assessed by the masses as one of the three elements, and continues to wear a four categories hat. He will be handed over to the masses for supervision and remolding, and sent down to do manual labor. His wage will be reassessed by the masses, and he will be given the chance to earn a livelihood."[39]

However, as the reports made clear, although Liao wore a four categories hat and was subject to mass control, neither the Nimu leadership nor the ordinary commune members considered him low-ranking. Not only that, both leaders and workers, from top to bottom, were mainly illiterate, and Liao was the only one who understood technology and engineering finance. One of the four categories or not, if they wanted to make a go of it and earn money, Liao was their only hope. This meant that although Liao was politically suppressed and restricted in regard to his personal freedom, his status was not perceived to be all that much lower than that of others in the commune. Although his income was meager, his life was not yet completely bad.

Liao used his technical expertise, including his ties in industry and his social skills, to help the Commune gain a large number of projects. So the leadership looked up to him and gave him a lot of freedom, including allowing him to work at home on documents. This aroused extreme dissatisfaction. The greater his competency and the more he was in receipt of treatment that one of his kind should not by rights have received, the greater the envy. This is clear from reports by Commune members. Most were poorly written, but the suspicion, jealousy, and loathing are palpable.

To be sure, these criticisms were no different from those voiced by the Commune leadership, so their impact on Liao's life and work was not great. Moreover, by that time, especially after his reduction in status, Liao no longer reacted to such accusations as sensitively and seriously as in the past. Each time his surveillance was discussed, he would say in all earnest: "I pledge absolute obedience to the masses' dictatorship over me and to their surveillance, and I guarantee not to make irresponsible remarks or act indiscreetly." "I swear that I will comply with the regulations concerning mass surveillance of the four categories, and that I will strictly abide by the requirements of the system for reporting on my thinking, requesting leave, receiving guests, examining and appraising, etc." "I will actively apply myself to studying politics and studying Mao's *Works* in my spare time, and I will regularly deliver study reports. As an important part of my thought reform, I will strive to achieve a double bumper harvest in my manual labor and my study, so that my hat can soon be removed and I can return to the ranks of the people."[40] But in fact, by then he no longer had much hope that his hat would be removed and that he would be allowed to go back to his original unit.

Naturally, Liao did his best to his realize his promises. If he made some small mistake, he would immediately criticize himself and request the chance to atone for his crime by performing meritorious service. For example, some workers exposed his regularly accepting invitations from project clients to dine with them, and to consume tobacco and alcohol. Although this was a necessary form of business entertainment, he nevertheless immediately admitted that it was "corrupt" behavior, and expressed his willingness to accept punishment. Although he was unable to compensate monetarily, he promised to "hand over one watch, as a disgorgement of ill-gotten gains. If that is not enough, five yuan can be deducted from my monthly wage, until the compensation is paid off."[41]

As for the other kinds of reports, he used the old "supplementary confession" method, seeking on the one hand to offer an explanation and on the other to make a self-criticism. For example, some workers couldn't bear the fact that he often worked from home, so he first admitted that this was a manifestation of his "fondness for an easy lifestyle and his aversion to work" and criticized himself for being afraid of disturbances, and then explained that a lot of paperwork in the Commune, including the preparation of engineering drawings and budget, was down to him; it was only because there were no quieter rooms in the Commune that he was allowed to work in the hostel. Others exposed the fact that when contacting people concerning projects, he wore the false hat of an engineer and an associate cadre, to which he "confessed" as follows: "I have made a personal investigation, and I found that I have never introduced myself or posed boastfully as an engineer or associate cadre." If the idea ever arose, it was because the clients were being polite and trying to flatter him. Naturally, he added: "If people flatter me, I should immediately declare my identity to them and correct their wrong impression. Otherwise, they might have wrong expectations, thus creating a bad impression. This is an expression of the vanity that stems from my social [experience], my dishonest attitude, and my vestigial thinking. It deserves severe criticism."[42]

DYING AT ONE'S POST

In 1966, the Cultural Revolution broke out. Longstanding four categories like Liao who had spent years under surveillance[43] were suddenly subjected to a ceaseless round of struggle meetings in various districts and units. Apart from the meetings, they were forced to sweep the streets, build roads, clear out the latrines with their hands, feed the pigs, and do strenuous and dirty work. But Liao did not, strictly speaking, suffer such treatment for long. Not long afterwards, the Nimu Cooperative merged into a residential construction company, and Liao was assigned to the ninth construction team to undergo labor reform on the production front. He joined one team after the other, always as a worker. But because he was too old to climb the scaffolding or do heavy physical work, the team put him in charge of transporting materials and other chores.

It is clear from the thought reports that Liao submitted to the regulatory authorities each month starting in the 1970s that around the age of 60 Liao, although still under surveillance, was in a much better state of mind than previously. Because of his special status, and because he abided by government policies, laws, and regulations, including the requirements at the ideological and moral level, he was far more conscientious than many workers and cadres and had a far deeper understanding.

The second construction team to which Liao was attached was constantly in deficit, and sometimes lost several hundred thousand yuan a quarter. Liao worked out the reasons for the loss. He pointed out that wages accounted for just 10–15 percent of expenditure, while materials and tools accounted for the remaining 85–90 percent, so the key to reducing losses lay in reducing waste and theft. He explained to the team again and again that losses due to waste and theft were serious and that it was necessary to develop ways of cutting them. He personally did his best to help resolve the problem.[44]

For example, on one occasion he found some workers had climbed up onto the roof to sleep or relax in a cool place and had broken some tiles, so that two of the workshops leaked, causing the machines to rust. To remedy the situation, regardless of his advanced age and doddery legs, he climbed onto the roof once it had stopped raining and replaced the broken tiles. The same happened the following summer: he once again climbed onto the roof and mended it.[45]

On another occasion, to prevent or reduce theft, he risked possible political retaliation by personally catching one of the thieves. When he saw that two workers were engaged in "furtive behavior," he quietly observed what was going on. When the two workers started to steal steel reinforcing bars and were getting ready to throw them over the wall, he rushed out and caught them red-handed.[46]

On yet another occasion, a construction team was sent to a military site to do some building. The team foreman pointed out that the soldiers were not particularly careful about the materials they used, and he asked Liao to come up with a way of leaving some of the materials behind and letting the foreman take them away. Liao was not afraid of offending the foreman, and said no. He noted in his thought report:

> This kind of devious hankering after petty gain is still quite widespread. For example, pulling apart reed mats to build private chicken coops; using straw bags to wrap coal for private consumption; and workers taking tinplate buckets and galvanized iron containers (which were production tools) without authorization and for private use in their own homes. The shortage of containers is especially detrimental. We are unable to meet our needs at work. More than fifty have gone missing. . . . I raise this sort of unhealthy tendency with the Organization. I propose that the Organization put an end to it, and that all common property be returned to its rightful place![47]

By then, Liao's ideological consciousness was far higher than that of most workers and cadres. This is obvious from his tireless submission of ideological reports to the Organization, especially his active criticism of bad people, bad things, and bad thinking.

There were two dictatorship objects in Liao's construction team, himself and another man called Chi Mujiang. Although both were under surveillance, Liao strongly disapproved of Chi's words, actions, and behavior. The reason was simple: in his view, Chi had not put his heart and soul into transforming himself.

For example, on the site for which they were responsible, the pipe to the septic tank was blocked and had started overflow, but Chi ignored it. Liao couldn't bear the sight of it, and used his Sunday break to clear the pipe and make a manhole cover using cement. Chi saw what he was doing, but said nothing. Nor did Chi regularly clean out the latrines for which he was responsible, so that some workers started complaining. The cadres in charge of hygiene, regardless of the facts of the matter, told Liao to find a solution. So Liao had to clean it up on his own. The team raised a few pigs, for eating at New Year. On Sundays and holidays, the workers had time off, and the pig workers also returned home, leaving Liao and Chi to feed the animals. But Chi always found an excuse to go off somewhere, so Liao, "without the slightest hesitation, bravely shouldered the task." In his ideological reports, Liao often sharply criticized Chi's "fear of dirt, fear of fatigue, and fear of death," and asked: "How can he talk about serving the people, how can he transform his world view and his thinking?!"[48]

Liao's heightened consciousness was exemplified by his daring to criticize not just fellow objects of the dictatorship like Chi but Party members and cadres in his own team. For example, Li, a Party member, led the rest, in violation of team regulations, to prize open the door to a meeting room on the third story of the hostel, where they removed the bed boards and gave them to the workers to use. Liao was affronted. He not only criticized the matter in his report but added further criticisms of other acts by Li. He wrote:

> Recently the head of cavalry was coming out of a meeting when he saw Li in the gatehouse reading a newspaper. He asked Li: 'So you don't go upstairs to join the meeting but stay here instead, reading the newspaper?' Li replied: 'Fuck the meeting!' Currently the brickwork on the third floor wall is a problem, but Li has gone home to get some rice, and won't be back for a few days. In the past, at the water transport site, when so-and-so from the construction team and Secretary Zhao had a big quarrel and so-and-so said the appraisal was unfair, Li said behind his back: 'Actually, lots of things are unfair.'

Liao wrote in his report: "It goes without saying that I don't have the right to talk about these things, but I still think that telling the Organization about words and deeds not conducive to socialism, to draw clear ideological boundaries," is necessary.[49]

Liao's transformation in the direction of ever higher consciousness had to do both with his getting old and his gradual physiological calming, and with his sense of gratitude toward the cadres and workers in his team for treating him without discrimination and for the general state of harmony. He could not but be grateful and rejoice at a good outcome when he thought back on the large number of counter-revolutionaries either shot or sent to labor camps in previous campaigns. He said: "A criminal counter-revolutionary element like me should by rights be resolutely suppressed, even death would not expiate my crimes, but the Party and Chairman Mao have granted me generous treatment and given me a way out. This is simply to give me the chance to redeem myself by good service."[50]

Strictly speaking, in the past Liao had had no strong attachment to home life. For many years, because he was under surveillance and for other reasons, he had almost never gone home, although his home was not far away. Even while on leave, he helped people by standing in for them or remained in the hostel to do jobs, or read the newspaper, as well as writing his own thought reports for the Public Security Bureau or his own unit. As he grew older, he gradually transferred his attention to his family and children. As he approached the age of sixty, he almost never mentioned his children or his family of his own accord in his thought reports and other confession materials. However, after the early 1970s, he began to mention them more frequently and to pay more attention to their circumstances. Although he had lived with them only briefly, he began to express warmth and affection for them, and he was grateful to the government for making possible a change for the better in his children's lives.

In February 1975, he talked more than ever about his children in his monthly thought report. He said: "Every spring, I think back on a misfortune that occurred in the old society." In 1936, after graduating from Y County Teachers Training College, he had, through an introduction by one of his teachers, got a job in a primary school attached to M Municipality's arsenal. However, to his dismay, on the day before the Lunar New Year, after he had left his family and gone to M Municipality, it turned out that he could not be employed, so he was forced to return in the freezing cold to K Municipality. His conclusion: "In the old society, graduation was tantamount to unemployment. Today, however, my children have all gone home, they are all working and studying, and they are fine in body and spirit." "The market prospers, prices are stable," and during the Spring Festival "the family reunites, with the addition of a new daughter-in-law. Everyone is elated, spirits are high, and all praise Chairman Mao and thank him for their good fortune." In the evening, the entire family watched a film together, and then he returned to the team to study the *Communist Manifesto* and *Communist Principles* for a couple of hours. He wrote: "In happily experiencing a revolutionized Spring Festival, I do not forget the Organization's solace toward me on this holiday," and he also felt "completely confident of the policies designed under Chairman Mao's leadership to educate and transform the people."[51]

In a report in September, Liao once again made an emotional reference to his son, who had been sent down to the countryside and, by then, been allowed by the Organization to replace Liao's wife on her retirement from her job as a sales assistant in a store. He said:

> Where in a capitalist society could you find such consideration? If a worker can no longer earn his living, he would have been kicked out. Take my wife, in her case, you can even better appreciate the thoughtful extension of differential treatment. It's very moving. Again and again the children are encouraged to listen to the Party, not to be particular about what kind of work they do or about their treatment, and to contribute their youth to the revolution." Today, "my four children all have jobs, and life and learning go well for them. This can only educate and encourage someone like me,

who has undergone transformation. I must strive even harder to transform myself, I must not relax my guard. I must stubbornly reform myself, so as not to hinder their progress.[52]

To a certain extent, Liao's attention to his own political consciousness was designed to transform himself in order to avoid getting his family and children into trouble. In late 1974, at a team meeting to review the four categories, some workers criticized Liao for having shown too little discipline in recent months. They said he had been going home during holidays and festivals a lot more than in the past. Liao immediately responded to the pressure. He said at once that he accepted the workers' warning. Why was it that he had rarely gone home in the past but in recent months had gone home often on Sundays? Because his eldest son was about to get married, so he wanted to be able to help manage things; on the other hand, it was true that he himself had significantly lowered his demands on himself. He said: "In future I will maintain strict discipline and follow the rules and regulations, I will strive to make a 180-degree turn."

On New Year's Day in 1975, Liao did not go home. Instead, he helped out in the team kitchen, repaired the stove, took the initiative to clean the stove and mop up the water, and covered the outdoor electric motor with asphalt felt. In the evening he read the newspaper, studied, and listened to the New Year editorial on the radio. He got ready to finish his December thought report within three days, and planned within five days to finish writing his annual report on his ideological transformation for the street neighborhood committees and the police. After that, he resumed his old practice of doing something to benefit the people on his days off. Later, he greeted the revolutionized Spring Festival with a militant posture and pledged to accelerate his reform in 1975.[53]

To maintain such a state of mind over a long period, especially given his greater years, inevitably led a man like Liao to transform ideological passivity into a dual "consciousness" in thought and action. In accordance with the CCP's theory of class struggle, Liao clearly believed that his "old ideological consciousness was pronounced and that his head was stuffed full of non-proletarian ideology"; "even his bones contained bourgeois toxins," and he definitely needed a thorough remolding. If in the past he had lacked a conscious understanding of his own reform, by the mid 1970s he had come to realize that it was wrong to transform oneself simply in order to have a hat removed: true transformation should not be for the removal of a hat but should aim at transforming oneself into a socialist new person.[54]

Whatever the extent of Liao's ideological awareness, one thing is certain: day by day and year by year, it far surpassed that of most non-four categories—even most advanced elements at the time probably bore no comparison. In addition to his daily labor, he spent the rest of his time, including his spare time, holidays, and days off, learning and working. As he himself said, in all things, whether on or off duty, whether at or after work, you should always strive to do useful things for the people as long as it is in your power to do so, adding that "if you can carry a hundred, don't carry ninety-nine."[55]

At the end of the Cultural Revolution, when class struggle stopped being the key link, Liao's colleagues finally began more and more to affirm his efforts. At review meetings workers openly recognized that Liao never asked for leave, never allowed small injuries or ailments to stop him working, and actively and enthusiastically participated in team affairs, whether during or after work.

For example, people mentioned how, on one occasion, a tricycle delivering glass had broken down and the boss had decided to get a vehicle to transport them to the site the following day. Liao saw that this would simplify matters, but the site needed the materials, and anyway it would be wasteful to use a vehicle to transport the glass and could easily result in breakages. So he insisted on pushing the broken tricycle himself. In all, it took him several hours to get back to the site.

Others mentioned how he had dredged the cesspit, cleared the water pipes, transported the soybean pulp, fed the pigs, and attended to environmental and sanitary issues on rest days or in his spare time. The septic tank in the team compound often overflowed, causing a terrible stink, and did so for years, but after great effort, much dredging, overhauling, and the building of open drains, he finally removed this long-standing problem.

When the praise started, Liao offered a straightforward explanation in his thought report. He said: "I have one dominant thought, which is to be of as much use as possible to the working masses so that they forgive me."[56] Obviously Liao's strong sense of guilt was due to his desire for forgiveness by the masses, but it is also true that he had spent all those years doing these things not just for himself but for others.

Whether or not he continued to hold out hope, the era of reform and opening up had arrived, and just around the corner lay the prospect of political liberation for all four categories. Liao had waited sixteen years for this—almost twenty-seven years, if one starts from his first wearing of the hat of a "backbone element of the reactionary Party." However, just a year before the Central Committee officially announced the removal of all four categories hats,[57] on January 9, 1978, he fell down from a bumpy lorry while transporting wood to the site and died, despite efforts to save him. He was sixty-two.

His sudden death raised a number of problems. How should he be put to rest, and what sort of funeral address was appropriate? Given his performance, one month after his death the team responsible for the annual review of objects of dictatorship proposed that the cadres should convene a special meeting to discuss lifting Liao's surveillance order and removing his four categories hat. Most of the workers were sorry about Liao's death and wanted him to be shown the same respect as a normal worker after his death, so that his children would no longer suffer the political opprobrium of being children of one of the four categories.

At the meeting, several workers and master workers gave Liao a relatively high appraisal. He had worked tirelessly and was not afraid of dirt, he didn't distinguish between work time and free time, he worked year in year out for the team, he was concerned about state property all the time. They all thought he had already achieved reform. They said, tactfully, that although Liao "remained our enemy up to his death," "we should, for his descendants' sake, take into account the fact that he had accepted reform, and remove his hat."

In their summing up, the cadres declared that it was the view of participants that "Liao, from the point of view of reform, had progressed year by year, had shown initiative at work, and had always shown concern for state property. No matter what the circumstances at work, he had always first of all told others of his status and put himself under the supervision and control of the masses. He always worked, whether he had been ordered to or not, so the masses believe, in accordance with Party policy, that his hat can be removed."[58]

After the team leadership, the company, and the local police station had done further research, on March 13, 1978, nine months before the Central Committee announced the removal of all four element hats, the team issued its last "four element examination and approval form" regarding Liao. It explained the removal of Liao's hat as follows:

> After gaining his hat and coming under supervision, Liao gradually recognized his crimes, accepted his punishment, and accepted supervision by the masses as a step toward reform. By the end of each year, his review had progressed. For example, at the end of last year the masses appraised him as × [word missing] category. In the course of various political movements, no further political or historical problems or concealment of guilt were discovered.
>
> While wearing the hat, and under supervision, Liao
>
> (1) persisted with his study, read books and newspapers, and seized the opportunity for ideological reform. To reform himself and become a new person, he personally subscribed to a newspaper and bought Mao's *Selected Works* and various study materials. In the course of his study, he was able find ideological links and identify gaps, to write about what he had learned from study, and to submit monthly and year-end reports. On holidays, he rarely left the site. He adhered to a program of half a day's study and half a day tidying up around the compound, feeding the pigs, etc.
>
> (2) He always did the work assigned to him. He took the initiative and was dependable. If the leadership told him to do something, he did it, and he even did things when not told to. In addition to his ordinary work, he used his spare time to attend to sanitation, repair the latrines and the lighting, dredge the sewers, and feed soybean pulp to the pigs.
>
> (3) He abided by the system of discipline. He arrived at work early in the morning and left late at night. During the rampages of the "Gang of Four," when

anarchistic thinking was to be found everywhere, some of the team's employees sometimes left work early, but he insisted on working a full shift and sometimes did not go home until ordered to by the leadership. Regarding ideological reform, he reported each month, and if something came up that required him to be away he asked for leave.

(4) He was able to put himself under the supervision and control of the masses to facilitate their supervision and his own reform. Wherever he went somewhere to work, he first told the people there about his political status, so that those who were unaware of it could supervise him.

The construction team's opinion was: "In accordance with Liao Xuechang's political behavior, the masses and the monitoring team decided after a discussion that his four categories hat could be removed."

The committee of K Municipality's second residential construction company issued the following ratification on March 24: "After research, the company's Party committee has agreed to remove Liao's counter-revolutionary hat, and asks the public security organs for their approval."

After the higher authorities and the local public security organs had issued their approval, Liao's four categories hat was finally, and posthumously, removed, and he returned to the ranks of the people.

The Consequences of Concealing History

How a Worker Cadre Came to be Classified as a "Bad Element"

The term "bad element" has long been used by both the Kuomintang and the Communist Party. At first, it was used in a general sense, of corrupt and opportunist elements, but later it became a technical term commonly found in CCP documents, meaning impure elements who had a destructive effect on the Party and its cause.

On March 10, 1956, the Central Committee issued an official document seeking to distinguish between counter-revolutionaries and "other bad elements." However, the document still stressed that "all counter-revolutionaries are bad elements." On this basis, it explained that other bad elements were, beyond the designation as counter-revolutionaries, also political swindlers, traitor elements, hooligan elements, elements whose intrinsic quality has undergone extreme degeneration to the point that it changes its nature, and so on.[1]

In 1957, Mao Zedong defined the concept for the first time within the ambit of criminal offenses. He said that dictatorship must be exercised over "thieves, swindlers, those who commit murder and arson, hooligan gangs, and the various sorts of bad elements that seriously undermine the social order."[2] Bad elements mainly "undermine the social order" indirectly, in which sense they differ from counter-revolutionaries, who directly oppose the Communist Party. So bad elements are usually sentenced slightly more lightly than counter-revolutionaries. However, since bad elements are still included among elements that "seriously undermine the social order," from the perspective of the class struggle the new regime continued to see them and class-enemy elements as jackals of the same lair. As a result, the policies directed against these criminal elements were, in essence, the same as those directed against counter-revolutionaries. That is why, after the founding of the People's Republic, landlords, rich peasants, counter-revolutionaries, and bad elements were lumped together as the four categories.[3] Apart from those shot or sentenced to prison, most were deprived of their political and personal rights for long periods of time, and handed over to lower-level authorities to perform manual labor under supervision and be reformed.

However, the definition of bad elements was too broad and complex. Few criminal offenders opposed socialism: many were not intentionally bad. Being bad was in many cases because of shortcomings of the system and policy flaws, so whether people convicted as bad elements were really bad, the extent to which they were bad, and whether or not they deserved sentencing and being placed on the Other register is, from today's point of view, debatable. Here, we are talking precisely about such a bad element. For whether toward the new regime or in regard to his personal feelings about the new society, he was at the very least never "bad." So how did he become "bad"?

A BRIGHT AND BEAUTIFUL FUTURE

Li Lesheng was born on August 26, 1925, in L County in J Province, into a poor urban family. His father was a petty clerk in charge of issuing grain-tax receipts. In 1937, Li's mother died and he acquired a stepmother. He had siblings, and the family lived off his father's meager income. Li only did six months of middle school before dropping out to make a living. At fifteen, he worked in a cigarette factory and was then apprenticed in a hosiery shop. He worked on a number of small stalls, became a trainee in the Highway Bureau, and worked as a bus conductor. His life was hard. In 1949, when Shanghai was liberated, he enlisted with the L County Grain Bureau and joined the training class at the age of twenty-four. He was influenced by the political climate of the time. Having sucked in the atmosphere in society under the new government, he performed well, and joined the New Democracy Youth League (later the Communist Youth League).[4]

In 1951, he was introduced to M Municipality's X Factory as a temporary worker, but because of his positive attitude, and because he was a League member, he was soon made permanent. Just after he joined the factory, Zhenfan took off. Li responded positively to the government's call and, upholding righteousness above family, reported that the landlord relatives of the man who had introduced him to the factory had gone into hiding and that his own uncle, who had twice helped him to find work after the Anti-Japanese Resistance War, when he himself had been entirely destitute, had an illegal firearm.[5] At the time, he was both working and, in his spare time, following a middle-school course. He also joined in the factory's literacy campaign. For three consecutive years, he was proclaimed an "excellent teacher of literacy." As a result, he was elected to the Youth League branch committee. In 1953, he became deputy branch secretary.

In 1956, the factory was told to move to Y Municipality. Li had just been married. Shortly before the move, his wife, an operative in a textile mill, had given birth, so she did not accompany her husband. However, Li was a League cadre, and the Party branch secretary in the factory trusted him. So he responded positively to the move, to set an example. The baby was just a few months old. According to regulations, he could have asked to stay in M Municipality, but he forswore all personal demands. He willingly bore the burden of office, and often exceeded the quota. In Y Municipality, he was elected deputy chairman of the factory union and attended a trade-union congress as a delegate. He won second prize as a union activist.[6]

After the relocation, he began to move toward the center of the political stage and his fate turned. The Party secretary was replaced, and this, coupled with problems caused by the relocation, angered some workers. The factory leaders launched a rectification movement, and called on the masses to criticize the cadres and oppose bureaucracy. The situation went to Li's head, and he made mistakes that, given his character and experience, he should not have made.

A GUILTY CONSCIENCE

Li Lesheng was not a tall person. He had long, delicate eyes and a smile played on his lips. He had an easy-going look. Normally, he spoke little. He was sensitive, with strong self-esteem. When he encountered problems, he was mindful of potential personal gains and losses. In the forms he filled out over the years, he was liable to mention this. For example, "I am swayed in my thinking by considerations of gain and loss," "I cannot endure attacks," "I am liable to petty-bourgeois cowardice." In organizational matters, he always "demanded progress" and "a positive attitude toward production," but he "lacked confidence in the struggle," "could not bear criticism," and had a "petty-bourgeois ideology."[7]

Li's character and his life experiences were closely related. Since joining the League, starting work at the factory, and serving as a cadre, he had experienced major political movements, including Zhenfan. He described his life as follows:

September 1938–June 1940: Missed schooling because of the Japanese invasion.

September 1940–June 1942: Attended primary school in L County, studied, graduated.

September 1942–June 1944: Studied in L County junior high school, dropped out due to family difficulties.

October 1944–June 1945: Worked in a hosiery factory in M Municipality as an apprentice, could not stand the oppression and left.

September 1945–August 1946: Worked as a student nurse in Zhang Town hospital in R County, was dismissed.

January 1947–June 1948: Trainee at a bus station under the Highway Bureau, was dismissed.

July 1948–March 1949: Unemployed, worked as a hawker.

August 1949–April 1951: Worked for the L County Grain Bureau and the city government, drew up accounts, helped out in the summer and autumn harvests.

April 1951: Joined a factory in M Municipality.[8]

But this was not a full list. Some things he concealed. And concealing history, as Li knew from movements and campaigns, put him under enormous ideological pressure.

In early 1953, Li was elected onto the factory's League committee, which, given his political ambitions, brought him satisfaction. However, the more he stood out, the more he drew the attention of senior political departments, and the more nervous he became about his concealment. So although he wanted to become even more active, he felt frightened when talking with League leaders. This went on for months, until finally he was no longer able to control his impulses. He wrote a letter of resignation, offering the following excuses.

> My own lack of political theory and work experience is an obstacle and takes away my confidence. My evening studies conflict with meetings, so at the time of the democratic reform movement I missed classes. My cultural foundation had not been consolidated and my results are poor, and I often miss meetings. My day-to-day contact with the masses is minimal. I can't go deep among them, so I have become divorced from them. Many in the League have criticized me. Some say I only care about my studies and am selfish. After I got married, there were problems at home, which took up my time. This makes me ideologically depressed. At work, I have become even more inactive. For the sake of my responsibilities at work, I request to be relieved of my League duties. The Organization can get someone else to lead young workers in their studies, make joint progress, and do mass work.[9]

As things then were, the technical level in a medium-sized factory of that sort was low. Most workers were illiterate, and only a tiny number had had even a primary education. Someone like Li, who had graduated from primary and junior middle school, persevered with his night-school education, started at senior middle school, and could write fluent reports, was a rarity. So the Party branch Secretary Fan sought him out for a conversation, to give him guidance and encouragement. Secretary Fan also found time to go among the young workers and play table tennis with Li and others, laughing and joking, to show Li by example how to operate among young workers. Li had no choice but to drop the idea of resigning. He started working hard for the League, and was appointed deputy secretary. Even so, less than a year later, he once again asked to resign and return to the ranks, on the grounds that he was too nervous and anyway, by then, too old for the League.

However, he hadn't realized that the experience of being League Secretary had made him different. In January 1955, he had to fill out a cadre history. This meant that, at a personnel management level, his status differed from that of a worker. Once the opportunity arose, the Organization might make him a cadre, and this worried him.

In the summer of 1955, Sufan was in full swing. Unlike Zhenfan, which was directed against local despots and special agents, the new movement aimed at purging cadres in the Party, government, industry, and mining. All historical stains or suspicious episodes fell within the scope of this all-embracing movement. As an ordinary worker, Li was not directly affected by it. However, his guilty conscience, together with the fact that the factory Organization had assigned him cadre status, meant that he could not help but see ghosts everywhere, take general comments as personal attacks, and connect them in his mind with his own circumstances. Seeing the historical problems of more and more people, including people he knew well, ferreted out, he could bear it no longer. In September 1956, he submitted a confession which said:

> When I joined the League in the early years of Liberation, my lack of education and knowledge led me to conceal my personal history. . . . I knew I had problems, but I was on the League committee and led the study team. I feared I would lose the leadership's trust and the masses would discriminate against me and mock me, and say that it is scandalous that a League member should have problems. That would have meant an enormous loss of face. I forgave myself. I told myself that my past historical mistakes were trivial, and that I hadn't been an apprentice or a trainee but had been unemployed instead. Outside, I'd only known a small circle of people, I knew nothing about the Party and hadn't even heard of it. In the past I had suffered. I'd been forced by circumstance to work in the factory, I'd done nothing against the Party or the people, and if anything was discovered, I could be forgiven. As long as I worked well things would turn out right. Because of the mischief caused by worrying about personal gains and losses, I couldn't summon up the courage to confess.
>
> After the democratic reforms, the leadership asked me to become deputy secretary. But the more the leadership trusted me, the more I experienced pain and shame. I was afraid that once the leadership knew about my problems, it would suspect that I had wormed my way into the Organization, and things could become even more serious. So I was never at ease. That was one of the main reasons I left the League in 1954. Sometimes I'm fine and cheerful, but as soon those shameful problems cross my mind, I'm depressed again.

At the end he wrote: In order to wash away these historical stains brought about by imperialism and the reactionaries, "I am today determined to confess to the Organization."[10]

HISTORY SEES THE LIGHT

What was Li Lesheng's "shameful" problem? According to his confession, it was as follows:

(1) During the Japanese and puppet period, afraid of being press-ganged, he deliberately under-reported his age by two years, and never corrected the omission.
(2) During the war, the Kuomintang army made him work as a nurse in a hospital. After he escaped, he had to make a living one way or another, so he signed up with a Kuomintang army health team for a while, and was introduced by someone he knew to help collect taxes.
(3) He and his associates became sworn brothers in a ten-brother team, under an "old man."

In this new confession, he rewrote his personal history. This version was markedly different from the previous one:

August 1932–June 1937: five years in the primary school attached to L County teachers' training school.

August 1937–June 1938: X Town, fleeing the turmoil of war.

August 1938–June 1940: Graduated from the model primary school attached to L County teachers' training school.

June 1940–September 1940: School stopped, lived at home.

September 1940–November 1940: Apprentice in a cigarette factory, M Municipality.

November 1940–August 1941: Unemployed at home.

August 1941–June 1942: Apprentice in M Municipality hosiery factory.

June 1942–April 1943: Nurse in the Eighty-Ninth Regiment's Hospital in R County.

May 1943–September 1943: Unemployed at home.

September 1943–June 1944: Nurse in the Eighty-Eighth Regiment's rear hospital.

June 1944–August 1944: Unemployed at home.

August 1944–May 1945: Jinjishan, X County, with the Eighty-Eighth Regiment's tax team.

January 1945–May 1945: Unemployed away from home.

May 1945–April 1946: Unemployed at home.

May 1946–January 1947: Hawker in E Municipality.

January 1947–June 1948: Highway Bureau trainee.

July 1948–March 1949: Bus conductor in X.

April 1949–August 1949: Cigarette hawker in L County.

August 1949–April 1951: Helped levy taxes for L County Grain Bureau.

April 1951: Joined the factory.[11]

Li naturally wanted to provide some sort of explanation. He said he had enlisted in the Kuomintang army in order to join the resistance behind Japanese lines, and that the first time he joined was when he was on his way to visit relatives. While he was travelling by boat to Zhang Town, the Kuomintang's Thirtieth Division seized him and sent him to work as a nurse. A few months later, he fled back home. Unable to get on with his stepmother or to stand the way people in the neighborhood looked down on him, he ran away to find work. However, he found none, so he again joined the Eighty-Eighth Regiment's health team. Nursing was hard work, so through friends he found a job with the Taxation Bureau—but only for three months, because of the danger of being seized by the Japanese.

Why was Li scared to confess all this? First, because he knew that having worked for the Kuomintang did not look good. True, the Kuomintang army was fighting the Japanese, he had stayed with it only for a short time, and he had never used a gun. But he feared the Organization would see it as a historical stain. Second, and more importantly, he had sworn brotherhood with ten others who revered the Kuomintang officer Yu as their old man. This would need to be investigated. Even in the absence of any blood debt or crime, this would count as having joined a reactionary secret society, a heinous offence. So he made a special point of emphasizing his youthful ignorance: "I swore brotherhood because in the past I had been influenced by old novels. I thought it was heroic, like in the greenwood stories. Revering the old man was because he was a hero who had not bowed his head. Stories about the Green Gang and the Red Gang drove my curiosity."

Li got on well with the factory leadership and the branch secretary, so he still had some illusions after his confession. He wrote: "I ask the Organization to deal with me leniently, and to educate and help me." After repeatedly hesitating, he added that he hoped the Organization would not make his confession public: "If it is possible for you not to make this public, please do so, to spare me mental pain."[12]

ASKING FOR TROUBLE

Li Lesheng's confession coincided with a period in which the leaders were mobilizing to move the factory to Y Municipality. Li was as active as possible. He put all his energy into the operation, to set an example. A few months later, the factory officially moved to its new site. There were many things to do, so Li's case took a back seat. The factory still depended on Li to help placate the factory workers during their migration and to resume production as soon as possible. This was why Li was not denounced but even promoted to deputy chairman of the trade union, as well as winning the title of union activist. For a year or so, no one took up Li's historical problems. Instead, even more esteem was lavished on him. Li got rather carried away.

For many workers, the move from M Municipality, a bustling metropolis, to Y Municipality, a backward, remote, and much smaller place, was hard to swallow, and created numerous difficulties in their personal lives. Before the relocation, Director Niu had described the new factory in glowing terms. He said the future was bright, things were cheap in Y Municipality, and it was a convenient place to live and work. But the workers found that things were a lot dearer than in M Municipality and the new plant was in the rural outskirts, more than three miles from town. Transport was poor, and so were facilities. It was even hard to get to the hospital. Nearly all the staff and workers were single and had no family to return to after work, but there was no entertainment. Feelings ran high, and there was a clamor to return.

Li Lesheng, as deputy chairman of the trade union, had to speak up for the workers. Secretary Fan, who had had confidence in him, had been transferred elsewhere, and the new Secretary, Deng Rong, was on poor terms with the trade-union cadres. Deng was rarely in contact with the workers, and immediately started criticizing the trade unions for only caring about workers' welfare and not doing anything to educate them. He criticized workers' discipline as lax, and blamed the union. Li looked down on the thin, small man. He had heard that his previous post had been at a brick kiln that had subsequently collapsed, which made him even more disdainful of the Secretary.

At that very moment, upper levels called for a free airing of views and encouraged the masses to criticize the cadres and bureaucratism, which encouraged the already dissatisfied workers to rush headlong into action and put up big-character posters everywhere.

Li's self-confidence returned. He had tried to help the factory placate the workers and had suffered abuse as a result, and he was not a Party member, so he was unable to attend important meetings. Aware that some decisions went against the workers' interests, he was filled with anger. Pushed forward by some of the workers, Li, with his senior-middle school education, became their spokesperson. He sorted out dozens of the workers' criticisms, and found some workers who could draw cartoons satirizing Director Niu. To judge by the contents of some of the posters, he himself had written one of them, criticizing Secretary Deng. The poster said that despite having in the past rendered great service, he never went among the workers. His brick kiln had collapsed, and the same was bound to happen to the factory.

The grass-roots rectification movement took place after the national anti-rightist movement, but it had a strongly anti-rightist dimension. As in the case of the national anti-rightist movement, the Party branch first encouraged the workers to step forward with their criticisms and help the Party carry out rectification and combat bureaucratism, thus deliberately exposing disgruntled elements, senior and junior, big and small. After that, the Party branch turned the movement against the critics. Several of them were labeled rightists. A few who had not put up posters but were known for their bad attitude and for running around on vicious errands during the movement were labeled as bad elements.

Li, as deputy chairman of the trade union, had not spoken out too sharply, so he escaped the calamity, but he was unable to escape self-criticism. In his written review of his criticism of the leadership in the wall poster, he explained: "The main concern was that Secretary Deng should go down to the factory floor to contact the masses. He had been at the plant for several weeks, but had only been to the paint shop once, and taken a brief look."

He also admitted that to write such a poster while rightist elements were attacking the Party showed that his "political consciousness was low, and seriously infected by rightist ideology and an inability to tell right from wrong." He went on: "In some places, the poster echoed the ideas voiced by the rightist bad elements. But for the movement, it might have developed in a dangerous direction." However, he stressed that, in the past, he had always placed himself on the side of the Party and government, upheld righteousness above his family, participated in various sorts of work, held various positions, and, when the workers began creating disturbances, helped the Party, etc. He said that although he "lacked ability, was not a good talker, and lacked experience," he "had always been loyal to the Party." He said: "I have never discussed with rightist and bad elements how to attack the Party leadership, I have never colluded with them," and the poster was "not an attack on the Party." Accordingly, he declared his willingness to accept the Party's criticism.[13]

A CLOSE CALL

The anti-rightist struggle in the factory was not yet over, and the Great Leap Forward had already started. The whole plant, from top to bottom, was the site of endless meetings, big and small. There were repeated expressions of determination to work extra hours, "to plant the red flag and pull out the white flag," and to go all out to make revolution. Li, whose education level was high, was transferred to the trade union, where he put together production reports, a daily newspaper, and briefings on the technical revolution. The economic situation was grim, human-made and natural disasters started happening, and famine was rampant, so Li, despite having stepped down as deputy chairman of the trade union, was still active on the factory floor doing cadre-type jobs such as recordkeeping and business accounting. His historical problem had still not been put on the agenda.

However, things soon changed. In August 1959, Ji, labeled a bad element in in the anti-rightist struggle, wrote a letter informing against Li. He said that during the rectification movement Li had abused his power as deputy chairman of the trade union to slander the leadership, and had produced lots of big-character posters, cartoons, etc. Ji said: "He personally told me that Secretary Deng's work style was very bad. At the first meeting of the factory committee, without distinguishing between the rights and wrongs of the matter, he criticized the factory committee. This sort of Party Secretary should change his style, or the same will happen as happened in the brick kiln, which collapsed. At the same time, he cursed Secretary Deng as an opium addict. He is deeply dissatisfied with Secretary Deng, and he constantly gangs up with Tang and Wan, I don't know what they're up to."[14]

Prompted by the informer's letter, in 1960 the Party branch turned its attention to Li's past confessions. While unable to verify several aspects of Li's past, it did acknowledge that Li had some serious problems politically, and started an external investigation.[15]

The external investigation looked into the following questions:

While working in Z County and X County, what reactionary organizations did Li join, what was his role in them, and did he engage in criminal activity?

In what circumstances was the sworn brotherhood of ten formed, and what was its purpose? After the revering of old man Yu ended, what happened to the old man's forces?

What organizations did Li join at the Kuomintang hospitals in Zhang Town and Tianjiashan, did he serve in any post, what was its political background, and did he commit any crimes?

What position if any did Li occupy in the tax office in X County, and did he join any other reactionary organizations or hold any posts?

Did Li join the Youth Field Service Corps or serve in any position in it, what activities did he undertake, and did he commit any crimes?

In 1945, when Li was unemployed in Z County and R County, did he do any other work, who did he do it with, what did he live off, and did he join any reactionary groups?[16]

Wang, who had a long-term working relationship with Li, was the first to be sent out to investigate Li's history. His trip lasted two months, and he was unable to track down most witnesses. But he did find another man called Ji, who had been with Li in the Kuomintang health team. Ji confirmed that Li had twice worked as a nurse and once as a tax collector.[17] However, Wang was not prepared to reach an immediate conclusion, and insisted that one should be skeptical about Li's confession and not lightly accept it.

He wrote: "Most of Li's past associates have a criminal or reactionary background, so some have been suppressed, some were sent to labor camps, and some fled elsewhere. Some died in labor camps, some fled to Taiwan [with Chiang Kai-shek] or Jiangxi, and the whereabouts of others is unknown, so I was unable to track them down. But it is clear from local Party bodies that such people were, in the past, members of reactionary organizations and colluded with bandits, despotic landlords, etc." His view was that when Li

> joined in reactionary activities he was still quite young, he didn't do so for long, he was a mere henchman. According to Li's associate Hong, there was no evidence that Li had committed any crimes or joined other reactionary organizations. But how did Li get in touch with these reactionaries and despotic landlords and become sworn brothers with them, especially in the old society of reactionary cliques, when it was not easy to join up with such people? At the same time these people controlled some evil forces, and Li did not talk in his confession about relying on evil forces. He said his life was hard and he was unemployed, but from an objective and a subjective point of view, the aim of swearing brotherhood was to share trials and tribulations, with the backing of evil forces. However, Li's confession says nothing about being contaminated by this. My personal view is that this matter is suspicious.[18]

Because Wang's investigation came up with nothing, the factory Party branch sent people hither and thither looking for anyone who might know something. They found the son of such a person, but all he could say, after several conversations, was that he had witnessed Li go to the Service Corps in search of work but could not prove that Li had joined it.[19] The Service Corps Li had been in contact with had only stayed in the locality for a couple of months, so the investigator believed Li hadn't joined it.[20]

Another name Li had come up with in a previous confession, who he said would be able to prove that Li was unemployed in the first half of 1945, was Cha, who had gone to another place. The factory spent months tracking him from Jiangxi to Xinjiang, before they learned that he had been sent to a labor camp. They then conducted an investigation by correspondence, but Cha insisted that he had "never heard of Li."[21] The Party branch was puzzled and disbelieving, so they wrote again to agencies in Xinjiang and asked them to help in the investigation, and to see if Cha still stuck by his story. The prosecutor in Xinjiang replied: "We checked with the hospital. He has absconded. If we get him back, we will tell you."[22]

The investigation of Li had come to a dead end, so it was suspended.

TAKING THE WRONG SIDE

In the second half of 1962, Li Lesheng was transferred to another workshop as production team leader. Because his fellow-townsman Chen was workshop director, Li spent only ten months in production and was then transferred out of it. After several months' training, starting in 1964, he was made a cadre and became a technical officer. He ran the workshop and the job responsibility system, as well as production management, quality, technical procedures, and other technical work until the Cultural Revolution.

However, Li's problems continued to weigh on his chances of promotion. Until the late 1950s, he was politically trusted, but after his historical problems emerged, especially during the anti-rightist movement in 1957 when he put up a poster about the secretary, people began to distrust him. Such was even the case with his fellow-townsman, who had been promoted to secretary of the factory's Party branch. Although Li was relatively well educated and by then a veteran worker, his political classification was only second rank. He was never informed about Party lectures and backbone-cadre meetings, and he no longer took part, as he had done in the past, in political work, propaganda work, and evaluating labor competitions.[23]

During the Cultural Revolution, Y Municipality split into factions, one representing the Red Guards headquarters, the other representing the August 31 Rebel Headquarters. At first, Li joined the Red Guards, because he despised the Rebels, who were "noisy and mischievous" workers who "loved to grumble," "were rude to the leadership," and would never achieve a good outcome. In his view, no ill could come of "standing together with the old workers and the Party and League activists."[24] Sure enough, the August 31 faction was repressed. But to everyone's surprise, it got support from the top, so the factory turned over and the Rebels seized power. They overthrew Niu and Chen. Anyone with the slightest power, from top to bottom, and anyone who had stood with the Red Guards became an object of struggle. Li, with his political and historical problems, was thrust into the open.

Li seems to have been ferreted out because of his relationship with Chen. The Rebels had branded Chen a "capitalist roader," and Li was exposed by the masses as Chen's "crony" and subjected to a fierce "bombardment."

To avoid falling into the political abyss with Chen, Li began writing big-character posters criticizing him, but he lacked the courage to face up to Chen at a struggle meeting. When some poster writers pointed their spears at him personally and mentioned him by name, he had no choice but to write never-ending criticisms of his relationship with Chen.

He stressed that he had only known Chen as a child, when they lived on the same street, and during two years at primary school. After that, they had no contact until 1951, when he joined the factory and discovered that Chen worked there. Even in the factory, they were rarely in touch, and didn't hang out together. In the early 1960s, however, Chen joined the administrative personnel and later became Party secretary and workshop director. He then transferred Li to a training role as workshop technician. They were constantly together, but only for two years or so. Chen had never talked with him about the Party. His role had mainly been to help Chen implement revisionist systems like the job responsibility system.[25]

Li did not link his own historical problems to the Rebels' interest in him. He said in investigations:

> I too was born into a poor family. At the age of fifteen I dropped out of school and went to work as an apprentice in a shop. I was beaten and scolded. I suffered inhumane treatment. After Liberation, I found a proper job and a secure life. In the old society I was a slave, in the new society I am a boss, so I hate the old society and love the new society. However, because I didn't study Chairman Mao's *Works* well, my world outlook was not thoroughly reformed. I blindly followed the local leadership. I did what I was told. I was deeply infected by Liu Shaoqi's stinking revisionist poison, and in the Proletarian Cultural Revolution I supported the bourgeois reactionary line. I am prepared to gain a profound understanding of my serious mistakes with the help of the Revolutionary Rebels and to strive for an early return to Chairman Mao's revolutionary line.[26]

HEMMING AND HAWING

On the evening of May 31, 1968, Li Lesheng was summoned to an office by a rebel worker and ordered to "confess his problems." Li hemmed and hawed, and gave a "poor performance." He was not allowed to return to the hostel, and was sent by the Revolutionary Committee to an air-raid shelter where suspects were detained to write confessions.

Li had a guilty conscience and was on edge. He was afraid he would be beaten. After thinking things through, at three o'clock in the morning he decided to escape. He walked to Hanzhuang and took the train to Y Municipality. At noon on June 1, he got off at a station but found nowhere to go. Practically penniless, he phoned his younger brother, who was still studying. The brother urged him to think again, and that night he returned to the factory. The next day, he wrote a confession addressed to the revolutionary workers admitting that his absconding was "another manifestation of his disbelief in the masses," and had "opened a gap through which the class enemy and people with ulterior motives could attack the Revolutionary Committee and the Revolutionary Rebels."[27]

On June 3, plagued by fear, he wrote a supplementary self-criticism addressed to the workshop service group responsible for watching over him. He said that he had "feared being beaten," and that the air-raid shelter was home to "swarms of mosquitoes." Staying there "was like being a prisoner, it was unbearable." As for Chen, although the two were from the same place and most people thought that he, Li, knew lots about what had been going on, in fact Li hadn't stopped blaming himself for "not having a high enough consciousness regarding the political line," for "having taken the wrong side, and for not having drawn a clear line with Chen." He said he knew that "the only way to return to Chairman Mao's revolutionary line was by drawing a clear line with Chen," but he didn't know the right things to say. He added: "I'm not very good at speaking. If I said nothing at the exposure rally, people would say I hadn't drawn clear lines; if I'd spoken up, I would have panicked and not been able to get the words out." He said he knew that some things, if raised to the higher plane of principle, would become serious, which made him even more afraid. So he had run away.[28]

Desperate to draw a line under things and put an end to the investigation and his confinement, Li racked his brains for every slightest detail of his contact with Chen over the years, and the materials steadily mounted up.

Li produced an eighteen-page exposé of Chen's "capitalist restoration" confessing his relationship with Chen. He cited examples of how Chen had done him small favors, promised him posts, recruited him into his faction, and "corrupted the workers' revolutionary spirit," quoting Chen's words since the start of the Cultural Revolution. The most serious charge was that Chen, at a meeting of leaders, had said that "people rely on education like cabbages on shit." This was to liken the Party's sun and rain to excrement, and "truly reactionary."[29]

But this was not what the Rebels wanted to hear.

On June 11, Rebel interrogators began attacking Li by innuendo, putting constant pressure on him for two hours, and none of the questions concerned Chen. They were all, in a roundabout sort of way, about Li, and the implications involved matters of high principle. The interrogators demanded that Li tell the whole story, in full detail, withholding nothing. All night he tortured himself wondering which problem had been exposed. Finally, he confessed to a "political mistake" that many people must have committed. He wrote: "In the first half of 1967, I listened to three Soviet revisionist radio broadcasts, the first time by chance, but also motivated by a sense of curiosity. The second and third time, I thought that as long as I listened with a critical mind, it wouldn't matter. I didn't realize that it was a serious mistake. If you listen for too long, you can slip into revisionism, enter the road of opposition to the Party, socialism, and Mao Zedong Thought, and turn into a revisionist."[30]

The Rebels were not satisfied. A struggle meeting was inevitable. Since the masses knew nothing of Li's historical problems, the denunciations and exposures continued to be about Li in the Cultural Revolution. So Li confessed in detail about how he had joined the Red Guards and opposed the Revolutionary Rebels. But because Li was not a leader, these utterances, including his confession that he had all along "been in cahoots with Chen," were trivial matters, even if raised to the level of principle.[31]

In late June, the Rebels organized a criticism and struggle meeting, and demanded that Li confess his historical problems. He handed over written materials. In July, he confessed to the whole factory and the "revolutionary masses" in a big-character poster. However, these confessions still did not satisfy the Rebels.

Aware that there was not enough evidence to convict him, the Rebels sent him back to do manual labor, while at the same time reopening the investigation of his historical problems.

NEW ISSUES CROP UP UNEXPECTEDLY

Originally, Li's historical problems were not particularly serious. At worst, he had, for a couple of months, worked as a nurse in the Kuomintang army, and he did not even count as an officially recognized Kuomintang soldier. Although he had sworn brotherhood with ten brothers and revered an old man, he had never actually done anything. However, as in the past with Secretary Deng, the Rebels did not believe that things were so simple. But whereas, in the past, the focus had been on the ten brothers and the old man, the new round of investigations uncovered some more serious facts that raised Li's problem to a new level.

The most important discovery came from Li's uncle Jiang Tao. He said in a statement:

> In 1948, Secretary Luo of the Highway Bureau handed out lots of forms at the bus stations, asking people to join the Kuomintang. Zhao and He asked me whether I was going to fill in the form and join. I replied: 'The deputy bureau chief is non-political, and I'm not interested in that sort of thing. We can just ignore it.' So neither of us filled it in. As far as I remember, Li said: 'It doesn't matter if you join or not, I joined the Youth Corps, but it meant nothing.' It was just a throwaway comment made while we were chatting about whether to fill in the form, I didn't take it any further. I didn't ask him where he had joined. At the time, Mao Benqing also worked in the station.[32]

This information stemmed from a query originally addressed to Li by an external investigator from Secretary Luo's unit. Li mentioned that, while employed at the Highway Bureau, he had seen a letter containing Kuomintang registration forms. He claimed that Luo had said he didn't believe in any party, so he didn't try to get them to join.[33] When Luo was asked about his relationship with Li, he could not fail to mention the matter. The only thing is that, while Li's statement could not harm Luo, Luo's statement caused Li no end of trouble.

To verify Luo's disclosure, the Rebels sent someone to question him. But by this time, Luo's answers had become vaguer. He said: "I don't remember the original words; as far as I understood it at the time, he had joined the Youth Corps, but I didn't pursue it any further."[34]

Although it was not easy to prove that Li had joined the Kuomintang or its Youth Corps, it was a useful lead in the struggle against him, and would doubtless become a big issue in the class struggle.

In late November 1968, the Rebels again organized an assembly of the masses to criticize and struggle against Li, and to demand that he confess his reactionary history. He wrote repeated confessions, but he stuck to his old line.

In one confession, he wrote:

Regarding the historical questions put to me by the revolutionary masses, I took the initiative to make a detailed written confession to the Personnel Security Section. I handed over a list of what I'd done and when, and of witnesses and their addresses. At the end of June this year, I wrote a confession for the spraying department's revolutionary committee. In July, I wrote a big-character poster in which I confessed to the revolutionary masses of the entire factory, holding nothing back. Now I provide an additional confession for the revolutionary masses to review. If I am found to have concealed any historical or criminal activities, I am willing to be severely punished.[35]

Because the interrogators raised further questions, Li made a supplementary confession. He explained that apart from the ten brothers and the old man, he had joined no further reactionary organizations. While belonging to the brotherhood, he had known only two of the ten, and he'd only met the old man twice. He'd not been active in the brotherhood, let alone done anything bad. "If I'm not telling the truth, I'm prepared to be severely punished."[36]

Since Li refused to confess to having joined the Youth Corps or the Kuomintang, the interrogators asked him point-blank. In a word-for-word repetition of his earlier confession, Li described in detail the situation when he was working with Luo. He said: "If I had been a member of the Kuomintang, I would not have been laid off in August 1948, and I would not have remained a trainee for more than a year and a half." He listed the people who had worked with him in the Highway Bureau and asked the Organization to conduct an investigation. He said:

I swear to the Party and Chairman Mao that I did not join the reactionary Party or any reactionary organizations, special-agent bodies, or peripheral organizations. I never participated in any political activities or any activities. I never bore arms. I was never in touch with the old man after our brief encounter. I was with a handful of the brothers on Mount Jinji, but I only met the other five twice, once at the swearing of the oath and once when bowing to the old man. There were no activities and we did no bad things. There's nowhere else I worked, and I have concealed nothing. If the investigation finds that I'm not telling the truth, my refusal to confess should bring even harsher punishment.

Obviously, he acknowledged that he should not have worked or collected taxes for the Kuomintang army, which was everywhere on the rampage, eating the people's grain, cheating and oppressing the people, and never actually fighting the Japanese devils. It was an army of the landlords and the capitalists, it was their tool, so it was extremely reactionary. Nursing its soldiers, dressing their wounds, giving them injections, helping its tax collectors cheat and oppress the people, feeding on the flesh and blood of the people, working hard on behalf of the Kuomintang reactionaries and the fascists, was counter-revolutionary. I joined the ten brothers and bowed before the old man as part of a gang of hoodlums. That was an even greater crime. I beg forgiveness from Chairman Mao and plead guilty before the broad masses. This revolutionary mass criticism is absolutely necessary. The general direction is entirely correct. I want to accept the punishment that the Organization deems appropriate.[37]

At the same time Li was being criticized and interrogated about his links to the Kuomintang and the Youth Corps, the Rebels' external investigators were continuing their work. However, they were getting nowhere. They had not been able to find Mao Benqing, whom Jiang had mentioned as a possible witness, and all the other people who had worked with Li at the time said they knew nothing about Li joining the Kuomintang. When they extended the investigation to the war period and people with whom Li had been in contact in the Youth Corps and the Youth Field Service Corps, these people also knew nothing about him.[38] The questioning and investigation had once again reached stalemate.

AN ATTEMPT AT SUICIDE TO ESCAPE PUNISHMENT

Li's problems did not go away simply because no verdict regarding his problems could be reached. Having been declared an object of supervision and control, he continued to be a target for exposure and criticism. In early 1970, the Central Committee started up a nationwide movement under the slogan "one thing to attack and three things to oppose."[39] It focused on cracking down on counter-revolutionary saboteurs and crime, so Li and other people with problems were dragged out and brought together in a "study class" and became the object of a campaign to attack saboteurs.

Because one of the spearheads of "one thing to attack and three things to oppose" was corruption and speculation and because Li's political problems could not, for the time being, be ascertained, the revolutionary committee saw his economic problems as a breakthrough, and got some leads from workers with whom, in the past, he had been on good terms. It was said that in 1962 Li, through a friend who administered the canteen, had substituted coarse food-grain coupons for millet on two or three occasions, and had used his authority to help that friend get a hardship subsidy and later used his name to borrow money to buy a radio.

After a fierce interrogation, Li was forced to admit that during the difficult years he "ate more than he was entitled to, served only his own interest, practiced graft and embezzlement, and lined his own pockets." He had used the name of the trade union and the workshop to get more cigarettes than he was entitled to; he had overcharged everyone by twenty cents for food coupons; taking advantage of the fact that he could obtain cheap washbasins from the factory, he had given them away in exchange for food and snacks; he'd borrowed steamed-bun coupons from the canteen and not returned them; and he'd taken cooking oil from the canteen.[40]

More emerged about Li listening to radio broadcasts from Taiwan. He admitted that in 1960 he had twice listened to the "enemy radio" in a workmate's home. The workmate had just bought a radio and could receive lots of stations, including Voice of America, Taiwan's Radio Free China, and Soviet and other stations. He hadn't paid attention to the content, and the second time he heard Taiwan radio he had switched it off after just a few sentences. In 1962, he had bought his own radio. Out of curiosity he'd listened a few times in October, but there was too much static on the Taiwan stations, although the Voice of America was clear, and he had listened to it only twice. In 1967 he had listened three times to a Soviet station, which was boasting about Soviet economic construction, the improvement in people's lives, and the fact that a Soviet delegation in China did not enjoy freedom of movement. But he swore that he had never deliberately listened to enemy radio in the company of others, and had never talked with anyone about what he heard.[41]

The most shameful and painful disclosure concerned his "crime of hooliganism." He had been sodomized by a platoon leader in 1942, while working as a stretcher-carrier for the Kuomintang. Later, he found that he had homosexual tendencies. After leaving the Kuomintang unit, he married and had children, so this tendency was suppressed, but he became separated from his family for a long period when the factory was relocated, and he again began forming homosexual relationships. So in dealing with the Organization, quite apart from his historical problem, Li faced this even greater secret worry and lurking danger. After his confession in 1956 of his historical problem, his continuing inability to face up to the authorities and his trepidation and anxiety whenever a new movement started was due to this. After the start of the Cultural Revolution, he did everything he could to meet privately with male friends with whom he had had sexual relations to make sure everyone told the same story, lest it slip out unintentionally. In the course of just two or three years, he had corresponded thirty-four times with twelve individuals and spoken with them more than thirty-two times.[42]

However, due to his guilty conscience, in December 1968 his interrogators bluffed him into making a half-concealed, hesitant confession. He was being asked about his roommates over the years, and said: "I have no other problems regarding my lifestyle, but I have touched male comrades' genitals, which is disgusting. I must mend my ways."[43]

In workers' dormitories such things happen. It's not so rare. There is a tacit acceptance of it by factory workers, although they might go on about it behind people's backs. In 1968, when the Rebels asked Li who he'd shared a room with, it was because there had long been rumors about him. With the focus on Li's political and historical problems, no special effort was made to investigate the matter. Now that the "one thing to attack and three things to oppose" campaign had got underway and the political issues could still not be resolved, the Revolutionary Committee was able to seize on this behavior, elevate it to a manifestation of "hooliganism," and attack him as a bad element.

After interrogating a worker who had shared a room with Li, the Revolutionary Committee identified several people with whom Li had had homosexual relationships.

On May 25, the workshop branch told Li that homosexual relationships were illegal and odious, and he must make a clean confession. Seeing that his "scandal" was about to be exposed, Li suffered extreme anxiety, fear, and shame. Unable to stand the mental stress, he made an attempt to end his life by taking poison, to put an end to it once and for all.

He left a message for his family and children in which he said he had committed a crime, that he apologized to the Party and Chairman Mao, and that he hoped his children would learn the lesson and study Chairman Mao's *Works*, obey Chairman Mao, and always follow Chairman Mao in making revolution.[44]

However, Li did not die. Someone heard his painfully struggling voice. He was taken to the hospital, and saved.

MAKING A CLEAN BREAST OF THINGS

After his release from hospital, Li, together with other members of the "study class," was put on a truck and driven to a rally in Y Municipality to support the fulfillment of policies and the honoring of commitments, and to accept on-the-spot education and, by telling the whole truth, receive a lighter sentence.

After returning, Li thought about things for two whole days and chose to make yet another confession. He wrote:

> In my mind were two kinds of fear. One was that if I confessed, the situation would become extremely serious, and difficult to handle; the other was that my mistakes implicated a lot of people, which I thought was unfair. These two thoughts battled away inside my head. Unless I confessed, things would get more and more difficult. The burden became ever heavier, so I could neither eat nor sleep. I could hardly breathe, I was completely dispirited and listless.
>
> The Party's giving me a second chance, in terms of my physical life, and especially its having saved and reformed me politically, the care it has bestowed on me, repeatedly explaining its policy to me, and summoning me to rallies and meetings—all this has helped raise my political awareness. It also takes great care of my life, it tells me to rest, to restore my health. If I am not loyal to the Organization and honest with

it, how can I be worthy of the Party and Chairman Mao and the revolutionary masses?[45]

However, Li was chancing his luck by not telling the whole truth and acknowledging only a small number of homosexual relationships for fear of harming friends. The Revolutionary Committee didn't believe him and tried to track down people by following up clues, widening the scope of the investigation, and interviewing suspects. The Committee twice dragged him before a city rally to receive on-the-spot "education," and the army representative Secretary Wu explained the policy to the various elements in the "study class." Li finally, bit by bit and with extreme difficulty, squeezed out his "problems."

By late July 1970, he had admitted to more than a dozen homosexual relationships.

In early August, he was forced to add Xiao, Xu, and Fan to the list. In late August, the Revolutionary Committee interrogated people with the aid of Li's confession, and some of his friends angrily denied having had a homosexual relationship with him and accused him of "framing" them. This plunged Li even deeper into a sea of remorse and dismay, and reawakened thoughts of suicide. On August 26, he slipped away from the factory and went to town to throw himself in a lake. However, on the way there, he remembered how two days earlier the small group had discussed the suicide of Zhang, and how one should be accountable to one's family, so he gave up the idea.

In September, Li accepted the masses' criticism. Seeing how impassioned the speakers were becoming, how they were stabbing around wildly on the basis of little or no evidence and "exposing" things that were a complete fantasy,[46] he began to realize that if he failed to make a clean breast of things, even more people might get implicated. So he carried on ruthlessly and regardless, made a "systematic confession" of "crimes associated with his lifestyle."

He admitted that, starting in the late 1940s, he had had homosexual relations with more than a score of people. His memory was excellent. He could trot out the year and even the month, as well as the location and the nature of the sexual act. He remembered every occasion with crystal clarity, and confessed them one by one.[47]

On September 16, Li wrote his longest and most painful thought report:

> Although I was not in the old army for very long, its bad style stained and influenced me deeply. A platoon leader in the stretcher team by the name of Nie took advantage of me while I was asleep to rape me anally. I was young and dared not resist. There were many instances of sodomy and masturbation. He hurt me, but I was young and ignorant. I disapproved of homosexuality, and had no interest in it. Given my ignorance, I began to masturbate, to vent my sexual urges. The poison had taken hold. I had fallen into the trap. . . . Later, I read some pornographic novels like *Secret History of the Qing Court, Fantastic Stories from Today and From the Past, Sexual Knowledge,* etc., about relations between men and women and between men and men. They were

filthy, and imbued with rational knowledge of that sort. These imperialist, revisionist, and feudal black goods seeped into my mind, took up positions along my ideological front, and deeply stamped my thinking with rotten bourgeois ideology. In the year before Liberation (1948), I was working as a conductor out of Kunshan bus station. I got along well with assistant driver Xu, and we became close friends. We were both around twenty-two and unmarried, and both of us had sexual desires. Because I had already been ideologically poisoned and had bad ideas, I lured him into a homosexual relationship and we committed the first offence. But all this happened in the old society. In the old society, you were surrounded by bad influences on all sides (I had been raped, I read pornographic novels, etc.), and I was young and ignorant, so I didn't realize it was a crime. As a result, I made mistakes. Everything can be attributed to the evils of the old society. After Liberation, however, Chairman Mao and the Communist Party saved me from my miserable life, guaranteed me a living, and gave me political status. By rights, I should have armed my mind with Mao Zedong Thought, swept away the remnants of the old society, and thrown myself into the three great revolutions (class struggle, production, and scientific experiment) and become a new person in the new society. However, one's world view does not change just because one wants it to. In society, there are still so many people who do not want to take the great socialist road. Li is such a person. In 1950, while working in L County, he raped me not only anally but orally, many times, which further poisoned my mind. To a certain extent, it shaped my future path of crime.

In accordance with Mao Zedong's teaching that external causes become operative through internal causes, Li's self-criticism highlighted the ideological roots of his crime. He believed that these roots lay in the word "selfish." It was because of his pronounced and deep-rooted selfishness that his words and deeds and his every move were for himself, not for the revolution.

> I went to night school for a few years, not for the revolution but so that I could get a higher wage and position; I made a study of production technology not so that I could do a good job but so that I could use my relationships to open back doors, eat more, engage in corruption, undermine the foundations of socialism, and sabotage socialist construction. Long-term abnormal homosexual relationships, even homosexual relationships that have replaced normal relationships between husbands and wives, can degenerate into criminal activity. All this is a manifestation of my bourgeois outlook on life, and of the contents of my life and of what I pursue.

He also criticized himself from the higher plane of principle and the two-line struggle, because, being decadent and degenerate "and not scrupling to listen secretly to jazz on the enemy radio or, on numerous occasions, to listen to enemy counter-revolutionary broadcasts, thus acting as a secret-agent squad of the imperialists, the revisionists, and the reactionaries, he had degenerated into a bourgeois representative of ideological backwardness and lived a corrupt and politically confused life."[48]

REHABILITATION AND MANUAL LABOR

Whether or not Li's political history was still suspect, his "hooliganism" was enough to make him liable to the same heavy punishment as a historical counter-revolutionary. In the winter of 1970, his case was closed as far as the factory was concerned, and he was transferred to the Military Control Commission of the Municipal Public Security Bureau for sentencing, punishing, and criticism. This body announced that he had been put under the interim control of the masses, to do supervised manual labor.

In 1971, Y Municipality's Public Security Bureau took over Li's case. Over and over again, Li confessed his crimes and wrote out confessions. The interrogation was completed within a fortnight. In accordance with regulations, he had to write a thought report at a set time every month, as part of the supervision process, while awaiting the outcome of his case.

He wrote:

> I have committed a heinous crime, which amounts to a contradiction between the enemy and the people. As an enemy of the people, I no longer qualify to be part of the people. I long for leniency, and for the government to deal with my case other than as a contradiction between the enemy and the people, so that even if I receive its highest punishment, such as expulsion from the factory, leaving the factory under surveillance, demotion and a pay cut, being paid only living expenses, being sent to the border region to engage in land reclamation, or being re-educated by the poor and lower-middle peasants, I will gratefully embrace it. If I am sentenced to wear a hat, I won't complain.[49]

The Public Security Bureau had already decided that Li did not need sentencing, so he was returned to the Municipal Light Industry Bureau's special team, with the recommendation that the unit itself finalize the punishment.

The special team approved the details of the case as submitted by the factory, and sent it to Li to check and approve. Li tried to defend himself on just a few points—that he had been dissatisfied with the relocation of the factory, that he had said there was "no way out," that he had used the rectification movement to attack Secretary Deng, and that he had frantically attacked the Party.[50]

In April 1972, the branch issued its conclusions and sent an official report to the Public Security Bureau for approval. It said:

> Li Lesheng worked for the Kuomintang Army's 30th Division as a nursing sergeant and a tax officer. Together with Xiang (an enemy major), Tong (suppressed by us after Liberation), Zhu (now in Taiwan), and others he formed a sworn brotherhood that revered Yu, commander of the Kuomintang's militia regiment, as its old man. He grabbed so-called taxes and engaged in other activities, as well as committing sodomy with the enemy health-corps platoon leader Nie. In 1947, while working as a bus-conductor, he masturbated and engaged in anal sex in the sitting posture, on

many occasions. After Liberation, he worked for the Grain Bureau in J Province and masturbated with Zhang; he also had oral sex with Zhang after getting him drunk. In 1951, after joining our factory, his hooligan behavior became even more serious. Up to the end of April 1970, he dallied with, masturbated, sodomized, and had anal sex in the sitting posture and oral sex with more than twenty workers, peasants, and young students. Seven were sodomized, five had oral sex, three had anal sex in the sitting posture, and liberties were taken with a female worker. When the worker Fan was sent down to the countryside, Li urged him to repay a trade-union loan. He invited Fan to his room for some fun, and they stayed there until late in the night. They had sex in the sitting position. Later, Li put vaseline on Fan's anus and sodomized him. After Fan had been sodomized, he kept on having to pass stool, and shat in his pants before he could get to the latrine. By laughing and joking with him, Li got a young worker in the hostel to have sex on repeated occasions. They masturbated, so that the young man ejaculated semen.

In 1960–61, at Li's home and in the hostel, he secretly listened to radio broadcasts by the U.S. imperialists, the Chiang Kai-shek gang, and the Soviet revisionists.

Apart from a historical problem to which Li confessed on his own initiative in 1956, he kept quiet about listening to the broadcasts until after he had been exposed; as for the sodomy and other activities, Li willfully tried to cover them up, and during the movement to 'purify class ranks' and the 'one thing to attack and three things to oppose' campaign, he established ties everywhere in order to conclude offensive and defensive alliances. After the Organization pointed this out to him, Li resisted by running away and trying to commit suicide. Only later, after the leadership had criticized and educated him and the masses had repeatedly struggled against him and criticized him, did he make a confession, moved and inspired by the Party's policy.

The factory's Party branch came up with the following method of dealing with him:

> Li is a veteran staff member. He swore brotherhood with ten brothers and the old man and played a reactionary role, which was to a certain extent evil. After Liberation, he continued to commit all kinds of outrages. He secretly listened to enemy radio, and he practiced sodomy, squatting sex, oral sex, and other criminal hooligan activities for twenty years. All this was serious, wicked, and criminal. However, seeing that Li is able to confess problems, the Party committee has decided, after discussing with workers and staff, to classify him as a bad element, put a hat on him, and hand him over to the masses for surveillance and labor reform.[51]

However, the Municipal Public Security Bureau considered that no obvious crimes had been committed. He had not listened to the enemy radio for reactionary reasons. His homosexual relations were consensual, and they were not only rather common among workers but the Supreme Court had clearly stated that it was 'not appropriate' to consider such behavior 'a crime.'[52] So as long as there was no evidence that Li had forced himself on others with criminal intent, the Public Security Bureau advocated education. The Municipal Public Security Bureau proposed that Li need not wear a bad element hat.

The factory's Party branch did not agree, but after mediation by higher authorities each side made a concession. The Security Bureau agreed to classify him as a bad element, while the factory agreed that he need not wear a hat and could do his labor reform in the factory. The Security Bureau declared that Li had been classified as a bad element, that he would not wear a hat, and that he would be dealt with as a contradiction among the people, in order to show leniency.[53]

<h2 style="text-align:center">FALLING INTO A TRAP</h2>

While waiting for their cases to be dealt with, Li and the others were assigned to rough, backbreaking work in the kiln, carting around huge quantities of bricks in dilapidated wagons. After the formal judgment had been passed down, the factory, given Li's technical ability, sent him to work in the spraying workshop.

From 1968 to 1972, during his four years of surveillance and of being locked up and controlled, Li had survived but had been denied the right to visit relatives, and he had nowhere to vent his sexual feelings. Once he returned to society and was granted freedom of movement, he started looking for partners. However, his old homosexual friends had been hurt, and no one dared contact him. He drifted into a relationship with Liu, another bad element in the factory. Liu had been a soldier in the Kuomintang, and had had a similar experience to Li. After joining the People's Liberation Army and being transferred to the factory, he too had sexual relations with other homosexual workers. This was why he, too, had been convicted.

Between August 1973 and July 1976, Li and Liu had sex more than a dozen times in the reception office, the air-raid shelter, the tea kitchen, and the milling section. But Liu was not Li's ideal sexual partner, so in 1976 Li had a sexual relationship with his fellow-worker Xiao's 16-year-old son. Li was infatuated with Xiao, and went during factory breaks to Xiao's home village to pursue his relationship with him. Li's behavior once again attracted attention. This time, he could no longer escape conviction.

In July 1976, when Li's behavior was exposed, the factory fetched him for interrogation. He admitted his sexual relations with Liu and Xiao. The Party branch and the factory leaders were furious. Sexual relations among the workers, especially among male workers after the factory's relocation, had been causing all sorts of problems. The factory leaders had had to deal with a great many cases, and they felt that the blame lay with bad elements like Li and Liu, who had imported bad morals from the old society. They gave Li and Liu notice of arrest. They said: "Li, despite the leniency shown him, has refused to repent. It is easy to learn from what is bad, and he has done serious damage to the physical and mental health of young people. In view of this, Li is classified as an incorrigible bad element who needs to be severely punished. After a discussion by the workers and deliberation by the Party and the Revolutionary Committee, we ask that the justice department arrest and prosecute Li and send him to jail, to appease the people's indignation."[54]

The criminal police conducted a preliminary review. They decided, in line with the principle that the public security system does not handle this type of lifestyle issue, only to carry out "policy education," and to send Li back to the factory to be dealt with.

When the case came out into the open, Li again flew into a panic. For a while, he was "on edge, and unable to calm down." The investigator had treated him kindly, and encouraged him to discard his mental blocks and strive to reform himself and thus to receive leniency. In a later thought report Li wrote: "I feel I have committed such a big crime that if I am not beaten to death with a club, if the Party leaders are still prepared to demonstrate patience and try to save me, to give me a clear direction, to do everything humanly possible to help me, I will feel to the bottom of my heart that Chairman Mao's revolutionary line is immeasurably wise and great. So I am once again determined to work hard at studying Chairman Mao's writings and to focus on transforming my world view and becoming a new person."[55]

But Li was too optimistic. The police had let him off, but the factory didn't. After stubborn insistence on its part, the Public Security Bureau accepted its opinion.

On December 27, Li's fellow criminal Liu was arrested. The factory held a rally where Liu was dragged up onto the stage by the workers' militia. His head bowed, he confessed his crime. The workers read out angry statements denouncing him. He was handcuffed, bundled into a police car, and driven away, to applause and cheers by an audience of hundreds.

Liu's trial left Li on tenterhooks and in panic for the rest of the day. On January 20, 1977, he learned that the factory was again about to deal with some criminal elements. The next day, he heard that a new person was going to take over his post. He realized his time had come.

On the 22nd, he told his younger sister that he might be arrested and imprisoned. That night, he told his younger brother, after he himself had gone to prison, to fight to overcome all difficulties and to do his best to get permission to go back to L County to visit their parents.

Having been fearful on so many occasions, Li began to calm down. He stopped thinking about suicide, and he even secretly hoped, after serving his sentence, that he might be able to return to the factory.[56]

Just a month after Liu's arrest, Li was arrested. Like Liu, he was dragged before a factory assembly. Charges were announced and notices were posted. The notice said:

> Li has repeatedly refused to reform. He has committed heinous crimes. His ideology is reactionary. His character is corrupt. He has reached a towering height of decadence. He is a remnant of the Kuomintang who has drifted into the ranks of our working class. To carry out the Party's basic line, to strengthen the dictatorship of the

proletariat, and to crack down on the sabotage committed by the "Gang of Four" and a handful of class enemies, the factory's revolutionary committee has decided to expel Li and to petition the public security organs to arrest him.[57]

Three months later, Y Municipality's People's Court sentenced Li:

Li is guilty of the bad habit of sodomy, left over from the old society. After Liberation, he failed to repent and was classified as a bad element, but he was not made to wear a hat. After being dealt with as a contradiction among the people, he offended again and again, committing evil and licentious sexual acts. To maintain social order and crack down on hooligan elements, we sentence the criminal Li to seven years in jail.[58]

Li's sentence was longer than Liu's, which he had not expected. He was sentenced in April 1977, at the age of fifty-two, and was sixty at the time of his release. Having been publicly expelled from the factory, there was obviously no point in him going back.

3

The Irremovable Hat

The Later Years of a "Historical Counter-Revolutionary"

On December 29, 1949, a Northerner wrapped in a long sea-blue gown, of stalwart build, with a big square head and wearing round-rimmed glasses, entered N Municipality Public Security Bureau and walked across to the "registration office for members of the reactionary Party or Youth Corps and reactionary associations wishing to repent." With utmost deference he handed over to the staff an already completed registration form, and there and then, using a writing brush, neatly wrote out a "written statement of repentance." Two weeks later, as instructed, he appeared at the police station on the street where he lived, to receive and fill out a "registration form for leading members of the reactionary Party, Youth Corps, or reactionary associations" and a "special household registration form," thereby completing the process of repenting his errors to the new government and entering his name into the register. He was Fang, a man in his early thirties, a doctor of Chinese medicine. He had been a member of the Kuomintang's county executive committee, which counted as belonging among the "reactionary Party's backbone elements."

It was eight months since troops under Liu Bocheng had captured N Municipality. That day, the CCP's military and political departments declared the establishment of a Military Control Commission, and that the "Chinese Kuomintang, the Three People's Youth Corps, the National Revolutionary Comrades' Association, the Chinese Youth Party, and the Social-Democratic Party are all reactionary organizations and should disband and cease all activities," while members of secret-service organs of the Chiang-Yan bandits "shall immediately report to the Public Security Bureau of N Municipality's People's Government designated by this Committee and its Sub-Branch and apply for repentance registration."[1] The

Commission then issued an even more severe notice, warning those who had not yet registered that if, by June 2, "you still refuse to register, and engage in sabotage, the People's Government will severely punish you, without mercy." Over the next few days, the number of people registering shot up from several dozen to more than two hundred.[2]

Fang had delayed registering largely because he was afraid. The Military Control Commission had made clear that the requirement to register applied mainly to six sorts of secret agent: Juntong, Zhongtong, the Second Department of National Defense, the command headquarters of Yan Xishan's special gendarmerie, political security organizations, and organizations affiliated with staff headquarters.[3] He had belonged to an organization affiliated with the Zhongtong, and was afraid to register for fear of being regarded as a secret agent. Even if not arrested, his rice bowl would be smashed. So, trusting to luck, he viewed himself as no more than a Zhongtong correspondent in the Party branch at the county level. He'd been in it for less than a year, and in 1948 he'd left the Kuomintang to make a living, so he thought that not registering was no big problem.

Six months later, N Municipality's Military Control Commission had issued a notice ordering Kuomintang members at district committee level and above and Youth Corps members at the level of deputy team leader and above to "forthwith and without delay take their ID card, household registration form, and two two-inch bareheaded photos to the district Public Security Bureau to apply for registration. They should surrender all remaining ID, documents, lists of secret Party members, archives, weapons, radio codes, and any public property or other items."[4] Fang could no longer hide. Although he hesitated repeatedly, after talking with old colleagues in the Kuomintang branch, he realized he had no choice.

He tried to explain this in the registration form. He said that after the Military Control Commission's notice, he had at first been undecided. Only after relatives and friends "encouraged him again and again" did he "joyfully" turn up to register. "Joyful" was of course hardly the word, but it is true that he had hesitated. However, his fear grew the more he hesitated. He would have ordinarily been careful about filling in forms and done everything possible to leave no loopholes, but this time he failed to do so because he was keen to gain the Government's trust. His attitude was positive, but his wording was indiscreet. He was lackadaisical even about basic information, and he was confused and incoherent. However, as the public security department was inundated with cases like his,[5] his form did not immediately land him in trouble.

For example, while filling in forms on three different occasions Fang listed three different workplaces, IDs, and details for his younger brother. The first time he said the brother worked as a farmer at home, the second time as a junior administrator in the inspectorate in Q County, the third time as a broadcasting officer in B Province. He gave his own age first as thirty-two and then as thirty-five, gaining three years in two weeks. He listed the occupation of a colleague in the Kuomintang County branch, who was also his best friend in N Municipality, first as a textile worker and then as a merchant. In the appendix to the "Special Residency registration form," he added a confession, to emphasize his acknowledgment of guilt. But it was obvious that it had been copied word for word from the "repentance form" he had filled out two weeks earlier.

After coming to power, the CCP was on its guard against five kinds of people left behind from the old society: secret agents, local bandits, evil bullies (*tuhao*), backbone cadres of the reactionary Party, and leaders of reactionary sects and secret societies. It not only subjected them to strict control but kept its various departments informed about their movements and followed up on them. The basic materials collected from different periods constituted people's personal files. The basic files on these five types of people initially consisted mainly of self-registration materials "pleading guilty to the people with heads bowed" (1949–50), and the historical leads they provided.

Relatively few "repentance" files relating to these five groups in 1949 and 1950 have been made public. Some of the main forms that Fang completed between 1949 and 1950 are therefore reproduced in detail below to help shed light on the situation.

REPENTANCE REGISTRATION

The materials were of two main sorts: "a letter of repentance by members of the reactionary Party and Youth Corps," and a "repentance registration form."

In the 1930s, the Kuomintang had required arrested Communists to write "statements of repentance," and now the Communists were using the same procedure against the Kuomintang. From Fang's forms, we catch a glimpse of the cultural level in rural areas and the nature of the education village children received.

The "repentance statement" was relatively simple. It was just one page long, and required a guarantor. Fang wrote:

> In the past, the writer of this statement of repentance, Fang Liren, joined the Kuomintang in S County and served as assistant secretary and administrative officer. Having served the Kuomintang's reactionary gang in its efforts to oppose the people, he confesses and repents in front of the people and pledges to become a new person from this day on, and to establish a worker's point of view in order to serve the people. If he does not keep his word, he is willing to accept the severest punishment.
>
> Guarantor Wang Ziming (his seal), repenter Fang Liren (his seal)
> December 29, 1949.[6]

"Repentance registration" is a rather lengthy procedure, taking up three pages. The form as completed by Fang is reproduced in Table 1.[7]

TABLE 1

Name and address	Current name: Fang Liren		Sex: Male	Age: 32	Profession: Practitioner of Chinese medicine
	Actual name: Fang Liren		Family class status: Poor peasant		Individual background: Chinese medicine
	Known as: [blank]		Education level: Elementary		Hobbies: [blank] Specialty: Medicine
	Origin	Xiguan Village, Q County, A Province.			Photo
	Current address	No. 9 Liuxiang (Hutong), Haizibian Street, Neiyi District			
Family situation	Real estate, assets and family composition	One brick house with two earth rooms and *six mu* of dry land. Father: Fang Guangxian, a doctor in the North China Military Region General Hospital, left home twenty-three years ago. Mother: disabled. Brother: Fang Libang, twenty years old. Resident in N Municipality, a total of four people.			
Education	Schools attended (where and when)	Xiguan Village primary school, four years. August 1926.			
	Training received (where, when and organizers)	October 1948, after Liberation, North China Military Region instruction corps.			
Personal history		Entered the county primary school in August 1926 (aged eight), and studied for four years without graduating. In 1932, aged fourteen, went to the county town and joined a pharmacy as an assistant. Began to study medicine. Successfully completed study in 1940, aged twenty-two, and began practicing medicine in September in Taigu County. Went home in June 1941 (when the Japanese invaders became more active and the medicine shop suffered damage). Both medicine and farming became impossible because of shortages. On February 28, 1945, aged twenty-eight, appointed by Q County government as a junior administrator. Became an assistant administrator in 1947, and assistant secretary of the Kuomintang branch in Q County in 1948. Left post in April 1948 due to a salary dispute. Came to N Municipality in July. A friend, Wang Yujiang, got me a job in the Huatang medicine shop. On October 7, became a medical worker with the Yangqu security police. On the 25th, after the Huangzhai campaign, liberated. Received training in Yangquan Municipality in the North China Military District for more than two months, and then went home. Since the Liberation of N Municipality, have remained with the Huatang medical shop, until now.			
Religious organization		Catholic			

Relatives and friends (including occupation and address)	Maternal uncle Chen Manyuan is a doctor in Q County. Cousin Shi Zhiming is a peasant in Zhang Village in Guan Town in Q County Town. Male maternal cousin Liu Youguang mends watches in N Municipality's Dudu Street. My friends Liu Liangchen and the merchant Zhao Xiansheng are in the Minsheng factory in Q County Town.						

Participation in organizations

Classification	Organization name	Place	Introduced by whom	Date	Document number	Unit	Position held
Pre-Liberation	Kuomintang	Q County	Zu Kang	March 1945	7	Q County Party Branch	
Post-Liberation							

	Name	Age	Origin	Occupation	Address
Direct supervisor	Zu Kang	42	Q County, Shanxi	Head of Secretariat	Address: Currently in Daliang receiving training

How the conspiracies were arranged	District sub-branches were set up under the county branch. Each sub-branch was divided into three groups. Each group of three to nine people had a district secretary, an executive officer, and a propaganda officer, later supplemented by another person. Based on district or street organizations. Due to hostilities in the Second War Zone, the above arrangements were not put into practice. The county branch had three groups: executive, propaganda, and organization. A separate group was put in charge of Yan Xishan's *Sheng* ("Voice") newspaper.
Sabotage you have committed	While serving in the Kuomintang, I carried out propaganda to influence the masses' thinking and make them loyal to the Kuomintang. I worked hard for the reactionary Kuomintang, I served the Kuomintang as general affairs assistant, I did accounting, and I opposed the people.
Weapons, ID cards, books, account books, charts, and other relevant material	[Left blank]
Registration vow	I absolutely confess that I have written down everything that I did in the past against the people and that from now on I will re-establish my worker's viewpoint in the service of the people. If there is anything false in my confession, I wish to be severely punished.
Notes for filling in the form	(1) If this form is not long enough, materials can be added. (2) In accordance with the Government's announcement, confess in good faith and add all necessary details. (3) Use a pencil or a writing brush, but write neatly. (4) This form must be accompanied by two photos.

(continued)

TABLE 1 (continued)

Colleagues who have led you or worked with you who belong to political parties—who are they? Say whether they belonged to the Party, the Youth Corps, or an association, and give the name of the organization, their name, age, address, sex, and occupation, and a brief personal history, including when they joined	Luo Liangchen, Q County branch of the Kuomintang, secretary and executive committee member, aged thirty-plus, lives in the Minsheng Factory in Guan Town. Ma Mingbo, Q County branch of the Kuomintang, executive committee and secretary, aged thirty-plus, a teacher in Pingcheng School, lives in the school on Chengmen Street. Liu Changliang, Q County branch of the Kuomintang, chairman of the free medical committee and secretary of voluntary work. Lives in Alley No. 2, now runs the Europe-Asia Pharmacy, in his twenties. Zhao Xiansheng, Q County branch of the Kuomintang, assistant secretary of voluntary work, thirty-plus, lives in the Minsheng Factory in Guan Town. Guo Shengmao, Q County branch of the Kuomintang, aged thirty-four, lives in Guogou Village in Q County, editor of Yan Xisheng's *Sheng* newspaper. Zu Kang, Q County branch of the Kuomintang, head of the secretariat, now undergoing training in Dalian Town. Fu Zhongxiu, Q County branch of the Kuomintang, in charge of general affairs, aged forty-six, now in Tangshan. Fu Hongshen, Q County branch of the Kuomintang, organizational secretary, aged twenty-five, now in Xi'an. Cao Weizhi, Q County branch of the Kuomintang, secretary of propaganda on the county committee, aged thirty-eight, now at No. 23, Huangmiao Street, in the county town. Zuo Youcai, Q County branch of the Kuomintang, director of the social services department, aged thirty-eight, lives at No. 2, Yijing Alley, Q County, now a merchant. Ma Dingren, Q County branch of the Kuomintang, assistant administrator of voluntary affairs, aged forty, lives at No. 10, North Village, Guan Town, in Q County, now at home. Shao Baozhong, Q County branch of the Kuomintang, assistant administrator of voluntary affairs, aged twenty-seven, lives in Sanhe Village in the county town, now a merchant.
People you know inside the secret-agent organization, their name, age, profession, address, brief personal history, sex, which organization and when joined	[left blank]

As well as registering with the Public Security Bureau and filling out the repentance form, Fang also had to register at the street police station. There were two registration forms: one for "leading cadres of the reactionary Party, Youth League, and associations within the jurisdiction of the third police station of the first branch of Public Security," and another titled "special household survey." Because the two forms differed, and were filled in on different days, Fang filled them in slightly differently, and in some places at greater length (Table 2).[8]

Finally, Fang filled in his "special household registration questionnaire (relating to Party, no. 130)" (Table 3).[9]

HIDDEN WORRIES OF A CADRE

Fang Liren continued to conceal the fact that he had joined the Zhongtong, the Kuomintang's secret-service agency. He had so far only confessed to having joined the Kuomintang in 1944, and having been a member of the branch executive committee in March–April 1948. At the time there was nothing and no one to implicate him, so he felt that he could swear "absolutely frankly" that "if what he said was found to be untrue, he was prepared to be severely punished." His life and work continued as normal.

However, the stormy Zhenfan movement that erupted in late 1950 and 1951 left him quaking. He had grown up in a Catholic family, been baptized, and, as a child, gone daily to mass. Later, while an apprentice studying medicine, his master was also a Catholic. He had rarely gone to church, but inwardly he was deeply religious. Such was his trepidation at the time that he went almost every day to seek God's blessing.[10] He later wrote: "During Zhenfan, as soon as I saw the notices about the shooting of members of the Kuomintang and secret agents, I was scared to death. I thought I was a suppressed object. I girded myself up and waited, I had nowhere to hide." After all, before Liberation he had spent several years in the Kuomintang and done many things that he now felt guilty about. So "when I looked at other people, I felt enormous shame and feared for my future."[11]

In the second half of 1950, in addition to his irregular job in the pharmacy, Fang had begun working as an acupuncturist in a convalescent hospital for city workers, and subsequently his appointment had been formalized. He considered himself fortunate. In his view, to work for the state was, under any circumstances, better than drifting around in the community, under the permanent gaze of the police. In a public hospital, his family also gained on-site accommodation, and his every move was known to all, so "it was an opportunity to become a good person."[12]

For the first time, he took the initiative in helping the new government. In 1951, in the district where he lived, a Three-Selfs patriotic movement was organized as part of the reform of the Catholic Church, and he was invited to take part. After reading newspapers and propaganda materials, he set about winning support

TABLE 2

Name: Fang Liren	Alternative name: Jiaming	Known as: [blank]	Sex: Male	Age: 32
Native place	Xiguan Village, third district, Q County, S Province.	Current address	No. 9, Liu Alley, Such-and-Such Street.	
Occupation before Liberation	May 1948, doctor in the Huatang Pharmacy, Mishi Street, N Municipality. October 1948, medical orderly with the public security force in P County, liberated during the Battle of Huangzhai.	Occupation after Liberation	After the Liberation of N Municipality and after finishing my training with North China Military Region instruction regiment, I returned in June to the Huatang pharmacy and worked as a doctor.	
Participation in the reactionary military group, and occupation	In 1944, my friend Zu Kang recruited me into the Kuomintang. In October 1945, I was appointed assistant administrator in the general affairs department of the Q County Party branch and started working as a doctor in the free medical service.	Family situation and health	My father left home twenty years ago. Now he is a doctor with the CCP's Central North China Bureau. My mother is crippled, she is with me in N Municipality. My younger brother Libang is a section member of the commissioner's office in Q County in S Province. He has six *mu* of land and a four-roomed brick house in Xiguan Village in Q County. He can live off his daily consultation fees. His average monthly income is around 150–60 pounds of millet.	
Counter-revolutionary actions you have undertaken	Since acting as assistant administrator for the Kuomintang, while checking residence cards together with the office, I often behaved badly and said bad things to people. Each time we held a meeting, I made propaganda for the Kuomintang and asked for donations to build military blockhouses and schools. Every day I loyally served the reactionary Kuomintang, for a period of more than three years. I took charge of accounting, general affairs, copying official documents, collecting Party dues, registering households, meetings, publicity, etc.			
Personal history	As an eight-year-old, I entered the village primary school, where I studied for four years without graduating. Due to flooding, the school stopped for a year. At the age of fourteen, I went to Guan Town in Q County, where I studied medicine at the Jude Pharmacy under Han Meifang and worked as a pharma-cist. I studied until I was twenty-two, and in September I went to T County to work as a doctor in the Xianghe Pharmacy. At the age of twenty-three, I went back to Q County, to work in the village as a doctor and do farming. When I was twenty-eight, the fields flooded, and life became more difficult still. In March, my teacher Xiao Guoliang introduced me to the construction depart-ment of the Q County government, where I worked as a second-grade officer. In October, I became an assistant in the general affairs department (assistant manager). In March 1948, when the Party and the Youth League merged, I			

	joined the executive committee. In April, after the merger, Party dues could no longer be collected, and there was a weeding out of personnel. I was unable to make a living any longer, so I left N Municipality and started working as a doctor in the Huatang Pharmacy in Mi Municipality. In October there was another reorganization, and Zhang Liangyu and friends introduced me to the P County public security brigade, where I did medical work. On October 25, we were liberated by the Huangzhai Campaign, and I went to Y Municipality to receive training from the Second Company of the First Battalion of the North China Military Region's Instruction Regiment. After the Liberation of N Municipality, I returned, and have continued working at the Huatang Pharmacy as a doctor until now.
Participation in the reactionary Party, Youth Corps, and associations	In 1944, after I met my friend Zu Kang (Secretary of the Party Committee in Q County), who had come back from X Municipality, he told me that while coming back through W County to recruit Party members, he had already introduced me to the Kuomintang [i.e., unbeknownst to me]. In August 1945, after the Japanese bandits had surrendered, the Q County branch moved back from W County to Q County. At the time, the Second War Zone was recruiting troops everywhere. I was then unemployed, so I volunteered to work for the county's Kuomintang office. In October, I was formally appointed as assistant administrator of its general affairs unit in Q County, while at the same time working as a doctor in the free clinic. In 1948, at the time of the merger, I was also on the executive committee. Starting in April, everyone had to take care of their own Party dues, and there was a weeding out of personnel. I no longer had a living, so I went away to fend for myself. In May I came to N Municipality, to work in the Huatang Pharmacy.
Family background and schooling	Four years at the national primary school in Xiguan Village in the third district of Q County. Didn't graduate. Studied medicine at the age of fourteen and finished at the age of twenty-two. Became a doctor.
Social relations	After the clinic, I spent the remaining time, apart from visiting the sick, with doctors, including Sun Changming, Li Beifang, Wang Shiwan, Liu Shiliang, etc., and with colleagues from the Party branch (Luo Liangchen and Zhao Xiansheng) and textile workers in Guan Town's Minsheng Factory. As for relatives, there is Bai Renyuan who sells goods in Ma Street, and Han Yunsheng, who weaves linen in Masheng Alley. As for friends, there is Xiao Qunfang, who runs a grocery store at the new South Gate, Yang Yusheng, who is an official in the N Municipality tax office, and Cao Xiliang, who is an accountant in the N Municipality steel works. Because of time constraints, I've gradually grown distant from my friends.
Ideological changes and understanding	When serving the Kuomintang, I listened to Party propaganda every day. It was called the Three People's Principles, but all I saw was people attacking each other, trying to win power, wallowing in the mire with each other, and being greedy and corrupt. It seemed to me that the Three People's Principles were not really being implemented, that politics was not on the right track, that it wasn't clear what was happening in the world. After Liberation, when I went to Y County to do training and noticed the strict discipline and the soldiers' hardship, I was amazed and lost for words. In my mind, questions arose. After three months of study, I realized that the greatest discipline was self-criticism.

(continued)

TABLE 2 *(continued)*

	I realized through regular study that hardship and great achievements are necessary for a revolutionary standpoint aimed at saving the people, and that I had to start it going myself, to take the lead. Everything that is for the majority of the people starts from justice, whence comes solidarity. In practicing solidarity, I came to recognize the hypocrisy of the Kuomintang, which would certainly collapse and be defeated by the strength of the people's unity. The Communist army's discipline as it entered the city, the purity of the staff of the organizations and factories that welcomed it—all that is without precedent in history. To summarize, it is public spirit in the service of the people, the weapon of self-criticism, that vanquished the Kuomintang. The standpoint of individualism was also vanquished. Only after a long ideological struggle did I realize that the Communist Party is the true heir to the tradition within the Party, so I submitted to the Communist Party, and would like to learn from the spirit of its members.
Behavior and meritorious service	On the way back to N Municipality, in places along the way, I explained to people the valuable lessons I had learned and the need for land reform. After reaching the city, I passed on to my friends all that I had seen and heard, using as irrefutable evidence the discipline shown by the army when entering the city and the purity of the welcome. Since registration, we can only thank the Party and the people for their leniency. After being encouraged to do so three or four times, I joyfully registered.

among patriotic believers at S Province University and X Middle School, and acquired a Catholic girlfriend. The two broke from the priests of the Three-Selfs movement and went over to the side of the government.[13]

After this, Fang's expertise in acupuncture and moxibustion was recognized by the Workers' Hospital and in early 1953 he joined the hospital staff as a full-time doctor.

In 1951, while employed at the convalescent hospital, he had moved once. In accordance with regulations, following his move the Public Security Bureau forwarded a copy of his registration materials to the police station at his new address.[14] In 1953, when he was formally transferred to the Workers' Hospital and moved for a second time to the hospital's staff quarters, the branch of the Public Security Bureau reported the change to the Municipal Public Security Bureau, which forwarded a copy of Fang's registration materials to the hospital's security section. The section was to inform the Municipal Public Security Bureau about Fang's new accommodation and any further changes in Fang's circumstances.[15] The section responded with the required information, and what it knew about Fang's history: that he "had joined the reactionary Kuomintang and acted as assistant administrator, and he had also joined the Youth Corps."[16]

By joining the hospital, Fang formally acquired the status of state employee. As a doctor, he qualified as a state cadre. Having joined a state unit, he was no longer

TABLE 3

Public Security branch bureau: Police station, No 9, Liu Street Alley		Household category	Party and Youth Corps	Head of household	Fang Liren
Name: Fang Liren	Sex: Male	Ancestral home: Xiguan Village, Third District Town, Q County, S Province.		No. of years in S	4 years
Other name: Jiaming	Age: 35	Date of moving to this address: 1945		Other places of residence in this city: [left blank]	
Education level and schools graduated from: completed higher primary school		Special skills: [left blank]		Special features: [left blank]	
Occupation and place of employment: Doctor, Huatang Pharmacy, Mi Municipality.			Places frequented regularly: [left blank]		
Family situation	Source of livelihood: My own income				
	Family members (name, occupation, relationship): Liang Xiuzhen (mother, 62), illiterate, household duties; Libang (younger brother, 28), broadcasting officer, R County.				

	Year started	Year ended	Place	Name	Position
Work experience	1926	1932	Q County	Primary school	Student
	1940	1941	T County	Xianghe Pharmacy	Studied medicine
	1945	1945	Q County	Government and county Party branch	Section member, deputy administrator
	1947	1948	Q County	County Party branch	Deputy administrator, executive committee
	1949	1951	P County	Defense force and pharmacy	Medical officer, medical practitioner

	Name	Relationship	Profession	Address	Current situation
Social relations	Chen Manyuan	maternal uncle	medical practitioner	Guan Town, Q County Town.	[Left blank]
	Shi Zhiming	elder male cousin	peasant	Zhang Village, Guan Town, Q County Town.	[Left blank]
	Liu Youguang	elder male maternal cousin	sells groceries	Mashi Street, this city.	[Left blank]
	Luo Liangchen	Friend	merchant	Tongsheng Factory, Liu Alley	[Left blank]

Suspicious points and sources of material:	[Left blank]
Appendix:	During my period of service, I opposed the people by making propaganda and influencing the thinking of the masses on behalf of the Kuomintang, loyally worked for the Kuomintang reactionaries, and acted for the Kuomintang as general affairs assistant and accountant.

an object of Public Security surveillance but instead an object of close scrutiny and examination by his own unit.

Checking on cadres was, in state departments and units, a matter for internal sections, and filling out forms and making assessments happened according to a regular timetable. In the case of new employees like Fang with historical problems, the checking was more stringent. So since Fang joined two different units, he had to undergo two examinations.

In June 1951, shortly after joining the convalescent hospital, he wrote a detailed autobiography in connection with his review. In October 1953, after moving to the N Municipality Workers' Hospital, he underwent an even more comprehensive review.

The review in June 1951 took place at the peak of the Zhenfan movement. A series of notices announcing killings, jailings, supervision orders, and show trials put Fang in a panic. As he later put it: "At the time, I was only just beginning to receive the Party's education. I knew little about the Party's policies, past fears weighed heavily on my thinking. I thought, given my history and background, and my crimes, there could be no leniency. So I kept it hidden, I didn't confess, I avoided the movement."[17]

By October 1953, when another cadre investigation took place, the political storm had already passed. Fang hoped that once things had settled down, and the Party had stopped checking cadres' history, there would be even less point in seeking trouble. So to avoid leaving incriminating materials in his file, he played down his historical problems.

On the one hand he was plagued by "ghosts," at the same time he was careless about keeping things hidden, thus setting up future problems for himself. For example, he made contradictory statements in his autobiographies.

In 1951, he said: "In June 1929, at the age of eight, I joined the village primary school. I stopped studying in 1933, during the floods, in the third year. I studied at home for two years, up to the equivalent of higher primary." In 1953, he changed the timeline to suggest that "from June 1929 through to 1935, I graduated at both levels from the village school."

Even though in 1949 and 1950 he had given two different ages, he claimed in both cases to have started primary school in 1926, aged eight, i.e., on the basis of being born in 1918. What's more, it worked better to over-report one's age. So he had "aged," from thirty-one in the first report to thirty-five in the second. When registering in 1951, he had given the younger age of thirty, and his year of birth as 1921; in 1953, he said he was thirty-one, born in 1922.

In the past, he said that he had started studying medicine at the age of fourteen, and completed his study aged twenty-two. In 1951, he said he had started aged fourteen and, "after studying for six years," "went at the age of nineteen to Taigu to be a doctor in a pharmacy," which could not be right.

In 1950, when filling in the section about "leading positions in the reactionary Party, Youth Corps, and associations," he said he had been roped into the Kuomintang in 1944, without his knowledge, and that he had not found out until 1945; but in 1951, in his autobiography, 1944 became 1941 and 1945 became 1943.

In early 1950, he said that in March 1948, when the Party and the Youth Corps merged, he had been appointed to the executive committee, but in April he had resigned and gone to N City, and had been on the committee for less than a month; in 1951, 1948 became 1947, and a month before the merger the Party's provincial branch had suddenly announced his appointment to the county Party's executive committee, so that between then and his departure in April 1948, he must have been on the committee for six months.

Other than the confusion of dates, the two following pieces of information seemed important from the point of view of the organizational department. One was that in 1951 he had claimed that in August 1946 he had attended a training course in N Municipality, where he had spent fifteen days. Another was that his cadre autobiography mentioned for the first time that he had been inducted into the Youth Corps.[18]

The investigations of Fang carried out in 1951 and 1953 seemed at first to have little effect on his situation. But unbeknownst to him, the organizational department in the Workers' Hospital had already formed negative opinions of him.

The materials from the investigations show that although the organizational department thought Fang's history was, broadly speaking, transparent, it believed that his record was politically sullied: "In 1941, he joined the Kuomintang; in 1946, he joined the Youth Corps. In his work as an assistant in the county Party branch, he demonstrated extraordinary loyalty to the Chiang Clique in the Kuomintang and to the Youth Corps, and was actively engaged." "His political record was sullied." The department's biggest concern regarded doubts about Party policy. Although Fang had managed, with help, to make a critical analysis of his past, his attitude was still insufficiently loyal and honest. The organizational department was even more critical of his behavior in the hospital in the previous year. It quoted patients' criticisms: "His style is frivolous, he is offhand, he doesn't pay attention, he says what he likes to women convalescents, he's not levelheaded when things go wrong, he's excitable and emotional, he's unable to proceed rationally (the patients say he's impatient)."[19]

In 1955, at the start of the nationwide Sufan movement, Fang was not yet a focus of investigation and was only listed as an "object for future reference." The security department said:

> The person concerned comes from a professional background. Although he was on the Kuomintang's county executive committee, he committed no serious crimes. After Liberation, he made a full confession, and his accounts are basically consistent. The conclusion: "His history is basically clear," and since Liberation, no evidence has been found of reactionary behavior. His thinking is backward, but it's mainly because

of the deep influence on him of the old society. His education needs strengthening. He can be put on record as "kept on file for future reference."

Comments regarding his future: (1) It is recommended that the unit strengthen his political and ideological education. (2) Write to tell Q County about Fang's role in the Kuomintang and get them to verify his confession material.[20]

However, as the movement intensified, and further incriminating leads emerged from Q County, by December Fang had been made the object of a special review:

(1) In 1941, Fang worked underground for the Kuomintang. He was on the executive committee of the Kuomintang in Q County and section chief of the Youth Corps. He actively developed Kuomintang members, and in 1947 he received special training from the Yan Xishan bandits. According to the registration form, 'I discovered a dozen Communists and handed their names to the Government,' so he is suspected of major crimes.

(2) Fang has done intelligence work for the Kuomintang, and in 1947 he participated in the 'Party investigation' (run by its supervision and investigation bureau) and was chosen as inspector for sixty Kuomintang members, all under his specific leadership.

(3) On the eve of the Liberation of Q County in 1948, Fang escaped with secret files to N Municipality. After Liberation he concealed his background as a special agent and his main crimes. He has close ties to Catholic Youth Society elements, and he has leaked our hospital's secrets. He is suspected of being a major secret agent.[21]

THE START OF SUFAN

Fang's secret 1947 stint as a correspondent for the Kuomintang's Bureau of Investigation and Statistics continued to prey on his mind. Ever since 1949, when the N Municipality Military Control Commission had demanded that all secret agents register as repentants, this had been among Fang's greatest worries. The longer he avoided registering, the more scared he was of doing so. The rise of every political movement pushed him ever closer to the edge.

The Workers' Hospital was in the second batch of suppression units, so the movement started late. Once it began to spread in 1956, the problems unearthed earlier in the localities and units were followed up in hot pursuit, and leads ferreted out in the units multiplied exponentially. The information fed back from Q County was unfavorable to Fang's case.

A report issued by the hospital's Party committee raised a number of points. The first concerned Fang's "reactionary status":

According to the Public Security Bureau's files on enemy and puppet forces in Q County, in April 1944, after serving as a member of the second branch of the county's Party branch, Fang was made a member of the Executive Committee, documents clerk, and so on. He was directly in charge of the supervision of branch members. The Public Security Bureau's materials written by prisoners X, X, and others show that, in 1947, after the Party and the Youth Corps merged, he was their section chief. According to X, X, X, and others, in 1947 Fang joined the Zhongtong as a secret agent, and was responsible for "investigation" work, as well as for action committees on culture, women, peasants and workers, and youth. In October 1947, he was sent by the Kuomintang's provincial committee to N Municipality to participate in the technical training of the Yan [Xishan] bandits' work teams. Training conferences were held twice monthly by the army, the government, the Party, and the Youth Corps. Communist activities were reported upwards, while Fang kept a secret copy.

The second concerned "criminal activities":

According to X, X, X, and others, Fang loyally attended meetings with the head of the Kuomintang Secretariat and, under the cover of medical work, collected military, political and other intelligence about us and the Japanese, and was responsible for developing its organization. After Japan's surrender, Fang's secret-service activities became even more frenetic. In 1946, employing toxic means, he brought about the downfall of a member of our Party's production section in the county. He personally led the "intelligence office" and was in charge of surrender procedures. Since then, under the leadership of X, head of a small group in the second section of the confidential bureau of the Pacification Bureau in Q County, we have actively collected intelligence about our side, the traitor organization, and comrades. In 1948, when Q County was about to be liberated, X and Fang fled with important documents to N Municipality. Fang stopped being a special agent and became a doctor working for a private pharmacy.[22]

A team appointed by the Health Bureau decided that Fang was "suspected of being a secret agent mole" and decided to "question and interview Fang." The main method of struggle was "peaceful negotiations, interrogation, and visits to attack [Fang] psychologically by engaging in a battle of wits to encourage him to confess. In case of recalcitrance, small-group struggle methods should be used, to apply the necessary pressure to force him to make a clean breast of each crime and accusation," and, "with the support of the security organs, secret investigations, and reconnaissance, to obtain an even wider range of materials."[23]

The secret investigation included arranging for a specialist to keep a lookout on Fang's every move. During the Spring Festival, when the team waged its struggle, it was even more important to monitor Fang's activities. Here are some reports:

I was on the night shift, and did not return home all night. Fang did not go out after arriving home. He spent the evening preparing for the New Year, making dumplings and so on.

On the first day of the first lunar month, I visited him in the morning, he was having a meal. He made four dishes, drank some alcohol, and ate dumplings (I also drank two glasses). Today he won't go out, he'll just have a nice rest, that morning he slept until ten. I visited him again that evening. He said that the next day he planned to go to town and walk around for a while, and go to the Chinese medicine hospital and the sanatorium. He received two guests this afternoon, they arrived at around two or three o'clock. It was his nephew and his nephew's wife. At around six they left. His nephew works in the steel plant.

Second day of the first lunar month. I was on duty when I noticed a guest arrive in the afternoon. By the time I'd gone to his place he'd already gone to town. His wife said he'd left around twelve. Someone from town had brought him a note and he'd gone immediately, without bothering to eat. He returned that evening and I sat in his house for a while. He said he'd been running around all day, that he had friends and relatives in the hospital and the sanatorium. He said he wouldn't be going tomorrow, he'd stay at home and rest, but the day after tomorrow he'd go to town again.

Third day of the first lunar month. I was on duty during the day and in the evening. I went back at mid-day to have a look, he was sleeping. I told him I was on duty and was back for lunch. I returned a book he'd lent me. He went back to sleep. I went to the hospital. When I went back for dinner at half past six, he was not at home. At ten past seven, when I went to the hospital, I saw him. I don't know what time he'd gone.

Third day of the first lunar month. I handed over to the next shift at around ten, the whole family had left, perhaps to town. Old Fang didn't return until the evening. Neither his wife nor his children returned. All day there had been no contact.[24]

Since mid-December 1956, Fang had been asked to work half time and spend the other half confessing his historical problems. After reading about Sufan in the press, he had been overwhelmed with anxiety. Immediately after the hospital launched the movement, Fang admitted to having concealed historical crimes and joined an organization subordinate to the Zhongtong.[25] As soon as the team began to question him, he panicked and was ready to speak. He feared that if he misspoke his guilt would be even greater and he would be in even more danger.

He admitted that at the end of 1949, when filling in his repentance form, he had not mentioned the amount of time he had spent in the Kuomintang and the Youth Corps, although he had admitted having been on its county executive committee. In 1951 and 1953, in reviews, he had added a supplementary account of his absorption into the Kuomintang in 1941 and into the Youth Corps in 1946, but had continued to conceal the fact that in 1947 he was a district leader in the Youth Corps and had joined a training class run by Yan Xishan's fake Party and Youth Corps and had worked as a correspondent in the Q County branch under the Kuomintang Provincial Committee's Investigation Bureau, during which time he had secretly reported a primary school teacher, participated on behalf of the Party in a conference to "suppress fakes," and voted for the execution of the director of a peasant association.

Fearful that he would be unable to explain his involvement in spying and be implicated in others' crimes, he worried for his wife and children—who would be there to look after them if he was jailed? Hampered by a deep sense of shame, Fang's confession was painful and somewhat unforthcoming. There were occasions where his memory had failed him, and was only jogged after prompting. Ultimately, he had no choice but to confess.

The special team alternated between hot treatment and cold. Because Fang feared losing face in a mass struggle, the team asked the hospital director to talk with him on an individual basis, and to tell him that if he made a good confession, he would not have to face a struggle; that if he made a clean breast of things and displayed a good attitude, he might get better treatment, and so on. With a nudge and a wink, the director said: "You'll have to confess anyway sooner or later, otherwise you'll end up in a more and more passive situation." The special team, on the other hand, waxed hot: "If you're unwilling to confess, no need to come, stop wasting our time!" After putting it off again and again, Fang spilled the beans.[26]

Fang's account mainly concerned the period in which he had been on the executive committee, when he had set up five Party committees under the county authorities and organized trade unions and workers and peasants' committees, etc., and the period in which he had worked for the Investigation Bureau as a correspondent. He had helped organize a network to monitor Party members, uncovered Communist activities among Kuomintang members and anti-landlord struggles, and written reports on Kuomintang activities. When Yan Xishan went to Q County in 1947, the county Kuomintang and the county government organized a protection team that he had helped lead, as well as five small teams, one of whose leaders he appointed, and taken over responsibility for law and order for a month.[27]

Some things Fang failed to recall. For example, he denied a charge in the externally collected material that he had betrayed Communists on behalf of the Kuomintang. He could not remember this. He was most ashamed of having "introduced" people to the Kuomintang. As he later put it: he himself had been dragged into the Kuomintang, by his relative Zu, who had hidden the fact of his registration from him—it was more than two years before he got to know. But while an assistant in the Kuomintang branch, he had played the same despicable trick on others. "I introduced forty members, all of them laboring people, some old teachers, some peasants. They were all my maternal relatives. What I did was unconscionable. I cheated them. I registered them as Party members, I sullied their unsullied histories. During the general check-up of Kuomintang members, I said there was no point in informing them, that I'd impersonated them, that I'd used their fingerprints, that I'd signed them up anyhow. I didn't make a true confession until Sufan."[28]

Fang's historical problems were soon established. The hospital's five-person team submitted its report to the municipal Party's five-person team: "The team's struggle and verification" confirmed that in October 1941 Fang was introduced by Zu Kang into the Kuomintang, and that he was recorder for the Party branch and an alternate member of the executive committee of a district branch, and that in

1942 he was elected onto the executive committee of the county branch and became a member of its monitoring committee. After that, under cover of acting as a medical practitioner, he did underground work for the Kuomintang. He gathered information about activities by the Japanese and the puppets and by the Party, and, in the name of the Limen Sect, recruited more than thirty people into the Kuomintang. He became assistant director in the branch and, concurrently, secretary of the first district branch, an alternate member of the local Kuomintang executive, and a member of the committee of the workers and peasants' movement. In 1946, he was attached to the Youth Corps unit (he himself said he was its leader), but was inactive. In 1947, he was appointed to the county Party's executive committee, while organizing and leading the women's and the peasants' mobilization committees, and he organized nine Party and Youth Corps members in those organizations. His main task was to collect intelligence on the army and Government, to participate in and organize the Kuomintang members' monitoring network, which covered some sixty members, and to handle reports. In October, he joined a training class, and he joined the Zhongtong as a correspondent. His main crimes were, in 1946, reporting teacher X as a suspect, causing the teacher to be detained for a month, and representing the Kuomintang at a suppression meeting that decided to execute one of the Party's peasant leaders. The leader was not executed but died in prison, of illness. In addition, investigations show that it was not Fang who brought about the defeat of our Party cadres and helped the Kuomintang capture our personnel, so this can be ignored. Some latent suspicions about Fang have not been proved, and Fang's going to N Municipality to become a doctor was for livelihood reasons. The report found no other suspicions. "We believe the case should be concluded with the decision that he was a historical secret agent."[29]

In accordance with this conclusion, the five-person team proposed:

> After coming to the hospital, Fang kept quiet for a long time about his background and criminal activities. During the early phase of the movement he voluntarily confessed to having informed against X and having joined the Zhongtong as a secret agent. Later, but only after having received the help of the masses, he made a confession regarding these issues. On this basis, we propose that the government exercise leniency and give him a two-year suspended sentence.[30]

The Municipal Committee's special team approved the closure of the case:[31]

> Before the movement, Fang confessed only to being a member of the Kuomintang's county executive committee and the Youth Corps, but concealed his having been an alternate member of the district branch, his attachment to the Youth Corps unit, and his having worked under the cover of practicing medicine to collect military intelligence about our side. He also concealed the special training he received and his participation in the Zhongtong as a correspondent with secret-agent status. He concealed the crime of having informed on X (later released). Accordingly, he should be

classified as a Zhongtong secret agent. He can, with help, continue to confess. His crime is minor, so it is recommended that he be exempted from administrative punishment.[32]

The hospital special team, the five-person team, and the Municipal Committee's five-person team all thought that Fang's problem was not serious and his crime was minor, so the recommended punishment grew lighter and lighter at each level. This is not surprising, for the hospital leadership had told Fang that his history had "already been clarified, there has already been a conclusion, historically it is up to par, but the Party committee feels, after the investigation and in line with the Party's policy of leniency in the case of confessions, not to punish you and not to make you wear a hat. You must work well and thank the Party and the people for showing you leniency." The personnel division told Fang that once the city had handed down its formal conclusion, it would be announced at a rally.[33]

After communicating with the Public Security Bureau and other departments, the hospital's five-person team approved the materials relating to Fang's suppression and dealt with the conclusions.[34] The five-person team of N Municipality's Municipal Committee announced, "This person has committed no few crimes, but they are relatively ordinary. In the movement, he volunteered a confession. He has been classified as a historical secret-agent element. It is appropriate to exempt him from administrative sanctions."[35]

For Fang, the decision could not have been better, but to everyone's amazement he proceeded to provoke a dispute and a great hubbub. The hospital's five-person team was furious.

UPPING THE PENALTY

Fang's family had a long tradition in medicine. There had been doctors on both his father's and his mother's side. His father had studied in Japan and understood both traditional Chinese and Western medicine. After returning home, he had opened clinics in the cities. Before the founding of the People's Republic in 1949, he worked at the North China Military General Hospital. In the Workers' Hospital, Fang was good at both medicine and organization. Patients sought him out, and he was easygoing and liked a joke, popular both in the department and among patients. However, because of his abundant experience and strong professional skills, he was self-important and easily swayed by emotion. People found him temperamental, even arrogant. On this occasion, unhappy about the section's salary adjustment decisions and having long held a grudge against the head of the Chinese medicine section, he took the lead in proposing a separate acupuncture section, and got into trouble.[36] Still a target of Sufan and a "historical secret-agent element," Fang was sure to suffer the consequences of such a bold move.

On October 5, 1958, the hospital's five-person team re-examined Fang's case and concluded: "After the movement, his reactionary nature had not changed. Not only did he fail to bow his head and confess and turn over a new leaf but he began to slacken at work, to go his own way, to vie for leadership, to vie for wages, to sow dissension, to undermine unity, and to set comrades at odds. To purify the ranks of the working class and stand firmly by national laws, we propose that the government sentence him to three years' control, and send him to the labor authorities for implementation." While waiting for higher authorities' approval, Fang was paid 46.50 yuan in living expenses (60 percent of his original wage).[37]

N Municipality's five-person team did not fully accept the proposal. It increased the penalty, but did not agree "to send him to labor agencies for its implementation," and instead sentenced Fang to two years in prison, suspended.[38]

The five-person team of the hospital's Party committee replied: "We agree that he should not be given criminal punishment. He will stay in the hospital, under supervision. His wages have already been reduced, no further change is needed."[39]

This happened just as the Great Leap Forward was getting under way, and people everywhere were responding to the instructions of Mao and the Central Committee to "plant the red flag and pull out the white flag" on the hilltops and in villages, offices, military units, factories, and cooperatives everywhere,[40] and to find examples of "red" and "white" in every unit. Fang's case was chosen by the hospital authorities as an example of an enemy "white flag." Fang was rebuked for creating disunity and vying for the leadership of the medicine section. He was criticized by the entire hospital and twice dragged out before a struggle rally.

On June 9, 1959, an official decision was handed down endorsing Fang's demotion and the reduction of his wages from 77.50 yuan to 49.50 yuan.

BECOMING A NEW PERSON

The successive political movements had no doubt put enormous strain on Fang. However, as someone whose skills were in high demand, overall he led a stable and secure life. He had married in 1952, had a son and a daughter, and he was able to bring his disabled mother from the village to the city, where he and his family got by on the wages of himself and his wife.

Fang's knowledge and experience helped him adapt. His Catholic faith was also a calming influence. With his family life and his work largely unaffected, this political and economic setback did not wipe him out but led to the onset of a greater maturity in his character.

Under the supervision system, he was at all times under the discipline of the Party branch, the security organization, and the mass control group. In June 1959, the three instances together met with him to let him know the decision, to admonish and educate him, and to develop a "Three Guarantees and One Guarantor" approach.[41] Fang came up with the first stage of a self-reform plan, and pledged to abide by it.

Every month at a given time Fang submitted a "brief self-reform summary" to the Party branch and the public security team, every quarter he submitted a "general self-reform summary," and every year he submitted an annual "self-reform summary" and a reform plan. His daily routine of seeing patients, attending clinics, and attending meetings was not subject to restrictions, so there were few real changes. However, because of the need to strengthen his self-reform, he spent a lot more time than before reading newspapers, Mao's *Selected Works,* and other writings. His self-reform summaries talked mainly about elevating his learning and his political and ideological thinking.

His goal was to "become a new person." His political aim was to study Chairman Mao's works and important documents of the day. Politically, he resolved to "report his own thinking to the Party and to receive its timely education and instructions"; "to report constantly to the supervisory team regarding ideological work, benefit from mass supervision, quickly correct errors, and promote self-reform"; and to "submit monthly summaries of my reform and quarterly work summaries to the branch and the hospital security team, and request the small group's appraisal." His plan: "Theoretical study: Monday, Tuesday, and Wednesday evenings for reading Chairman Mao's works and political literature"; "midday for reading the newspaper and important reports, to be continued in the evening if necessary"; "Thursday, Friday, and Saturday evenings for professional study, i.e., Chinese medicine review time." His work plan: "Regarding diagnosis and treatment, study advanced methods and do everything possible to improve quantity and quality, eliminate errors, and carry out more than fifty medical consultations each day"; "actively and conscientiously implement the tasks with which the Party has entrusted me, assist young people studying Chinese medicine, and contribute my own theories and experiences"; "spend my spare time on patients with acute illnesses and family members who have difficulties in getting to hospital, and be on call night and day"; "work hard to develop scientific research, summarize my own experience and understanding, make health care available to the hospital, and continue research."[42]

Fang worked hard at realizing his plan. He read the newspaper and studied political writings every day, and because he lived in the hospital, he spent much of his time diagnosing and treating patients, regardless of whether it was within working hours or in his spare time. Most days he saw more than fifty people, and after that he often went over to the clinic to examine other patients. Every month after hours, he saw at least a few dozen and sometimes as many as a couple of hundred. In 1960, he developed an instrument for neural diagnosis and other scientific advances, aimed at treating occupational diseases with two kinds of prepared Chinese medicine, and successfully applied his findings clinically. He handed over more than a dozen folk remedies that proved effective, and he used a combination of Chinese and Western medicine to treat more than 180 people suffering from edema. To save patients hit by cocklebur poisoning, he successfully used acupuncture and moxibustion on one child having convulsions, and saved another with a swollen liver by applying Chinese medicine.[43]

The Party branch and the supervision team initially viewed historical counterrevolutionary elements like Fang with disdain. Even so, their reports show that in the end they could not but admit that Fang's self-reform and professional work were basically good.

In 1959, the security people appraised him as follows: "Fang's reform does not comply with acceptable standards, and in the Chinese medicine section he is stirring up trouble about wages. He does not behave well at work, even though he improved after criticism. He treats workers and cadres differently, and he is insufficiently bold. He actively participates in technological innovation, but waxes hot and cold." The branch offered an even more radical opinion: "This person is a troublemaker who causes disunity at work and quarrels about wages. He improved after receiving criticism, but his behavior waxes hot and cold. He lacks real talent, and does not stick to the rules. We agree that he should be removed."[44]

However, after a few months, everyone's views had changed. At the end of 1959, the medicine section started emphasizing that Fang had, "since 1959, become clearer about his own mistakes and reform. Ideologically, he has accepted reform." Praise was lavished on Fang's greater boldness in his work and scientific research. He had written seven papers describing the Chinese medicine approach to chronic hepatitis and bronchial asthma; he had used acupuncture and moxibustion to cure a young deaf-mute; he had saved two patients said to have been on the point of dying and whose liver and kidney functions were thought to have failed; he used herbal medicine that he himself had developed to treat chronic hepatitis, and had achieved good results; to pursue his study on the main and collateral energy channels, he had stayed at work every night until past midnight; and so on.[45] Accordingly, they proposed that Fang's counter-revolutionary hat be removed.[46]

On March 28, 1960, the laboratory branch and the supervisory team still thought as follows:

> In the first quarter, this person behaved well. He actively transformed his ideology, and in addition to submitting timely reports to the branch and the supervisory officials regarding his thinking and his work outside, he was able to unite with comrades in the section and to listen with an open mind to firmly expressed opinions. He works hard, he is not afraid of hardship or of dirt, he thinks actively about the section's tasks, and he takes the initiative in developing plans and doing scientific research. He has made achievements in one quarter, actively participating in campaigns such as completing the savings task by exceeding the target. He fell from a great height, but he was not bothered by the fall and kept on fighting hard. In addition to completing his own daily schedule, he is able to help the section leadership and others in their work.[47]

The report issued by the supervisory team was even more specific:

Ideology: he punctually delivers a brief monthly summary, and urges the section to hold an appraisal meeting. He participates each day in political study.

Work: He has changed greatly, mainly due to comrades' help in pointing out problems, such as being overcautious. He has made some big achievements, for example by cooperating with the departments of internal medicine, gynecology, and dermatology. He has helped treat vaginal trichomoniasis and scarring in the surgical department, with good results. He recently drew up a one-year plan for scientific research and analysis, and plans to work on treating chronic hepatitis.

He has sacrificed his spare time to give lectures and tutorials to help doctors trained in Western medicine to learn Chinese medicine. Every Tuesday and Friday evening, he gives the doctors a class on acupuncture, and from seven to nine o'clock in the morning he helps them understand Chinese medicine. He takes on jobs on his own initiative. The supervision of a number of trainees is left entirely to him. Apart from doing his own outpatient work every Wednesday and Thursday afternoon, he gives the trainees lectures, and goes about it very positively and conscientiously.

Manual labor: Every morning from eight-thirty to nine o'clock he cleans up everything, in readiness for the clinic. After work, he sweeps up, actively participating in manual labor.

Defects: His attitude to work is not entirely dependable. Comrades in the section feel that during working hours he keeps on disappearing, no one is quite sure to where, and sometimes he's away for as much as half an hour. If you keep an eye on him, he behaves well, but if you don't, he can be a bit slippery.[48]

Because of the improvement in Fang's performance and his role in the section and the clinics, he gained himself a few more years in the hospital.

By late 1960, Sufan was basically over in the hospital. When sorting out counter-revolutionaries unearthed in the movement, the hospital Party committee, given that the Central Committee and the provincial committee had laid down a policy on the internal retention and continuing employment of counter-revolutionary elements and bad elements,[49] thought for a while about sending Fang "back to the villages for labor reform under the supervision of the peasants," but the Party branch disagreed. It argued that while under supervision, Fang's behavior had been good. He was a backbone doctor, so he should stay in the hospital for supervision and reform. The hospital Party committee rethought its decision. It made clear its new position in a report:

The Party committee, in accordance with the policy set by the provincial Party committee, decided to send Fang to the villages for reform through supervised labor. Now the Party branch in the clinic proposes that Fang, after quarrelling with colleagues and being subjected to criticism and struggle, has been able to accept reform, has been creative in the field of technological innovation, has expertise in the field of Chinese medicine, and is trusted among the masses, and that during the period of his reform he is able to report his thinking to the Party branch. In accordance with the recommendations of the clinic's Party branch, the Party committee agrees that he can stay in his unit for supervision and reform.[50]

On August 5, 1961, after the document had travelled back and forth, the five-person team gave its approval: it "agreed to his retention on site for labor reform under supervision."[51]

BAD LUCK STRIKES

In November 1960, when the Party committee changed its mind about sending Fang back to the villages for labor reform, Fang was not necessarily aware of it, but he seemed noticeably less bold. In August 1962, talking with a leader of the Party committee, he said: "I worry that I'll make another mistake, so I can't be bold at work, and I'm always afraid that something will go wrong. I'm scared to open my mouth when I'm with comrades, I'm afraid they'll start asking things. I'm even more frightened of the canteen and the storeroom. I'm afraid some problem might pop up and I won't be able to explain myself; I don't even dare go to places where there aren't many people, for example toilets. I'm afraid there'll be reactionary slogans, and that they will create trouble for me. I worry that I'm a person with problems, if things heat up, I'll be the first to suffer, I might get locked up, I might lose my job, I might be suppressed, I have all these ideological worries."[52]

Ever since 1959, Fang had stayed on the straight and narrow. Desperate to perform outstandingly, in terms of technology and professional activity he was much more active than in the past. He treated chronic diseases by integrating traditional Chinese and Western medicine, thought up new ways to innovate, and achieved repeated breakthroughs. During the Three Hard Years, he used the results of his own study of the science of channels and collaterals, combined with his specialist knowledge of acupuncture techniques and the integrated application of Chinese and Western medicine, to treat arteriosclerosis, hypertension, hemiplegia, and chronic hepatitis, and was especially successful in curing oliguria, gangrene of the finger or toe, cholecystitis, vertebral neuritis, and other illnesses. His reputation grew. In 1961 and 1962, leading cadres with apparently intractable illnesses flocked to him for diagnosis and treatment, and unanimously affirmed his efficacy.

To allow even more patients to benefit, he taught young doctors Chinese medicine, and imparted to them his experiences in using acupuncture. He gave regular classes in Chinese medicine. Apart from teaching the science of channels and collaterals and acupuncture techniques, he used his own acupuncture charts to give students clinical guidance. In the case of leading cadres who could not attend clinic or hospital, he visited them in his spare time, so as not to disturb the normal routine of outpatient and ward work. The outpatient department assigned him a young assistant to train and study under him and to help him observe patients and make a proper record of their diagnosis and treatment.

In early 1960, the Central Committee began removing hats from batch after batch of people classed as rightists.[53] Units everywhere started removing hats from people classed as counter-revolutionaries or bad elements who were behaving well at work. In early 1962, Fang was fortunate enough to be nominated by the hospital for hat-removal.

A meeting of the clinic branch formally adopted the following motion:

> This person has, since coming under supervision in 1957, shown that he is prepared to accept reform, recognize his crimes, and appreciate the Party's generous treatment of his problems. To resolutely reform and become a new person, he has actively participated in all kinds of political study. His ideological consciousness has risen. In addition to humbly accepting the supervision of the masses and regularly reporting his work and thinking to the Organization and taking the initiative to remain close to the Organization, he has been diligent year in, year out, and done everything with his patients in mind. If there are many patients in the section but few doctors, he ignores quotas and works beyond his allotted hours, and never once complains. If people seek him out after hours, even in the middle of the night, he responds appropriately. To relieve patients' pain, he digs deep into his research, so three deaf-mutes were cured and two patients with renal failure were saved, whereupon they demonstrated their deep gratitude. This person is deeply concerned about the next generation. An enthusiastic teacher, he has passed on his techniques in recent years to four young Chinese medicine doctors who have embarked on clinical work and shown great promise. Given his behavior, and given the Party's policy, we conclude that he should be removed from penal supervision if the higher Party committee sees fit.[54]

On March 13, with the agreement of the hospital's Party committee, the security section proposed a formal report on the question of Fang's hat:

> Since he started wearing a hat, his behavior has been consistently good. In the course of reform, he has punctually exposed his thinking, taken the initiative in seriously implementing his brief monthly summaries and the system of seasonal appraisal of his reform, and achieved a more correct understanding of his historical crimes. As a result of his daily technical study, his professional standing has improved greatly, leading at work to a series of outstanding achievements. For example, between December 1961 and February 1962, he treated X's spondylitis. An examination done in accordance with Western medicine suggested that the disease had developed to the point where the patient's joints were so stiff that they could no longer move, but after fifteen days of acupuncture, the patient was cured. In April 1959, Fang cured a deaf-mute aged sixteen (who had had apoplexy before the age of four and in October 1958 had been treated several times to no effect) by applying Chinese medicine that replenished the blood and got it to circulate across all the acupuncture points, and by

applying acupuncture on just two occasions. The patient's hearing and speaking ability was restored. The deaf-mute was able to shout out 'Long live Chairman Mao.'

This person's basic resolution was to serve the people and achieve his own reform. In his spare time, he attended to patients waiting to see a doctor, and repeatedly published accounts of advanced methods of therapy. He atoned for his crimes by his achievements, he alleviated patients' suffering with medical treatment, and he received praise from the masses and the leaders. After studying the matter, we agree that Fang's counter-revolutionary hat can be removed, that his penal supervision and manual labor can be rescinded, and that his wage should be adjusted from the current living allowance of 46.50 yuan to 67 yuan (medical grade 17).[55]

Two weeks later, the Party committee of the Hygiene Bureau expressed its approval: "We agree that his counter-revolutionary hat can be taken off and his salary adjusted to 67 yuan."[56] However, after this opinion was forwarded to higher authorities, its implementation was delayed. One reason was that Mao Zedong had previously expressed concern at the large number of people having their hats removed, and had proposed putting a stop to it.[57] That year, Mao spoke even more often and more sharply about class struggle. In September, he again referred to class struggle as all-decisive and something that should be "stressed year in year out, month in month out, day in day out."[58]

Even under these circumstances, Fang's supervision and reform team, the clinic branch, and the security section continued to believe that his hat should be taken off. The supervisory team reaffirmed his good behavior, and the security section drafted a report noting his "positive behavior" and his "readiness to take the initiative at work." Even the hospital's Party committee expressed its agreement.[59] However, when the report was passed on to the second office of the Municipal Public Security Bureau, the reply came back: "The opinion is that the hat should not, for the time being, be removed, and that it should be considered during the current Four Clean-Ups."[60]

The situation was again fraught with class struggle. The Central Committee was launching the Socialist Education movement (also known as the Four Clean-Ups), which stressed the struggle between two classes and two roads.

In 1964, the movement, which had originally focused on the villages and village cadres, spread to urban factories and offices. The main task was to rectify and clean up the Party's grassroots organizations, and to ensure that basic-level leading cadres "wash their hands, and take a bath." The movement's basic method was to clear the way through class struggle, make the four categories in the units the first target of attack, carry out a thorough check-up and criticism, and wage a "struggle by argument and reasoning."[61] The movement aimed mainly at the Party's grassroots cadres, so the higher authorities launching it sent out Four Clean-Ups work teams composed of soldiers, workers, and cadres. The Party leadership and the administration stepped aside and waited for things to be sorted out. The same happened in

Fang's hospital. During the campaign, the Four Clean-Ups work team had the final say.

Of the four categories retained in the hospital, Fang's problems were by no means the biggest. He inevitably became a target, but when the spearhead turned toward the hospital's leading cadres and corrupt elements, he was basically extricated, and allowed to go about his usual business. In the summer of 1965 the movement entered its final stage, and when people began summing up the investigation, Fang was asked to write a set of detailed inspection materials for the Four Clean-Ups team to appraise.

In the materials, he admitted that "I have committed crimes against the people and am a historical counter-revolutionary," and went on to enumerate his past crimes. He said that in the hospital his own crime was "the biggest and most serious. Because of the Party's leniency, I was not suppressed, but that was through the grace of the Party, which did everything humanly possible to help me." He was deeply grateful to the Party, and determined to reform all aspects of his life. He went on to talk about how he had read Mao, studied politics, and at all times and in all places reported to and requested instructions from the Party organization, the security section, and the supervisory team, to make sure he stayed on the straight and narrow. He described how he had single-mindedly bent his efforts at work to serving the people, and he listed his main achievements:

(1) With the help of doctors trained in Western medicine and the comrades of our own section, he managed, mainly by using Chinese medicine, to save two patients suffering severe liver and kidney failure, so that after another two years of treatment, they were able return to the workplace.

(2) In collaboration with leaders and comrades, he was able to save nearly 150 children who had suffered poisoning, and did so using Chinese medicine, acupuncture and other methods, so that all the children were eventually declared out of danger and restored to health.

(3) By combining acupuncture and Chinese medicine, he cured a sixteen-year-old deaf-mute.

(4) Using a traditional approach, he cured a woman suffering from nephritis, which had already led to a severe case of ascites, and restored her to health.

(5) He explored the use of acupuncture therapy, and cured a male patient of hemiplegia and convulsive spasms.

(6) On the basis of long-term research and clinical experience in the motherland's science of channels and collaterals, he produced in preliminary form a volume titled *Doctrines of Meridian Channels and Acupuncture Points,* in which he summarized and expanded on existing knowledge and put forward a relatively new method of treatment of balanced acupunctural stimulation. He arranged twelve volumes of teachings based on his experience treating various diseases and symptoms. He developed patent Chinese medicines.

But in his review, he was careful not to forget his problems. He mentioned how, during the Three Hard Years, he had attended to his own self-interest: "I did not behave morally, I did not abide by the law and know my place, and I undermined the nation's supply policy by secretly using the back door." He added that he had violated the nation's laws and his personal integrity as a doctor. What he meant was that, through a patient, he had managed to buy some slightly better-quality meat without having to queue, together with some turnips beyond his ration quota, and that he'd given leading cadres special treatment. Although he sacrificed his spare time and even went to the clinic on an empty stomach, sometimes he had thought it might help him buy a sewing machine, or a better cut of meat, and so on.[62]

Fang submitted this review on June 16, 1965. Five days later, the Four Clean-Ups group held yet another meeting to discuss his hat. The review had already been distributed to participants, so Fang only made a brief statement. The meeting criticized him for "going by the back door" and for saying one thing and doing another. It also criticized him for "not working hard enough," for "not making good use of his brains," and especially for not behaving equally to workers and leading cadres: "For example, you treated a patient with severe ulcers by moxibustion. That was very careless, you show too little sympathy for workers." Some speakers made it clear that they did not want his hat removed, and others advised waiting. However, the section leaders stepped up and asked people to stick to the main point, so in the end sixty-four people agreed to remove the hat, with just one against.[63]

The Four Clean-Ups group summed up the meeting:

The masses discussed all aspects of the ideological reform of the historical counter-revolutionary Fang ... over the past few years, and brought up these points:

(1) Ideological aspects: He has been able to accept reform, he has reported punctually, every month he has written brief summaries of his reform, he has been relatively honest in his reform, he has not engaged in sabotage or made reactionary comments, he has not joined any improper organizational factions, his ideology has been all right, and he has regularly accepted the views of his supervisory group.

(2) Work: He has been active and taken the initiative, he has atoned for his crimes by meritorious service. At work he knows how to deal with problems and to make timely summaries of the treatment process, he has published papers in journals, and he has taken the initiative in contributing folk prescriptions and secret remedies. A patient who had been deaf and dumb for years was able to shout "Long live Chairman Mao" after Fang treated him. Fang has all along been at patients' beck and call, whatever the time of day. In his daily work activities, he abides by the medical system, accepts the work assigned to him, and fulfils his allotted tasks.

(3) Problems: In the Party's difficult period, given that his bourgeois thinking had not yet been fully reformed, he sometimes went by the back door and failed to treat workers and cadres equally and without discrimination.[64]

The clinic's Party branch also "agreed to remove the hat."[65] The Four Clean-Ups work team quickly called a special meeting to discuss the proposal.

Its submission affirmed Fang's reform over the previous few years. It stressed that he had been able to comply with the implementation of the reform system, and pointed out that he had behaved responsibly at work and devoted much of his spare time to treating patients, curing deaf-mutes, and helping hemiplegics get out of bed and speak. It added, in a special note: "Over the past few years he has cured more than two hundred patients suffering severe illnesses, including four patients snatched from the jaws of death." He had passed on secret remedies, published a dozen papers in relevant journals, and conveyed his techniques to others, "so that the masses repeatedly praised him."[66]

"The meeting agreed unanimously that since first receiving his punishment in 1959, his behavior has for the most part taken a turn for the better. The team agrees that his counter-revolutionary hat can be taken off."[67]

On July 8, 1965, the Four Clean-Ups team and the hospital Party committee jointly drafted a report on the removal of Fang's hat:

Since getting his hat, despite one episode of poor behavior, he has demonstrated his determination to reform. His behavior at work has been good, he has complied with the reform system, and he has achieved results. Although he has sometimes favored cadres over workers and has, in difficult times, gone by the back door, he has not engaged in sabotage or refused to submit to reform. He was an object of assessment in the Four Clean-Ups campaign, and now, in accordance with the spirit of the Party's policy and the opinion of the masses, and in view of his performance in ideology and work, it has been resolved after discussion to remove his counter-revolutionary hat.[68]

However, the comments on Fang's historical crime and his attitude to his own reform were plainly adverse:

Participated in the Youth League, and served as a district leader; joined the Kuomintang and served as section leader and secretary of Q county branch Party. Participated in and helped organize the Kuomintang monitoring network, collected intelligence about our local militia and army, and reported to the fake Party's provincial headquarters; in 1946, attended the Q county meeting to suppress the fake forces, participated in the decision to kill Chairman X of our peasant association, and secretly reported on our primary school teachers; in 1948, again participated in the Zhongtong as a special agent. During the movement he was designated as a historical special agent, but because he was able to confess on his own initiative and his attitude was honest, he was exempted from punishment. However, because his nature as a counter-revolutionary remained unchanged, he continued with his activities despite

108 CHAPTER 3

his lenient treatment. As a result, in 1959, he was publicly given a hat and put under supervision. In 1959, when he was handed over to the masses for supervision and reform, he did not bow his head and confess his guilt, and he said openly to the workers and staff: Wearing a hat is not important, it's because I and the leadership can't get on. He incited the masses, he said the work made him tired, that it would be better to return to the village to do farming, and so on. In order to subdue the enemy, in 1960 various big and small meetings were held to present the facts and argue things out, and for the masses to reason things out and conduct struggles. This happened three times. Only then did this counter-revolutionary with his blood-debt bow his head, recognize his guilt, and express his determination with these words: 'In future I will be frank and honest, and submit to supervision and reform. Hereafter I will gradually progress from bad to good, actively respond to the Party's call, improve my behavior in the various movements, act more seriously and responsibly at work, and strive to achieve things.'[69]

These comments were in stark contrast to previous assessments of Fang by the clinic's Party branch, the hospital security section and the Four Clean-Ups special team, which were all positive and made no mention of any provocative behavior since wearing the hat. The current report presented Fang in quite a negative light, making it difficult for any reviewer to have a good impression of him.

Those responsible for leading the Four Clean-Ups in the hospital issued these instructions: "After discussion by the Party Committee of the work team, Fang's historical crime is serious. Although his behavior at work has not been bad, his political attitude is unclear and he should continue to wear a historical counter-revolutionary hat, undergo supervision and reform, and give further thought to his own ideology."[70]

A few months later, the Cultural Revolution broke out. In the localities and units, the first revolutionary act was to criticize, struggle against, and drive out the five black categories. Fang and other elements in the hospital wearing hats and being held under control were driven out into the villages. In September, Fang was forced back to his native village, to undergo labor reform under the supervision of the poor and lower-middle peasants. He and his disabled mother, in her eighties, together with his three children, still of school age, had to live off the 60 yuan a month earned by his wife.

THE ROAD TO APPEAL

For the first year or two in the countryside, Fang Liren did not dare act rashly. Although the brigade had health stations, this was not the sort of post available to a counter-revolutionary wearing a hat. However, since the medical level of the doctors in the health stations was low, more and more cadres sought out Fang's help. This upset the doctors and some cadres, who picked quarrels with him. Fang, who had never in his life engaged in manual labor, not only had to work with his hands day after day but, as a punishment, was made to join other five categories in sweeping the streets, collecting dung, and building earthworks.

After the first storms of the Cultural Revolution in the countryside had blown over, he wrote again and again to the Party committee, lodging appeals and requesting a change in his treatment. In his view, his situation was due to his "historical counter-revolutionary" hat. Unless that was removed, there was no chance of any change. Again and again he mulled over the course of events starting with his exemption from punishment and ending with his award of a hat and his being placed under supervision, and he felt all along that there were questions about the process. What he remembered best was what the Party secretary had told him, to his face, that the Organization's political recommendations would be shown to him and would be signed, sealed, and announced at a rally. As far as he remembered, he had never seen the Organization's conclusions, let alone seen them signed and sealed.[71]

During the Cultural Revolution, everyone was rebelling, seizing power, and rebelling again, so the hospital leadership never settled down. Not surprisingly, Fang's appeal was ignored. Not until August 1973 did the hospital finally respond. The review, stamped with the seal of the hospital's Party committee, said: "In accordance with the spirit of the notice of the Central Committee of the CCP forwarded by the Military Control Commission of the Beijing Municipal Public Security Bureau on March 18, 1967, the hospital Party committee decided after study not to return this person to the hospital. He is to stay in his native place performing manual labor under the supervision of poor and lower-middle peasants."[72]

The Beijing Military Control Commission's notice mentioned in this statement referred to the "Measures for the handling of persons returned to Beijing after being sent home during the Cultural Revolution." It declared that "poorly behaved" five categories, including those whose hats had been removed, were not allowed to return to Beijing; and if they had returned, they must leave again immediately, or they would be forced back by the revolutionary mass organizations and the public security organs.[73] Fang was not only still wearing a hat and under supervision but his political appraisal would undoubtedly have been "poor." So during the ten years of the Cultural Revolution Fang stood no chance of returning to the city.

Finally, after years of suffering and deprivation, the Cultural Revolution came to an end, and Fang resumed writing a quick succession of letters of appeal. On hearing that wrongs were being righted on a wide scale and five categories were losing their hats, he wrote to the Provincial Committee's Policy Implementation Office, the *People's Daily*, and other institutions: "Although I have serious historical problems, I already confessed during Sufan and the Organization concluded that there had been neither concealment nor omission, that I had undergone serious reform and committed no new errors. To contribute my medical techniques to the great socialist motherland and spread medical knowledge to the broad mass of medical workers" and at the same time to take care of his family, "I request, in accordance with Party policy, that I be returned to N Municipality and that work be arranged for me."[74]

In 1978, after spending twelve years in the countryside and having reached the age of sixty, Fang had a heart attack. His mother had died in the last stages of the Cultural Revolution; his wife was suffering from chronic hepatitis and anemia; his son had become disabled at work and, as a paraplegic, had been sent to Shanghai for treatment; his daughter had a factory job, but she was unable to leave the factory at night, because of the three-shifts system and the distance between home and work. A family shattered by death, disability, and distance.

To help Fang's son regain his ability to earn a living, the hospital, in response to a request from the family, sent the son to Shanghai for treatment and provided a testimonial requesting that Fang be allowed to accompany him, so he could treat him with acupuncture. The hospital's Party committee announced on May 24, 1978:

> Fang Liren belongs among those wearing a historical counter-revolutionary hat. According to the provisions of article 5, paragraph 10, of the document issued by the CCP's Provincial Committee, 'those designated as enemies who have technical expertise and behave well are permitted to return to their original units to do appropriate work'; in the spirit of the disposition of that those who are 'old, weak, sick, disabled, and without support in their original places and cannot live alone but need relatives to support them in the city,' the Party committee proposes to let Fang, whose home is in the city and who is a practitioner of Chinese medicine, return to practice Chinese medicine.[75]

The hospital sent someone to the Q County public security department to obtain relevant materials, in order to submit them to higher authorities. However, the "evidentiary materials" provided by the brigade where Fang worked were highly unfavorable:

> We hereby certify that Fang Liren, now in our brigade, wears a historical counter-revolutionary hat and, since returning to the brigade in 1966, has refused to submit to reform, has violated the brigade's security system, and has privately received patients. When the brigade found out about this, it paraded him through the streets and denounced him publicly. In 1971 and 1974, it twice reviewed his historical counter-revolutionary hat, but did not remove it. A few years ago his son was injured at work and he applied to the brigade's political and security council for no more than a fortnight's leave, but it was more than a year before he returned to the brigade, thus violating his leave conditions. In terms of abiding by the law and performing manual labor, his behavior is the same. I hereby certify.[76]

In the conditions of the day, Fang's political status was still that of a "historical counter-revolutionary," so he could only be acknowledged as someone the removal of whose hat "is unclear, and who should be treated as not wearing a hat." It was still necessary to get the evidence from the brigade before further steps could be taken. Without an indication of "better behavior," the door to Fang's return might be open but the path was blocked.

The Fang family became anxious. Fang was in Shanghai with his son, so Fang's wife had to get the daughter to issue an appeal to the relevant authorities. She did so, indicating that in his spare time her father treated people from the brigade and from neighboring villages and even communes, and even cadres from outside the county. She explained the relationship between him and the brigade cadres and the complex reasons for it. She ended: "I earnestly request the provincial and municipal leaders to solve my father's problem."[77]

In late September, Fang was called back to the brigade and wrote to the hospital's Party committee. The letter made a point of the hardships suffered by his family. He said that his family's difficulties were overwhelming.

> As long as I am in the village, I can neither help my sickly wife nor solve my son's crippling illness, nor can I share my daughter's worries about her mother, her brother, and her father. I therefore request the leadership to transfer me back, so that I can work hard, putting my forty years of medical knowledge at the service of the Four Modernizations, and, together with my wife, take good care of our children and create the conditions for them to thrive, so that my wife and daughter can act concertedly and make an energetic and due contribution to the people, while at the same time sharing the burden of my son, currently borne by the leadership, his work unit, and his comrades.[78]

The Party committee, after studying the evidence submitted by Fang's brigade, decided to approve the report. They once again sent someone to show Fang their decision allowing him to return to his family and resume work. Fang signed without hesitation. The Party Committee of the Health Bureau and the Political Department of N Municipality's Trade and Industry Bureau issued a formal reply: "Fang is to return to his work and his family at his original wage level."[79] The brigade's resistance to Fang had been basically overcome.

A month or so later, the Central Committee's policy began to change. At the start of 1979, the Central Committee and the Ministry of Public Security issued a series of resolutions "on the question of the removal of hats from landlords and rich peasants and the question of the children of landlords and rich peasants," as well as other documents requiring a practical solution to the problems of four categories and their hats.[80] In October, the Ministry of Public Security issued further instructions urging all localities to implement the work of removing hats from four categories. Fang finally received a piece of paper headed "Notice regarding the removal of four element hats."

In the spring of 1979, Fang moved back to N Municipality. A year later, he re-joined the Workers' Hospital. He was already in his late sixties; his working days were almost over. Problems regarding his wages remained, and the family continued to face difficulties.

He had spent three decades scared and worried. Now, at least, he had nothing left to fear.

4

The Price of "Reaction"

The Emergence and Discovery of an "Active Counter-Revolutionary"

Mu Guoxuan lived the most miserable life imaginable. Born the son of a bureaucratic landlord in 1933, at first he could not have been more carefree. Then, unexpectedly, just as he was growing up, the Japanese arrived, and his whole family was displaced by war. To avoid losing its land, in 1941 the family was forced to return to live under Japanese occupation, and its living conditions plummeted. At the end of the war, Mu was twelve years old, but his family could no longer afford to send him to senior primary school, so he went to live with his brother, who worked in the county town, and relied on him for support. He managed to scrape through middle school, but the civil war caught up with him. It was hard enough anyway to get into University at a time when the whole of China was changing color, and in his case he lacked the means to do so. For a living, he gained admission to a cadre school, but he didn't like the work he was assigned, so he sat the examinations for the School of Hygiene.

He was desperate to stay in the provincial capital, but after graduation he was sent to work in a remote county sanatorium. To get back to the provincial capital, he and two classmates wrote letters to provincial and municipal hospitals, but failed to achieve their aim and were forced to criticize themselves at a mass rally. In 1955, during a study movement at the time of Sufan, he was again investigated for making "reactionary comments" and colluding with others in a "reactionary clique." He confessed his reactionary thinking, and, as a token of his honesty, gave the Organization his diary, in which he had complained about the new government. To his surprise, his problems multiplied as a result. The most "reactionary" bits of his diary were disseminated throughout the hospital for people to criticize. He was kept in quarantine and investigated for further possible counter-revolutionary activities, while his unit sent people to his village to confiscate his parents' criminal possessions. The Organization discovered that he had written not only a reactionary diary but some "reactionary slogans" and "reactionary anonymous letters." In June 1956, he was labeled a "counter-revolutionary element"; the following March, he was sentenced by a court to two years' re-education through labor, and the sanatorium announced his expulsion. Two years after the expiry of his sentence, he returned to the system, and was assigned to work in the radiology department of a county hospital. However, he quarreled with his colleagues, and in March 1960 he regained his "counter-revolutionary" hat and was returned to the countryside to do manual labor under supervision. He continued to appeal throughout his twenty years under supervision, and in 1985, he was partly rehabilitated. His unit agreed to let him return to his family and his work, but the greater part of his life had already been wasted.

Mu's experience was special but by no means unique. His misfortune was a result not only of the changes brought about in environment, identity, and thinking by the passage from old to new but was intimately linked to the political climate of the time, with its emphasis on class struggle and on individual rule as opposed to the rule of law. His stubbornness was also a major factor. In such times, under such a system, strong personalities often come to grief.

Mu's personal files have been salvaged from the waste bin, but there are big gaps in the record. The following summary is shaped by the existing materials, which it does its best to bring to life and make speak. Unfortunately we do not have a complete picture of Mu's life as he lived it, as many details had to be left blank.

ORIGIN OF THOUGHT

From the very start of his career in early 1953, Mu's status was that of cadre. In China in the 1950s, anyone who wanted to be a cadre had to fill out a cadre's personal history form, and to make a clean breast of his or her past. A comprehensive reading, comparison, investigation, and analysis of a cadre's efforts at self-accounting over the years can often help to explain in some depth a person's social history and the changes in his or her thinking.

Unfortunately, Mu's dossier preserves only two "historical autobiographies," both written during Sufan. One is the diary he handed over, written in the period before his isolation and interrogation; the other concerns the period after he took the decision to surrender his diary, after the nature of his problem changed, and after he became the unit's key focus in Sufan.

The first set of materials focuses on the family's economic situation and the effect of family upbringing on the author's outlook. Regarding ideology, it mentions only two points: one is his father's helping him to aspire to become a scientist, the other is his family's stopping him at a very early age from playing with workers' and peasants' children, so that he "only wanted to get close to people with manners and to intellectuals, and was unwilling to get close to worker and peasant elements who talked crudely and behaved unreasonably." Politically, he mentioned having joined a "comrades' society" at middle school and having heard the Three Selfs Lectures.[1] This "influenced his psychological fear of the Communist Party, so that from Liberation through until today he continues to doubt and question it."[2]

The subsequent historical autobiography speaks about his family and his history before 1949, but because he was in isolation and under investigation, the writing is in some respects insincere and sometimes ascends to the higher plane of principle and the two-line struggle, under the interrogators' influence. It is unfortunate that the materials cannot be replaced or supplemented; however, their narrative method reveals much about modern history that is worth knowing. I cite at length from Mu's writings so that readers can learn about his experience of growing up and studying:

> I began remembering things at around the age of five, but even at four I had a notion of the family's general situation. In 1936, when father was an officer on the General Council of the fake Pacification Office, he did not actually work but merely occupied the position. Every month he went to the provincial capital to fetch his salary (more than 1000 yuan a month), and once a month or once every few months he attended meetings, although he spent nearly all his time at home. The family had five ordinary courtyard houses and many *mu* of land (I don't know how many). Each season we received a big income from rent. We lived partly off father's salary and partly off rent, so we were prosperous. Our staple food was wheat and rice. We wore silk and satin, wool, fur, etc. We employed three cooks, a maidservant, and a guard. I was spoiled and pampered. I could eat and dress as I pleased, everything without limit. My mother often beat the maid. Though I was young, I also developed bad habits, and I too beat and cursed her. From an early age, I acquired the mentality of a ruler. That was the reactionary and backward side of my family. But my mother also loved and cared for the poor. We had many cotton army uniforms at home, and when winter came and beggars or people without clothes started turning up, mother doled out uniforms. That was her good side. But it had little impact on me.
>
> The family had numerous social connections, including father's colleagues from the old days, mostly old-style army officers (in uniform, bearing weapons), but I was young and disliked strangers, so it meant little to me. We had photos of Sun Yat-sen, Chiang Kai-shek, Yan Xishan, and so on, and I remember father telling people: 'These are the leaders of China.' That started me thinking. In July 1937, when war broke out, father mentioned Soviet military aid to China, and the Japanese protests against it. Japanese aircraft were bombing daily, so with tenants' help, he went to X to hide, and every few days he went down to the village to take care of things. After the

Mid-Autumn Festival, with the Japanese Army drawing closer, we all fled by train to X, returning only in 1940. We took up temporary residence in the courtyard of a shop, but the Japanese bandits' primary school teacher took it over, and we moved to an adjacent courtyard. I was eight. All I knew of life was the grief and distress of poverty.

We lived off the rent from our land and houses. Father spent all day at home, with nowhere to go. In the summer, he grew vegetables for our own table. In 1939, mother contracted lung disease and died in the winter of 1941. The family became chaotic in the absence of a woman, so one was hired to care for the family. She cooked food for me to take to school. Not long afterwards, in the spring of 1942, the Japanese gendarmerie turned up, on the pretext of checking our household registration. There was a police captain, two military policemen, two fake police inspectors, an interpreter, and some other policemen. The Japanese police captain, adopting the tone of an interrogation, asked father about his past activities, and revealed that his purpose was to get father to help the Japanese and puppet authorities. But father said that he had not fought against the Japanese and that he was an old man. In the end, he managed to refuse the job.

In the spring of 1941 (when I was nine), I began boarding in the First Xinmin primary school, set up in the Japanese and puppet era under Japanese leadership. Apart from the principal, who was Japanese, there was one Japanese advisor for every two classes, and in year two we began learning Japanese. I was good at it, and was praised by the Japanese teacher. When I got home and told father, he scolded me. He saw it as a form of enslavement. He said there was no need for intensive study, knowledge of written Chinese and mathematics was the main requirement. In the second year, we were transferred to the Second Xinmin school. We commemorated Japanese anniversaries and held ceremonies for Confucius and Wu. Father explained: 'Now China is in temporary retreat because of the Japanese invasion. Wang Jingwei's government is a government of traitors, its politics are of enslavement. Our real government is in Sichuan, and will come back in future.' At first, I loved to watch the Japanese do their drill. When I told father, he said: 'Our armed forces, our Central Army, will be much stronger than them.' With that, I established my idea of the nation. I believed that the national government and Chiang Kai-shek were China's leaders. They would return and things would become better. Japanese enslavement by education would be abolished. So from then on, I tried get away from school.

In 1942, father remarried. An old friend used to come to our house to chat about current affairs. He and father often talked about the Anti-Japanese War. For example, they talked about the Battle of Nankou, the Battle of Taierzhuang, the Battle of Xuzhou, the Battle of Wuhan, the Battle of Changsha, and the Battle of Luoyang, and they also mentioned the Battle of Pingxingguan and the Fuping campaign. They noted Japan's losses and China's victories, and spoke highly of Chiang Kai-shek's military skills, and how the Japanese wanted to destroy China and had repeatedly met with resolute resistance by the Central Army. All this left a deep impression on me. I was convinced that China would not perish and that Japan would be defeated. Thus my faith in Chiang Kai-shek was slowly born.

THE PRICE OF "REACTION"   117

In 1946, I graduated from senior primary school, but father was unable to afford my school fees, so my brother helped me get to the provincial capital, where I gained admittance to middle school. Brother constantly checked my grades, and hoped I would become an engineer. After the victory over Japan, Chiang Kai-shek called on young people to become primary school teachers, pilots, and engineers. Father agreed with him, and so did I. In the period leading up to Liberation, we spoke about his time in X during the anti-Japanese years, and also about the situation as it then was, and our fears of a Communist victory. We hoped that the Central Army would send a large force to relieve the provincial capital, and we believed the rumors about Chennault's Flying Tigers, although they turned out to be false.

My middle school served a dozen surrounding counties. I've already explained about the curriculum, but not about the teachers' political attitude. The Chinese-language teacher was a graduate of Beijing's University of Law and Political Science. He talked about Chiang Kai-shek's personal qualities (filial piety, etc.), so my respect for Chiang grew even stronger. Apart from slandering Communism in his lectures on socioeconomic problems (I confessed this earlier), the teacher said that the Communist Party recognized no law or morality, and that if the rich and poor went to court, the rich were always in the wrong. He said our Constitution did not distinguish between rich and poor, and that it was common for sons to beat fathers in Communist areas during land reform. This made me even more hostile to the Communists. The Director of Political Training said in a philosophy lecture: 'The Communist Party regards people as things—dead objects. It does not distinguish between different levels of intelligence, it views everyone as equal, so society remains backward and people prefer leisure to hard work.' I've already confessed the other political courses. This sort of thinking instilled in me a deep hatred of the Communist Party. After Liberation, it seemed to me that the Party's putting worker and peasant cadres in key positions was exactly what the fake director of political training had implied, so I was even more opposed to it.

In 1947, a comrades' society sprang up at the school. An oath was sworn a fortnight after I had filled in the membership form. I still remember the organizational principles, 'a system of democratic collectivism: the minority was to submit to the majority, and lower levels to higher levels.' In the spring of 1948, we started up the Three Selfs, meaning self-cleansing, self-defense, and self-government. Classes stopped for three weeks, and students were organized into groups of between five and ten with a set proportion of members and non-members. Everyone had to investigate their lives starting from the age of seven, the age at which memory begins. Three students were from a disputed area in conflict with our army, so they weren't approved and were made to attend a rally at which they were subjected to a struggle. Because I was a member, I took part in the interrogation. After the struggle, we stood guard over them at night. Later, after instruction, the three underwent self-cleansing for a month and then returned to school.

After Liberation, I was no longer able to pay my school fees, so I was forced to consider joining the cadre school. This school only did politics, so we studied 'The Present Situation and Our Tasks,' 'The Chinese Revolution and the Communist Party,' 'On

Coalition Government,' 'On New Democracy' (Mao Zedong's works), 'On the Party' (Liu Shaoqi), 'The History of Social Development,' 'Political Economy,' 'A Critique of the U.S. White Paper,' and 'Dialectical Materialism and Historical Materialism.' The schedule was tight (more so than in general schools), and we learned songs, including 'Make Revolution to the End,' 'The Chinese People Praise Mao Zedong,' 'Go! Follow Mao Zedong,' 'Without the Communist Party There Would Be No New China,' 'Unity is Strength,' and 'We Workers Have the Power.' But given my reactionary stand, my hatred grew apace. It seemed to me that what had been said in old China was true, and what was said in new China, by the Communist Party, was all about power.

In February 1950, we graduated, and the provincial committee assigned us to new posts. The job to which I was assigned was not to my liking, and the location was intolerable. My thinking had not changed. I was afraid that in the distant future, after a coup, I would not be able to work for the Kuomintang, so I did not accept the assignment and returned to the countryside.

In the summer of 1950, the medical college started enrolling, and father saw this as a good opportunity for me. I applied and was admitted. Because medical study was publicly funded and concerned natural science and technology, there was nothing to put me off. But my dissident views on politics did not go away. I disliked the newspaper course and the political course, and never took notes. For exams, I mugged up at the last minute and scraped through. Knowing that the Communist Party, in all circumstances and at all times, will always force people to study politics, I concentrated hard on specialist matters, for I felt that science and technology were subjects in their own right and could do no harm. Political study could lead to problems after future changes. I set out to find friends with whom I could deepen my specialist knowledge, and I avoided people who liked to join in social activities. I sat behind my books all day and kept quiet. The students I was close to never spoke about politics, so all they knew was that I preferred specialist questions to politics. They had no idea how reactionary I was.[3]

As a focus of Sufan, what Mu has written here accords by and large with the requirements of the special team working on his case, and may have been written to order. The reason for digging deep into one's personal history was to detect the influence of historical roots and social relations on the subject's "reactionary ideology." It is easy to see what the special team wanted Mu to identify. The main thing was to get him to dissect his own "reactionary ideology," his reasons for supporting Chiang Kai-shek, and why he hated the Communist Party.

YOUNG AND UNHINDERED

In 1955, Mu Guoxuan was twenty-two. Why did he become the main focus of Sufan in his unit? First, because he was young, unhindered, impulsive, liable to blurt things out, and sarcastic. For example, when he was assigned to the sanatorium in 1953, he found it hard to settle down. "The main reason was that I felt relations among workers were unequal, conditions were poor, and it was impossible to deepen one's understanding of specialist theory. There were too many administrators and meetings. All this ate into my self-study time, so I was unhappy with the Party committee. On a number of occasions I put forward ideas and wrote letters."[4] The Party committee did not accept his views. In addition, he was loath to leave the city for such a small place, so he began to make plans to leave.

During the three-year war against the United States and in defense of Korea, the sanatorium was extremely busy. Many wounded were brought in from the battlefield to rest and recuperate. But the sanatorium was poorly equipped. Medical professionals were outnumbered by political and administrative personnel, and people with specialist training and qualified doctors were in short supply. The sanatorium managed to get a batch of graduates from the province, but they were poorly qualified. The sanatorium was so over-stretched that people were being recruited at random to tend the wards.

When Mu first arrived at the hospital, he was not yet twenty. He had never actually met a patient, let alone dispensed clinical treatment. Left by himself on the ward, things kept going wrong, and he was under constant psychological pressure. He had grown up spoiled, with contempt for the uncouth and uneducated. The convalescents had come straight from the front. Their injuries were serious and they were liable to fly into a temper, which put Mu even more on edge. He said the sight of new convalescents in uniform arriving day after day made his head spin.[5] Then, by chance, he was joined by a newly assigned student with ideas similar to his own—similarly afraid of making medical mistakes and being blamed for them, and similarly unwilling to stay in the sanatorium; and another who, being married, itched to rejoin his wife in the provincial capital. The three, joined by spiritual affinity, flung caution to the winds and, alone and jointly, wrote requesting transfers.

Initially, the hospital sympathized with their difficulties, but gave them to understand that the hospital was beset with problems and they could only go if the province found suitable replacements. The hospital knew this was impossible. Mu and the others had no alternative but to carry on sending joint letters to the authorities, with Mu writing most copiously, once or twice every two days, ever more clamorously.

On May 6 he wrote to the provincial deputy chairman. His tone was relatively mild. He said: "When the health department assigned us our jobs, we were neither consulted nor informed. Our names were ticked off and we were sent to the sanatorium. I'm from a student background, and I've never had a job. Since arriving here, I've written more than a score of letters to the health department and the general hospital requesting a transfer, but because of their bureaucratic style of work, no solution has emerged. In a state of utter helplessness, with the convalescents in a dreadful situation, I came up with the idea of writing to the provincial leaders."[6]

A letter dated June 6 was more impetuous: "The approach of deputy secretary X in the sanatorium represents one hundred percent selfish departmentalism, narrow vision, and short-sightedness. He thinks only about the sanatorium and ignores other factors. I beg the director to consider this issue, in order to avoid harming us. Otherwise, our years of training will have been in vain, and the loss to the state and the individuals concerned will be incalculable."[7]

On July 9, he wrote: "Now not only the patients but the hospital leaders are against us. If the leadership refuses to see us as humans, I will not force myself to eat the millet of the people. Please resolve this quickly, or I will resign."[8]

Mu and the others continued demanding a transfer, even threatening to complain to the Central Committee,[9] causing turmoil at higher levels and in the sanatorium itself. In late 1953 the sanatorium leaders launched a campaign of ideological rectification, directed at Mu and the others. The Party committee announced at a series of meetings that the emphasis should be on the subordination of individual interests to the state and to the overall interest, and that it opposed the tide of bourgeois individualism. Mu was named, and was forced to carry out self-criticism at a rally. Mu did as asked, and stopped requesting a transfer. But his anger remained, and he continued to address cynical comments and complaints to colleagues implying criticisms of contemporary society and praise for Chiang Kai-shek, as well as openly using publicly owned radios to listen to broadcasts from Taiwan.[10]

After the Spring Festival in 1954, Mu hid his resentment and spent more time studying. His father had always wanted him to apply to an engineering university. Mu liked the idea, but he was even more anxious to get into Whampoa military school, so that he could serve the country. His father told him about his own experience. He hated himself "for not having studied science and technology, and instead following an old-style military career," and that the only thing was to master technology in the service of the state.[11] Mu made a clear choice for science and technology, and grew anxious when the civil war prevented him from going to university. In his view, in the "new society whoever has ability can work in a good place."[12] Because he still hoped to study at some point, he drew together a small number of colleagues in a study group, where they used the opportunity provided by the drop in the number of convalescents and the resulting increase in free time to study medical problems.[13]

In July 1955, at the start of the campaign against the Hu Feng clique, the Central Committee launched Sufan. The sanatorium set up an "office to clear out counterrevolutionaries," organized a special Sufan contingent, and established a system of boxes for letters of denunciation, in order to mobilize the entire workforce to inform on counter-revolutionary activities. Some of Mu's activities became targets of public criticism. Bad things he had said or done were exposed, and the charge spiraled into one of "extreme reaction"; even his study group was suspected of having acted as a "small clique."[14]

The "office to clear out counter-revolutionaries" concentrated on the following aspects of Mu's case:

(1)   His attitude to work was poor. "He started causing trouble immediately after his assignment to our hospital"; with two other malcontents, "he expressed his disgruntlement, demanded a transfer, and was unhappy with the leadership"; "he was hostile to convalescents when they raised issues with him, and refused to consider whether they were right or wrong. He would say, 'Take it up with the leadership.'"

(2)   His ideology was "extremely reactionary." "When he first came to our hospital he hated the fact that there were political officials, he thought they were of no use." "He considered that the hospital leaders attached too little importance to professional matters and too much to politics," which led to confrontations. "He despised worker and peasant cadres, and said they were uncouth. He preferred people with a certain refinement. One day, X said: 'Premier Zhou is truly great, how wonderful it would be to see him.' Mu said: 'Don't be so silly!'" "He disliked having to perform manual labor, and said: "Doctors and nurses both perform labor, there's no difference."

(3)   "In studying Sufan, his attitude is incorrect, and he says disruptive things." During collective study sessions he read *Zhonghua zazhi* (*China* magazine); after study, he read a comic about Hitler's attack on the Soviet Union in the Second World War. When other people spoke at meetings, he gave cynical smiles, or looked out of the window. When people were inside the room, he sat outside, and when people were outside, he sat inside. He grumbled about the study campaign: "Can studying a document ferret out counter-revolutionaries?" When discussing someone who had written reactionary slogans: "It wasn't necessarily one of our people who wrote them, people here are complicated." He said: "Now the hospital is in turmoil, the doctors can't find time to study their profession. How can technology improve?"[15]

Everyone knew that his remarks and "ideological tendencies" were reactionary. So Mu owed his suspect status mainly to his section and the study group, which exposed him, criticized him, and struggled against him. However, because more and more people pointed spearheads at him and agreed that his "reactionary ideology" was tied to a not-yet-exposed "reactionary history," Mu, who had pretended that his family were not bureaucratic landlords but middle peasants, lost his composure.

In August 1955, Mu made a self-criticism. He had no choice but to confess that he had studied at cadre school in 1949–50 and dodged his subsequent assignment. He admitted that his family was not middle peasant but bureaucratic landlord. However, although his father had sat on the council of the fake Pacification Office as a military officer, he had resigned after the start of the Anti-Japanese War to take care of the household, and from then on had no longer taken part in military affairs. After 1940, the economy collapsed, and after the Anti-Japanese War things became difficult and he couldn't afford his tuition fees. Only his two brothers continued to work for the old government. But because they were more than ten years older than him and didn't live with him, "I didn't think they had any effect on me." He said he knew nothing about their situation: "If they did anything and I failed to report it, I am prepared to accept any punishment the Organization thinks appropriate."[16]

As for his own ideological problems, on the basis of his ordeal during self-criticism at the time of the rectification campaign he had slavishly copied the existing model of self-criticism, based on the "higher plane of principle" and without any attempt at originality. The difference was that the core issue in the rectification movement had been selflessness versus selfishness, and even though it had escalated to the plane of "reactionary bourgeois and petty-bourgeois ideology," it did not stretch to actual "counter-revolution." In Sufan, however, non-revolutionary meant counter-revolutionary, not to mention reactionary, and the plane reached was that of "counter-revolution." Mu was insufficiently knowledgeable or ideologically prepared to know the risk he faced. He even believed that as long as he displayed a sincere attitude, as the Party secretary had said at the rally, and bared his heart he would again be forgiven by the Organization and the masses.

In his self-criticism, he classified his thinking as "supra-class," a "wrong world-view." He said this was mainly due to having been influenced by the negative social philosophy of certain people, which had convinced him "that there is no truth in society and anything goes. This had produced world-weariness and escapist tendencies in me," which, in today's world, "can easily be used by counter-revolutionaries." He confessed his habit of "seeing new problems from an old point of view, which was a counter-revolutionary sentiment." He had always thought that the Nanjing Government was orthodox, and did not recognize Premier Zhou's statement that the People's Republic had taken over from the Republic of China. He also believed that Zhang Xueliang and Yang Hucheng had betrayed the nation in the Xi'an Incident,[17] and that Chiang Kai-shek's policy of maintaining internal security and repelling foreign invaders was correct; in the Second World War, victory was due to the Anglo-Americans rather than to the Soviet Union; he had always wondered why newspapers in the old society could satirize the government but not in the new society; he had always thought that the electoral system under capitalism was more democratic than under socialism; he was disgusted when Party and Youth League members praised the film *Life of Wu Xun* only to turn against it after *People's Daily* criticized it, etc.

Finally, he said that, seeing how often he had complained about the Party, "I would like to hand over a reactionary diary to show my will to reform, in the hope that the leadership will educate me and save me from the counter-revolutionary mire."[18]

REAPING THE FRUITS OF ONE'S ACTIONS

The day after Mu's self-criticism, he handed over a diary he had kept since joining the hospital. He explained that once the study movement began, "I only wanted to hear people mock the Party." "Only after the entire group had formed a preliminary opinion of my attitude did I realize that this movement applied to reality, and that if the vilification of the Party in my reactionary diary was worse than Hu Feng's abuse, what then?" Although the Party secretary issued a report supporting Sufan, Mu felt that "the Communist Party would not lightly let go of a reactionary, and that although it would be dangerous not to hand over the diary, it would also be dangerous to do so," so he continued to hesitate. He said later it was because he saw at the rally how everyone helped a comrade with a historical problem, and especially when he heard the leader say: "Hiding history and 'having a small problem but not confessing it will lead the Party to suspect a big problem.'" He also said: "I reconsidered my concealing of the cadre school and its consequences, and I realized that unless I made a clean breast of things, the leadership would always suspect me and I would miss out on training. If there was to be no restoration of reactionary rule, why incur losses for a lifetime by delaying a decision? With these old and new ideas wrestling in my mind, I boldly surrendered the 'reactionary diary' and my concealment of my history."[19]

The Party committee and the purge office had an inkling of Mu's backwardness and reactionary thinking and were planning to use the movement to discipline him, but they had no idea that his problem might escalate to the plane of counter-revolution, so at first they did rank him as an object to be suppressed. When they read his diary, they got a big shock: an element even more counter-revolutionary than Hu Feng!

The suppression team spent a few days copying out the diary's reactionary bits. After sending them to the people in charge of the review, they mimeographed them as a book. They distributed the book to use for criticism, while commenting:

> Mu Guoxuan's reactionary diary provides evidence that exposes Mu's hostility to the Party, the people, and the revolution. Why does Mu oppose the Party, the people, and the revolution led by the Communist Party? Because he is from a reactionary landlord and bureaucratic family. In 1948, he joined a bandit comrades' society, such is his nature. Here are a few excerpts from his diary, together with some of our notes. See what kind of person Mu is![20]

The purge office edited the excerpts, mostly from 1954, into eight sections. Strictly speaking, it was not a diary but a miscellany of thoughts and brief essays. An early article, titled "Being fake is not to surrender," was about his own attitude and perceptions in a time of change. Referring to himself as "Xiangfu," he wrote:

> Several years had passed, within which time the semi-independent marquis had coerced Xiangfu into committing dishonest deeds. But that was the early summer of

the thirty-fifth year of the Republic, and the troubles caused by those deeds were not great, and not yet reviled by the master [meaning Chiang Kai-shek]. At the bidding of his father, Xiangfu had attempted to join the school sponsored by the master, but he failed to do so due to the obstacles put in his way by the marquis. A lifetime opportunity was thus missed, that is the greatest regret of my life.

Another year, a new turn of events. The marquis departed, and the nobleman arrived. He wasn't much better than the marquis, and had many even worse qualities. He could barely support the situation, but he depended on their group, just as the marquis did. His *modus operandi* was to try by all means possible to monopolize the wealth for their group. Those who were not members of this group could not survive, and even if they do evil, they can be used again. This is called curing a poisoned patient with poison. On a certain day in a certain month, Xiangfu also had to join the group. However, he did so not as a heartfelt act but under life's pressures. The situation was akin to that of an Islamic terror mission 'whereby the scriptures are held in the right hand and a sword in the left hand, and those who do not submit will be killed.' The commoners had no choice but to join, and they did not really convert to Islam.

Sighing for home, frequently thinking of the South China Sea [meaning Taiwan], I do not know on which day the master will arrive. In these circumstances, one cannot say that I have submitted to the kingship [meaning the CCP]. This article is proof of what lies closest to my heart. If the master one day returns, please do not blame me.[21]

Another essay titled "The resonant role of a betrayer of the golden mean" describes his attitude toward the intellectuals' shameful surrender to the new government:

Among our original patients was a senior middle school student, outwardly benign and elegant but at the same time able to mingle with the mob [meaning members of the CCP], as if he had become a worker or a peasant. However, regardless of whether workers, peasants, intellectuals, thugs, docile citizens, or loyal and outstanding persons, under the present circumstances all resonate with the authorities. The mob and the docile ones also resonate, but it is especially the poor who succumb to the gun in the hands of the apostate. Particularly pitiful are those apostates under the gun who succumb halfway. From the point of view of qualifications, those he resonated with could not even compare to his students. This resonance is born of curiosity and of a wish to be on the state payroll.

The role of a betrayer of the Neo-Confucian golden mean is like that of the scholars of Duke Wen of Jin,[22] who in order to help their master to plunder the people's wealth were willing to sacrifice their silver tongues. Compared with the village scholar who helps someone to write a letter, their sins were even worse. So in order to receive an emolument, they must flatter this generation of rulers, and their resonating function can last only for the duration; otherwise, they will forfeit their emolument and their resonating function will come to an end. This is something the renegades must beware of. Pitiful, pitiful![23]

Another essay, titled "A Devil's Cover," is about Chinese diplomacy:

The newspapers have been carrying a lot of bad news. This news explains why the Chinese people don't want to continue living in this unreasonable way, especially in the interests of foreigners [the Soviet Union]. Some wise people are disappointed that Chinese just drag on, without knowing the destination. But due to the restrictions imposed by the situation, they have no way of expressing their ideas, so they read between the lines and scour the papers for news that is in our own interests. This is so-called 'anti-imperialism.'

When the Geneva Conference was coming to an end, diplomatic activities around the world showed who liked war and who wanted to annex the world. So the tyrants' [the CCP's] representatives—diplomats, now visiting Europe, now hurrying off to Asia—sow discord, confuse truth and falsehood, and want to be like Zhang Yi,[24] to persuade nations that do not love war to join with them in the criminal endeavor of destroying peace in the world. So that, unexpectedly, some unwitting nations abandon their neutrality, swell the devils' chorus, and threaten the world. These facts fully conform to the actions of the entrusted merchant depicted above. These unwitting nations might gradually take the same path to the Kremlin and be charged with doing business with the trusted merchant.

The wretched world is small, and it turns out that the tyrant asks foot soldiers to consider serving him, as future ministers and generals. However, the tyrant merely places their names on a list, and uses them as cattle and sheep that shiver before him. For example, was Beria[25] not loathed by the tyrant and driven tired into the slaughterhouse? Do you imagine that you, an alien foot soldier, will go to the palace to drink chicken soup? You will be trampled without batting an eyelid.[26]

In 1955, Sufan started up. Mao had ordered the publication of three batches of Hu Feng and his friends' correspondence, and declared them a counter-revolutionary clique. Hu Feng and his friends had been left-wing writers and literary critics. Many had joined the Communist Party and opposed Chiang Kai-shek. If such people could, on the basis of criticisms uttered in letters, be branded counter-revolutionaries, what chance did Mu stand, a man from a bureaucratic landlord family who in his diary had denounced the new regime? *People's Daily* made it clear, in the Hu Feng case, that if, after reading that kind of material, you could still not see that they were "a counter-revolutionary black gang," you were either a counter-revolutionary sympathizer or a hidden reactionary element.[27] Given Mu's comments, it was obvious how the Party committee and the purge office would react.

On the day that the purge office handed out Mu's "reactionary diary" to the workers and staff, it reported to higher authorities: "After graduating in March 1953, Mu was assigned to our hospital. He has never been at ease. He behaves irresponsibly, and when put on the wall-poster committee, he said that was for Party and Youth League members and refused to do it. He roped in people to engage to

write letters vilifying the leadership and wrote a reactionary diary. Our preliminary judgment: he is a counter-revolutionary element."[28]

DESPERATE MOVE

After realizing how reactionary Mu's thinking was, the purge office was determined to delve further into his activities. It warned the hospital that Mu had all
along been a reactionary. He had "longed, in vain, for the bandit Chiang to make
a comeback," so he must have "carried out secret nefarious activities." "What
exactly is Mu's purpose and what is he organizing? Who is his master? Comrades
must carry out further investigation, and Mu must make a thorough confession."[29]

In early September, when Mu's diary was made available, there was no immediate
announcement of a struggle against Mu's organization. Instead, people were mobilized to hold big and small meetings to struggle against him, while awaiting instructions from the purge section. In late September, when instructions were handed
down, a special team was set up and people went to search Mu's village home.

Mu knew he was in big trouble. He was terrified, "first, of the misunderstanding
that there had been an organizational connection; and, second, that if an organizational connection could not be established, he would be arrested and punished,
and even implicating his family."[30] But he remained resistant, and told everyone
that "doctors all have problems."

This went on until early October, when the special team began its interrogation.
Several people took turns at questioning him to tire him out. He particularly
despaired when he was fiercely attacked on the question of the "small clique," his
current activities, and the source of his reactionary ideas. Initially, he said next to
nothing, and when he was eventually forced to say something, his attitude was
impatient. He was especially aggrieved when the "reactionary small clique" came
up, and he started arguing: "All this happened because I handed over the diary. If I
hadn't, who would have known?" "I handed over the diary in all sincerity, there was
not a glimmer of a reactionary organization, why keep asking the same question?"[31]

He was convinced that "the University and his personal future were over."
When the special team resumed digging, he believed that he would never be able
to vindicate himself, and there was no way out for him. On October 11, he swal-
lowed a bottle of sleeping pills. In a suicide note, he listed his dissatisfactions with
the government, and stressed that he had to commit suicide "because neither the
Kuomintang nor the Communist Party trust me."[32] But the act was discovered, and
he failed to die. Through his "death," Mu achieved a "profound realization," and no
longer battered his head against the purge committee.

At the suggestion of the team, he wrote some reflective pieces confessing his
past and reviewing his behavior. He admitted that he had pinned his hopes on the
Kuomintang and thought that the Kuomintang's defeat was only temporary and

that Chiang would raise a new army and "make a comeback." He said: "My reactionary diary was not just for my own eyes, once things had developed, I would have made it known. After reading it, people would think about what it said, go on to find out about counter-revolutionary organizations, and get ready to join them." He admitted that his actions were "odious and dangerous," and said that he was willing to give up the five or six years of his "dead-end life" and "dead-end thinking" in order "to thoroughly clarify everything, to confess everything," "to emerge from the darkness," and to accept "legal sanctions."[33]

By late October, the purge office had collated Mu's various sins, of which there were more than a score, and the evidence for them.

Regarding historical crimes, someone had dug up materials to show that in 1947, at the age of fourteen and while still at middle school, Mu had been sent to the county seat to write materials for military intelligence slandering land reform in the liberated areas and accusing the Communists of killing and punishing people; someone else had discovered that he had joined the Kuomintang's "comrades' society," made ten new recruits, and was an activist in Three Selfs training; someone else had found that he petitioned the Kuomintang authorities to put an end to the students' movement; someone else found that in 1948, under the leadership of the director of political training, he had participated in the "bandit army's" military training.

Regarding current criminal activities, ransacking his family home had unearthed the following.

(1) A reactionary magazine and cap badge (with a portrait of Chiang Kai-shek, political manuals and journals, an infantry training manual, and military cap badges advertising the spirit of the Iron Army and the Kuomintang), etc.

(2) A sheet of paper on which was written "the bandit Mao deserves to die" and "all support and long life to the national government of the Republic of China."

(3) Several reactionary letters: "For today's disaster we must thank the hooligans Zhang Xueliang and Yang Hucheng for their evil plotting, what a shame that Chiang put those two bandits in charge of the northwest"; "the Communist bandits are now running amuck and the people are in dire straits, it's scarcely less chaotic than in the days of the bandits Li Zicheng and Zhang Xianzhong in the Ming Dynasty."

Other revelations:

(1) While attending cadre school, he mocked and attacked progressive students, and had said that the head of the student association was "simply catering to everyone's interests to get praise for himself, so he can join the Party."

(2)   He argued with classmates about newspaper propaganda concerning the United States occupation of Taiwan, saying: "It's true that Taiwan is Chinese territory, but so are Mongolia and the Northeast, so why, in 1946, did the Soviet Union insist on Mongolian independence and on occupying Dalian? If the United States is occupying Taiwan, how is that different from what happened in 1946?"

(3)   He told students: "The Korean War is a case of Chinese manpower, Soviet firepower, and North Korean grain; both China and Korea obey the Soviet Union."

(4)   He used to say that the United States was good, and that he knew a professor who had graduated from Harvard and wore an American watch.

(5)   He listened to the hospital radio and switched to shortwave, so he could receive the reactionary Taiwan station.

(6)   He criticized the sanatorium for its "low technology, none of which was worth studying," and said the hospital "was sub-standard, if you worked there, the patients got angry with you, it was pointless."

(7)   He said: "What's the point of studying politics? It doesn't help in your work, or professionally, and in future people won't want you."

Mu confessed:

(1)   In 1950, he returned home and found that his younger sister was joining in school cultural activities, singing revolutionary songs, joining the Young Pioneers, and wearing a red scarf, and he refused to speak to her.

(2)   He said to the head of the village militia: "If in the next few years the Kuomintang does not come back, we will have nothing to eat except atom bombs, collecting signatures for peace won't help."

(3)   When the Korean War broke out, he said that Kim Il-sung had attacked Syngman Rhee first, that "China was standing in for the Soviet Union, and that in the Battle of Inchon the United States was representing the United Nations, its presence was reasonable, ours was unreasonable."

(4)   When he heard that the Kuomintang General Wei Lihuang had returned from Hong Kong to the Mainland, he called it an act of treason that caused Chiang Kai-shek to lose face, and said Wei lacked integrity and was not fit to be a military leader.

In Mu's oral confession, two crimes stood out. One was when, after returning home from the cadre school, he wrote anonymous letters to the school, roundly cursing it; another was during Zhenfan, when he wrote reactionary slogans on the medical school's toilet wall.[34] These two instances came to light at the prompting and as a result of the pressure exerted by the special team, which caused Mu to dig deep into his memory. Unable to recall much specific content, he "recalled" the general contents of his anonymous letters and the slogans. The letters cursed the cadre school for "lying to people and lying to itself" and insulted China's leaders, concluding that things would end badly. He said "Long live the Republic of China! Long live President Chiang!" This was mainly to express his dissatisfaction with Zhenfan.[35]

After the internal interrogation and Mu's own confession, the next step was to send investigators to other localities for external investigations. The special team found it necessary to clarify some discrepancies, and confronted him:

Q: Since you wrote these letters, why go to the cadre school looking for work?

A: I had no work, I had nothing to live off.

Q: What did the head of the organization department ask you about the letters?

A: He said, the letters you have written are awful, they are highly reactionary.

Q: Did your family know about the letters?

A: My father knew. When I wrote angry letters, father asked me who they were to. I told him they were to the cadre school, I'd cursed the director. Father didn't stop me.

Q: Did the medical school find out who had written the slogans?

A: There was no announcement.

Q: Where were the reactionary slogans written?

A: On the wooden wall in the toilet, in the middle of the night, in pencil.

Q: Why didn't you talk about the reactionary slogans written in the medical school when the movement started?

A: I thought they were less important than the diary problem, and dishonorable.

Q: Is it true that you spoke with the militia leader?

A: Yes. It was because a plane flew over the village and the militia head said, so the Communist Party has planes? I said it's not worth one tenth of the Kuomintang's.

Q: Are the things we've been talking about all true?

A: Yes, they're all true.[36]

TWICE PUNISHED

On November 8, 1955, the special team drafted an outline program for the external investigation component of Mu's case. They sent people to the cadre school and the medical school and wrote to his old middle school and his village, to gather further evidence on Mu's numerous problems.[37] But the external investigation inevitably dragged on. Messages kept flowing back and forth through until the following spring. This confused Mu, who came to believe that he had escaped prison and would be dealt with by his unit. To avoid harming his future chances of employment, he even wrote to the purge office[38] politely suggesting that "as long as my problem remains unresolved, it's perhaps best not to announce it at a rally."[39]

After months of internal and external investigation, Mu's historical crimes could still not be thoroughly ascertained, first because he had been too young at the time and second because most of those in charge lacked a clear memory of what had happened. Mu's active counter-revolutionary crimes were also hard to prove. The "reactionary slogans" found in his home were written with a brush in an exercise book, and it was impossible to determine the date of writing (Mu said he had written them while at middle school). There was no way of establishing criminal intent in regard to his family and social ties, or to his private discussions and his retention of the Kuomintang cap badge. The possibility of establishing criminal intent concerned three items: the letters, the slogans, and the diary.

The diary was easy to prove but the letters and the slogans less so, for "no additional witnesses could be found." Regarding the letters, the political director of the cadre school said: "I'm sure there were such things, but the situation was chaotic, so it was difficult to say who wrote them, and it's hard to find conclusive evidence. As for the slogans, a school official said "slogans did appear," but there was no evidence of their content. But the special team said it could establish Mu's guilt, for he "hadn't repudiated his confession and his behavior since Liberation had conformed to type."[40]

The special team concluded that Mu's main crimes were as follows:

(1) In 1947, he had joined the "bandit comrades' society" and had recruited to it; in 1948, he had been active in Three Selfs training, and had struggled against and taken into custody so-called "disguised elements."

(2) After Liberation, driven by resentment as a result of his lack of opportunity to study, he was admitted to the cadre school, where he gathered a "small clique" to sabotage learning. He worked closely with secret agents of the [Kuomintang] Bureau of Investigations, reviled our relations with the Soviet Union, which he abused as one of "father and son," and called the school a concentration camp; after graduating, he refused work assignments, and at home he wrote letters and reactionary slogans.

(3) In September 1950, he sneaked his way into medical school, where he gathered together backward elements to attack progressives. During Zhenfan, he wrote reactionary slogans in the toilet.

(4) After his assignment to the sanatorium, he was unwilling to wear a military uniform. When he saw soldiers, he got a headache. He couldn't bear worker and peasant cadres. He sowed discord between medical and political people, and masterminded collective letters cursing the leadership, while at the same time secretly listening to the Voice of America. He also caused two medical accidents.

(5) After arriving at the hospital, he wrote more than reactionary diary entries and poems, cursing the Party leaders and the Soviet Union. His attitude was

one of "deeply ingrained class hatred, and he engaged in reactionary behavior. He managed to confess his problems of his own accord, but his reactionary position had not changed, and he undermined the movement by trying to commit suicide."

"PROPOSAL FOR TREATMENT: RE-EDUCATION THROUGH LABOR."[41]

On June 1, 1956, after revisions by the hospital's five-person group, a decision was made for dealing with Mu's suicide attempt. It said: "Mu tried to commit suicide. We decided that he did so for the following reason: he had made a confession, but the small group was continuing to investigate his status as a special agent, so he was afraid." Their proposed treatment was in line with the hospital's recommendations:

> This person is a counter-revolutionary element of the enemy class. After Liberation, someone in his family was attacked and he was unable to realize his dream of attending the Whampoa Military Academy and going to America, so he believed the Communist Party had destroyed his hopes. He hankered after a capitalist restoration and hated the Party. Despite joining the revolution, he continued to adhere to his standpoint, and wrote reactionary slogans and a diary; he slandered our Party and our leaders, and engineered accidents among the patients. He was consistently dissatisfied. His crimes were heinous. During Sufan, his attitude was honest, and with the help of the masses he confessed his crimes. An investigation suggested that his confessions were frank and honest. Therefore he should be shown leniency. We propose education through labor.[42]

The county court sentenced Mu to "two years of control, to be implemented by the re-education-through-labor organs." A week later, the sanatorium passed a resolution striking Mu off the roll.[43] He was sent to serve his sentence.

Two years later, Mu was freed and returned to the hospital. He was assigned by the provincial health department to a radiology department in a county hospital. However, his old habits had not died. He was still full of resentment, which he found it hard to conceal. During probation, he failed to understand much of what was going on in the hospital. His relations with some colleagues and the leadership were strained. One day, while he was X-raying a patient, a young doctor ran into the X-ray room and started whispering with the nurse but forgot to close the door. Mu lost his temper, abandoned the patient, and went off to find the leadership. The young doctor escaped criticism, because Mu was accused of sparking a "medical incident" by abandoning the patient in the X-ray room and was suspended and put under investigation. Because he was still on probation, the hospital escalated the issue to the higher place of principle and the two-line struggle, and subjected Mu to mass struggle. The hospital decided that Mu should "resume wearing a counter-revolutionary hat, stop his probation, and return to his original place of supervision."[44]

THE PROCESS OF REHABILITATION

Mu Guoxuan was sent back to the countryside in April 1960.[45] He lodged appeals, but there was no response. In 1979, after the start of the reforms and opening up, his appeal attracted the attention of the hospital authorities, who organized a review.

Mu's appeal was as follows:

> In March 1959, after the expiry of my sentence, I went to work in the county hospital as a probationer. Because of an altercation with a member of the staff, my probation was ended, my case was escalated to a higher political plane and blown up into a contradiction between the enemy and the people, and I was forced to wear a counter-revolutionary hat and sent back to the countryside. For me and my family, the consequences were dire. For seventeen years I have been without formal work. I don't think my punishment has been in line with Party policy. I have repeatedly appealed for a reopening of my case.[46]

The review concluded:

> Mu came to our hospital on probation. He behaved arrogantly, lost his temper with staff and patients, stopped working (to the direct detriment of patients), and did not do a good job. In 1960, he was told to wear a counter-revolutionary hat, but the judicial authorities did not approve the decision. The hospital Party Committee decided, in March 1979, that Mu's behavior, which has been generally acceptable, does not warrant his again wearing a counter-revolutionary hat or being sent back for manual labor. Nevertheless, he did not behave well during his probation, so he should not be allowed to resume his old position.[47]

In 1980, the Central Committee rehabilitated the Hu Feng counter-revolutionary clique and the Beijing Municipal Higher People's Court declared Hu Feng innocent. The news revived Mu's dream of rehabilitation. He said: "Today Hu Feng is no longer a counter-revolutionary but a member of the People's Political Consultative Conference. Should I, an ordinary citizen, be condemned to living death?"[48]

In 1981, in a new appeal that he distributed far and wide, he said: "During Sufan, I surrendered my diary, in accordance with the Organization's requirements and of my own accord." After surrendering it, "I was quarantined and interrogated, and, though just a young man, struggled against at meeting after meeting, denied my wages, and humiliated and insulted. I couldn't stand the pressure to confess, so I wrote an explanation of the diary and affixed my seal. The hospital sent three or four people from the political work section to ransack my parents' home." After that, his admissions regarding the letters, slogans, etc., were prompted by the special team. He was "on tenterhooks and in a suicidal state, and prepared to admit anything." As for the "reactionary anonymous letter," he explained there was nothing political about it, it was just an attack on irresponsible leaders. If it had had a political content, the school would have handed him over to public security. On the "reactionary slogans," he explained that the matter had been resolved. They had been written by X, posing as a Red Army veteran, and the case had been dealt with.

He proposed that the sanatorium "should not use the materials I handed over to the Party as evidence, and thus make me suffer all over again"; "the sanatorium should not use the slogans that appeared at the medical school or describe the letters I wrote to the Organization Department of the cadre school as anonymous, or use them to prove that I was a counter-revolutionary"; "given that there were no differences between what I was punished for in 1957 and what I was rusticated for in 1960, clearly I was punished twice on a single count"; "in 1979, the hospital recognized that my punishment in 1960 mixed up two different types of contradiction," and that "as a result, my case was treated as a contradiction between the enemy and the people, so it need not assume responsibility for my losses."[49]

The hospital where Mu had been on probation in 1959 did not deem itself responsible for looking into his appeal. It defended its previous decision, and concluded that Mu's problem had nothing to do with Hu Feng, and that it was right to put a stop to his probation because his behavior did not stand up to the mark.[50]

In the next three years, provincial, city, and county authorities all received letters of appeal from Mu. In 1983, the county health bureau launched an investigation into Mu's case, sending people out on missions and writing letters to relevant units and officials responsible for classifying Mu as a counter-revolutionary.

A letter from the Party committee in the original sanatorium read:

During Sufan, some people exposed Mu's reactionary talk and diary, and he was classified as an object for suppression. He surrendered his diary. It attacked the central leadership, so he was classified as a bad element. The county court sentenced him to two years' re-education through labor. As for the reactionary slogans in the cadre school and the medical school, there was too little evidence. We hope you can undertake a serious review. But the decision was based mainly on the diary and the reactionary comments. His problem can be resolved in accordance with Party policy.[51]

A leader of the former special team assigned to Mu's case wrote:

One day during a study meeting Mu said that after study, his awareness had improved, he believed in the Party, and he wanted to make a clean breast of things. He said his thinking was reactionary and he was dissatisfied with reality, and he handed over his diary. He did so voluntarily. An investigation showed that the diary was reactionary, but it belonged to the category of voluntarily surrendered objects. I remember going with X to report on this to the head of the provincial Party propaganda section. X said Mu's problem was serious but it belonged to the category of voluntary surrender, so it was all right not to proceed. I no longer recall why the case went ahead.[52]

In June 1984, the County Health Bureau issued a report on the Mu case:

(1)   According to the political commissar in the sanatorium originally in charge of the case and a witness at the original court hearing, Mu's reactionary diary was surrendered to the leadership by Mu. There was no evidence of his having circulated it.

(2)   In January 1950, after graduating from the cadre school, he refused his assignment and, after returning home, wrote anonymous letters to the cadre school. In 1951, during Zhenfan, he wrote some reactionary words to the medical school, but we only have his word for this, there is no corroboratory evidence.

(3)   On October 2, 1955, while his parents' home was being searched, reactionary writings were found. At present, we are unable to verify whether they date from before or after Liberation, and they were not circulated.

The sanatorium's case against Mu was based on insufficient evidence. According to document no. 29 (83) and document no. 122 (83) of the Central Organization Department, the Party committee of the Health Bureau decided on June 6, 1984, to propose to the people's court that the case be reheard.[53]

After a year of toing and froing, in March 1985 the county court reviewed the case:

> The original verdict against Mu regarding reactionary anonymous letters was based on insufficient evidence, and is rescinded; the original finding that Mu had written a reactionary diary at home and reactionary words on the school toilet wall was based on Mu's voluntary confession during Sufan. It was wrong to sentence him as a counter-revolutionary. We hereby revoke the court's decision of March 20, 1957.[54]

The County Health Bureau decided: "Comrade Mu Guoxuan should return to work and resume his residence, and his wages should be raised by one incremental point from their original level of 54 yuan. This applies from the date of sanction. His seniority should be treated as continuous. His wages should not be paid retroactively. He should be given a hardship payment of 800 yuan."[55] As a result, Mu was able to return to work, to his place of residence, and to his job. He wanted to bring his wife and children to the city and felt that his salary, having stagnated for years, was on the low side. The Health Bureau decided in 1987 to raise it to level 12, or 87 yuan.[56]

The "Fall" of a Branch Secretary of the Communist Youth League

How a Young Teacher Became a "Bad Element"

Chi Weirong grew up in the reddest years. Born in 1937, at the founding of New China he was a middle school student in A Municipality. After being admitted to industrial college, he was sent in 1957 to X mine in Q Province as a trainee. Unable to adapt, he returned to A Municipality in 1958. He worked as a casual teacher at the Qixian Cultural School, then as a technical teacher in the medical glassware factory, and served as secretary of the school's Communist Youth League. Just when he was beginning to sail with the wind, win the trust of the leadership, and lay a stable foundation for his career, disaster struck. He was criticized for a teacher-student love affair, after which he gave himself up as lost, turned corrupt, stole things, went absent without leave, and tried to flee to Hong Kong. He became the glass factory's typical "bad element." Whenever a movement started up, he was brought out and criticized.

Chi's experience was not particularly rare. However, most people born since the Cultural Revolution, or brought up in a different environment from that of Chi, would find it, including that of those who contributed to his corruption, strange indeed. Here, by way of an introduction to the vicissitudes of Chi's life, I will try to identify the factors in grassroots society that produced his downfall.

AN UNEXPECTED ATTACK

Chi graduated in July 1957 from the mining class of the Nonferrous Metals College, and in August he was assigned to X mine in Q Province. He and six classmates declared that the jobs did not match their professional qualifications. Moreover, they were unable to adapt to local life, the local diet, and the working conditions, and asked to be transferred back. The mine did repeated ideological work on them, but to no avail, and it had to agree to let them return and find other occupations.[1]

After his return, Chi's personal file was sent to the local street office. With its help, he was introduced to the Qixian Cultural School as a part-time teacher. Five months later, at the height of the Great Leap Forward, he was introduced by the committee to the middle school of the glassware factory.

At first, Chi was very active. He was serious about his work, and was intelligent and articulate. He became a popular teacher who was good with students and put them at ease. The leadership recognized his value and made him secretary of the Youth League branch.

The Great Leap Forward soon ended in failure. This affected Chi. At the age of twenty-one, when his appetite was at its peak, the food ration was just twenty-eight pounds of grain, plus some meat and eggs, so he was in a state—for the first time in his life—of semi-starvation. Then his father fell ill. His mother, a shop assistant, earned little, and his two younger siblings were still at school, so the family was in dire straits. His family was unable to help him—on the contrary, he had to help them.

Chi came up with an idea. Having lost confidence in the factory, he asked permission to apply for university. His idea was to escape the mess he was in. He told the students, causing a great shock. He was a form teacher, and his relationship with his students was good, so "the entire class burst into tears."[2] His application was not approved. Seeing no hope for himself, he became more and more negative. He no longer attended to his work with the same seriousness. He was seen to be "inattentive during working hours, and as soon as lessons finished, he would get on his bike and leave." His work for the Youth League meant even less to him.

Another problem was that he fell in love. He was twenty-one, but had never had a girlfriend. As a teacher and League secretary, with many girl students around him, he fell in love with a girl called Fu Xiumei. She was young and playful, and it was the first time for her too. Chi ignored his teacher's status and went around with Fu as a couple. The other students inevitably talked. But Chi argued: "Did not [the writer] Lu Xun marry his student? Why shouldn't I have a relationship with Fu Xiumei?"[3]

In September 1959, higher authorities launched a rectification movement to oppose rightism. The school had no real rightists, so the students were mobilized to engage in mutual criticism, to rectify the school ethos. Some took the opportunity to criticize Fu and, indirectly, Chi. Chi confronted the criticisms and defended himself and Fu, scolding the students for gossiping.

The Youth League had long known about Chi's romance, and was determined to use the rectification campaign to attack him. They hadn't counted on Chi dismissing their criticism. The secretary of the Youth League went to the school to organize a criticism meeting, but Chi refused to attend.[4]

The Youth League submitted a disciplinary report to higher levels asking for Chi to be dealt with. The report was approved, and the branch sent someone to announce the decision.

The report said: When Chi first arrived, he was keen to do Youth League and administrative work. He followed the leadership, concentrated on his work, and got on well with the students and his peers. However, "since May 1959, this comrade has no longer kept his mind on his work, and asked leave to apply to go to university (it was not granted). He became dilatory in implementing League resolutions, and created difficulties for the League leadership. He was not close to all the students, just a few of them." Because this comrade was unable to set an example, school discipline became lax, and relations between students and teachers suffered. When the factory launched the rectification movement, Chi was branch secretary. "He should have led from the front and been the first to make a self-criticism. Instead, faced with criticisms, he spoke out in his own defense, and threatened to take revenge on the critics. When people tried to help the student Fu Xiumei, his attitude was poor. He did not admit his faults or accept them and even stood up for Fu. Because of Chi's threats, few dared criticize him during rectification, except by way of covert insinuations."

The League decided to "punish Chi Weirong by stripping him of his membership and of his position as secretary." They said: "He rarely shows any interest in studying politics, doesn't care about the students, and shirks his responsibilities as a leader. In leading students to engage in rectification, he has compromised his principles. He fails to support students' fervent criticism and even attacks them and threatens revenge. He is not loyal to the Organization in regard to his relationship with Fu Xiumei."[5]

BLIND FLIGHT

Chi's ejection from his positions was a bitter blow. His dream of attending university was dashed. If he stayed at the school, it would make no difference whether he raised his head or lowered it, and it would even be difficult to maintain his relationship with Fu. Pride made him even more reluctant to stay. On the surface, he still laughed and joked with the students, but inside he seethed with resentment. He published a poem in the school newspaper, of which he was editor, titled "Courage," which reflected his state of mind:

> Whose heart has never burned, who says no to an everlasting spring and summer?
> Compare your heart to mine, who can forget affection?
> The moon is missing from the sky but is still round,
> the grass roots are withered but still grow,
> the wind opens your suffering breast, suffusing it with melancholy.[6]

Chi had always liked dancing, photography, and watching films, and he now began to indulge himself. He could always get hold of dance hall tickets. After class he used to go ballroom dancing with five or six students, and they danced the night away. At weekends he bought students cinema tickets, and talked with them about life in Hong Kong. Under his influence, many started watching Hong Kong films.[7]

Chi had another hobby, travelling. He opposed the factory's calls on students to participate in manual labor, and encouraged them instead to have fun, on the grounds that "to have lived a whole life in this world without having travelled or looked around would be a life lived in vain." To enable the students to have collective fun, he contacted the D Municipality medical school on the pretext of bringing some students to do training, but in reality he took them to L Municipality and D Municipality on outings. He gave them a good time. He was always praising the merits of L Municipality and D Municipality to his students, and encouraged them to seek opportunities for travel. The students enjoyed the scenery by day and danced by night. After that, the students were even keener to go on visits with him. So he contacted a unit in Beijing, with the intention of taking his students there to "train."[8]

By that time Chi intended to flee the factory, for a change of scenery and to start again from scratch. He thought of X mine, and secretly wrote asking if there was any chance of him returning. The League sent him to help set up a school in a commune, so he used the opportunity to remove his household registration and food ration from the factory.

In the spring of 1960, Chi and two other similarly disgruntled colleagues began secretly scouting for work elsewhere. He proposed going to Guangdong, saying that there were lots of mines there and they paid well. One of the students worked in the mining bureau there, and would be able to help. His two colleagues thought differently. One proposed going to Xinjiang, having heard that there was a labor shortage there; the other had heard that Xi'an needed electricians, which was also an occupation with great prospects. In the end, both backed out of the venture because their families refused to let them go. Just at that point a letter arrived from X mine agreeing to take Chi back, so he resolved to follow his own plan.

He lacked the money to go south, so he started looking around. After his "training" in D Municipality, the medical college sent him a food bill for 206 yuan, which he misread as 266 yuan. The factory gave him 266 yuan to send to the D Municipality college, and the college returned 59.4 yuan of it to Chi (60 yuan minus 0.6 yuan postage). Chi kept it for himself.

After returning from D Municipality and while getting ready for the Beijing trip, he failed to give back the three to four hundred pounds of grain in food stamps that he had saved from the earlier trip. The factory refused to allow him to contact Beijing or to permit a second trip, but Chi kept the food stamps. He used some of them on the students, but he kept stamps worth more than a hundred pounds of grain to use on his way south.[9]

THE "FALL" OF A BRANCH SECRETARY 139

To help pay for his trip, he also asked colleagues, even Fu Xiumei and two other female students, to lend him money. He bought a ticket to Shaoguan in Guangdong for the night train. But he unexpectedly received notification that his presence was required on the same day at the Three Antis study group.

The Three Antis movement in 1960 was part of the struggle against corruption. Chi suspected that being sent for such study had something to do with him embezzling public funds and food stamps. Scared even to return to his college accommodation, he enlisted the help of two female students to collect the things he needed from the dormitory and to take them to the railway station, and to burn the rest.[10] He also sneaked into the school, prized open a drawer, and helped himself to three pre-stamped template introduction letters, with details left blank that could be filled in later, and two sheets of stamped paper, to facilitate his journey south.[11] On the evening of his departure, he did not dare wait until eleven, but boarded the seven o'clock train with his girlfriend. His girlfriend accompanied him as far as J Municipality and then returned to A Municipality. In Beijing, he missed his girlfriend and sent her a telegram asking her to come to Beijing. The two went on outings in Beijing and Tianjin and he took her to Shanhaiguan, after which he returned to his own affairs.[12]

Chi had intended to get help in Beijing from the Ministry of Metallurgy to relocate to a new post. To his surprise, the Ministry did not handle work assignments and told him to sort it out with the school from which he had originally graduated or with his old mine. Chi had no choice but to continue southwards, first to Guangzhou, where he sought out the personnel department of the Mining Bureau. They told him they could only help after contacting his factory. But if they did so, "not only would he not get reassigned but he would be sent back." So he no longer dared enter the Bureau building. Finding himself in an impasse, he revived the idea of escaping to Hong Kong.

Going to Hong Kong required a legal permit. You could go illegally, by paying 70 to 80 yuan, but he "no longer had any money, and even if he did, where would he find a smuggler?" He remained in Guangzhou for a few days trying to arrange an illegal crossing, and wrote to colleagues in the factory complaining about things and sounding out the possibility of getting money. But all to no avail. He therefore returned, by way of G Municipality in Q Province, to X mine. However, a few days after his arrival the mine started shedding personnel, because of the economic crisis in the wake of the Great Leap Forward. Anyone who had joined the mine since 1960 had to go.[13] Chi's hopes of a job were dashed.

A TEST EASILY PASSED

Two days after Chi Weirong went AWOL, the Party branch reported to the District Office of the Three Antis movement.

The report said:

Just when the Three Antis movement in our factory entered its concentrated learning stage, the suspect Chi, a technical teacher in our school since July 1958, engaged in opportunistic behavior and made illegal use of students' food stamps. It is clear from disclosures by the masses and the Organization's own soundings that the said person has committed acts of embezzlement and theft. The Organization has therefore singled him out as a key Three Antis target. This person has long had problems. He is unable to set his mind to his work, and he has repeatedly written to the Organization asking for a transfer. His day-to-day behavior is poor and he is unhappy with the Organization (there are other problems too). Just when this campaign began, he took fright, and on the afternoon of the 17th, when the Organization informed him there would be a concentrated study session that same evening, he vanished. The next day, the Organization sent people to his home and asked his relatives where he was, but no one knew. He had accommodation in the factory, but he had not returned to his room. His household registration and his luggage had been moved in advance. We concluded that he had probably absconded to avoid punishment.[14]

Three weeks later, the factory's security section came up with some leads, and cited three aspects of the "problem":

(1) Ever since joining the factory in 1958, his attitude to work has been negative. He has opposed the leadership, and written to F, a classmate (a teacher in the Mining Bureau's miner's lamp factory) voicing his discontent, viciously attacking the Party. This year, while leading students in manual labor, he incited them to go on lecture strike.
(2) The said person consorts with thieves. In 1959, when Fu Xiumei, a former pupil in the school run by the chemical glass factory, stole items, he harbored them on her behalf.
(3) Between 1958 and 1960, he took students on a tour to D Municipality and, while engaging in manual labor in villages, abused his authority to obtain food stamps amounting to more than 220 pounds of rice. On the eve of the Three Antis campaign, he did not confess and even spoke openly about taking aggressive action against various individuals. When the Organization summoned him for a session of concentrated study, he absconded.

The factory's security section asked the public security organs to arrest Chi. "Recently two public security bureaus have notified us that the said person has fled to Guangzhou, and might escape abroad. We request the sub-bureau to give instructions for his detention, so that he can be brought to justice."[15]

However, before the A Municipality public security organs could approve his arrest, Chi used his last few yuan to buy himself a ticket home on December 6. His return to the factory helped somewhat to turn his case around.

Back in the factory, he was held in a cellar and ordered to confess. He realized that the problem was serious and could see no way out, so he confessed everything. During the Three Antis campaign, the factory had unearthed no few cases of corruption, so Chi's 59.4 yuan and food stamps seemed trivial by comparison. The security section's other two suspicions did not meet the conditions for filing a case, so the factory released Chi and demoted him to common worker, under the supervisory control of the workshop leader and several backbone workers. In August 1961, a conclusion was reached in the case against Chi. Even his absconding to the South did not receive a mention. The factory identified just two issues: "(1) In May 1959, the D Municipality Medical School returned an over-payment on meals of 59.40 yuan, which the said person kept for his own private use. (2) Some students went to D Municipality on a tour and received food stamps worth 1,100 pounds of grain, but only used 560 pounds. Around 300 pounds were returned to the students, but the said person corruptly retained 240 pounds' worth."

The report concluded: Although Chi had fled fearing punishment, in the end, in response to an appeal and with the patient help of the Organization, he realized the seriousness of his error and volunteered a confession. The said person had changed his behavior and resolutely returned all the money. Because of this, the office of the Three Antis movement has, "in accordance with the Party's policy of leniency in the case of frank confession and harsher punishment in the case of refusal to confess, classed the said person as belonging in the category of ordinary corruption, and will spare him punishment."[16]

SMASHING A POT JUST BECAUSE IT'S CRACKED

Chi Weirong did not learn the lesson of this experience. He still thought himself rather grand, and not only wanted to get to a better unit but was still thinking of applying for university and upping his status by a notch or two. Much of his unhappiness in the technical college was because he felt insufficiently valued. One can imagine how he must have felt after his demotion from technician to a sweat-covered furnace worker, too tired to stand up straight.

Around this time, Chi's father died. Chi's wages had plummeted, and his father's death meant one less income. The factory helped him with a few dozen yuan during his father's illness and funeral and allowed his sister to join the factory, but still he saw no hope.

Chi's father was also a middle school graduate, and had worked as a primary school teacher, accountant in a foreign firm, and clerk in the Kuomintang's District Office. After Liberation, he was first unemployed, then drove a coal cart for a few years, and eventually got the chance to work in a factory as an accountant.[17] For Chi's father, life after Liberation was extremely hard, leading to his untimely death in his forties. This was too much for Chi. The family's reversal of fortune and his own irreversible loss of face convinced him that he might as well write off his situation as hopeless and act with abandon.

Chi had always hankered after a life of pleasure, and this time he cut completely loose. He used to say that "only fools torment themselves with pain."[18] Most teachers in the college had serious interests and pursuits, so he turned to socializing with students. After his demotion, he found that many young workers had nothing to do after work, and given Chi's love of entertainment, he had much to offer them. They became his friends, and they started going on outings, taking photographs, playing poker, watching films, and eating at restaurants. They began causing a ruckus wherever they went, and became notorious. Sometimes they posed as cadres, engineers, or the sons of high officials, flaunting their status just for fun.

After the Three Hard Years, the authorities cracked down on the dancing craze and it became hard to organize dances, but the passion for dancing remained. Chi's dancing style captivated many young workers, and everyone wanted to learn from him. He used to tell his friends: "However badly I behave, people like me."[19]

Idling away one's time in search of pleasure was a luxury ordinary workers could not afford. Going out for a meal cost as much as 6 yuan, whereas the monthly salary of a worker just out of his apprenticeship was less than 40 yuan. Chi initiated much of the activity. His expenditure was naturally greater than that of most. His difficulties increased, and he often went without food.

In January 1962, his friend Yin Mingde received 52.4 yuan in wages and health care but failed to bank it. The following morning, while Yin was away from the dormitory, the dormitory door and a drawer were prized open. Yin's money vanished. The security section identified Chi as the chief suspect. Chi flatly denied the theft. He shouted that he had been wronged and even wrote a suicide note, saying he would die in protest. But after being repeatedly pressed, he was finally forced to admit that he had stolen the money. He paid back 40 yuan, and the remainder was withheld from his next month's wages.[20]

His prestige among the young workers, and his bonding with them, directly affected relations between the workers and the factory leadership. The factory canteen had never been run well. There was little variety, and few non-staple dishes. Few workers had dared to complain, but after Chi's arrival, they put up wall posters criticizing the size of the food ration and calling the management passive and muddleheaded. The Party, the League, and the administration all believed that Chi was behind the unrest, and hated him for it. Following their apprehension of Chi after the theft, the security section filled out a criminal charge form and asked the factory to hand Chi over to the Public Security Bureau. The report said:

> In 1960 Chi Weirong embezzled students' food stamps, committed theft and absconded to Guangdong. As someone on a low wage, he often goes out eating and drinking. He has made backward elements dissatisfied with the Party, and written to friends vilifying our Party. In the school, while working as a teacher, he spread his

ideas in newspaper form. He and Yin Mingde were close, and last year they ganged up together in a small backward clique that expressed dissatisfaction with the leadership, fanned discord, and went out to places of entertainment.[21]

Because the evidence cited by the security section was thin, the factory did not allow it to be reported to the Public Security Bureau, and the matter was dropped. But the security section continued to identify Chi as a thief. Two more people reported seeing him steal things. On one occasion, he had prized open the drawer of the custodian of a mutuality fund but ran into the League secretary and his attempt failed; on another occasion, someone in the dormitory lost thirty-two feet of fabric, and another saw Chi stuffing fabric down his waist. But Chi denied it.

After the New Year in 1963, several young male and female workers asked Chi to teach them dancing, and they danced until two in the morning. They then went to the female dormitory to sleep, and pressed up against one another. Chi even "engaged in an improper act" of "kissing" a married female worker. Because this happened in the factory, the security section criticized it. Chi made light of things, saying that since the factory wouldn't organize dancing during the holidays, the workers couldn't be blamed for doing it themselves. At the Spring Festival, Chi and several male and female workers spent the evening playing poker at the home of one of the workers, and afterwards they spent the night together.[22]

Such close interactions between male and female workers were likely to lead to problems, and Chi and his group were a case in point. Although Chi's activities did not lead to group sex, they did lead to some young men and women going off the rails. This alarmed the security section and the factory leaders. The security section had long been frustrated by the lack of progress in solving the pilfering cases. After the Chi business, they fixed their attention on him, convinced that all the thefts that had occurred in recent times were his doing.

After further investigations, the security service again requested that Chi be subjected to re-education through labor. Their report combed through all his crimes:

> While working in the technical school, the said person formed intimate ties to some female students on the pretext of caring for them. He spent the night with them and engaged in improper relations, especially with the student Fu Xiumei, with whom he had sex, seriously undermining the school's internal order.
>
> Employing means such as destroying receipts, he embezzled food stamps worth 240 pounds of grain meant for the students on a visit to D Municipality, and 59.4 yuan in cash.
>
> He silenced students wanting to raise criticisms and sabotaged the rectification movement. The Organization removed him from his post as League secretary, but he was unrepentant.
>
> He stole 59.89 yuan belonging to Yin Mingde. At first he denied it, but under pressure from the masses he admitted his crime.

In 1963, at New Year and during the Spring Festival, he organized a dance in the dormitory. He organized immoral activities and infringed dormitory rules, which had a very bad impact. After dancing late into the night, he and three other men and women slept together. A certain woman slept by Chi's side, another woman pressed against a male thigh. One woman 'kissed' Chi and engaged in improper relations.[23]

The security section went on to enumerate Chi's criminal activities, including theft, and proposed that "in accordance with regulations of the State Council, we have decided he should be sent for re-education through labor."[24]

The report and the proposal were approved by the factory, but failed to obtain approval from the municipal public security department. Chi had again escaped disaster.

FINDING ONE'S OWN WAY TO WEALTH

By now the factory was convinced that Chi had committed theft on its premises. He didn't see stealing as something to be ashamed of, and even said so publicly: "People are too poor, if they don't steal, what else can they do?" However, he realized the danger of continuing down that path. He knew that if people nurtured evil habits and embarked on the road to theft and deceit, they would probably end up dead.[25] He didn't want to make the same mistake.

Because the factory saw Chi as the instigator of bad practices in the unmarried quarters and a thief, he was sent back to live at home. There, he continued to think of ways to solve his money problem. Soon, together with his relatives, some local unemployed, and some poorly paid workers looking to supplement their income, he devised a scheme to buy goods from corrupt officials and resell them at a profit.

Chi started by illicitly peddling food and cloth stamps and selling cigarettes at the bus station. He promised Labor Reform elements he knew from childhood that he would help them get work permits. He also borrowed money and food stamps from them. Later, he was introduced by a female cousin to Wang Heting, the Shandong leader of a group of unemployed migrants, and the two started reselling scrap copper. Wang had long lived off trafficking vegetables and peanuts and knew the tricks of the trade, so Chi learned from him. Wang had no fixed abode, so Chi secretly arranged accommodation for him in the factory. First, they identified purchasers in A Municipality for scrap materials or acquired "scrap copper" from people who stole it from the factory, and then took it by train to sell it in H Province or E Province. Because of a discrepancy in the copper trading price in the two places of 0.5 to 1 yuan a pound, a load of thirty or forty pounds brought a profit of 20 to 30 yuan. For the first time Chi tasted sweetness. While on night shifts in the factory, he would run from place to place collecting scrap copper. He spent the weekends travelling north by train to sell it on.

The state did not yet allow private trading. Long-distance trafficking in scrap copper was illegal, so Chi and the others acted with extreme caution. Even so, they were sometimes checked by trade and industry officials. On such occasions, they abandoned the goods and fled. On average, each earned less than 20 yuan.

In May 1965, unbeknown to Chi, Wang Heting had been detained by public security, who were preparing to send him home. After waiting in vain for Wang to turn up, Chi used his wages to buy forty pounds of copper in A Municipality to resell in E County in E Province. Unfortunately for him, he was arrested by officials of the local industry and trade department. Chi gave a false name, and said he was a probationary technician from X mine, on his way back to A Municipality to visit relatives. He said the scrap copper had been collected by his father, who had heard there was a market for it in E Province. His father had told him to use his days off to sell it, to supplement the household income. That was why he was there.

He wrote in his confession: "I really didn't know that it was wrong to sell, or I would never have done it. I considered that father had picked up these scrap materials over the years, what was the point in them simply lying there, I might as well sell them. That's why I brought them here." Now he realized that he shouldn't have done this, and he said that "after getting back I will tell father not to pick up things that the state was temporarily not interested in acquiring, it is wrong to throw the market into disorder. I should study hard, raise my consciousness, go back to the factory, and dedicate myself to hard work."[26]

The market officials lacked the power to detain smugglers and could only seize illegal goods, so Chi was released after confessing. When the officials checked up on the name and address he had provided, they found that it was false. So they turned over Chi's copper, together with 76 yuan confiscated from him (they had left him 5 yuan for the fare home), to the state.[27]

Chi had spent all his wages on the copper and returned home penniless, without even enough for food. He then sold his uncle's bike behind his back. He used the takings to buy a secondhand stopwatch and handed the rest to his family to live off. Afterwards, he told his uncle he'd exchanged the bicycle for a watch.[28]

THE ENTIRE FACTORY CRITICIZES CHI

Over the years Chi had been repeatedly let off by the factory, despite his petty thieving and scamming, because up until then his problems were only seen as those of money and lifestyle. In 1965, however, A Municipality's mines and industries joined the Four Clean-Ups movement. While the focus in the countryside was on cleaning up work points, accounts, warehouse stocks, and property, in the urban factories and the mines it was on cleaning up ideology, politics, organization, and economics. Work teams sent out by the municipalities stayed in the workplaces and targeted workers, with the goal of ferreting out the "monsters and freaks" among them. Needless to say, Chi became a focus of the investigation.

Apart from his economic and lifestyle problems, the team determined that Chi resisted social norms and harbored resentment.

After his removal as League secretary, Chi had made comments that could be seen as "reactionary." Unhappy with the factory leadership, he expressed his dissatisfaction with the Communist Party and the new society. After his demotion to the rank of worker, he had more than once said to students and workers: "What sort of Communist Party is this! Do you still think the Communist Party is good?"[29]

Fueled by growing resentment, humiliation, and a sense of hopelessness, he began to sympathize with viewpoints critical of the political environment. He listened to Taiwan's Voice of Freedom and took delight in programs that sneered at the food shortage on the Mainland. He read *Reference News*, noted that in Western countries people could oppose the president, and saw this as a reflection of the freedom those countries enjoyed. He read materials attacking bourgeois rightism, and was very interested in the rightists' satirical couplet about the bureaucratic system in the new society, which he quoted endlessly: "Mighty lord, mighty lord, my mighty lord, ascending to the thirty-third level of heaven to tile the roof for the Jade Emperor; humble servant, humble servant, your humble servant, descending to the eighteenth level of hell to dig coal for the imps."

Among workers, Chi was undoubtedly an intellectual. He was cultured, bold, uninhibited, and good at making friends, so workers liked his company and paid scant attention to his problems. Regarding the workers' own problems, he answered all their questions and said what he thought.

When a worker raged at the lack of goods on sale, and asked whether the shop was not actually a shop but a museum, and why the press didn't talk about the shortages, Chi replied: "Didn't the rightists say that the Communist Party's newspapers only publish good news?"

Another worker said he couldn't understand why propagandists never told the truth and asked whether it had been the same throughout the dynasties. Chi replied: "All propaganda serves those in power. Before Liberation, the Kuomintang filled the walls of A Municipality with slogans like 'When killing pigs, remove the bristles,' which served its rule. Today we say other countries are ruled while our country is led, but what's the difference? If the Communist Party leads China, doesn't it also rule China?"[30]

Chi's cousin was in Hong Kong, so Chi was well informed about the standard of living there. His cousin had just graduated from school and was on a salary of 390 Hong Kong dollars. When his uncle's elder brother died, the funeral cost more than 2000 dollars, and friends and relatives contributed more than 1600 dollars. So he didn't believe the propaganda about people in capitalist societies living in an abyss of suffering. Ideologically, he envied the "free world." Privately, he told workers that life in Hong Kong was great, that you didn't need stamps to buy things. He told them about the skyscrapers in New York and patent leather shoes. He reminded them that at home food was rationed, and people toiled for watches, bicycles, sewing machines, and radios (the "four big things" of the day). In the West and Hong Kong, cars had long since replaced bicycles, television had replaced radio, and electric sewing machines had replaced pedal-driven sewing machines. In Western countries speech was free, and in the United States you could criticize the president. In China, there were plainclothes men everywhere, and the people could not speak ill of the government.[31]

The work team found out about all this. Initially, because there were others who had clashed with factory leaders on far more serious grounds than Chi, Chi's case was ignored. However, after the start of the Cultural Revolution, which came out of the blue for many, some oppressed and battered grassroots cadres and workers, swept along by the revolutionary tide and the idea that it "was right to rebel," rose up and began writing wall posters, directing their spearheads at the "capitalist roaders," i.e., the Party and administrative leaders and the Four Clean-Ups team. The Party branch and the work team, not to be outdone, branded a certain Zhang, who had taken the lead in writing wall posters, a "counter-revolutionary," and then, making clever use of black material gathered in the course of the Four Clean-Ups, organized Party and League backbone members to put up posters revealing unknown facts about worker cadres, diverting people's attention to the lower ranks. Thus the work team was able once again to focus on dealing with those elements "that love to criticize the leadership, whose family background is bad, or who have returned to the factory after re-education through labor."[32]

Wall posters exposing cadres and workers started going up throughout the factory and the criminal records of individuals previously investigated by the work team were released, so that the rebels started feeling insecure. Many switched targets. Chi's problem became widely known and he became an object of the factory masses' "criticism and struggle." For a while, posters exposing and criticizing his crimes "against the Party and socialism" went up everywhere. Chi was forced onto the platform at criticism rallies organized by the work team, his head was pushed down, his clothes were torn, his arms were dragged behind his back, and he was forced to bow and to accept his assailants' impassioned criticism and scolding.[33]

In mid-July, the work team compiled materials on Chi's "opposing the Party and socialism," and submitted them to the branch for discussion. The materials summarized Chi's problems:

(1) He is hostile to the socialist system, he has viciously attacked the Party and attacked and slandered the Central Committee and Chairman Mao.

(2) He actively prepared funds to defect to the enemy and commit treason.

(3) He has listened to enemy radio broadcasts, propagated rightist views, engaged in slander and vilification, trumpeted Hong Kong's and America's way of life, expressed his dissatisfaction with present circumstances, and dreamt of restoring reactionary rule.

(4) He is morally corrupt, upholds a bourgeois philosophy of life, advocates supporting pernicious vestiges of bourgeois rule, and uses every opportunity to corrupt the youth.

(5) He disregards the nation's laws, rampages around inside and outside the factory, commits evil deeds, masquerades as a state cadre, and disrupts social order.

(6) He is a speculator and a profiteer, he is corrupt, and he steals things and harbors evil people.

The report proposed: "In the spirit of the provisions of the Central Committee regarding objects of dictatorship, Chi belongs among the fifth of the six kinds of objects of dictatorship, that of ideologically reactionary elements. To educate him, raise the masses' awareness, and remedy the losses he has caused the Party, he should be handed over to the masses to overthrow him and destroy his reputation."[34]

The Party branch decided that Chi should be classified as an "anti-Party and anti-socialist element." Together with other reactionary elements, he joined the Cultural Revolution's first batch in the factory of enemies of society.[35]

GETTING TO THE BOTTOM OF THE PROBLEM

Materials and testimony gathered by the factory in June and July 1966, and denunciations by the masses, boiled down Chi's problems to the following.

He was dissatisfied with the leadership, he was a negative thinker, and he made backward comments. He often denounced the leadership's intervention in his own and the students' lives and its criticisms and sanctions, which he described as an attempt to give him a hard time. He believed that the leaders only liked those who fawned on them, and that they liked to control people, to rule over them. Kuomintang or Communist Party, their leaders were all the same. Mainland China was inferior to Hong Kong and to Western Europe and the United States, its economy and technology were backward, and its people lived in poverty and were unfree.

He led a wasteful and extravagant life and was sexually promiscuous. Many people spoke of Chi's likes for food, drink, and entertainment, his seeking pleasure from women of ill repute, and his setting of a bad example. They spoke of his inappropriate relations with the student Fu Xiumei, that they cohabitated in the factory and were intimate in public. Particular note was made of the fact that in the school and the workshop, Chi had often stayed in the dormitory with male and female students or workers, and had even shared a bed and a quilt with them, cuddling and embracing. This attracted the greatest number of denunciations.[36]

He had engaged in theft and swindling, and was dishonest. Li Fengyi, a student, revealed that in 1960, before going south to Guangzhou, Chi had swindled five or six students out of cash, "even as much as 20 yuan."[37] Yin Mingde revealed that in 1961 he and Chi, pretending to help unload a vehicle, had jointly stolen a load of potatoes and sweet potatoes; and Chi had stolen Yin's entire wages and health-care money, covering a whole month.[38] Li Yanjun revealed that Chi had illegally resold copper but often used an old ticket to get to A Municipality and H city, by repairing the hole made by the ticket collector.[39]

Nearly all the students and workers who criticized Chi agreed that he had many social connections and was popular. For people who had never even seen a Hong Kong or a Taiwan stamp or remittance voucher, he could get hold of one. He knew people in all the cinemas in A Municipality, and all the dance halls, and could always get tickets for films and dance evenings. This was because, for various convoluted reasons, he knew some of the hoodlum gangs that frequented such places, could talk with them, and knew which gangs hung out in which places. Having grown up in such an environment, he had relatives and friends everywhere, lots of whom had close relationships with the gangs. In his own words, these gang people "are all known to me, I know what they are up to, and when they get arrested."[40]

His close childhood friend Wang Hongcai was a habitual thief. When Chi was studying at technical middle school, Wang was sent to a reform school. But Chi never avoided or despised him. Every time he turned up, Chi would go out to dance clubs with him, and borrow money from him to spend.

Another of Chi's neighbors was Wang Hongfa, also a thief. He was first detained for seven days by the District Public Security Bureau for stealing a watch from his uncle. After his release, he wandered around stealing, and was again arrested. He was arrested again and again over the next several years, and was eventually sent to a labor camp. He knew Chi's brothers well, and Chi's younger brother, influenced by these people, also learned to steal, and was arrested.[41]

Most of Chi's problems were related to the challenges faced by those at the bottom of society. Many workers and city poor lived on meager incomes. Unable to clothe or feed their families and with limited recourse to means of livelihood, they were driven to gangsterism, theft, speculation, and profiteering. On the other hand, the opportunities for consumption and entertainment had been significantly reduced. The reason gangs could exist in the cinemas, clubs, and dance halls and in the department stores was because in such places allurements were available. That was why so many hookers could seduce men out enjoying themselves and get cash from them. The women selling their bodies did so in exchange for a half-pound food stamp or 0.5 yuan.[42] This shows how low the standard of living was.

Quite a few workers and urban poor survived on very little, and there were big differences between rich and poor in terms of material consumption. A letter from X mine regarding Chi and his five colleagues' refusal to accept their work assignment shows that their "fall" was to some extent the result of the impact of society. An unsuitable environment or temptation can easily lead people along a road of the sort Chi followed.

This letter illustrates the attitude and behavior of the six:

Chen and five comrades, after their assignment to the mine, almost immediately applied for home leave. They spent most of the time in the guest house, having fun, playing ball games, and causing trouble. After persuasion and education, Chen spent five days at work, but Cui and Wu worked for only three days and Tang Xixian for only one day, while Chi and Zhao never worked at all.

The Organization, aware that they were from the northeast and had not yet got used to life in the south, gave them much help and care, and, as far as possible, met their requirements. They said they had brought no clothes with them, so they were given additional clothing stamps; they said they had no money, so loans were approved; they said they were unwell, so they were taken to the hospital for examinations and x-rays, and told that if they were really ill, and got a doctor's note, then appropriate care would be taken in the allocation of work; they said they weren't used to life in the south, so they were allowed simply to observe for a while, until they had got used to things. We did all we could to take care of them. But they continued to make trouble. They refused assignments, they didn't want to go down the pit to take part in physical labor, they screamed that they were ill, that the air in the hostel was bad, and that there was a serious silicosis problem in the mine. They cursed the Organization and administration in their original school as 'liars,' and claimed that they'd been tricked into coming. We continued to hold to the view that we were responsible to the Party, and to them, and our mine director and Party secretary, our cadres and our leading comrades held countless conversations with them. However, they continued to disregard the stipulations of the State Council and the Ministry of Metallurgy, and unreasonably asked to be excused from going down the mine and doing physical labor. They advanced all sorts of objectively unfeasible arguments that caused the Organization numerous headaches. For example, they were afraid of silicosis, and they demanded gas masks before going down the mine. Otherwise, they were not prepared to stay, and wanted instead to go home, or to go back to the school to pick a fight with a teacher. Our mine asked permission from the bureau to grant their request and let them go home and find work, although it did not agree with their returning to the school. In accordance with regulations, we gave them the money to get home.[43]

GETTING A HAT

Yin Mingde put up a wall poster exposing Chi Weirong in June 1966, and the work team handed the job of investigating Chi to the security section. The security team sought out students and workers who had had dealings with Chi, to get them to speak out and say all they knew about Chi's reactionary words, deeds, and crimes, while holding back nothing.

After sorting out a pile of evidence and going through the necessary proce-dures, the security section put up a wall poster bombarding Chi and dragged him out for mass criticism. They brought in secondary targets to accompany him, the primary target, and interrogated him ceaselessly. The interrogators included a good cop, who repeatedly advised Chi to confess cases of theft in the factory that had not yet been solved, saying: "Admit what you have done, I know your life has been very hard, I'll make sure you don't lose out, we all count on you, we're not going to punish you. We're all old comrades, you can trust me." Then there was a bad cop, who shouted, wrangled, swore, and said: "You're a cunning bastard, you can stop playing games with me, we know all about your problem, don't think you can get away with it. If you don't talk, we'll give you what for. Do you want to go to jail? It's up to you. If the masses say you did it, then you did it. Can you deny it?"

There followed countless struggle sessions and countless threats. In early August, at a struggle rally, Zhang was charged with "resistance" and delivered to the security authorities, who announced that he would be brought to justice. That gave Chi a big fright.

Chi was subjected to criticism and struggle at a small rally in the workshop, and forced to confess his thieving, including having stolen Yin Mingde's watch, Cai's thirty-two feet of fabric, etc. Chi realized that he had no choice but to confess, and after returning to the custody room, he asked for pen and paper and wrote an obsequious "statement of repentance":

Dear Party comrades, dear worker comrades:
    I am guilty, I ask the Organization to deal with me severely. I apologize to the Party and to my worker comrades for my heinous crimes. The Organization not only punished me, just as the masses repudiated me, but patiently helped me, again and again. They enlightened me and guided me. But I remained stubborn, I confronted the Organization and caused trouble, my attitude was dishonest, I failed to acknowledge my crimes, I resisted the movement. I am an extreme sinner, I should be brought to justice. But today, after listening to group leader Zhang's report, my heart was touched. The lenient treatment accorded Li Jianzhong made me even more convinced that the Party's policy means what it says. Today, I thank the Party from the bottom of my heart. Dear Party, you are closer to me than my parents. If I do something wrong in front of my parents, I expect to be beaten and scolded, but you, the Party, have always taken meticulous care of me. For the last seven or eight years, I have not spoken with the Party from my heart. That's as if for

seven or eight years I hadn't said daddy, mommy. Today for the first time I shout out the words daddy, mommy, and I feel particularly close. Dear Party, what I am about to tell you is that I thoroughly confess my guilt. In the past, I did wrong things, so deal with me strictly, or my heart will be even more troubled.

He admitted stealing Yin Mingde's watch and Cai's cloth, and confessed to speculating in scrap copper.[44]

However, the factory's security section, which had never managed to stop the thefts, was not satisfied. They took advantage of their victory to launch a further attack, and dragged up case after case. Since Chi had already started confessing, he couldn't care less if a few more offences joined the list, so he added some new details. Yes, he had stolen Chen's cotton-padded overcoat from his bed, he had stolen Tao's quilt and Hu's blanket, he had made off with 4 yuan, taken from a colleague's overcoat in the communal showers, and so on.[45]

After the great progress made in exposing Chi's thefts, the cadres began to escalate his problem to the political plane, pointing to reactionary remarks his colleagues said he had made. Chi had no choice but to own up. Naturally, he knew that political problems were graver than theft, and that you could end up losing your head if you didn't deal with them effectively. So he did all he could to make some excuses for his comments.

Yin Mingde revealed that Chi did not favor workers working hard or soft-soaping people. Chi's explanation was that he was dissatisfied with the Organization, that people could work themselves to death and still get nowhere. He said that Yin always tried to be a sycophant to get the leaders' trust, but that disgusted Chi, and he thought Yin was wrong to use such methods to get close to the Organization.

Yin Mingde also disclosed that Chi had said that under no circumstances, even on pain of death, should truth yield to despotic power. In Chi's view, it was impossible in the glass factory to appeal to reason. Saying that was his way of refusing to succumb to pressure.

Yin Mingde revealed that Chi had said the Communist Party ruled the country, just as the Kuomintang had. Chi explained that he meant that under any system propaganda served the ruler—in the Kuomintang period it served the Kuomintang, under proletarian rule, it serves the proletariat.[46]

Only after Chi had been shown the allegations and denunciations did he finally realize the trouble he was in, and that if he wanted to be treated leniently, he should "spill all the beans from the bamboo tube"—he should withhold nothing.

To gain sympathy, he wrote a thirty-page confession that began:

Honestly speaking, from the bottom of my heart I don't have anything against the Communist Party or the socialist system. The Party has taken great care of me. My life has been difficult, and the Party has helped me out. When I lacked money to buy food, it gave me money; when my father fell ill and I had no money to pay for him, I received a subsidy of 60 yuan; when my father died and I had no money for a coffin, the factory knocked one up for me; I have a big family, and it has always been difficult to buy clothes, but the Party gave me cloth stamps and cotton cloth; when we had no food to eat, the Party gave me rice at a bargain price. It's not that I wasn't grateful, I was, from the bottom of my heart. But I didn't realize my mistakes, so was always ready to complain, I was dissatisfied with some leaders and made comments complaining about the Party. Those comments gave the impression that I am opposed to the Party. Because of that, I want not only to confess all my reactionary words and deeds but to carry out self-criticism and raise these issues to the plane of principle.

He arranged his "anti-Party and anti-socialist comments" into the following sections: (1) Propagating the lifestyle of capitalist countries. (2) Disseminating and carrying out reactionary propaganda. (3) Spreading discontent about reality, by word and deed. (4) Spreading rightist views.

Other issues included "being unwilling to work, secretly absconding, betraying the country," engaging in "corruption, theft, and speculation," spreading "moral corruption, sabotaging the system, and disturbing public order." As for the allegations in the new poster exposing his thefts, he admitted seven or eight infringements, such as taking away people's newly purchased coats and wearing them as his own after changing out of his factory clothing; stealing 11 yuan from the shop next to the cinema while watching films with younger workers and spending it on them; with others, stealing brooms and light bulbs from the factory warehouse and stealing an old violin and an *erhu* and a *jinghu* from the workers' club; together with others, stealing sweet potatoes and potatoes from the factory and, while doing manual labor on a farm, stealing a sack of rice; in conspiracy with others, stealing books from the factory library; etc.[47]

In September 1966, the wave of mass struggle ebbed. The criticism rallies directed against Chi lessened. He began to feel uneasy about the confessions he had made, and feared being further attacked. He worried that the work team and the factory leaders would, given his own highly inaccurate confessions, reach a verdict on his case. So he tried to tell the work team and the cadres of the security section the real truth, and to modify his confessions.

His efforts greatly annoyed the factory authorities. In October 1966, the work team and the general branch reached a conclusion about how to deal with him. The report said nothing about corruption and theft but identified Chi's main problem as political. It said that he had (1) attempted to defect and commit treason; (2) carried out reactionary propaganda; and (3) spread discontent. They concluded: "On the basis of the above-mentioned errors, during the Four Clean-Ups and the Cultural Revolution he continued to be dishonest even after the masses had criticized him, he continued to stand up to the masses, and he made confessions at rallies that he later withdrew. He has not bowed his head or repented his crimes, so after discussing with the masses, we determine him to be an ideological reactionary and require him to wear a hat. He should stay in the factory to do manual labor under supervision."[48]

The same day, Chi, just before appearing on the platform to receive it, dashed off a petition:

(1)   The poem titled "Courage" that appeared in the school magazine was not written by him.

(2)   The comment in his diary that "from now on I will begin to steal, rob, and cheat" had not been written or even said by him.

(3)   As for posing as a state cadre, he himself had not done this. Other workers had done it, and he had criticized them.

(4)   Yes, his uncle had given him some remittance vouchers, but he was a relative, so why was it a crime?

(5)   The letter to Gao telling her to await her opportunity and asking "what sort of party is the Communist Party" was not something he had said. He had intended to sneak away and could barely look out for himself, how could he have told her to await whatever opportunities?

(6)   He was supposed to have said that American tennis shoes were good and that his uncle had sent him a pair from Hong Kong, but they had been exported from Shanghai, he'd never said they were from the United States.

(7)   It was not true that during the movement he had formed an offensive and defensive alliance with reactionaries. He had hoped that others would help him to think of problems that he had not confessed, but how can that count as an offensive and defensive alliance?

(8)   He was said to have been dissatisfied with the food policy and to have incited people to write wall posters. But who was he supposed to have incited? The fighting in the canteen was because of problems caused by queuing and had nothing to do with people being dissatisfied with the food policy.

(9)   He was supposed to have lauded Chiang Kai-shek to the sky, but he had been talking about how Chiang killed his elder brother and Chiang's family background, he had said that Chiang practiced mean and despicable tricks—how was that lauding him?

(10)   He was said to have made preparations to rebel and defect, but that was not true. In 1960 he had been notified by X mine that it was all right for him to return to the mine to work, so he had got part of his wages together and borrowed a bit, but not in order to commit treason.

(11)   He had admitted stealing from the unmarried quarters in the factory. During and after the struggle meeting, with the masses and the leadership piling on the pressure, he had admitted whatever allegations were made, but only because he was scared of being beaten. He hadn't stolen Yin's watch,

nor had he stolen Cai's cloth, Chen's coat, Tao's quilt, or Hu's blanket. If you checked his time of arrival, he could not possibly have stuffed thirty-two feet of fabric down his pants and made off with it. His confession was full of contradictions and clearly false.

Chi did not ask for the whole case to be overturned. At the end of his letter of appeal he wrote: "Apart from the above, which I didn't do, I did do all the rest."[49]

Once again, Chi had an unexpected stroke of luck. Just as his problem had been reclassed as political, the tide turned against the Four Clean-Ups work team. They had implemented a "reactionary line," wrongly pointed the spearhead of the struggle at the masses, and shielded the "capitalist roaders." The suppressed cadres and workers in the factory ganged together in a rebel organization and turned the struggle against the factory's leading cadres, confiscating and destroying black material manufactured by the work team. Chi's problem was again put aside. Some in the factory, including old cadres in the security section and the workshop director, stuck by the work team and the factory branch's earlier resolution and refused to recognize Chi's rights, but Chi was anxious to try to overturn his case.

In December 1966, he put up a fourteen-page wall poster denouncing the work team's "bourgeois reactionary line" and exposing various practices of the security section and the work team, including the use of trickery and coercion to secure confessions. He argued that the team should return to the factory and make an investigation. He withdrew his forced confession and destroyed the black material.[50]

However, it was too late for Chi to change the fateful course of his life. Even a rebel organization would find it hard to view a villain like Chi as their own. At the end of 1968, the revolutionary committee reconsidered Chi's problem, but did not reach a conclusion. In 1970, the Central Committee announced its attack on counter-revolutionary sabotage, issued its directive opposing extravagance, waste, corruption, theft, and speculation, and launched the movement "one thing to attack and three things to oppose," that is, it argued that it was necessary to oppose words and deeds "against the Party and socialism," embezzlement, and speculation. Chi again became an object of scrutiny and a target for attack.[51]

The contents of Chi's file did not extend to the final verdict. Old people working in the factory at the time can no longer remember what became of Chi, so it is impossible to tell whether a verdict was reached in his case or what his fate was. One can only hope that Chi, in his thirties at the time, went on to experience yet another reversal of fortune.

6

Weighty Files

What Happened When a Cultural Teacher Handed Over His Diary

Your file determines your life. Before the opening up, Chinese society was highly organized. Virtually no one was beyond the Organization's control. However, under the system of ownership by the whole people and collective ownership, there were differences in the way each person was organized. Individuals under the system of ownership by the whole people were the most stringently controlled. Each was subordinate to a unit. One of the most effective ways the Organization could control an individual within a unit was to set up a file on that person, a file invisible to everyone. In it was a cursory or detailed record of everyone at every stage of his or her life, including every action taken and every word uttered at every major turning point. Your file followed you like a shadow. Transfers, promotions, joining the Party or the League—it recorded all the important steps in your life. Everyone's life is different—not all files are equally thick. Regardless of thickness, however, if it recorded criticisms or blemishes, they followed you around, and could get you into trouble.

Below is a letter from a cadre who had suffered on account of his file, asking the leader of his old unit to help him remove a blemish:

Commissioner Ma:

Hello! I have a problem. Ever since 1955, I have carried a heavy ideological burden. I am not a rightist, but my situation is worse than that of a rightist. I was particularly affected by the ten-year Cultural Revolution. So were my wife and children. My whole family suffered a tragic misfortune that can hardly be expressed in words.

According to Central Committee policy, the rightist problem has been resolved, but my problem has not been resolved (the verdict was a problem of ideological understanding). I have written several times to the military unit, but received no reply. Now my unit favors a resolution, but problems that arose before the Cultural Revolution must be resolved by the original unit, and if that unit no longer exists, they can be handled by the present unit. I have asked the original unit to resolve the problem, but have received no reply.

You were in charge of my problem at that time, so I beg you to resolve it for me. You are a senior cadre. I believe you will, in the interests of the Party, the people, and the nation, seek truth from facts to resolve it. For details, please see the attachment.[1]

The contents of the attachment are summarized here:

From the autumn of 1947 right up until the Sufan movement in 1955, I wrote several thousand entries in my diary. Most of the views expressed in it were correct. I later formed some erroneous views, for example, that the army's policy on intellectuals wasn't properly implemented, that the peasants' life was hard, etc. In 1955, at the start of Sufan, I saw a chance to resolve my ideological problems, and after reading some diary entries to a meeting, I took the initiative to hand the diary over, from the period of Kuomintang rule (1947) to after my joining the army. Because my transformation was poor and my understanding inadequate, I misunderstood the Party and the army on several points. The Organization subjected me to review, which was reasonable.

But there were problems with the review. During it I was quarantined, and, though a revolutionary, was considered not to be a revolutionary. In the verdict, I was quoted out of context, and evidence was sought to prove a prejudged opinion. After the material in the verdict was entered into my file, not only was my personal progress held back but so was that of my family, so we suffered unduly. In consecutive political movements I was labeled 'backward,' 'reactionary,' and so on.

In accordance with the current spirit of the Central Committee, I hope you agree that materials regarding my ideological understanding are not appropriate for the file, and can be withdrawn from it.[2]

The writer was Shang Haowen, who joined the revolution in 1949, joined the army in 1950, and left the army in 1956. He had a spotless history, but he was made to wear a hat and put under surveillance. His misfortune was that his file contained a portion of his diary, together with materials that his original unit obtained during the investigation triggered by his diary.

What did the diaries say? Why should a personal diary be handed over to the Organization? What parts of the diary were put in the file? What other materials sufficient to destroy Shang's life were put in the file? Why did they have such a big impact?

THE PROBLEMATIC DIARY

In early 1949, Shang risked his life to flee to a liberated area, where he "remained staunch, in peacetime and in war." Although not everything was to his liking and he had some disappointments and doubts, he never doubted the Party's revolutionary ideals. His diary expressed dissatisfactions, but he was eager for the Organization to help him resolve his ideological confusion. That was why he always said that the diary contained "both correct and wrong understanding, with more of the former than of the latter."[3]

However, in Shang's file we see not thousands of entries but just two sections: fragments of fourteen entries from the Sufan period, excerpted by his then military unit, about how to classify Shang's problem; and bits from the period when the struggle team was preparing to launch a struggle against Shang. Of the thousands of entries between 1947 and 1955, fewer than one percent were selected. All those chosen were "seriously problematic," and none showed Shang's "correct understanding."

So what problems did the diary entries put into Shang's file exemplify?

JANUARY 27, 1950

To attempt to turn white into black, to turn the coalition government into a one-party dictatorship, to reduce the sphere of mass activity to the sphere of clique activity, to call one's own policy by a fine-sounding name, to pretend not to discriminate against people while actually saying that if they don't join my organization, they are not progressive, is that real action? Bones pile up, blood flows like a river for victory to be realized, is that all for a clique's amusement?

JANUARY 28, 1950

Chairman Mao in the coalition government is very reasonable, he frankly points out the disasters suffered by the Chinese people. The gentlemen he leads are duty-bound to implement his policies and be loyal Communists. Why, when they find that others express their individuality (but not against the people), do they take fright? Why do they make all sorts of excuses to exclude others, and even to block them with fine-sounding words? Are such people revolutionary activists? In the new society, people should have new ideas, or it will be impossible to build a society that 'rights wrongs in accordance with heaven's decree,'

JANUARY 30, 1950

Although the peasants have been allies in this proletarian revolution and climbed up from the eighteenth circle of hell, that merely shows that they are the democratic base led by the working class. Mr Mao said that peasants are the source of the Chinese army and soldiers are peasants in uniform. Peasants are the main force in China's democratic politics, and if democrats do not rely on the assistance of the 360 million peasants, they will accomplish nothing. His poignant comments explain the great role played by peasants, one that we can never forget, and for which we are deeply grateful. This summary is reasonable, for peasants now and in the future must follow that road and, by themselves, create their own glorious history. That is the peasants' present and future direction, to win back their own leading position, to take as their own the appeal for labor to create the world.

FEBRUARY 5, 1950

Lenin was deeply aware of the peasant problem, and peasants were one of his most reliable supports. If Lenin had not early on grasped the basic problem of the dictatorship of the peasantry and the proletariat, his revolution would have failed. However, gentlemen in the Soviet Union who distort the peasant problem willfully switch targets, abandoning this foundation, slighting the peasant problem, and denying the peasant movement revolutionary significance.

JANUARY 5, 1954

In earlier times, cadres were the product of imperial examination, whereas now they are trained at special schools; but old-style prime ministers could change at any time, whereas the present-day prime minister holds his title for life, and would never let a talented and virtuous peasant become prime minister or a talented and virtuous soldier become commander-in-chief.

MARCH 20, 1954

I went to Shenyang station to buy a ticket. A crowd of people lay asleep, in rags, each face as if covered by a layer of black ash. X has attendants crowding round and plenty of food and clothes, while these people lie in the chilly mud. How tragic!

OCTOBER 27, 1954

Why do people want to retaliate—a tooth for a tooth, blood for blood? Will murder be permissible? In my view, that day will come. People who go against the prohibition on killing are the public enemy of humankind, a disgrace to themselves.

DECEMBER 25, 1954

The people, especially peasants, are, from the day of their birth, full of hope. Up until now, those hopes have not been realized, and people have been used as capital. Today, what has taken away their hope? The narrowly conceived mass line, the idea of the Organization. They are stable in appearance, but in reality they are restive and disordered, they have been separated, so the peasants' hopes turn to ash.

Zheng Guangrong's elder brother said that seven of them 'harvested ten *shi* of grain, more than three *shi* were officially procured, how can they survive? They eat chaff, and kill livestock. Such is the case in the northeast, it's probably worse elsewhere. The northeast is an old liberated area, rich in produce. Fellow citizens, we have been cut off from reality. This is what the peasants get for tilling the land.'

JANUARY 4, 1955

In my opinion, they are loyal. They spend their days working, and they do not fawn over the authorities. Orders that should be obeyed are obeyed unconditionally; those that should not be obeyed are rejected, and suggestions are provided. They do not abuse or exploit those below them. They do not blow their own trumpets to their superiors, nor exaggerate their achievements. But others crawl like worms. Certain higher-ups (who shall remain nameless) possess none of the right qualifications, and lack talent and virtue. Their ingratitude, though not equal to Qin Hui's treatment of Yue Fei,[4] is at least reminiscent of it. Of course, there's another sort of person given to bragging and toadying, that pretends to be progressive, and whose ambition is furthered every day.

MARCH 4, 1955

How it was in the beginning! How feverish, how ready to sacrifice ourselves we were! But reality has failed to live up to my illusions, today's encounter has taken me back to past misery. People disappoint me! In the wretched present, I turn things over and over in my mind, I regret that I was too naive, that I waved the flag and shouted slogans, that I followed Zou Rong,[5] that my blood boiled so furiously. I wanted to live a hard life and suffer with the people, why did I not become a peasant, why did I join the army? Haowen, why do you weep? Why are you so listless? You are an intellectual, a worthless individual, you joined the revolution for opportunistic reasons, in search of glory and a way out for yourself. You are a vile and worthless rice-bucket, people should despise and humiliate you, jeer at you, the hardships that you tasted in the past are nothing to what you should taste now. You should witness again the supercilious disdain you witnessed in the past. People now look sideways at you, avoid you, are afraid that you have a problem, they won't let you attend meetings, when they cut meat they give you the bone, they give you inferior housing, if things are distributed you receive the worst, people want to give you nothing, people resent the fact that you get too much subsidy, and they want to extort some of it from you. Haowen, don't you know that when living under another person's roof, you are at that person's mercy, and you have no right to make decisions for yourself? As soon as you speak, others want to review your actions; as soon as you do anything, to study your thinking. Even if something is untrue, you must own up to it, or you're against the proletariat. According to the rules of conduct, you must never abandon your aspirations; for the sake of beauty, conscience must be not be breached; for things to flourish, the people's sufferings must never be forgotten. You are not a Manchu, you cannot slap a hat on someone and kill that person. You are in the year 1955, you must respect universally accepted truth and justice. Facts show that truth and justice will be victorious, while tyrants who abuse the people will be defeated.

MARCH 9, 1955

When can your fate be like the vast clear sky, when can you unburden yourself of all your bitterness, my peasants![6]

These diary entries must have appeared shocking to anyone in the Organization. Even so, Shang's utterances were not unreasonable.

The diary placed in Shang's file covered early 1950 and 1954 to early 1955. This suggests that no particularly serious problems were found in the diary before 1950 and up to the end of 1953. The excerpts used by the Organization show that the changes in his thinking occurred mainly in two periods: after the founding of the PRC, especially at the beginning of 1950; and after the end of 1953, when the government implemented a state monopoly over the purchase and marketing of farm products. After that, the ideological ferment persisted for quite a long time, from early 1954 to 1955, before the handing over of the diary.

The contents of Shang's diary could not be tolerated by the Organization. His dissatisfaction was manifested in three main regards. First, at the systemic level, he found it difficult to accept inequality and the lack of democracy. Excerpts from January 1950 and from 1954 express views on inequality not unlike those expressed by Wang Shiwei in Yan'an. Second, at the policy level, his identification with the peasants made him deeply uneasy about their fate. The entries from January and February 1950, March and December 1954, and March 1955 reflect his dissatisfaction with the position of the peasants after the revolution, especially their living conditions. Third, at the personal level, he was unhappy with his unit and the policy toward intellectuals. This is clear from entries in January and March 1955.

EXPOSÉ MATERIALS

The file also contained materials and exposés relating to political movements. To grasp how these materials came about, we need to look at Shang's personal history.

Shang was born in 1930, admitted to university in September 1948, and ran off to the liberated areas a year later. In July 1949, he was admitted to the Military and Political University, in October he joined the Southward-Marching Work Regiment, and in March 1950 he became one of the army's cultural teachers. Although there were changes in his role, he remained at platoon level. He did not join the Party, nor did he get promotion. In 1955, when Sufan started, he had already been working at company level for five or six years as a cultural teacher. Many of his colleagues, people who had enlisted with him, had already been promoted to several ranks above him.

Shang had failed to be promoted for two main reasons. One was his family background. Before 1949, his family had owned twenty-five *mu* of land, as well as a sugar refinery, a donkey, and six thatched huts. That did not amount to much, but his father was a teacher and a businessman, as well as a fortune-teller. The family did do manual labor, but it had a long-term hired hand, so after land reform it was designated as a well-to-do middle peasant family, and later as small landlords and merchants. That wasn't Shang's only problem. Soon after land reform, the father was dragged off to be struggled against, and while in the hands of the peasant association he died (some say he hanged himself, his family say he died of fright). Shang stated vaguely in his form: "My family background is landlord class, my father died of illness during the 1952 land reform." At the time, having a relative who had undergone "political repression" was a sensitive issue for anyone joining the Party or seeking promotion. Shang's vagueness got him into trouble. As soon as he turned up for an examination of his political record and promotion to the rank of cadre, he would almost certainly have been asked whether his father had died as a result of political struggle.[7]

The other reason had to do with Shang's own political behavior. His diary gives us a glimpse of a man who, in daily life, liked to moan and pass comments, and who resented adjusting his behavior to people's expectations or engaging in flattery. In a regime of strict discipline, in a military unit in which all actions are subject to command, such a person inevitably stood out. The longer he stayed at grassroots level, unable to join the Party or be promoted, his complaints grew, rendering him ever less trustworthy to the Organization.

In early 1955, during a movement to examine cadres' personal history, he had caught the unit's attention. "His behavior while on home leave" got him earmarked for investigation.

In the spring of 1954, Shang returned to his home region to visit his family. He complained to numerous people about the disaster his home region had suffered, the government's failure to provide relief, the peasants' hunger, his mother's suffering, and the fact that everywhere he went people wanted to sell him their watches, saying "everyone at home is starving, I'll sell it for a few yuan." The soldiers' thinking became negative as a result of their families' suffering.[8]

This made his unit suspicious of his family history and political attitude. They wanted the investigation to clarify: (1) "The said person claims to have supported the Communist Party. Is this true?" (2) "Why did he join the army, and go to our Military and Political University?" (3) "When the struggle began against his family, did he harbor feelings of discontent? What was said, and to whom?" (4) "When his father died in the struggle, what was the said person's behavior after returning home, and what did he talk about with his mother?" (5) "Has he shown feelings of discontent toward our Party's policy of grain procurement?"[9]

The movement had barely begun when the campaign against the Hu Feng counter-revolutionary clique broke out, followed by nationwide Sufan. The two movements were combined into one, which changed their nature.

The movement aimed to clarify cadres' history and background, ascertain their political attitude, "purge from the Party and government organs counter-revolutionary, alien class elements and degenerate elements that have sneaked into it," and provide reliable data for promotion. The review was mainly by way of investigation behind closed doors; it did not generally extend to open mass criticism and struggle.[10]

Sufan also had a review, entailing exposure by the masses, internal and external investigation by the Organization, and mass criticism and struggle. The Central Committee's directive stressed the need to "give free rein to the masses" in order to come up with the necessary leads, and to unearth hidden counter-revolutionaries and bad elements.[11]

Sufan entailed three steps:

(1) Study, discussion, and mobilization. Unit members had to undertake repeated readings of the Preface, Annotation, and Editorial Note to the book *Hu Feng's Counter-Revolutionary Clique* and to discuss them at mass rallies and in small groups, link them concretely to the situation in the unit, and analyze how hidden counter-revolutionaries could have sneaked in and spread rightist ideology, liberalism, individualism, sectarianism, and dissatisfaction.

(2) Reporting. Intense discussion, a mass meeting, a leader's report, mobilization of the masses to expose and criticize, and the setting out of policy. "Leniency for those who confess, severe punishment for those who conceal; if you don't tell the truth, others will; if you know of a counter-revolutionary but don't report him or her, that is harboring. If discovered at some future point, Party members will be expelled and the persons concerned will be implicated—it is better to report a counter-revolutionary than not."

(3) Cleaning up. After the receipt of confessions and reports, cases were classified in accordance with their nature and degree of seriousness. A detailed evaluation followed, and, on the basis of investigation, distinctions were made between right and wrong and degree of seriousness. Counter-revolutionaries were to be separated into primary, backbone, and general categories, those capable of reform and those who would not repent, and dealt with accordingly.[12]

Despite Shang's landlord background, his father's unexpected death, and all the "nonsense" since 1954, his work unit did not have enough on him to make him a target. However, grassroots military units were required by the Central Committee to identify 5 percent hidden counter-revolutionaries and bad elements, which was hard to achieve. So Shang's problematic ideological tendencies placed him in an unfavorable position.

Following instructions from above, Shang's unit organized reading, study, and discussion groups to great fanfare. Activities aimed at exposing wrong views and dissatisfaction with the Party led to the uncovering of Shang's problems. At the confessing stage, leaders preached "leniency for those who are frank, severity against those who are evasive" and explained that "failure to speak up about a counter-revolutionary equates to covering up counter-revolution." This prompted even more cadres and soldiers to expose him. Shang, who up to then had been nonchalant, became anxious. He realized that some of things he had written in his diary were more serious than the problems exposed by his peers. Living communally, where everyone did all they could to expose and report anyone and anything, he knew that it would be impossible to hide the opinions expressed in his diary. If they were discovered, the punishment would be "severe." But if he confessed and handed over the diary, things he had said about the case against Hu Feng's counter-revolutionary clique might come to light, and the consequences would be equally disastrous.[13]

Shang decided to come clean. For the most part the thoughts and views expressed in the diary seemed correct and he had rarely stepped over the line. They merely showed that weaknesses remained in his thinking, and that he needed the support of the Organization. Handing over his diary would be a plea for help. So he decided to use the occasion of a small-group meeting to read out bits from his diary that reflected correct thinking, while at the same time explaining that his thinking was blemished in other regards.[14]

Most of materials relating to the exposure of Shang dated from around 1955. They can be divided into two parts—reports by cadres and soldiers, and records of small-group meetings.

The reports mainly concerned wrong terms used by Shang after 1953. For example, on returning from a visit to his family, he had complained that "in the past, under the old society, even the poorest peasant would be fed and clothed. Every year they could afford a pig or two. Now, things have become much worse, some people can't even get food or clothes." When someone asked Shang what happened to the crops harvested by the peasants, he replied: "How much would they have harvested, not even enough for handing over [to the state]!"

Someone said Shang had criticized the Organization at a conference of youth representatives, describing it as "a wooden statue floating in the sea, with only its neck above water."

Another said that Shang, as vice-secretary of the Youth League, treated young soldiers who applied to join coldly, and said, "It doesn't matter whether you join or not, you'll still make the same progress." He exhibited the same attitude toward young people carrying out Party studies: "It doesn't matter whether you attend, it's all the same. Branch member or not, you still get to eat."

Another said that Shang, while speaking in class about the "direction for the transitional period," explained that the policy for the reform of private industrial and commercial sectors was "let's drain them by taxing them, once the taxes become too heavy they will say silly things, which we can then use to expropriate them." Talking about the need to cross over into socialist society, he said, "Who knows what society will become once we reach communism!"

Another said that Shang had still been complaining on the eve of Sufan. He had declared that "there are no prospects in the military for intellectuals, the higher-ups never trust you. Had I known earlier, I would not have studied. If I'd been a simpleton, I wouldn't have ended up like this." "We are missing just two words—Party member. Otherwise, we would have changed profession a long time ago!"[15]

Even Shang's girlfriend wrote to his military unit to say that he had not got on well with his instructor and had not put his mind to his work, so his thinking had become backward. She had disagreed with many of his opinions, and had tried to break up with him. She wrote: "Although I am in a romantic relationship with him, I have already—under the guidance and nurturing of my work unit and the Party branch—clarified my stance, and I wish to fight resolutely against any counter-revolutionary element (our class enemy). Even if he is my lover, I will report him and expose him without hesitation." "I will not regard him as my comrade, but rather as my enemy. To my enemy I will not show a shred of sympathy. He has written many letters expressing backward views. Should the Organization require them, I can send them for review."[16]

The records of the small-group meetings mainly concerned Shang's "confession" and participants' criticism. Shang talked about the origins of his thoughts and problems. At university, he had adopted Confucius' idea that "the world belongs to all"; he had become dissatisfied with Kuomintang corruption; and he had taken a centrist position. His basic inclination was to be progressive, but having seen the hustle and bustle of the cities, he had wanted to climb upwards. After joining the revolution, this desire remained, and he felt lost and disappointed. In 1954, he gave up the idea, and "developed the individualist viewpoint of wanting to write books and become famous, in the belief that as a democrat and a non-Party personage he could still carry on all the same. Isn't Guo Moruo[17] still a revolutionary?" He admitted that he had sunk deeper into "individual heroism" and extreme democracy. He felt that "if you are better than me, I must become better than you," and believed that "outside work, one should never approach one's superiors; with colleagues—if you come to me, I respond, otherwise I ignore you." He used to say: "I have read about Wang Anshi. He was a pauper, and became chancellor. What about me? After ten years I can't even become a branch cadre."[18]

He insisted that he had gone to university and joined the army and the revolution in pursuit of progress. Before joining the revolution he had read articles by Sun Yat-sen, Mao's autobiography, "On New Democracy," etc., and at school he had started to admire the Communist Party. After the Hu Feng incident, he had written articles criticizing Hu Feng's colleague Lu Ling, but they had not been published.[19]

Interrogation and criticism were organized in advance. Questions centered on Shang's history, his family circumstances, his father's death, and the sources of his dissatisfaction with the Party and reality. The meetings started in August 1955, and took place nearly every day until early September. Later, a struggle group made a thorough study of Shang's diaries. Struggle meetings lasted four days.

Shang Haowen initially explained his father's death like this: "He'd been ill, and was terrified of struggle meetings. Once at a meeting he saw three people get shot, so he was scared to death." When young, he had not felt emotionally close to his father,

who beat and scolded him. Only after Shang entered university did his father's attitude change. Already in his sixties, he continued to work at his business so that he
could help with Shang's tuition fees. After Shang joined the army, his father walked
nearly three hundred kilometers to Shang's base to visit him. During the visit he
urged him to return home and get married, and on leaving he cried. Only then did
Shang realize his father loved him. Recalling the moment when he had received
news of his father's death, he said: "I thought to myself, he supported me throughout
my studies, without him there would have been no me. So I felt sorry for him."[20]

The redistribution of his family's land meant nothing to him: "Some people
owned no land, they should be given some." However, he was puzzled by the
reclassification of his family from "rich middle peasants" to "small landlords." He
found the treatment of his mother even harder to accept. After his father's death,
the peasant association took her to struggle meetings to denounce her. Shang
thought that was wrong, since his mother was from a poor peasant family. They
also confiscated her belongings. Shang's mother was in poor health and had no
one to care for her, so she nearly took her own life. This upset Shang: "She came
from a poor peasant family!" "She has never done anything wrong!" "What has she
done to deserve such suffering!" While visiting home during the Spring Festival in
1954, he saw that his mother was unable to care for herself, yet he could do nothing
to help. He felt sad. All he could do was comfort her: "In future, once I have the
means, I will take you with me."[21]

Shang clashed frequently with his interrogators. He admitted to being unable to
change his view that life was hard for peasants. He thought that the Organization
was out of touch with what was happening at the grassroots: "By only relying on
reports rather than seeking out the facts, the Central Committee becomes cut off
from the rural population." Policies like state control of the procurement and distribution of crops were wrong, and made it difficult for peasants to feed and clothe
themselves. Peasants should have control over their own labor and reward. He
insisted that he had never been against the Communist Party: "I support communism, but I suspect the Party has abandoned the peasants," "I have ideological
doubts about whether revolution is really for the people." Otherwise why, since the
establishment of the People's Republic, had the focus been on developing cities
rather than rural areas? He said: "If this is really in the peasants' interests, I will
reverse my position."[22]

Speaking of Communist revolution: "I am sure the Communist cause will be
achieved," "ideologically I wish for communism to be realized, but I am not willing
to take part in a bloody battle, I prefer arguments." He saw himself as a humanitar-
ian: "It is difficult ideologically to accept the act of killing." He said everyone is
born human and should be treated equally. A country is like a big family, we are all
brothers and sisters, if someone makes a mistake we should help them, not kill
them. Regarding Zhenfan, he agreed that "if in the people's opinion someone

should be killed, then they can be killed. Otherwise we should take the approach of education and rehabilitation."[23]

He admitted not concentrating on work, and liking to compare himself with others. On one occasion his superiors had announced promotions that did not include him, and he felt humiliated. They had previously mentioned that the position of cultural teacher would be scrapped. Shang worried that "as I get older, without a secure job my future seems troubled. I have written to my superiors to complain," but that had not solved the problem. He thought his negative mindset could be attributed in part to his earlier progressive thoughts. He had always thought of himself as more progressive than most, and had taken part in student strikes and read progressive books, so mentally he found his predicament hard to accept.[24]

The small group held a meeting to report on Shang, chaired by higher authorities. It was agreed that the progress made in one week had "reached the projected goals, that Shang had admitted being hostile toward the Party and slandering it," and that "the masses have seen through Shang and their hatred has been ignited." However, the meeting also found that Shang's arrogant attitude "had not been completed defeated," and that his "true colors had not been fully revealed." According to Commissioner X, "on the whole, his thoughts are negative. He was not born a peasant, and his ideology has been shaped by his closed mind. He was born a landlord, and he has no sympathy for the peasants. He (1) sabotages socialist construction; (2) sabotages the organization of the branch; (3) distorts and sabotages the Party's policies; and (4) stirs up trouble in relationships and sabotages unity." Commissioner X demanded further investigation to clarify Shang's political motivation and background.[25]

The small group studied Shang's confessions line by line. They even managed to force Shang to talk about the curses he had uttered in his sleep and the complaints he had made in letters to his lover. Shang was forced to admit that he had had many political problems, and that he had been "unsupportive" of the Party. He had failed to support the policy of bloody struggle and the objectives set by the Party. He had criticized elitist rule by cliques, a mass line that was out of touch with reality (i.e., bureaucratic), a system that did not allow free speech, and policies that prioritized urban over rural areas.[26]

The struggle group found that Shang's diary (1) slandered the Party as elitist; (2) did not recognize leadership by the working class, and maintained that the right to lead belonged to the peasants; (3) distorted the Party's policies, and propagated extreme democracy; (4) opposed state control of procurement and distribution, thus spreading discontent; (5) was dissatisfied with reality, leading to sentiments of extreme pessimism and despair; (6) and undermined leaders' authority, stirring up trouble between superiors and subordinates, talking himself up, attacking others, etc.[27]

The struggle group went on to examine the motivation behind Shang's thinking and its historical sources. Attempts were made to bully Shang into admitting that he grieved at the death of his landlord father and had come to harbor hatred for the Party.

Shang Haowen: Recently the problem that's been bothering me most is 'fear of sanctions': demobilization, reform-through-labor, being placed under control. What if I get sent home? Or sent for reform through labor, or placed under control for years? Yesterday they asked me to write some material, I'm afraid the sanctions will be implemented soon.

On Saturday they said my problems have not yet been addressed. I only have two more problems worth talking about. Apart from that, I have nothing more to say.

As for the things I said in my sleep, about being hostile to the Organization, I never entertained such thoughts. I feel that the leadership, and everyone, has helped me time after time, so why would I feel hostile? They have all the material, and threaten to impose more sanctions if I don't speak out, but I truly feel no hostility. As for the alleged cursing in my sleep, I have always had this habit, though it's not clear to me who I would be cursing.

In the past, for a short while I sympathized with my father, but overall I had a bad relationship with him. Our relationship only improved after 1948–49, when he gave me financial support and stopped beating me. After I joined the army he came to visit me and cried, which moved me, but we did not have a strong relationship.

Regarding my motivation for joining the army in 1949: (1) revolution; (2) to become an official. My father died in 1952, I only received the news half a year later, and I only found out the details last year, when I visited home. My father was still alive when I joined the army, so I could not have been motivated by revenge. It might seem that I felt sympathy for my father, but I did not. I only felt sympathy for the peasants, I had no strong feelings toward my father.

Q: You once said that your father died during the struggle, which was better than being executed by shooting. Was this sympathy or not?

A: He was old, and could not work, to die was not a bad thing, I didn't have any problems with it. That had nothing to do with sympathy.

Q: You say your father could not work, so he would be better off dead. This shows you were worried that your father would have to work, isn't this showing sympathy?

A: If you put it like that, then yes.

Q: You are saying your father was old and it was his time to die, death would be better than living in pain, and better than execution by shooting. Isn't that sympathy?

A: In principle it is sympathy.

The questioner reads from Shang's diary:

"O Dad, oh my kind and loving father, from today I have lost another loved one!" Is this sympathy for your father or not?

(Silence.)

Shang later addressed his relationship with his father in a confession:

Father had written to explain that the alcohol distillery had closed down. I tried to comfort him: 'Without the distillery we can still get by. We also get to avoid wasting food, so the prohibition by the government is just. The Communist Party is reasonable, problems can gradually be solved.'

Regarding father's death, once I had received news from home, I felt that he owed no blood debt and I was unaware of him being guilty of anything, so I felt he did not deserve to die during the struggle. I only found out about his guilt when I went home. Exploitation, engaging in lawsuits on behalf of other people, idleness.

When I was in the army, father walked three hundred kilometers to see me. I felt he was good to me. We chatted, and I told him about the army. He wanted me to return home to get married. His visit moved me. I felt a father's love for his son, and realized that the beating had been done out of love.

On hearing of his death, I felt that he had raised me in vain. He did not get to enjoy a single day of my caring for him, in return for his caring for me. I felt that he was innocent, and had died aggrieved. Later, on my return home, mother wept while recounting stories to me. There were people around and I was afraid that reports would spread, so I stopped her. I said 'better this way than being shot, please don't continue.' She wanted me to burn some incense for father. I said it was inappropriate, but we could go for a walk instead. Later I visited father's grave together with my elder brother. I thought: 'Who would have guessed that our reunion at the military base would be our last meeting? You raised me in vain. I have never poured a glass of water for you, I never attempted to fulfill my duty as a son.'

After joining the army I received several years' education about the revolution, but I still felt sympathetic toward my father. I worried that people would say I was the loyal offspring of a landlord. I was afraid that they would trace my origin and say that I stood firmly with the landlord class and defended its interests. I was afraid to confess, for they might put a counter-revolutionary hat on me. Father had been found guilty. To show sympathy would add to my guilt. The more people pursued such matters, the more scared I became.

My sympathy toward my father was limited to what I have just said, it did not go further. After returning to the base, I did not dare speak to anyone about it, although I did mention that I felt sorry for my mother. Yesterday I was worried that I would be sanctioned, but now I have said everything there is to say. If people don't believe me, they can go ahead and sanction me. The things I said in my sleep had nothing to do with avenging my father.[28]

CONFESSION MATERIALS

Shang Haowen's file consisted of a large number of confession materials, written at various stages of his review. The three confessions referred to so far were written in 1955.

The first dealt with Shang's family and history. Regarding his father's occupation and "sins," he wrote: "Father's occupation was teaching and doing business, including much shady dealing. His sins, as far as I know, included helping others with lawsuits, which he did on two occasions. Once against a colleague of my uncle's, which he won; and once on behalf of Factory X, which he lost. An example of exploitation is his diluting alcohol with water. He also did some clerical work for the Kuomintang local government."

Regarding his ideological problems after joining the army:

> At first I was full of passion about all things new, but I knew nothing about the revolution—the paths to it (new democracy to communism), the methods (policies), class struggle, who leads the revolution. Whatever I knew was distorted. Because I never took part in the revolution, I had been poisoned by my imaginings about Communist society—I thought that as soon as the revolution had succeeded the world would belong to all, classes would cease to exist and everyone would be equal. I thought the alliance of workers and peasants led by the working class was unfair, and it was not right that the peasants should be led. I thought that historically the peasants had contributed more to the revolution than the workers, so they should be the leaders, or least should have been equal. I searched everywhere for writings by revolutionary leaders—when I read their comments about peasants, it seemed to me that they were affirming that peasants should play a leading role in the revolution. I thought: 'revolutionary leaders recognize the peasants as leaders, so why is this not implemented?' I corrected these 'extremely erroneous views' during the rectification movement—after reading the leaders' theses about the forces and relations of production, I understood the difference between peasants and workers, the latter progressive, the former backward.

Regarding his dissatisfaction with the peasants' living conditions:

> In recent years I'd seen the peasants struggle and felt sorry for them. I kept asking why it is so hard for them. I had wrongly come to believe that the peasants should have been able to freely allocate the fruits of their own labor, which they worked so hard to obtain, whereas instead these fruits were taken from them by the state. I began to wonder whether our revolution had abandoned the peasants, and started to have doubts. I thought, the rural area is in such a state, why doesn't the country understand? Is it because no one has visited the grassroots to find out what's going on, rather than merely rely on reports from lower levels? I thought that such reports did not necessarily reflect the truth, as they had been through a process of analysis and weren't original materials. This led to a gap between the central government and the countryside.

He later admitted: "This type of thinking is against the people. It displays a lack of trust in the Organization, and is wrong." He asked himself: "Does not each level of the Organization work to serve the people and implement the Party's policies? Of course it does. Each level is vital for linking up with the masses and serving the people, it in no way resembles capitalist governments or organizations. This was a mistake of basic stance."

In response to repeated questions about whether his father's death had roused sentiments of class vengeance in him, Shang denied such feelings:

After land reform, I did not have much of a reaction. The Organization can confirm this by looking at my correspondence with my family. After my father's death, I had wrongly thought that I owed him my life and the chance to study. I felt that after university he had treated me well, and had visited me after I joined the army. But then I thought, he never lifted a finger, so where did the money come from? It must have been from exploitation! It only looked as if he had supported my studies, in reality the working people did. In any case, his death was not untimely. He was an old man, so why should I have feelings? After that, I was able to let go. Toward mother, however, I felt true sympathy. This was a class error, it showed that my consciousness was not high enough. Why did I feel sympathy? Because I did not think about her exploiting people, I merely thought about her family background and how good she had been to me. My class stance had been replaced by my relationship with my mother.[29]

In his second written confession, Shang analyzed his ideological problems. He acknowledged that enemies of the Communist Party can be separated into the enemy that can be openly defeated and those who, though never engaging in hostile actions, are nevertheless mentally reactionary. The latter desperately resist new things, they criticize everything but themselves. "I am of the second type. I am reactionary by nature. My goal is to sabotage the revolution."

On struggle: "I think everyone should treat others as human beings, everyone is equal and free, no one should oppress others. Those born in the same country are like one big family, all men are brothers, and all women sisters. All internal problems in a country (with the exception of the Chiang Kai-shek bandits) should be resolved through reasoning, without resorting to violence; nor should we kill our enemies." He said he now realized that

[I]t's not that we don't treat people as human beings, and it's not that we are crazed killers, it's that our enemies want to kill. In the past, have they not killed countless of our comrades? They don't treat us like human beings, they humiliate and kill us at will. Are we then not justified in killing those executioners from the past and those who orchestrated them? In this world, as long as classes are not abolished, class struggle will continue; and as long as class struggle continues, bloody fights will be inevitable. By repudiating bloody struggle, I repudiate class struggle. Only the capitalists and Chiang bandits refuse to accept the existence of classes.

He also examined his sympathy for the peasants:

We are the same people, why is it that rural living conditions are so much worse than in the towns? The reason is that villages are different from cities (I have maintained this view ever since student days). I argued that the countryside should be constructed in the same way as the cities—whatever cities have, villages should also have. Currently most construction is in the cities, and does not extend to the countryside. I think this is unreasonable, and it has made me dissatisfied with the Party. After my return to the countryside last year, I witnessed the life of rural people. This reinforced my reactionary thoughts, and led to my distorted view of rural living conditions. I thought the Party did not cherish the peasants, it had abandoned the peasants, and the peasants had been 'deceived.' On the issue of 'state control of procurement and the distribution of crops,' I said the peasants should be allowed to control the fruits of their own labor, and use them to construct the countryside. State control of the procurement and distribution of cotton has restricted people's choice of clothing. I had not understood the peasants' new life after the land reform, but had simply noticed the shortcomings, compared to life in the cities. What does that demonstrate? I was behaving like the enemy, who never mention the advantages of our regime, I was behaving provocatively. As someone born into a family of landlord hegemons, how could I ever sympathize with the peasants? I was doing it in name only, in reality I was sympathizing with the defeated landlords.'

He continued to criticize his "sympathy" toward his landlord family, and said:

As long as a person sympathizes with landlord hegemons, that person will never feel sympathy for the poor and suffering. Is a 'father' such as this worth feeling sorry for? Aren't the lives of the millions who have died under the whips, knives, and guns of the landlord hegemons equally worthy? Why did I only feel sorry for the death of my landlord father? Obviously, I still thought like an exploiter, I still believed in landlord ideology and feudal morality. Why could I not face up to my father's sins? I was covering up his heinous crimes in order to excuse my sympathy. What kind of person would see his death as unjust? Someone from a landlord family, someone like me. As for mother, she was the wife of a landlord, and I not only ignored her past exploitation but exaggerated her poor origins. Ought she not to have participated in labor? In the past, she had exploited people, now she could no longer do so, and had instead to work for herself. How was that 'suffering'? Only a member of the landlord class would engage in such slander. The things you say stem from the position you take— I am well and truly a 'dutiful offspring' of a landlord hegemon!

He dug deeper for the source of his thinking. He believed that his reactionary thinking was in one respect the result of "the long-term capitalist education I had received, I had been fed a diet of capitalist idealism. This had created an erroneous foundation, both in my ideology and my actions, and had set the conditions for me to follow a reactionary path." He traced his thinking back to Rousseau's philosophy of natural right: "Rousseau's theories interested me immensely. I thought he was right: people should be born equal and free, and should have rights; it is wrong for people to oppress one another or kill one another. I thought that this was the ideal I should pursue. I have maintained this ideal up until now." He also said that he "had been poisoned to a degree by Confucius, whose ideas about 'the world belonging to all' and 'those who excel at learning becoming officials' struck deep roots in my mind. I saw the society in which 'the world belongs to all' as Communist society. I agreed that 'those who excel at learning should become officials.' I thought posts should be filled by scholars, since learning reveals reasons, and officials should be reasonable. I had always hoped that after joining the revolution I would get an official post. Once reality set in, my attitude turned to disappointment." He identified the other source of his reactionary thinking as his membership of the "reactionary landlord class":

> The clearest example of this was my sympathy for my father and mother after the struggle against them. When sympathizing with the lives of the peasants, what was my standpoint? Was I really arguing for the sake of the revolution? No. I was aiming to serve the landlord class, I was not out to consolidate the revolution but to sabotage it. Attempting to sow disunity in the workers and peasants' alliance and to shift the focus of the Chinese revolution to the peasants and the focus of construction to the villages was to resist the idea of the Party leading the peasants. Having been born into a landlord family, how could I have acted in the interests of the people? Assuming that I had at some point acted in the interests of the people, why would I then be dissatisfied with the Party? My reactionary ideas were born of my class background, for reactionary ideas are themselves a reflection of reactionary being.

It wasn't enough to analyze his thoughts and trace their origins. He also needed to discuss the objectives and motives of his "reactionary nature." His analysis ran as follows: he was dissatisfied with the old society, but he was also dissatisfied with the new society. The key problem was that "up to now there have been too few progressive theses to improve society." "I therefore came up with some sinister reactionary plans. My plan was, in ten to twenty years' time, to write a book about the reasons for the success and failure of the revolution. Once I had finished it I would get a lot of royalties, and I would no longer need to be a teacher. I would concentrate on academic research, set up a small library, and live in isolation from the world."

What new theory did he want to create? "As far as I can see, at present Marxism and Leninism are progressive philosophies, but they have shortcomings. I want to use Marxism-Leninism as a foundation, and to enrich it, to make it more complete. That could be done in two ways: (1) by adding elements to Marxism-Leninism; (2) by developing a new system based on the existing foundation." His goal was to create a theory to resolve social conflict and oppression, "so people can live in a world free from the death and horror created by humans, one in which there would be no danger of political oppression, and in which people can—collectively—do whatever they want." He doubted whether the Party, following its current trajectory, would be able to lead the people to communism. "If you cannot lead, someone else will. Once my reactionary theory achieves results, others will be able to implement it. I cannot predict who that might be. This was my motivation, with the goal of opposing the Party's current direction and creating new theories to depose it. I formed these views in the second half of 1954, motivated by the bloody struggle, freedom of speech, peasants' living conditions etc."[30]

The struggle group reconvened to criticize Shang's confession. This put Shang under enormous pressure. On October 3, Shang managed to respond calmly to the questioning. By the 4th, he had grown impatient with the endless repetition and hat slapping. He said again and again that he had answered the questions. Then someone banged the table and said his thoughts and words were as reprehensible as those of murderers and arsonists. He lost his temper: "Yes I have killed! I have killed myself! I'm dead anyway, blame everything on me!" Someone else loudly denounced his attitude, and he shouted back: "I have nothing more to say! You can deal with me now, give me your verdict!" There was a lot of yelling back and forth, and the note-taker wrote: "He was hostile. He ground his teeth and said: 'Even my piss smells bad, whereas your piss smells good. I can do no right!'"[31]

The meeting was resumed on the 5th. Shang's attitude remained the same. At first he was reluctant to say anything, but after repeated scolding from the chair he declared: "I have nothing more to say. You have seen my attitude, draw your own conclusions. I have confessed everything. No matter how shameless I am, I can't make up problems that I don't have!" When someone told him to take responsibility for his actions, he replied: "That's what I'm doing! I'm taking responsibility for myself, I'm being responsible!" When someone warned him that he risked antagonizing the struggle group, he answered: "That's fine. If you want to kill me, get it over with!" "I have no more problems, do whatever you will."[32]

MATERIALS RELATING TO THE SUMMONS

Shang's antagonistic attitude angered his military unit, which led to an escalation of his problems. The five-person group of leaders approved the establishment of a special task group to investigate his "ongoing counter-revolutionary" case. Although he had never previously worn a hat, his file contained oral material of the sort used in criminal cases.

Although Shang's problems had escalated, after ten months of confrontations he no longer cared about being subjected to criticism from the higher plane of principle. The special group's interrogation style was quite different from the previous stern approach, so Shang was more forthcoming.

The opening interrogation focused on his family and personal history: "Explain your family's economic situation, composition, and political outlook before and after Liberation." "Detail your experiences before joining the army, concentrating on when, where and what." "Describe your visit home in 1949, and your objectives in organizing a fellow-students' and fellow-townspeople's association during the visit." "During your time at school, what reactionary organizations did you join?" "During your time at university, what reactionary organizations did you join?" "At university, did you get to hear of any progressive organizations?" "What ideology compelled you to seek out our progressive organization?" "What progressive books did you read at university?" "Where did you get the progressive books?" "What other books did you read at school, and how did they influence you?"[33]

The second interrogation concentrated on his diaries.

Q: Why did you oppose the leadership of the working class in your diary?

A: When I first joined the revolution, I had no understanding of its methods, or who was to lead it. Later, I heard it was led by the working class, but this puzzled me. Previous revolutions had been initiated by peasants. Peasants were the most effective class, and many in number. So I thought the revolution should have been led by the peasants. Later, after two Party rectifications, I grasped the issue. I realized that the working class possessed no means of production, so they would be more resolute in the revolution. Once we have reached Communist society, the peasant class will no longer exist. The issue was thus resolved.

Q: Why did you say in your diary that Chairman Mao said that China lacked a peasants' party, and that Lenin said peasants were the leaders and motivators of revolution? Why did you write that?

A: I can no longer remember! If they did not say it, then I must have distorted Marxism-Leninism. However, at the time I really wanted to get to grips with this problem.

Q: Why did you say that you seemed already to have reached your ideal? Is the socialist order, the society we have today, not your ideal society? In what respect is it not your ideal?

A: I felt that peasants' lives were hard in the past. Several years after the revolution their lives were still hard. Our Party only constructed the cities, not the villages. The rural people were still suffering. In my view, the Party did not allow freedom of speech, what appeared in the newspapers was all positive and never negative. If you were not careful about what you said, you could end up a suspect. The Party should not have treated intellectuals as it did—looking after the ones that are still useful and ignoring the rest. Under the old society I could not speak, now I still lack the freedom to speak. In our army unit, nobody wanted to approach me or help me with my problems. That's why I became pessimistic.

Q: Why did you say our writers have succumbed to power, why did you insult them as 'dogs'?

A: It seemed to me they only talk about how bad things were in the past. They should write about today, about everything, bad as well as good. Before Gao Gang was exposed, nobody criticized him. Only when there is freedom of speech can science develop. Only through debate can we reach the right conclusions. Merely criticizing someone does not show what is wrong. We should be allowed to see the wrong side. I did not insult writers as dogs, I just gave an example, it should not count as an insult.

Q: You asked in your diary when would the peasants control their own destiny, when would their suffering come to light? What did that mean?

A: I was mainly expressing my dissatisfaction with the peasants' living conditions.

Q: What does 'controlling your own destiny' mean?

A: Destiny refers to the peasants' hardship. When will their livelihood improve?

Q: We think you are implying something else—that the peasants' destiny is not in their own hands. Because they don't have the power to lead, they have not become the masters. When they become the masters, their destiny will be in their own hands!

A: I didn't mean that. If that's what you think, there is nothing I can say. I have already explained what I meant. Forget it, whatever the Organization decides, I have no objection.

Q: You said that you had long since stopped opposing working class leadership, yet in 1954 and 1955 these problems were exposed. How can you claim to have changed your mind?

A: These things can't be linked with 1950. I really had changed my mind. Since 1954, these thoughts stemmed from my dissatisfaction with various policies, as well as with the hardship faced by my family and by rural people, and the fact that construction did not extend to the rural areas. They had nothing to do with the worker-peasant alliance.

Q: You accused the Party of cronyism, is that supporting the Party? You said the Party was using the peasants, and that peasants did not control their own destiny. Isn't that proof that your ideology has not changed? You should be honest about your true thinking.

A: If the Organization takes that view, there's nothing I can do about it. Let's move on to conclusions and sanctions! I have no objections. These were my thoughts at the time. On closer analysis, it does sound as you say, but it's wrong to connect these two things.[34]

The third interrogation focused on the death of Shang's father and his visit home. Regarding the impact of his father's death, Shang's statement did not change. Regarding his own "spreading discontent among the masses in his army unit after his visit home," he said he had done nothing more than speak the truth, and had not tried to spread discontent.

He declared: "I said only that my family was living a hard life. I wanted my superiors to realize that I was not rich and I was suffering, so they would help me. I received no help, which upset me. I thought my family was having a difficult time, so I should be helped!"

Q: Soldiers from your unit have reported that you said that 'the government only talks about assistance but never provides it. Who knows where all the food has gone.' Is that true?

A: How could I have said such things in front of soldiers? I only said that my family was suffering. During the previous small-group struggle I had been under pressure, and it had seemed to me that 'if I had said no such thing, why would the soldiers say I did?' So I thought maybe I had said it, and confessed it. But even now I still can't recall saying it.

Q: In the past you said things like 'joining the Youth League made no difference to whether you progress or not,' didn't you?

A: Yes. I was not trying to stop people joining the League. It was because I had applied to join the Party and not been approved. I was unhappy, that's why I said such things. I was trying to comfort them, to explain to them that there was no hurry.

Q: Why did you come up with such reactionary thoughts?

A: When I joined the revolution I was dissatisfied with the Party's cadre policy, which treated intellectuals differently. When things failed to meet my expectations, I became even more unhappy. That was mainly because of things I had learned under the old system, especially 'natural rights theory' and 'the ways of Confucius and Mencius.' I had been influenced by my family, though not to any great extent. Yes, I had some reactionary thoughts, but I have always supported the Party. In my previous confessions I said I was against the Party, but that was nonsense, I was coerced into saying it.

Q: Why did you accuse the party of cronyism and say that you were living in a cruel world, that you opposed the Party's policies? What did all that mean? Can that be interpreted as supporting the Party?

A: That's your opinion. Whether I support the Party or not, at least I don't oppose it. Let the Organization handle this as it sees fit. Deal with me as you like, I have no objection.[35]

THE VERDICT

If Shang Haowen's diary, together with his uncompromising attitude during the latter part of the small-group struggle, had been linked to the Hu Feng case, he would have been branded a "counter-revolutionary." However, the five-person group went easy on him, and his sanctioning took a dramatic turn.

In early 1956, after the special group delivered its report, several senior leaders (including the five-person group) talked separately with him, and listened to his explanations. He admitted his problems, and promised to study hard and reform his ideas. The five-person group rejected the special group's recommendation that he be severely punished, and even decided not to punish him at all.

The five-person group reached a conclusion on June 19, 1956. The verdict noted the opinions expressed in Shang's diary, but they did not label them as "reactionary" or "counter-revolutionary." On the other hand, they found that his problems were "due to his opposition to some Party and army policies." They concluded that "after joining the army Shang had at times worked well, completed his tasks, and made some achievements." His problems stemmed from "his severe capitalist individualistic ideology, as well as arrogance and dissatisfaction following his failure to realize his personal ambitions, which festered in him. His sympathy for his landlord family, the death of his father, and the suffering of his mother were also factors." They commented: This comrade does not yet fully appreciate some of the problems he faces, but as a result of "numerous conversations and meetings, and repeated education, he has shown a marked improvement." "Overall, his problems are ideological in nature, and were exhibited through his diary. There will be no punishment."[36]

Once the report was submitted to the Party committee, some argued that at least some punishment was necessary. In the end, the five-person group amended its verdict, changing the term "opposition" to "reactionary ideology." Shang's problem therefore became one of "reactionary ideology," and he was charged with being "arrogant, harboring a severe capitalist individualistic ideology, believing that his talent had not been utilized, and having a mentality in which dissatisfaction developed into a positively reactionary mentality." The recommendation also changed. The final verdict is recorded in Table 4.[37]

In accordance with this decision, the Youth League Committee also issued a statement: "In light of the above, we confirm that although on joining the army he received education from the Party and higher levels, he was unable to abandon his old class stance and displayed hatred toward the people's government and Party policies. To educate him, a decision has been made to monitor him within the Youth League, for one year."[38]

Not long afterwards, Shang was reassigned elsewhere. Although he had always wanted to be reassigned, with such a file it would be difficult for him to achieve anything, whichever unit he ended up in and no matter how hard he worked. In the various political movements that followed, including the Cultural Revolution, Shang's file and the contents of his diary were used by interrogators or activists as ideological targets, and even as class-struggle targets. During activities such as manual labor that had nothing to do with political movements, people would quote from the decision on Shang in their evaluation of him. For example, in the summer of 1960 Shang and his workmates were sent to the countryside to do three months' manual labor. Shang was hardworking. The small-group evaluation confirmed that he had performed well in all areas, including labor, study, and relations with the masses. However, it added that "because Shang was to a large extent a bourgeois individualist, after realizing he was sick his heavy ideological burden became apparent and his morale declined, which had an impact on his temperament. He is not sufficiently modest when receiving criticism. He does not demand enough of himself, he is not good at relying on the Organization, and he is easily irritated."[39]

TABLE 4

Nature of the problems	Arrogant, harboring severe capitalist individualistic ideology, believing that his talent had not been utilized, and having a mentality in which dissatisfaction developed into a positively reactionary mentality.

Conclusion and recommendations:

The said member, before joining the army, had been deeply contaminated with capitalist democratic and liberal ideology. Between August 1948 and May 1949, while studying at S City, he became disenchanted with the corrupt and authoritarian Kuomintang regime. In pursuit of a better society and democracy, as well as in pursuit of his own personal success, he joined our army after Liberation.

Periods of good behavior followed. However, after 1950 he became dissatisfied with the people's government and the leadership of the working class, claiming that "the fruits of the revolution achieved by mountains of bones and rivers of blood have become the plaything of a clique [meaning our Party]." In his opinion, the government should be led by the peasants, of whom he regarded himself as a representative. He criticized himself on this account two years later, but after visiting his home in early 1954 he claimed that his "sympathy for the peasants" had revived. He opposed the Party's control of procurement and distribution and became a blind humanist, for whom the peasants were "suffering too much" and "continued to be oppressed and dominated." He expressed the view that our Party "does not allow freedom of speech," that its "politics are undemocratic," and that Zhenfan was "an act of revenge and murder."

In 1952, while carrying out regional assistance work, he was upset when the Organization did not approve his request to get married. He believed that the army did not value or properly utilize intellectuals and that he "lived in a cruel world." He was dissatisfied with the Party's cadre policy and believed that "talented peasants cannot become prime minister"—this was even worse than the "imperial examination system." He later developed these thoughts further.

He was not only suspicious of and dissatisfied with our Party but he expressed sentiments hostile to the Party, labeling its leaders as cronies and suggesting that in some respects "the new society exceeded the Kuomintang's reactionary rule." He wildly claimed that he wanted to "improve" Marxism-Leninism.

The motivation and source of the said comrade's ideological errors were mainly his own severe bourgeois individualism and wild arrogance. After joining the army, he failed to achieve his personal ambitions, and his feelings of dissatisfaction led him to adopt a reactionary attitude. His sympathy for his landlord family, his dead father, and his suffering mother was also a factor.

When Sufan started, he repeatedly insisted that he had no problems, and he read out to the masses some positive parts of his diary, to demonstrate his innocence and progressive character. During the small-group struggle he shouted out: "Damn it, people who are ideologically backward are counter-revolutionaries, why don't you just execute me?" Despite the army's and the five-person group's repeated urgings and exhortation, and the criticisms of his reactionary thinking, he has yet to carry out a thorough review, and he does not acknowledge his mistakes. He does not appreciate the severity of his problems, insisting that for him "it is not a matter of position" and that he "supports the Communist Party 100 percent." He quibbles, and he attempts to disguise his wrong thinking. We would have punished him severely, but given that for the most part he expressed his ideas only in his personal diary and his activity had no negative outcome, he can remain a member of the Youth League and will be monitored for a year, in preparation for reassignment.

These burdens continued to weigh on Shang. Finally, in June 1980, his military unit decided:

> During Sufan, Comrade Shang Haowen handed over his diary to the Organization. He thus opened his heart to the Party and put his trust in the Organization. The diary contained some wrong views that reflected shortcomings in Shang's ideas and understanding. The previous finding in this matter is hereby revoked.[40]

This correction happened too late for Shang, who was already in his fifties, but better late than never. Only then did those files become ineffective.

"Non-Political Detention"

*A Person Who "Went Through The Back Door" and
Became a "Violator of Law and Order"*

When the Cultural Revolution started in 1966, city dwellers deemed to belong to the five black categories were sent to the countryside, along with their families. Many who had undergone reform-through-labor or detention were also moved to the countryside. Che Shaowen had never worn a five categories hat, but he had undergone reform-through-labor. It didn't help that he was unemployed, so he too was sent to the countryside.

Che Shaowen was born in 1916. The exact date of his rustication is unclear. It was probably around 1969, and he would have been well past his prime and not fit for manual work. He also suffered numerous illnesses. He had been committed to reform-through-labor in 1960, but was sent back on medical parole. He struggled to carry out even a moderate workload, let alone physically demanding farm work.

Che's file had been transferred from his commune to the county authorities in March 1970. The timing was odd. The spring of 1970 was a critical juncture, when people were "preparing for war," "digging deep tunnels, piling up stores of grain," and "preparing against natural disasters." Large cities had begun conducting evacuations in readiness for war, and cadres and staff were being dispersed to the countryside or inland. It was unusual that Che's file should have been brought from the countryside to the city at such a time.

After its transfer to the countryside, no new information had been added to Che's file and it was returned to the police station in C Municipality in its original state. Had Che also been returned to the same police station, there would have been some sort of record of his activities or state of mind. That was also odd.

Che, whose health was already failing, probably died soon after being sent to the countryside. Perhaps there was not enough time for his commune to keep a record on him, so the file was returned untouched. As he was no longer alive, the county's public security authorities took their time in processing his file. The file was transferred back to the public security authorities in Che's city of origin. Eventually, it was returned to the police station near his original address. Once the police received the file, they must have left it together with the other closed files, apparently never to see the light of day again.

How did someone in poor health end up being sent to the countryside in the first place? Being sickly and on a meager income, he must have struggled to support his family. What became of his family after he was sent away? Below is some information from Che's file that helps shed light on these questions.

STUDYING AT THE CADRE SCHOOL

Che Shaowen's record at the C Municipality cadre school dated back to July 1951. The application form said he was 35 years old, had completed junior high, was married, and was a rice merchant with skills and experiences in the grain trade. Between 1935 and 1950, he had worked as an apprentice and then as a clerk in a grain store. After becoming unemployed in 1950, he did some voluntary work around his neighborhood. There were eight people in his household, including his mother, wife, two younger sisters, and two children. After Che lost his job, the whole family lived off the income of one of the younger sisters, who worked in a government organization. Her monthly salary, worth about eighty-five kilos of rice, was occasionally supplemented by income from two of Che's older sisters.[1]

Che scored a "B" in his interview, and an "F" in his physical examination. Che said in his application form that (1) he had worked as a clerk and completed junior high; (2) his level of awareness was average, and he was doing voluntary work; (3) he was born into a merchant family, whose business had closed down, and he was supported by the wages of his sister and brother-in-law; (4) and he would require financial assistance during schooling.[2] The cadre school issued a letter of acceptance. Che was assigned to Unit 2, Squad 5.

Che put a lot of effort in getting into cadre school for one and only one reason—to gain employment. On his first day, when he saw the slogan on the wall ("Welcome new schoolmates joining our big revolutionary family"), he was skeptical. He thought: "I came to this school to learn about trade, and when I graduate I will work in a state-owned company and earn a wage to support my family. I'm not joining the army, so what does it have to do with joining a big revolutionary family?"[3] When he was asked to write an autobiography a few days after joining the school, he admitted that his main motivation was to get a living.

He said he had graduated from junior high in wartime and never had a steady job. After 1950, he was again unemployed, and the family relied on his younger sister's income, with the help of two older sisters (who had already left home). He decided to try a state-owned enterprise as a last resort. During the second half of 1950, he joined some neighborhood reading groups and did voluntary work. A year later, he obtained a letter of recommendation from his district and got the chance to apply for cadre school. He intended to get through the four months of study, graduate, and then find a job in a state-owned enterprise with the cadre school's help.

Che was unfamiliar with the new political jargon. After attending political classes, he came to understand that autobiographies must incorporate political elements. He therefore added a few sentences at the end of his autobiography. He said: "My sole purpose in joining the cadre school was my own survival, I had not thought about learning for the sake of the people. After several days' study I realized that in the past the U.S. imperialists cloaked themselves in religion in order to anesthetize Chinese youths, and that reaction and nonresistance have created the environment in which I find myself today, covered with stains. I must reform my ideology and learn for the sake of the people—only then will I avoid mistakes."[4]

Che's autobiography shows that he had very little political awareness when he first joined cadre school. A week later, he had scarcely changed:

Question: What kind of people did you admire in the past? What kind of books did you read? What ideology did you follow?

Answer: I admired Ye X and Chen X (grain-store bosses in C Municipality); I liked reading classical novels, including *Romance of the Three Kingdoms*, *Outlaws of the Marsh*, and *The Three Knights-Errant*; I espoused individualism.

Q: What was your life plan?

A: My plan was to be a good apprentice, and to open a small grain store.

Q: What are your views on the Soviet Union, the Chinese Communist Party, the Kuomintang and Chiang Kai-shek, and American imperialism?

A: I don't know much about the Soviet Union, only that during the war against Japan they gave Chiang Kai-shek planes and anti-aircraft guns and fought against the Japanese. As to why they assisted the Chinese Communist Party after the victory against the Japanese, leading to internal conflicts within China, I don't know. I think the Chinese Communist Party cares more about seizing power and exacting personal revenge. Chiang Kai-shek is not a bad person, but his subordinates are corrupt evildoers. As for the American imperialists, they are a civilized country, industrially advanced. They produce high quality goods and can help China develop its education. Their president is elected by the people once every five years.

Q: What were your views on the revolution in the past? Why is revolution necessary? Is revolution good? What is your attitude toward revolution?

A: Revolution is fighting for power, revolting for the sake of personal vengeance is no good. It has sent commodity prices through the roof, and it's impossible to do business.

Q: What have been the changes in your ideology from Liberation until now?

A: The army does not bother the people, and it returns what it borrows. The soldiers help the peasants with harvesting and building dams. When food is scarce and there is little grain for sale, the Central Committee brings out its rice stock to restore the market and provides relief for the people. In wintertime, warm clothes are distributed to the poor; roads and irrigation works are maintained; children of the needy can go to school for free.

Q: Since you joined the school, which shortcomings—in terms of ideology, lifestyle, approach, and attitude to learning—have you identified?

A: I wish to learn new terminologies and sort out my livelihood, I'm not used to living in a group, I can be disorganized and out of touch with reality, sometimes I have strange thoughts regarding family life.

Q: What is your understanding of, and attitude toward, the Korean War?

A: We must not let America occupy our territory. Korea is our close neighbor and our gateway, we must not let thieves in to rob us. We cannot stand by and watch a repeat of Japan's Nanjing Massacre [in 1937], and let the American imperialists seize Chinese resources and money. Helping the Koreans fight the Americans was the right decision.

Q: What is your understanding of, and attitude toward, land reform?

A: Under land reform, every peasant gets land and is fed, so they can lead stable lives. Agricultural production grows, and industry develops. China doesn't have to buy food from other countries, we can be stronger and more prosperous.[5]

After two weeks, Che's political awareness had risen. An exam on political subjects was held after the completion of the course. There were three questions: (1) Why do we say that the Kuomintang counter-revolutionaries are general representatives of the three big enemies? (2) Why is it necessary for the working class, not the intellectuals, to lead the revolution? (3) What is the nature of the present phase of the Chinese revolution, and how does it differ from the old democratic revolution and socialist revolution?

Judging from Che's answers, he had familiarized himself with the language of the regime. His response to the first question extended to more than six hundred characters. He clarified the relationship between the Kuomintang counter-revolutionaries and imperialism and discussed the Kuomintang and the feudal landlord class. Although he missed out on the relationship between the Kuomintang and bureaucratic capitalism, the two points he made were consistent with the new regime's views.

In response to the second and third questions, he was also able to reproduce what he had learned in class and reports. He was able to recite all the arguments for why the Chinese revolution must be led by the working class and to explain why China was not in a position to go over immediately to socialism. Che's responses were approved, and he scored four out of five.[6]

At the end of the second part of the course, each student had to say what he had learned. By now, Che knew how to combine his past sufferings with his love for the new society:

When the Japanese imperialists came, my family fled to Liuhezhen. Following my father's death, my elder brother took on the burden of supporting the family. He bought cigarettes and alcohol from Liuhezhen and re-sold them at Puqiao. The feudal chiefs and traitors Zhang Fang and Ye Cheng were county heads and lapdogs of the Japanese. One day, some of their underlings and their Japanese associates were returning from duck hunting when they ran into my brother. They said that my brother had not paid tax and that his goods were of dubious origin. They took him to the county headquarters and detained him for two nights. He was released, but his cigarettes and alcohol were confiscated. He travelled overnight and returned to Liuhezhen, blood dripping from his mouth. He continued to vomit blood for ten days. My family could no longer survive in the countryside, and had to return to C Municipality. After Liberation, when three hundred or so people were suppressed, I saw that the list of the accused included Ye Cheng, and I rejoiced. He's the one who confiscated my brother's goods, and he was the cause of the illness from which my brother died. I thought at the time that only the People's Liberation Army could avenge my brother. That was my turning point. During the second half of the course, we learned from Director He that when the Japanese imperialists invaded China they got military supplies from the British and American imperialists. The imperialists took away China's agricultural resources and handed back small favors like opening schools and spreading religion to lull Chinese youths into acquiescence. I now realize that at school I had been infected with lies fed by the imperialists, through education and religion, which made me ignorant and backward.[7]

Four months later, Che was already able to use the new regime's language to criticize his background and ideology. He filled out half a dozen forms, and wrote essays on "ideological examination," "the process of changing ideology," and other forms of self-criticism:

My father co-owned a rice shop with a friend, and my elder brother opened a rice shop after finishing his apprenticeship. The shops were able to support the family's daily needs and my education. We had no other income, but we lived comfortably. Father used to say, "You must study hard, so that in future you can manage a shop. I won't be able to support you forever. If you don't study well, you will only be able to work for someone else and never be your own boss." I concentrated on my studies, so that I could open a shop and be the boss.

I attended a Christian primary school, and I was influenced by the American imperialist priests. I thought Jesus was a real God, and everything in the world was ordained by God. When the Japanese imperialists invaded northeastern China after the Mukden Incident in 1931, schools organized demonstrations in protest, but my school did not take part. The priests told us that the northeasterners did not believe in God, and this was God's punishment. I thought this was true, so I used to go out with the priests to preach. I received sweets and toys from the priests. I was envious of the Western houses they lived in, the suits and leather shoes they wore, and the milk and bread they ate. To me these were luxuries, and I wanted to get closer to the priests so that I too could one day work for the mission and enjoy the same luxuries.

When I became an apprentice, I didn't like to hear my father going on about how our family had been merchants for generations and that doing business was in our nature. After visiting the grain store, I saw that for the bosses every meal was a feast and that they got their apprentices to do everything on their behalf. I began to appreciate what my father had said. From then on, I worked hard and tried to learn from the boss.

My family and my experience in the grain store instilled in me from an early age the belief that study was the only way to make money, and helping others got you nowhere. Only bosses had a future. I had abandoned my principles and become a loyal lapdog of the American imperialists. After the stories of the Sacred Heart Orphanage and Cardinal Antonio Riberi came to light, I began to see the true colors of the religion of the imperialists. They were trying to pass off dog meat as lamb, killing off Chinese children and paralyzing Chinese youth, turning them into their lapdogs. I learned that China had been invaded by foreign imperialists over one hundred or so years and become a semi-colony. I see the true nature of imperialism. I now know that the world is created by the working people. There is no such thing as God, or Jesus. In the face of this imperialist concoction, I declare that I will no longer be deceived by you.[8]

He carried out a detailed self-examination of how his ideology had changed over time:

When the Japanese were defeated, I returned to C Municipality to work in the grain store, and business flourished. I thought, had it not been for Chiang defeating the Japanese imperialists, how could we have prospered? I admired the Kuomintang and thought Chiang Kai-shek was wonderful. He made friends with the rich Americans, that was really something. When the Kuomintang troops were taking back the northeast, the reactionary *Central Daily* reported that the Communist Party were blocking the troops and allowing the Soviet Union to remove machinery and take it to Russia. I detested the Communist Party. Not only did it not resist the Japanese, it interfered with the Kuomintang troops taking back the northeast and allowed the

Soviet Union to take away machinery. It was selling out China. As for the Soviets, they were just like the Japanese, looting our wealth and betraying our trust, unlike the United States, which helped us defeat the Japanese imperialists. The United States was a real friend. During the Huaihai campaign, the Kuomintang said that the Communists were murderous arsonists, press-ganging able-bodied men into the army left, right, and center. The men would become soldiers, and the women would serve as auxiliaries. I bought into these lies. When C Municipality collapsed into the turmoil of war, I became anxious. I advised my younger sister to flee to Taiwan, so that she would not have to serve as a women's auxiliary. When C Municipality was liberated, I saw that although the Communist troops weren't well-dressed, they were disciplined. They were also approachable, unlike the Kuomintang army. Yet I still had my doubts: maybe it's because the Communists have just arrived and are trying to win people over. The grain store closed down and I became unemployed. I thought the government was no longer issuing licenses and wouldn't let us do business. Did that mean that a salary earner like me would never get to run his own business? Under the Kuomintang, you could open a shop and run a business. The Communist Party was making it hard for us poor folk. Due to this conflict of interest, I again became resentful of the Communist Party. I told friends that the Communist Party used the carrot and stick, and that it was impossible to do business under them. Without the Kuomintang we would suffer. When the time for Zhenfan came, I saw it as the start of the Communist Party taking revenge. I thought their methods were diabolical, and saw no end in sight. One day 376 people were suppressed, and I was frightened to death. Once I saw the list of accused, however, my mood lifted. The traitor Ye Cheng was on it. That made me very happy. The memory of him beating my brother until he spat out blood flooded back. Under the Kuomintang reactionaries, I had reported Ye twice, but to no avail. But the Communist Party avenged my brother, which exceeded my expectation. I knew that the Communist Party would need evidence to execute someone, but I also thought that among 376 people there must have been at least one person who was innocent. After witnessing a meeting at which a local tyrant was executed, I gained a better understanding and realized that suppression could never lead to wrongful conviction of an innocent person. When the government released the first batch of counter-revolutionaries, it showed that they killed people only when they had evidence, unlike the Kuomintang, who killed indiscriminately. Two years of rebuilding C Municipality—roads, bridges, river channels, etc.—showed that the Communist Party acts in the interest of the people. The textbooks about reconstructing the Chinese economy introduced me to the ideas of 'giving consideration to both public and private interests' and 'benefitting both labor and capital.' This made me realize that my old business was wrong and illegal. The government looks out for the interests of individuals and prevents profiteers from controlling the market. The government looks after the employees' interests, and the employees would not be exploited or sacked for no reason, as they used to be. From now on I must follow the Party, never cease learning, and reform my tainted ideology of greed and exploitation.[9]

POLITICAL EVALUATION

Studying at the cadre school was not simply a matter of imbibing four months of history and ideology, learning to write an autobiography, and getting a job in a state organization. It was essential to evaluate the political awareness and behavior of each student, so there would be no problems or hidden surprises further down the track.

There are several accounts of Che's political behavior at the cadre school. Not long after joining, he was deemed by the small group to be "unwilling to reveal his shortcomings, unwilling to accept criticism from others or to correct mistakes. He is vain but keeps up a pretense of amicability. He is nostalgic about the Chiang Kai-shek period. He is strongly committed to his family, which struggles to make ends meet. He is resentful of our Party."[10]

At the cadre school, each course ended with an evaluation by the small group. Soon after joining, Che was judged to be a "lower-middle member": he "was not active, liked to hang out with backwards elements, was eager to please, and was two-faced. He would say one thing in front of the cadres and another behind their backs. He didn't join in discussions, was reluctant to reveal his ideology, was not helpful, and was out of touch with reality."[11]

A summary of the courses, approved by the small group in December 1951, reflected the impression Che had given at the cadre school:

COURSES ONE AND TWO:

Able to comply with school rules. Not active. Behaved well during the first few days. Initially, he was worried about being laughed at, and was embarrassed about joining in. He had applied for the school out of concern for his family's livelihood. He had been unable to understand why, under the Japanese, no one lost their jobs and people lived quite comfortably, whereas after Liberation there was hardship. He urged smokers to switch from foreign to local cigarettes in order to 'save money to donate for making planes and guns.' He said: 'I am not happy about others criticizing me, and I am unwilling to discuss my weaknesses.' To some extent he resented our Party. He fell in with two backward elements. During the second review he adopted a false attitude. He laughed during the review in front of his classmates, and said privately that 'this way others won't take it so seriously.'

COURSE THREE:

Able to comply with school rules. Not active. Likes to hang out with a backward element, they play chess and leave school together during breaks. Two-faced, eager to please, says one thing in front of the cadres and another behind their backs. Only keen to help others when it's in front of the cadres. Timid in exposing problems. Does not help classmates. Wary of the Organization. His performance is falling behind. Takes his studies seriously, and didn't do badly in his theory test. Had some problems and conflicts with his class leader.

COURSE FOUR:

Since X was transferred to another group, Che has had fewer chances to contact him. He has become closer to backward elements and drinks with them, instead of spending time with progressive students. He quarrels with people over trivial matters. But he has studied hard, and spends hours each day copying notes. He respects hygiene in the dormitory. He does not reveal his thinking, and he said at the general discussion session following the ideology review that 'I no longer have any ideological baggage.' He said that the economic policy of New Democracy is to expropriate the capitalists.

IDEOLOGICAL SUMMARY:

Before conducting the ideological summary, he falsely claimed that 'I no longer have any baggage.' After being criticized by cadres, he revealed that he had once associated with the Green Gang, and that he was still wary of the Organization. In one-on-one conversations he expressed his opposition to the backward elements, and said only good things about the small group. He likes promoting his own interests. He does not reveal his thinking and thinks a lot about his chances of employment.[12]

The small group was clearly dissatisfied with Che's political behavior, and began to pay greater attention to his historical problems.

In November, the cadre school began investigating its students' historical problems by making enquiries at police stations and workplaces. An official letter read:

X, a student at our school, is a resident of your District. We are writing to you as we have identified certain historical ambiguities concerning this individual, and we are unable to determine his political affiliation. Please assist in collecting information in all regards (while ensuring that this is done discreetly so as not to alert the individual or his family or associates), to help us gain an understanding of his political affiliation, attitude, motivating factors, etc., for the benefit of his education and reform. Each student only studies with us for a short while, and upon graduation is allocated to work, depending on his or her individual attributes and operational requirements, so we request that the material be sent within one week. If there are difficulties in ascertaining the information, please notify us urgently, so we can get the information through other channels.[13]

The school wanted to know whether Che had been a traitor during the Japanese occupation, and why he had "not exposed" anyone during Zhenfan even though one of his sisters had been a Kuomintang Youth League member and her husband a defense department employee during the occupation who'd later gone to Taiwan (Che had claimed that he had "gone missing"). The investigation raised four questions: (1) Has Che belonged to any reactionary organization? (2) What did he do during the Japanese occupation? (3) What contacts did he have during the Japanese occupation and since Liberation? Did he have any relations with reactionary elements, and if so, what? (4) What was his relationship with Fang X, Li X, and Yang X (arrested as counter-revolutionaries)?[14]

These questions stemmed from Che's own admissions in late 1951. The admissions were made in response to repeated criticism and exhortation by Che's supervisor and classmates.

For example, Che admitted that he became an apprentice in August 1933 and, worried about losing his job and eager to find "lifelong backing," had followed Chen, an employer in the rice trade, as his master, and joined the Green Gang.

He admitted that during Zhenfan in 1950 he heard that one of his old neighbors, Li, had been arrested for having fought against the Communists. He was shocked. Green-Red Gang member or not, "Li was a good guy," and a skilled railway man. Che thought that the Communist Party needed skilled people, and "people like Li could have been reformed rather than executed." He felt it was "such a shame."

Che admitted that an uncle he had never previously met approached his family for help during Land Reform. Land Reform was about to start in this uncle's village, and he wanted Che's family to move there, so he would have a big enough household to keep his land. The uncle promised Che financial support to start a business. Che agreed, but it turned out that the uncle could not register Che's family, so the arrangement fell through. Che felt "very disappointed."

In the autumn of 1950, Che met a grain merchant, Yang, from another province. Yang was a landlord, who had fled to C Municipality with his family following Land Reform and was struggling to make ends meet. Che failed to expose Yang and even gave him five buckets of rice. He told Yang that "when Chiang Kai-shek returns, all the land will belong to you again." Yang was arrested and sent back to his village. When Che heard the news, he thought that "the land has already been taken away from him, so why break his family apart?" Che "hated the government for being too cruel."[15]

In December 1951, Che completed his last ideological summary at the cadre school. The small group, the squad, and the unit conducted their evaluations of his performance.

Che had been repeatedly questioned in the "ideological summary" phase about his activities during the Japanese occupation, so he admitted a brush with corruption during this time:

> When the grain store closed for business in August 1937, my family took refuge in Liuhezhen. Father fell ill and passed away. In 1939, I returned to C Municipality to work in the grain store. In 1941, the Japanese started to control the distribution of grain, so there was hardly any business and I was fired. My brother died after vomiting blood, so life was hard. In 1942, an uncle's neighbor helped me get work with the Japanese. Initially I worked down a mine, for about four months. I then managed to get transferred to a cooperative, looking after an agricultural plantation. The director was a Japanese. I sold produce and kept the books. My monthly salary was two *dan*

of rice. I sold it on the market and shared the proceeds with other employees. I managed to put some money aside. I returned to C Municipality to get married. The Japanese director gave me 100 yuan, I was grateful. From then on I worked even harder. After getting married, I relocated my mother, younger sister, wife, and nephew to X, to save on living expenses. The town flooded and my dormitory was under water. I went to stay at the office, two *li* from the mine. Du X said to me: "The [Communist] New Fourth Army on the opposite bank are not so bad. I'll take you across to check them out." Then Du and I went over. A member of the New Fourth Army cooperative asked how we managed the books of our cooperative. I explained. We spent two hours there, and he invited me to visit again. The goods sold by our cooperative were all made in S City and M City. The Japanese director took me along when he went to purchase supplies. Every time we went to a Chinese shop, he asked me to discuss falsifying the receipts to make the goods appear more expensive. He gave me money and asked me not to tell anyone, and promised to take me on the next shopping trip. On one occasion, when the company was running low on wood and charcoal, he asked me to buy some for him. The area occupied by the New Fourth Army did not accept banknotes of the puppet regime, so I arranged for people to bring over some fabric, handkerchiefs, socks, and shoes to exchange for wood and charcoal. I made some money from the deal. The Japanese director was good to me. As long as I saved, I would have enough to start a business even if they fired me.

After the victory over Japan in 1945, I arranged for my family to relocate back to C Municipality. I stayed behind to tidy up the books and take stock. It was no longer possible to purchase things with banknotes of the puppet regime, and the merchants had stacked away their goods. The company was low on rice, and we could only obtain rice in exchange for the salt we kept at the cooperative. I discussed the future with two colleagues: "Now that Japan has been defeated, what if the Kuomintang come back? That won't bode well for us. If we can't find jobs, how will we survive?" We decided to swap the remaining salt for ten *dan* (five hundred kilograms) of rice, and fled to C Municipality by boat.

The old society raised me to be money-hungry. I became a lapdog of the Japanese, pandering to their whims and colluding with them for personal benefit. I exploited the blood and sweat of the working masses for my personal enrichment. I harmed the interests of my people and my country. I swear to toil to atone for my sins.[16]

The small group had seventeen students. Its evaluation reports had to be countersigned and sealed by the relevant individuals, so the comments were largely positive. Che's evaluation highlighted his strengths: he was "dedicated to labor, undertakes regular cleaning," "complies with dormitory rules and school rules, does not arrive late or leave early," "studies hard, as reflected in his notes, written documents, and questions," "upright in his behavior, not disorganized or undisciplined," and "responsible and able to complete the tasks given by the Organization in a timely manner." As for his weaknesses, he was "reserved in his thinking," "unable to engage in criticism and self-criticism," "unable to apply theories to practice," "not an enthusiastic contributor to classroom discussions," "only helps fellow students in some respects," "impatient," and "individualistic in his study style."

Comments by the squad mirrored those of the small group: Che was "able to comply with dormitory rules, dedicated to labor, and responsible in his work," but "unable to expand or reveal his thinking, unable to get close to the Organization, reluctant to report relevant circumstances, and unable to engage in criticism and self-criticism."[17]

The closed-door evaluation was another matter. The squad made a separate evaluation of Che's historical problems, without his knowledge:

> As an apprentice at the grain store, he joined the Green Gang and took advantage of its support. During the Japanese occupation he worked in a cooperative and earned the trust of the Japanese devils. He was in close contact with traitors, and was one himself. After Liberation, his lifestyle declined as a result of unemployment, and he dreamed of a return of the Kuomintang. He harbored a fugitive landlord, hoping that once the Kuomintang came back he could rely on him to get into the grain trade. Since joining the cadre school, he has been backward in his behavior, suspicious and apprehensive of the Organization, and reluctant to reveal his thinking. He has a hazy political understanding. He fantasizes about the Kuomintang and is nostalgic about his comfortable, 'prestigious' lifestyle under the Japanese. He has not fully explained his historical problems during the Japanese occupation.[18]

The comment about Che's "close contact with traitors" came from reports by public security officers. They reported that Che had had run a grain store before the war. During the Japanese occupation, Che was sent by his brother to a workers' cooperative run by the Japanese. He was "closely connected with the traitor network, and knew many traitors." After victory, he returned to work in the grain store. After Liberation, grain sales came under state control and he lost his job. "As for his participation in the [reactionary] Yellow Union and reactionary political groups, as yet we do not have a full understanding."[19]

Che's having joined a gang, sought out a master, and helped Yang (a fugitive landlord and a relative) was corroborated by the investigation. Che's sister and nephew confirmed that he "had joined the Green Gang," and sought out Chen, a director in the ice industry, as a "teacher."[20] However, there was no documentary evidence that Che had "close contact with traitors," or that after joining the cadre school he "fantasized about the Kuomintang and was nostalgic about his comfortable, 'prestigious' lifestyle under the Japanese." The small group concluded that Che's "involvement with the Green Gang has been explained," but his "history during the Japanese occupation remains unclear." Referring to his encounter with the New Fourth Army, the small group expressed the view that "he may have engaged in actions detrimental to the interests of the people and the revolution, and been a traitor."[21]

This appraisal caused Che trouble later on. He had joined the Green Gang and harbored a fugitive landlord, and was possibly a traitor. Even more troubling were his current ideological shortcomings. The appraisal had linked Che's attitude after 1949 (revealed through admissions made during his self-examination) with his backward behavior at the school, and concluded that he continued to "fantasize about the Kuomintang" and "reminisce about the Japanese occupation." This stopped Che getting a job and earning the trust of his workplace.

NEAR DISMISSAL

In December 1951, Che was assigned to work as a clerk in a local company. When his file reached his new workplace, the Three Antis movement was in full swing and the Five Antis movement was gathering pace. Che was immediately on the radar of his new workplace. He was assigned to the company as a cadre, so there should have been no probation requirement. However, his paperwork said he was "on probation." An external investigation listed Che's past as a traitor or foreign agent.[22]

Che was assigned to the copper products section to look after dispatch. The section reported that he was careless and unreceptive to criticism. Dispatches were often late, and fifteen kilos of copper plate went missing. When the leaders criticized him and urged him to take more care with public property, he went on a rant behind their backs: "So what if fifteen kilos of copper went missing? Even if I sold three wives I wouldn't have enough to pay it back!" He made excuses, such as problems with the scale. He said the same scale was used to weigh different types of copper, including copper plate. Why did the scale always give a uniform weight in the case of other types of copper, but not for copper plate? Che was transferred to work in a warehouse and reported for forming dubious social networks. He was said to be familiar with many locals, and had meetings with the owners of rice stores—he "acted sneakily" and "stayed out until late at night." On one occasion when the director made a random check, he was absent from his post.[23]

By then, the Three Antis movement had started "hitting tigers," and many people were categorized as small or big "tigers" and subjected to intense struggles. One of Che's brothers-in-law worked at the hospital and had been a member of the Kuomintang. He was ousted during this movement, but denied corruption and committed suicide. Another brother-in-law had worked in the Kuomintang's defense department and fled to Taiwan. These family histories made things even worse for Che.

Apart from problems with Che's past and his social networks, his personality became an issue. He admitted that he had made many mistakes in the past, and that during class struggles he was never able to put aside his connections. Even though he knew that his brother-in-law's suicide was an act of "resistance to the

Three Antis movement and refusal to reform," he admitted that "when my sister became sad I did not try to make her understand the policy, and I sympathized with her." Instead, he should have informed the Organization at unit meetings. But because of his petty-bourgeois mentality and vanity, he was unwilling to do so. He admitted that he was often headstrong, "thinking that none of my comrades' suggestions were as good as my own. I would sulk and lose interest if they ignored my suggestions." When he met with the slightest rebuff, he "felt dejected and lost the urge to carry on." He worked hard on tasks he liked, but otherwise acted irresponsibly.[24]

By June 1952, the Three Antis movement had ended, and Che filled out a form summing up the movement. For his job title he still wrote "clerk," and was positive in his self-evaluation. He said he was "hard working, always ready to work, able to take the lead, not self-centered," "planned ahead, and was able to adapt." He was "engaged politically, and keen to progress." His shortcomings included "not taking a strong enough stand, not yet being able to draw a clear line with the enemy on some issues," "no strong sense of team, subjective and unable to accept feedback from comrades," "unable to see tasks through to the end, blowing hot and cold," "not political enough, infected with petty-bourgeois vanity, unable to criticize others and myself," etc.[25]

Those responsible for investigating Che said they had not uncovered any problems: "From Che's history, there seems to be no problem. From the material we have gathered and discussions with him, he was dishonest in discussions, and he might have been a traitor."[26]

Che was still listed as "on probation." At the end of his probation, his manager reported that he was not up to standard, and he was put on the list of "non-staff."

Che was among those to be dismissed. An assessment of his "daily work performance" contained numerous comments—they exceeded the allocated column and required a half-page attachment. The gist was that he had complex social networks, performed poorly at work, and should be "sent for further political study or expelled." The Bureau of Commerce and Industry recommended that Che be "given some allowance and sent home."[27] Higher authorities approved the recommendation and asked Che's company to provide him with an "application form for staff requesting discharge." Che's company had given the following explanation for his discharge: "This individual was a member of the Green Gang. While working at the company warehouse he often returned home after midnight. He is not hardworking or responsible. When items went missing, he made excuses. The leadership and his colleagues have urged him to pay more attention. He ranted behind their backs."[28]

After the Three Antis and Five Antis movements, industrial and commercial enterprises shut down in large numbers and unemployment increased greatly. Party and government leaders demanded an all-out effort to restore and expand production in order to curb unemployment. This was the context in which the "application form for staff requesting discharge" was issued to Che. After going to such lengths to get a job, Che was not going to give up without a fight. Despite efforts to persuade him, he refused to fill out the form. The company retreated. Che was taken off probation and given a permanent position. After this, he became much more careful, and did his best to be humble and keep his temper. He worked diligently and avoided further trouble. Within three years, the opinion of Che had changed. Although he still "had complex social connections and during the Japanese occupation was a traitor . . . whose traitorous activities must be further investigated," he was "hard-working with a positive approach and the ability to endure hardship." However, he still "waxed hot and cold, had a low level of awareness and changed his tunes depending on who he was talking with." Overall he was categorized as a "third-category good person" with a dubious history.[29]

In those days, it was common practice for workers in government enterprises to take advantage of their positions, at least to some extent. Che was no exception, particularly since his large family lived in poverty. He started to earn a salary in 1952, but his and his sisters' combined income could barely sustain the family. Later, when the sisters moved out, Che's wife found casual work that paid too little to maintain a family of six or seven. Life became even harder. Every time Che had to travel for his unit, he tried to spend less than the budget and pocketed the difference. According to his admission years later, between 1953 and 1957 he made an extra 11 yuan in this way:

> Business trip, July 1953—the buses weren't operating, so I had to walk. When I claimed reimbursement, I included 50 cents in travel expenses.
> Business trip, July 1954—I spent virtually nothing on food as I was hosted by friends. Yet I claimed 60 cents in meal expenses.
> Business trip, September 1954—the trip lasted several days, I claimed an extra 4.2 yuan in expenses.
> Business trip, September 1955—the trip lasted three days. I ate steamed buns and spent little on food. I claimed the usual meal expenses, an extra 2.1 yuan.
> October 1955: I went to a conference. I had no meal, but I claimed 70 cents.
> November 1955: I went to a conference. The meal allowance was generous. I claimed an extra 2 yuan.[30]

CLEARED OF SUSPICION

In early 1955, the movement to examine cadre history and Sufan started across the country. As Che had complex social connections and was suspected of having been a traitor, he became a target.

In March, after having been spoken to several times by the five-person group and his work unit, Che produced more detailed confessions.

The investigation dug deeper. Had Che been a traitor? Anyone who might have known Che in X Town was contacted, but nobody could provide concrete details—just a few blurred recollections. Someone knew "he had got rice and oil from the welfare agency, and had worked in the butcher's, barber's, and tofu shops, all signs of corruption. I don't know any more details."[31]

Some said that most people Che interacted with at the mineral company were mine workers. They could not remember the details of Che's work at the cooperative, let alone his involvement in purchasing goods. "I seem to remember Che as a Green Gang member and a follower of the town police chief."[32]

Some said that they had worked with Che and gone gambling with him. Che had asked the police chief to be his godfather. The police often bought things from him. As to whether Che had engaged in other activities with the police chief, the respondent had no idea.[33]

The investigation extended to Che's encounter with the New Fourth Army. The Organization had urged Che to come clean, and he had written detailed confessions, but none had mentioned his visit to the New Fourth Army. This led the five-person group to question his honesty. Had he spied on the New Fourth Amy? The investigation probed whether he visited the New Fourth Army base "under particular instructions or circumstances," had he "been a spy for the Japanese," or had he "committed other sins, etc."[34]

The investigating officer reported that "discussions with Du X revealed that Che was popular, everyone knew his name, but Du was not aware of his having joined any reactionary groups. Che might have kowtowed to the police chief once (Du could not be sure). As for the trip across the river to the New Fourth Army, Du had been there himself, and was certain that Che had not crossed the river with him. There were no gangs or organizations at the mine."

The officer went to talk to Che. Che admitted that he had asked the police chief to take him under his wing. However, despite prompting, Che was unable to recall visiting the New Fourth Army. He only recalled the incident after the investigating officer brought up Che's revelation at the cadre school. Che said that he had lied about it "to gain the trust of the Organization."[35] He added an amendment admitting he had lied. This was because he "did not have a high awareness, and did not understand the Party well. I thought that telling lies would show my understanding of, and positive attitude toward, the New Fourth Army."[36]

The investigating officer issued the following recommendation:

(1) The information provided by Du and Wu (former colleagues) largely corresponded with Che's confession. There was no espionage and there were no reactionary organizations at the mine. Du was adamant that Che never crossed the river with him.

(2) Che has adopted a fairly honest attitude. He volunteered information about his involvement with the Green Gang, and admitted that he had not been loyal

enough to the Organization. He prepared statements swearing that he never crossed the river.

(3) Further investigation confirms that the above is likely to be true. I recommend that the suspicion be removed.[37]

Before a final verdict could be given, the movement to examine cadres' history began. The examination team continued the lines of enquiry followed by the cadre school and the police, and insisted on "the need to further clarify this employee's historical background during the Japanese occupation." A later investigation in March 1958 reached the same conclusion.[38]

The conclusions: although Che had worked in the mineral company, he had not participated in any political activity. The cooperative "was a Japanese enterprise run only by Japanese." As Che had arrived at the cooperative earlier than other employees, "the Japanese went to him more often, but it was only as part of a daily routine." "We recommend that Che be cleared of the suspicion of having being a traitor."[39]

Any remaining doubt had been quashed. The recommendation was approved by various authorities, unanimously agreeing that Che be cleared of suspicion. Che was officially notified of this verdict by the office of the examination of cadre history team.[40]

GETTING IN TROUBLE

This decision lightened Che's mental load. The political movements carried on, but none of the anti-rightist movements between 1957 and 1958 affected him. After the start of the Great Leap Forward, the "plant the red flag, pull out the white flag" movement and the rectification movement also bypassed him. By then he was working as a clerk in the wholesale department of a local company. He had accumulated years of experience in the agricultural trade, and was capable and hardworking.[41] He was a highly valued worker and part of the company's backbone force. However, he was still unable to shake off bad habits. In 1958, in an ideological summary, he admitted that he had "never reported his thinking to the Party." This was partly due to vanity and partly because he felt, being a member of neither the Party nor the Youth League, that he had no right to criticize comrades, and he wanted to avoid retribution. He worried that the Party would not believe him, and that by expressing opinions he would only invite trouble: "I always thought that if I criticized others, others would criticize me in return. I always appeared amicable. Even when I noticed someone doing the wrong thing, I might say something, but if he argued back, I would retreat. I am unable to stick up for my principles, for fear of offending others."[42]

For Che, born into a family of small merchants, life had always been about making money. He saw everything through a business lens—was it cost-effective and profitable? He was also like this in his public life. During the Great Leap

Forward, the whole city was mobilized to produce steel and iron, but Che could not stand seeing iron gates and pots being destroyed to make pig iron. He thought it a waste, but he did not dare say anything. The company repeatedly called for "bulk purchase and bulk sale" of goods. Being in charge of operations, Che was "worried about getting into trouble for overstocking, and would rather be out of stock than overstocked," and was "only concerned about profits." So he ignored targets set by the leadership. As a result, throughout this tumultuous movement, Che did some things right but also messed some things up. Che had no choice but to publicly examine himself. He might not have agreed deep down, but on the surface he criticized himself for "stressing the business side and overlooking the political side," and for "causing loss to the Party."[43]

Che continued to approach his work in the manner of an old-style merchant, networking, wheeling and dealing, and exchanging small favors. It did not occur to him that this would land him in hot water. In May 1960, the Central Committee launched the Three Antis movement in rural areas. It ordered a review of grassroots cadres in rural areas and of cadres in the trade sector. People who had "taken small advantages, misappropriated public funds and engaged in corruption on a small scale, or erred on the side of being overly bureaucratic" were to be educated and saved; "seriously corrupt, wasteful, and bureaucratic" cadres were to be "struggled against resolutely and given the necessary punishment. The minority whose mistakes are severe and who are detested by the people must be sacked (and, in the case of Party members, expelled from the Party) and criminally prosecuted."[44]

For the whole of May Che was ill in hospital. On his return, he was still unable to devote himself 100 percent to his job. The Three Antis movement was in full swing: staff were mobilized, views were aired, reviews were commissioned, and symposiums, debates, and exhibitions were held. Everything was targeted on corruption and waste.

In June, Che was reported by a Party member in the canteen: "He goes through the back door and sells goods unavailable on the market to friends and relatives, at wholesale prices." "If any of his acquaintances want something, he always helps. In return, he gets food, and can buy other things as well."[45]

Many of the company's problems were exposed during the Three Antis movement, including dealing through the back door, using company goods to buy favors from outsiders, and gaining personal advantage at public expense. These practices were widespread, so Che's behavior did not initially come to the attention of the rectification office.

However, a fortnight into the investigation, instances of Che's exchanging public goods for personal favors were uncovered. Personnel from other companies said Che set a high value on relationships—no matter what you requested, as long as it was within his control, he would do his best to get it for you. In return, the contacts offered him discounts and even gave him things for nothing.[46] One factory listed fourteen occasions on which Che had gone through the back door to obtain bones, oil, duck liver, and pork liver, totaling more than 20 yuan.[47]

The investigation gathered pace. By mid-August, a dozen people in the company had accused Che of violating supply policy, acting without authorization, using public goods to gain personal favors, and going through the back door. One reported that a buyer had been close to Che, and that when Che was sick he sent him food. This was because Che had helped procure goods for the buyer.

Another said that a clerk from a fruit and vegetable company had visited Che at home while he was sick. He gave Che tinned food, biscuits, and pork liver. He did this because Che had allocated 200 pots of preserved tofu, 2500 kilos of bean paste, and other sauces (which were in short supply) to this person's company.

Another said that Che went through the back door to sell goods at wholesale price to relatives and friends. X from the Central Restaurant often came to buy fruit and vegetables. Once Che sold him 5 kilos of bamboo shoots and .5 kilo of tree fungus, products unavailable on the market. Che sold them to him at wholesale price. In return, X opened the back door to Che. Che often went to X's restaurant to buy meat (which was rationed). He bought meat for others too, and didn't even have to use meat coupons or queue up.[48]

In late August, Che was isolated for examination, to explain his wrongdoing. He made a "frank confession." He had sold more than 1000 kilos of rice noodles, 100 kilos of pickles, 100 kilos of dried bamboo shoots, 75 kilos of dried fruit, and 150 kilos of fruit to food processing factories and distilleries. He had gone through the back door to help the canteen procure 10 kilos of pig trotters, 20 pairs of duck feet, 25 kilos of fresh fish, and 25 kilos of tofu dregs, helped the materials section procure an engine and 350 kilos of iron, helped the secretary buy 5 kilos of sweet sauce, helped colleagues buy 10 cartons of cigarettes, and helped the section head buy 7.5 kilos of salted fish. He had dined at several companies, and bought oil, fresh fish, pork, and cigarettes.[49]

He produced a further list of transactions carried out between 1959 and 1960 in which he had sold and procured goods through the back door. He admitted having dined out on a dozen occasions since 1960, as well as "taking advantages and accepting gifts," etc.[50]

On August 21, under instruction from the investigators, Che again went through his work connections, one by one. According to him, he had only engaged in corrupt behavior on three occasions, when he had misreported meals and travel expenses. Under repeated questioning, he admitted that when he was away purchasing stock in 1957, he had brought back a reimbursement of 20 yuan. No one from the finance department was around at the time, so he left the money in his office and eventually spent it.[51]

On August 22, he remembered that the Cultural Bureau had donated several theater tickets. He took two of the tickets and went along with another colleague.[52]

On August 23, he remembered that in 1954, 1955, and 1959 he had on three occasions over-reported his travel and meals expenses.[53]

On August 26 and 27, he confessed to six or seven instances over the years when he had over-reported travel expenses.[54]

On September 2, he admitted the unauthorized sale of 2500 kilos of rice noodles, 750 kilos of pickles, 750 kilos of bamboo shoots, 50 kilos of MSG, 500 kilos of dried fruit, 25 kilos of day lily, and 250 kilos of apples. In the first few months of 1960 alone, he dined out around twenty times with colleagues at others' expense. Sometimes there were enough diners to fill two tables. He had received gifts through his connections. The gifts included chickens, eggs, oil, sugar, cake, etc., to the value of more than 16 yuan. He admitted to other instances of over-reporting meals and travel expenses "totaling 45.10 yuan" starting in 1953.[55]

On September 8, the company issued a "report concerning Che's violations of law and order, corruption and bribery, which have caused great loss of public property": "Che has been consistently irresponsible. As warehouse clerk, he accepted goods without weighing them. When he was responsible for receiving copper delivery, the company lost fifteen kilos of copper plate in just one month. He complained and said strange things. He had been investigated by the Organization in 1952. In his current post, he is arrogant and boastful, and he reeks of old-style merchant ways. He claims that others do not know business as well he does, and he disrespects the section head. He acts without consulting others."

The report identified Che's three main problems.

(1)   He "seriously violated supply policies, and unlawfully supplied scarce goods." When in charge of goods allocation, he had "recklessly supplied various work units with controlled goods, up to a value of 160,600 yuan."

(2)   He "was irresponsible regarding work, and caused loss to public property." He "complied in public but not in private, created chaos, built up excess stock, and wasted capital, causing loss to public property." There were more than twenty charges pending against him, involving merchandise in transit for longer than expected and going off or going missing, to an "estimated value of 61,469 yuan."

(3)   He "abused his position to dine out for free, and engaged in corrupt transactions."

Factory A had given Che a chicken and thirty eggs, and Che had supplied the factory with 30 tons of soy sauce. Company B had given Che a kilo of white sugar and .5 kilo of pickles, and Che had given the factory 12.5 tons of sauce. Che had dined at work units around fifty times. His contacts "used Che's authorization to purchase things not only from Che's company but from other work units."[56]

Che's company submitted an "application seeking approval of the sanctions following the determination of the Three Antis case." It said: "Che Shaowen has performed poorly. He is irresponsible and backward in his ideology. He undermined the Party's supply policies. He usurped the Party's authority. Our preliminary view is therefore to arrest him and commence criminal proceedings in pursuit of a severe punishment."[57]

THE CASE FOR REFORM-THROUGH-LABOR

Che's bribes had not amounted to much. He had received small quantities of cake, pork liver, etc. and had over-reported allowances totaling around 40 yuan. The damage to goods in transit was not entirely Che's fault, and could be mitigated, so it was not a complete write-off. "Dining for free" and receiving discounted or free goods was hardly new—most employees did it. All the employees in Che's company had carried out self-reviews, and some had behaved more or less the same. So there were insufficient grounds for criminal charges. The authorities raised objections to the application and demanded more evidence.

Che's company submitted "supplementary material." In it Che was said to be "suspected of stealing and selling goods." He was greedy and dined out often. His lifestyle did not match his income. Given his numerous contacts and murky relationships, it was probable that he stole goods from work.[58]

However, suspicion alone was not enough. The "supplementary material" failed to convince the authorities to refer Che for prosecution. The investigators thought that the accusation of "stealing and selling the merchandises" was groundless.[59]

The investigators again went through Che's files, to see if they could find more evidence, but all they could come up with was 71.7 yuan, made up mostly of travel allowances, which might or might not have amounted to corruption. Actual corruption was confined to the 20 yuan in reimbursement that Che confessed to spending in 1957.[60]

News of Che's case spread across the company, and received a lot of publicity for a month or two. Many staff members were exposed on similar grounds. However, Che was unique as someone with complex relationships who allocated scarce goods without authorization and caused management chaos. As a deterrence, he had to be punished. As criminal prosecution was not an option, the company decided to request that he be "reformed through labor." This request was approved by the municipal Party committee.[61]

The final verdict on Che was that he had "violated law and order" on four main grounds: "(1) Violation of the government's supply policies and opening the back door" (examples were given, but not quantified). (2) Abusing his position, "getting food and drink, accepting bribes, and helping others to make arrangements for the receipt of expired goods, contrary to policy" (the loss was estimated at 116,000 yuan). (3) "An irresponsible attitude to work, publicly complying with orders but disobeying them in private, and causing serious loss to public property" (an

estimated loss of 61,469 yuan). (4) "Accepting bribes and engaging in corrupt practices" (61.60 yuan were thought to have been embezzled). Che was labeled a "violator of law and order"—not one of the four categories, but not a law-abiding citizen
either.[62] The People's Committee of C Municipality issued a decision to reform Che
through labor.[63]

Che was arrested by the Public Security Bureau and sent to a farm. Reform-
through-labor was not yet standardized. The system was organized in accordance
with a directive of the Central Committee from August 1955 ordering the "rounding
up those who cannot be criminally prosecuted but who are politically unsuitable
for the workplace and would contribute to unemployment if left in society" as well
as "counter-revolutionaries and other bad elements" "to perform manual labor for
the government and receive a wage."[64] But the system lacked legal procedures, and
in effect was a highly subjective and politicized form of punishment. The Central
Committee granted reform subjects certain political rights, but the authorities
responsible for administering reform decreed that "the period of reform and the
wage need not be specified."[65] When Che arrived at the farm in December 1960, no
one informed him of the length of his sentence, his wage, or his rights.

Having learned from experience, Che was anxious not to say or do the wrong
thing, and did not even ask about the length of his sentence. Despite his gastric
ulcer and heart disease, he threw himself into manual labor. He was rated as
"reforming well." Six months later, he was given a form requesting "approval" of
the length of the reform-through-labor to which he had been sentenced. It turned
out that reform-through-labor in Che's case involved first sending the reform subjects to a farm and then deciding on the term of the punishment after further
months of observation. The length of the sentence was determined less by the
seriousness of the initial offence than by the farms' evaluation of the reform subjects' behavior. Luckily Che had performed well, and the cadres' comments were
largely positive:

> This individual recognizes the seriousness of his errors and is grateful for the oppor-
> tunity to reform. Since his arrival at the farm, he has admitted his sins and obeys
> commands. He is committed to reform and never complains. He is the first to engage
> in manual labor. Once when he was told to cut one hundred kilos of reed, he cut 175
> kilos. Once when he was planting rice seedlings, the weather was cold and the others
> hesitated to get into the water, but he jumped in and motivated the whole class to do
> the same. When planting crops, he would inspect the quality of the work. He consults
> and cooperates with other members when undertaking production tasks. He abides
> by the farm rules, and has not attempted to escape. He is rated as "performing well."[66]

But these positive comments seem not to have influenced the decision on Che's
punishment, for they were never submitted to higher authorities. Che was given a

"fixed three-year" sentence, which was relatively severe. The three years started not from the time of Che's arrival at the farm in December 1960 but from October 1961, the date of sentencing.

MEDICAL PAROLE

Che Shaowen did not raise any objections to the decision. However, manual labor (in the harsh wintery conditions) exacerbated Che's gastric ulcer and his hemorrhoids, and he became unwell. According to the farm doctor, Che had a chronic heart condition and needed rest. He experienced palpitations, shortness of breath, and heavy sweating. His weight plummeted, and he began to exhibit other symptoms such as edema and anemia.

In June 1962, Che was sent to the city for a checkup and diagnosed with chronic pulmonary heart disease. The farm proposed that he be given medical parole,[67] and a request was submitted (Table 5).

This further demonstrated the irregularities in the system. As Che was no longer able to "perform manual work for the country," the farm was not obliged to care for him, and could return him to society whether or not he would "add to unemployment." To support its recommendation, the farm underlined the seriousness of Che's medical conditions but exaggerated the income of his family. In fact, Che's wife could only find casual work from time to time, and could earn 10 yuan a month at most (a far cry from the "around 30 yuan" claimed). It was also untrue that Che's two sisters could contribute 20 yuan a month. Only one was unmarried; the other scraped a bare living.

The request was approved in just two days. By July 6, Che was on his way back to C Municipality. The guards took him to the Public Security Bureau, along with a parole notice, and their mission was complete. The notice said:

> Che Shaowen, male, age 46, resident of 112 Xiang Chun Li 3rd Lane, City East District. As a result of corruption and theft, he was sent for reform through labor. He is medically paroled due to various illnesses. Enclosed is a dossier concerning Che. Please notify his family and parole officer, and allow his residency to be re-registered so he gets his quota of food and oil. Tell residents about this individual, and instruct him to abide by the law, undertake to reform, and regularly report on his thoughts. Thoroughly monitor his reform. In the event of a full recovery, or of further offending, contact Farm X.
>
> This individual was initially sent for three years of reform, starting in December 1960. He has already received his quota of food and oil for this month. He is a smoker.[68]

The notice was garbled. It mistook the time of Che's return for the time of his arrest and gave a wrong date for the start of his three-year reform.

TABLE 5

Name	Che Shaowen	Other name		Sex	Male	Age	46	Current work unit	X Farm
Category		Date received	Dec 20, 1960	Term	3 years			Length already served	5 months
Place of birth	__Province, __City (County), __ Street (People's Commune), __Lane (Brigade), __ Number (Squad)								
Address	X Province, X City, City East, Xiang Chun Li 3rd Lane, No. 112								
Family composition	A wife who does casual work and receives a monthly income of around 30 yuan. Three children. Two younger sisters who contribute 20 yuan a month to family income.								
Reason for reform through labor	Corruption and theft.								
Behavior during reform	He has been fairly contrite, and regularly engages in exposing ideology, criticism, and raising awareness. Approaches manual labor with enthusiasm, and regularly reports on the reform of his ideology and work.								
Main illness and treatment history	Main illnesses: (1) gastric ulcer; (2) chronic heart disease; (3) hemorrhoids. He is emaciated, his lower limbs exhibit moderate edema, he is severely anemic, he often has stomach pains, and he suffers from heart palpitations and is too weak to walk. After an extended period of rest and various treatments his condition has not improved.								
Medical evaluation and recommendations	He suffers from chronic heart disease, gastric ulcers, and hemorrhoids. These are chronic diseases that have not responded to extended treatment, so we recommend medical parole. Farm X Medical Clinic (official seal).								
Views of the work unit	Reform-through-labor Farm X (official seal).								
Views of the responsible officer									
Director's decision	Medical parole approved. It is also recommended that some support be given to assist his day-to-day living.								
Note	This individual is seriously ill and has not responded to a long period of treatment. After consultation with local authorities, medical parole was recommended. Responsible officer: X, July 2, 1962.								

UNABLE TO ESCAPE

After his return, Che recuperated at home, and reported every month to the police station on his thoughts. During this time, his mother died. The family, two adults and three children, now relied solely on Che's wife. She could only find casual work here and there together with some business on the side, which brought in just a few yuan a month. They managed to get by with a monthly subsistence from one of Che's sisters, of 10 to 15 yuan a month, and by selling what they could from their belongings.

In October 1962, Che started to feel better. He found a casual job on a building site through a friend. He stuck at it for three months. During this time, he neglected his reports to the police.[69]

The local police were unhappy about the reform-through-labor department sending Che without prior consultation. Now that Che had breached his conditions, they viewed his parole negatively. However, Che's neighborhood committee, which was responsible for monitoring his day-to-day living, was more concerned with the welfare of his family. They knew that Che was being careful, and avoiding his old business friends. He was even afraid to go to the market, for fear of stirring up trouble. They also knew that he had had agonized about not being able to find a stable job and was depressed.

The divergence between the views of the police station and the neighborhood committee was apparent in their reports, issued nine months after Che's return. Che, the police, the neighborhood committee, and the public security officer all produced reports about the progress of Che's medical parole.

The local police expressed dissatisfaction with Che's behavior:

> This individual has behaved poorly. There have been some improvements in his medical condition. Soon after his return he started breaching his reporting obligations, while he was busy at home attending to a small business with his wife. When asked to report, he said he was not able to do so as he could barely scrape a living.

Noting Che's "poor behavior," the report recommended he return to reform-through-labor.[70]

The report by the neighborhood committee took a different approach:

> Since his return, Che has mainly been at home recuperating. The family has struggled financially, so he took casual work for a while. However, he had to quit when the weather got cold. The family's main source of income is Che's wife's business. The local government provides some help. Che stays at home, and never goes to the market. In the early days after his return he rarely reported to the authorities, but lately he has reported once a week. He has not participated enough in study groups, mainly due to his worries about his family's livelihood and his resulting depression.[71]

The public security officer's report was neutral:

> He rarely goes out. His sister-in-law got him a temporary tiling job, but he no longer does it. His wife sells local produce to support the family. He stays home to look after the house, and receives some help from the local government. He reports to the public security officer once a week, but has not studied much. He is worried about his family's livelihood, and he gets depressed.[72]

The reform-through-labor sentence was passed by the local authorities, so the final say in Che's parole rested with the street committee. It supported the neighborhood committee:

> According to the neighborhood committee, Che is still unwell and unemployed. He has many children, and the family struggles with day-to-day living. It receives a government subsidy of 10 yuan per month. In our view the medical parole can be continued.[73] After criticism from the local police, Che became more careful and handed in his thought report every week, no matter how tired he was. These reports shed some light on how difficult day-to-day living is for Che's family.

On 17 July 1963, Che himself reported:

> On my way to work last month, I took a tram at 4:30 A.M. When the tram arrived at Stone Bridge at 4:45, it caught fire. The driver was unable to open the door, so the passengers had to jump from the windows. I jumped, and hurt my left foot and received a cut to the head. I was bleeding a lot, but I could not afford to go to the hospital for treatment, so I took another tram to South Gate to seek out my sister. My foot was swollen and I could no longer walk. My sister had to take me home. I am not able to walk, let alone work. It's been like that for more than a month, so we are struggling at home, and we have had to sell furniture and clothes. There is work available outside the city, but bedding and food costs would be a problem.[74]

He reported on 20 August:

> I have been unable to find work. We have finished the food assigned to us for the second half of the month, and we are in no position to buy from the market. We are living off field pumpkins, which we buy with the money we get from selling our winter clothes. We are struggling to get by. I am unable to respond to the school's demands for school fees, let alone attend to my own studies. We can't go on like this. Thinking about it depresses me. I would like to request the leadership to help find my wife a job, or perhaps give her a small business permit, to help us get by. I am grateful for the leadership's consideration.[75]

In September, the authorities helped Che's wife find work making paper boxes from home. Che submitted a report expressing his gratitude. He said that he had sold a cotton coat to pay one child's school fees, and asked the authorities to ask the school for a partial exemption for the other two children.[76]

Che's behavior won the approval of the local police. The term of his reform was three years, starting in November 1961 and ending in November 1964. Che's old farm wrote to the police in September 1964 notifying them of the imminent expiry of Che's sentence and enquiring about his behavior.[77] The police asked the director of local security to write a letter:

> Since being granted medical parole in 1962, Che Shaowen has recuperated at home, and has from time to time undertaken casual work. His wife and three children struggle to make ends meet. His wife works for a private factory, earning 10 yuan a month. The factory does not operate on a permanent basis, so sometimes there is no work. Che rarely goes out. We are not aware of him having engaged in any illegal acts. He receives 3.40 yuan a month, so life is difficult. During his medical parole, he has not acted against the law. We support terminating his reform-through-labor.

The police station said "the description of the director of security is on the whole accurate."[78]

Farm X agreed to "release him on schedule."[79]

This should have completed Che's journey back to freedom. However, just as he was being released, the Four Clean-Ups movement began sweeping the country. Many four category elements were hauled before struggle meetings. Luckily, Che was only a "violator of law and order" and had no four categories hat, so he was largely spared. From time to time, he was able to get some casual work.

But his luck ran out when the Cultural Revolution started. People like him, no matter how ill, how poor, or how well behaved, could no longer escape victimization and purging. It was also no longer possible for those banished to the villages to take advantage of the "medical parole" system.

8

The Curse of the "Overseas Connection"

How a Former Technical Worker Became an "Active Counter-Revolutionary"

What initially stood out about the "counter-revolutionary" Luo Guozheng's file was its sheer volume. It was a foot thick. Yet someone with such a voluminous file, the subject of countless internal and external investigations, turned out to be not a "counter-revolutionary" at all.

The "review finding" of August 1979, prepared by Luo's work unit for his rehabilitation, read:

> Luo Guozheng, male, 69, high-school education, previously worked freelance, now works as a mechanic in our department. During the Cultural Revolution, arrested by the Military Control Commission of the Public Transport Bureau as a counter-revolutionary, and taken into detention pending criminal proceedings in November 1968. During detention, he sympathized with fellow inmates and talked indiscreetly. In November 1971, the Revolutionary Committee put an 'active counter-revolutionary' hat on him.
>
> We find that while Luo has said and done some wrong things during the Cultural Revolution, he did not fundamentally oppose Chairman Mao, the Communist Party, or the socialist order. Since he had no counter-revolutionary motives, his problems should have been dealt with as a contradiction among the people, not one between an enemy and the people, and he should not have got the hat. This is hereby rectified. Luo's political status is restored, and his monthly salary of 68 yuan will start up again, backdated to November 1968. Documents inconsistent with this finding are to be disregarded. This finding is final.[1]

The review begged many questions. It did not say why Luo was arrested in the first place. Why was he remanded for more than three years before his case was heard? Why was he convicted for "talking indiscreetly" with fellow inmates?

THE REVIEW'S FINDINGS

Like many "problem persons" of that era, Luo Guozheng had a troubled history. In its 1979 report, the Party Committee of the Public Transport Bureau provided the following biography:

> Between 1921 and 1926, he was a student at primary school and the railway school in J Province. He became an apprentice at a cotton mill in 1927 and joined the Preparatory Squad of the military school in 1928. Between 1929 and 1930 he was a member of the 11th Division of the fake army, in which he served as a clerk and an officer. He received training between 1931 and 1940 in telecommunications, taxation, and ground-to-air liaison; he also held other reactionary positions. He joined the Kuomintang on two occasions, in 1932 and 1939. He was captured in 1940, and later worked as a station manager and technician for the Salt Bureau's radio station. Since December 1949, he has worked for the Communications Department in X Province. He first worked in the provincial department, and later transferred first to the Public Transport Bureau in X City, then to the Bureau's farm, and finally to a print works.

The report makes no mention of any punishment before his detention in 1968, nor of his experiences since 1949. It explains that Luo's troubles mainly stemmed from the fact that he "persistently attacked the Party's policies, madly opposed Mao Zedong Thought, attacked the Chinese People's Liberation Army, sabotaged the Cultural Revolution, fanned discontent against the Organization, and sabotaged the movement to 'grasp revolution and promote production.'" Luo's conviction came about as a result of his "reactionary behavior" during his detention (1969–71), so he was probably not deemed to have engaged in counter-revolutionary behavior before then.

The report quoted these "vicious attacks":

(1)   Chairman Mao led China's revolution to success. However, in his later years he stopped caring about the people, and only cares about becoming a global revolutionary leader and establishing his authority.

(2)   The current constitution is useless, so is the People's Congress. The people aren't free to migrate, associate, assemble, or work.

(3)   This Cultural Revolution is destroying culture, just as Emperor Qin Shihuang burned the books and buried scholars. It has caused chaos, to the point where the army had to step in. Many places are under military control.

(4)   After the three years of natural disaster, the economy recovered due to Liu Shaoqi's economic policies.

During the Cultural Revolution, the law was applied inconsistently. Convictions for expressing wrong opinions were commonplace, and punishments varied. While Luo's work unit might have requested his conviction as a counter-revolutionary, the public security authorities probably saw things differently. Luo was convicted for incidents that occurred between 1970 and 1971, during the nationwide "one thing to attack and three things to oppose" movement. His punishment was "severe." Had he not said "Chairman Mao has led China's revolution to success," he would have suffered an even worse fate and been sent to the countryside to do labor under supervision.[2]

It was never Luo's intention to "oppose," so he felt aggrieved. Once the reforms started and the Central Committee ordered hats to be removed and wrongful convictions overturned, he asked for a review. Luo's main ground for appeal was that no clear reason had been given for his arrest in 1968.

Luckily for Luo, he lived long enough to have his conviction overturned. The review team examined the records. It concluded that Luo's conviction was mainly due to his ranting during pre-trial detention. Although his rant "involved Chairman Mao, and was a serious political mistake, most of his comments were in the early stages of the Cultural Revolution and at the height of the factional struggle."

Luo's comments included:

(1) "My background is superior to yours [addressing Party members and the factory director]. When I was deputy platoon commander, Premier Zhou was at the Whampoa Military Academy, and Guo Moruo was an officer in the Kuomintang's Department of Political Affairs. You call me a platoon commander, but that's to promote me. You need to rehabilitate me."

(2) "We learn to combat liberalism on the one hand but commit liberalism on the other. What we learn is useless for resolving problems, I don't want to study any more." Regarding Chairman Mao's axiom that Communists should be conscientious: "Must we be conscientious about everything? If so, we should recognize that even water can be poisonous."

(3) During a meeting to "recall sufferings in the old society and contrast them with happiness in the new society": "I have no sufferings to discuss. I was an officer before Liberation. I made money and lived well in the old society."

(4) In a private conversation: "Two of my brothers were nurtured as rightists by the Communist Party." "Starving on meager rations, constrained by the government." "The Great Leap Forward was a big mess, and the mass steel production campaign led to big losses." "Our products are not as good as those of capitalist countries." "The Red Guard raid on my home was wrong." "The police are swine."

The review team found that Luo's comments, including his criticisms of Chairman Mao, stemmed "from his objections to past policies (the Great Leap Forward, the Anti-Rightist movement, household registration, etc.) and their implementation

THE CURSE OF THE "OVERSEAS CONNECTION"   211

by the local government and military authorities. He was unhappy about his detention, and thought he had been pushed toward the enemy. Discontented and resistant, he made wrong comments about Chairman Mao and the Party, because of his
unrealized personal ambitions. He was unaware of what was happening in the Party
and blamed Chairman Mao for chaos created by Lin Biao and the Gang of Four."

The Party Committee and the Public Security Bureau agreed that Luo should
not have been classified as an active counter-revolutionary, and he was rehabilitated.[3]

A COMPLICATED LIFE

During the Cultural Revolution, many people got into trouble for saying wrong
things or blaming the wrong people, especially if the "wrong things" or "wrong
people" involved Chairman Mao. When "mass dictatorship" was in vogue, some
died. Compared to them, Luo was lucky. Those who convicted him probably realized that he "did not fundamentally oppose Chairman Mao and the Party." Most of
his "reactionary comments" were cynical remarks made in private or out of anger.
People at all levels of society made similar comments. Why did Luo end up in jail
as a counter-revolutionary? It had a lot to do with his political history.

According to Luo's autobiography, he was born in 1911. His grandfather was a
scholar in the late Qing Dynasty and a magistrate in X County. His father was a
lawyer. Even so, there were many people with similar family backgrounds. Luo was
not born into a life of privilege but went through hard times as the family declined.

Soon after Luo's birth, his grandfather lost his magistracy and the family's
income fell. Although by then a qualified lawyer, Luo's father rarely worked. The
Luo household—grandparents, parents, and seven children—lived off the father's
income. The family was forced to sell off the ancestral home. By the time Luo
entered primary school, his father was unable to pay school fees and the boy
switched to the village school.

When Luo graduated from primary school, his father found a school that
charged modest fees. However, the school closed down, so he went to work as an
apprentice in a silk factory. When the Northern Expedition reached the Yangtze
River, the workers went on strike demanding better conditions, but the factory
owner shut it down. So Luo lost his job.

Thanks to the influence of his father and grandfather, who valued education,
Luo was an excellent calligrapher. When he joined the Kuomintang army, his talent
was discovered, and he was assigned to assist clerks in copying official documents.
After two years, he too became a clerk, and earned enough to support himself.

However, Luo's grandfather and father died, so he had to send money home to
supplement the family income. In 1932, he trained as a telecommunications officer,
and was rewarded with steadier and better pay. He always had money to send

home, and ample jobs to choose from, as his skill was in high demand. After the Japanese invasion, Luo's unit was disbanded, and he held civilian jobs here and there and was able to maintain a basic livelihood. He met his future wife through a colleague. They married and had three children. After the war, he found a job in the Salt Bureau. When X City was liberated, the Salt Bureau's Communications Unit was abolished, but Luo could still work as a general technician. He was transferred to the newly established Provincial Communications Department. His income fell, but he was still able to support a family of six (including his mother).

Luo's troubles can be traced back to his complicated work history (Table 6).[4]

INITIAL CONFESSIONS

In 1949, the new government initially retained "old" employees left over from the previous regime, while screening them politically. The local military committees urged all who had been involved with reactionary groups or espionage to register at designated locations and seek the opportunity to repent. This put huge pressure on Luo's family. Luo's wife had, years previously, trained as a journalist in the International Affairs Research Institute, a subsidiary of the Kuomintang army. The institute conducted intelligence work. Though a student, she was suspect by association, and had to register. This did not apply to Luo, but every time he joined a new work unit he duly disclosed his Kuomintang membership. However, like many others, he did not tell the whole truth. He mentioned that he had moved around army units, and that on two occasions his unit had joined the Kuomintang collectively. As he had not joined voluntarily, he was never a full-fledged member: "In 1932, my unit joined the Kuomintang. I left the unit before I was able to collect my card, and I never participated in any activity. In 1939, during the Anti-Japanese War, when I worked for the radio station, my unit again collectively joined. I left the following year to work at the Salt Bureau, so again I never received a membership card."[5]

In 1951, Luo's work unit started a two-week training course for "old" employees. They received political education and were interviewed as part of a thorough vetting.

Luo was naturally a suspect. He was sent on a cadre training course. The goal was to learn about rectification and elicit further confessions. After two months of collective learning and confessions, and against the background of a campaign to capture and kill counter-revolutionaries, Luo had no choice but to bring up his past.

On the "registration form for previous members of reactionary parties, spy organizations, and feudal gangs," Luo admitted that the first time he collectively joined the Kuomintang he had in fact received a membership card, but it had been destroyed in a big fire in C City.

TABLE 6

Month and Year	Work Unit	Position	Salary
January 1927–August 1927	X Silk Factory	Apprentice	
November 1927–May 1928	Military Academy Preparatory Team	Soldier	
October 1928–May 1929	11th Division, 64th Platoon	Soldier	
June 1929–March 1930	11th Division, 61st Platoon	Clerk	
April 1930–August 1930	11th Division, 61st Platoon	Officer	
September 1930–January 1931	2nd Division (teaching), 4th Platoon	Officer	
February 1931–November 1931	4th Division, telecommunications technology training class	Student	
November 1931–April 1932	4th Division, signal battalion radio company	Officer (engineer)	
May 1932–February 1933	52nd Division, 5th Platoon	Lieutenant/ Aide-de-camp	
March 1933–September 1933	98th Division, 307th Platoon	Lieutenant/ Quartermaster	
November 1933–October 1935	Tax Police Corps, 1st Division radio station	Second Lieutenant	42 yuan
November 1935–January 1936	Tax Police General Division, radio battalion	Second lieutenant	42 yuan
February 1932–November 1936	Tax Police General Division, telecommunications training class	Student	42 yuan
December 1936–March 1938	Tax Police General Division, radio battalion	Second Lieutenant	60 yuan
April 1938–June 1938	40th Division, radio platoon	Second Lieutenant	60 yuan
July 1938–August 1938	Wuhan Officers' Division, ground-to-air liaison training class	Student	
October 1938–September 1939	184th Division, radio station	Captain	80 yuan
March 1940–September 1940	First Group, Military Communications Battalion	Captain	80 yuan
October 1940–April 1942	X Salt Transportation Department, radio station	Chief Engineer and Announcer	80 yuan
May 1942–March 1944	Small business/unemployed		
April 1944–November 1945	Xianggu transit station	Manager	
December 1945–February 1946	Unemployed		

(continued)

TABLE 6 *(continued)*

March 1946–July 1946	Salt Bureau (head office) radio station	Chief Engineer	100 yuan
July 1946–December 1949	Salt Bureau (branch) radio station	Chief Engineer and Station Head	100 yuan
January 1950–January 1951	XX Provincial Communications Department	Technician	Varied between 53 and 58 yuan depending on the work unit
Any training, awards or punishments received	Has on three occasions (in 1931, 1936, and 1938) received training in telecommunications and ground-to-air liaison. Has received commendations for singlehandedly maintaining the radio station while also taking on the role of announcer, and ensuring the smooth running of the station for several months.		

The school demanded that past sins against the people must be declared, so he handed in a confession detailing ways in which he had "treated the people as an enemy"—by fighting the Red Army and press-ganging men into the Kuomintang army:

In October 1931, I graduated from the fake army's training class and was sent to work as an engineer. We were stationed at Hankou. The division became a special branch of the Kuomintang, all its units became sub-branches. The supervisors collectively signed up to the Kuomintang. We then set out to attack Kuang Jixun's Red Army unit. Our radio company maintained communication between brigade and division. Commander Zhang Lianhua was killed at the front during a battle, so we retreated. We press-ganged twenty or so men and hurried off to Hankou.

In January 1932, the 19th Route Army launched the Anti-Japanese War in Shanghai. We were transferred to X. I had reported my battalion commander for corruption, so it was no longer appropriate for me to continue in my position. I took extended leave and headed to Q Province to serve as an officer (I had received my Party card, serial number 00117, later destroyed in the September fire). I followed the troops around southern Jiangxi. I thought, given that I had the backing of a senior officer and was a full-fledged Party member, that I would go far in the army. I loyally served the fake army and was determined to destroy the Communist Party. Once the Kuomintang's rule has been consolidated, I would rise through the ranks. So I engaged in press-ganging and transporting supplies and ammunition.

Later, I was transferred back to X for training. I joined a team inspecting residence permits. We arrested anyone not on the register or who appeared suspicious, several hundred in all. Some were released after producing documentation or a guarantor, the rest were sent to headquarters to be dealt with, I can't remember the exact number. Soon after that, we attacked the Red Army. A Party unit had been established in the regiment. Two Party members came to assist. They painted slogans while the army was on the march, and mobilized civilians for sentry duty. I was one of their assistants. When we reached L County, we were re-routed. Commander Li Ming was killed in action, and the Commander Chen Shiji was captured. I was also held captive. On our release, the Red Army told us to stop fighting our own people. I hadn't realized that they were our own, and I was still keen to report to the reception center set up by Chen Cheng. I was sent to X for training.

In the autumn of 1938, I joined the 8th Corps as a radio engineer. We were short-staffed and busy, and I thought of quitting. An old classmate, Chen X (who commanded a Communications Battalion), asked me to join him, but I was not allowed to leave, so I went AWOL and joined anyway. I became a radio engineer. I was worried that the 8th Corps would come looking for me, so I changed my given name to Liang. The following summer, the division again joined the Kuomintang collectively. As I had changed my name, I joined a second time under the name Luo Liang. There were no cameras, so our fingerprints were taken. However, before I could collect my Party card I was captured by the Japanese. I was held prisoner until my escape in 1940. After that I never went back to the army, and I lost touch with the Party. In C City the Kuomintang held numerous registration drives, but I never re-registered.[6]

Luo's tie to the Kuomintang army caused him much trouble and made him an object of suspicion. In twelve years, he had served in ten units, almost one a year. He had been promoted quickly and received specialized training. He could not but stand out.

AN IN-DEPTH SELF-EXAMINATION

Luo's self-examination paints a picture of the internal workings of armies in the Republican era. They also shed light on Luo's mindset. He explained why he "treated the people as enemy":

I diligently performed my role as officer.

(1) To ensure timely supply of foodstuff and ammunition, in each county I worked with the authorities to enlist porters, sometimes by force. We took a dozen at a time. I found a room to lock them up in, and sent guards to watch over them. If they resisted, they were beaten. Though the beating was by the guards, they were under my supervision.
(2) When we were on the move, logistical staff travelled ahead to set up camp. I was well versed in that role. I set up camps in residential areas. We looked for nice houses, and didn't bother to get permission. When we moved in, the residents moved out.
(3) Two platoons dispersed a group of Red Army soldiers and intercepted large quantities of oil, salt, candles, cigarettes, matches, boots, etc. We took what we

needed, what we could carry. We didn't want to leave anything behind that might "aid the enemy," so we burned the rest.

(4) On another occasion, all the civilians had fled. At first we could get food from nearby places. Later, we took it from nearby villages. We killed livestock at will and took away anything edible.

(5) Our platoon was fictitiously inflated by two-thirds. When headquarters demanded a roll call, I got the authorities to round up civilians to make up the numbers.

(6) The division had a section that wrote slogans on the march. I helped out.

(7) Once, at lunar new year, I joined in a residence check. Anyone not on the register was detained, more two hundred in all. Most were bailed out. A dozen or so who had no one to bail them out were sent to the division.

(8) I looked for ways to make money. When reporting purchases, I inflated prices and kept the difference. I also pocketed payments meant for the laborers. If a laborer had been away from home for a fortnight, he was desperate to return. I allowed them to escape and pocketed the money. My income grew, and my lifestyle became more decadent.[7]

In another confession, Luo wrote:

In 1931, I was warrant officer. I heard that the division was planning to set up a tele-communications training class, which I thought would be a useful skill. I was sent for training.

(1) Organization of the training:
The class comprised forty soldiers from various units, including me, and a company of high-school students. The class had a head teacher and a deputy. The director was Wang Wenguang, from Guizhou. I had met him on the battlefield in the early days of the Anti-Japanese War, when he commanded a communications company. The commander of the student company was Fang Pingzhang, from Zhejiang. The principal instructor was a German called Stoelzner. He lectured in German, and Zhang Yunji interpreted.

(2) Contents of the training:
We started with basic military training, including military science, infantry operations, field service, night watch, shooting, cartography, rules, regulations, etc. Only the essential elements were taught. Technical training was also provided: radiology, electromagnetism, electrical engineering, communication tactics, telegrams, semaphore communication, telephony, flash communication, cloth board signaling, carrier pigeons, messenger dogs, and so on. Stoelzner taught various technologies. Sometimes we held memorial meetings on Mondays and learned about Sun Yat-sen's legacy.[8] The instructors were outstanding soldiers or leaders from various regiments.[9]

In his description of the training, he mentioned only that "it was brief, just four weeks."[10] Two months later, he provided a more comprehensive account of his actions during the Anti-Japanese War, including an account of the ground-to-air liaison class and his capture by the Japanese in 1939, which nearly ended in him becoming a spy.

He wrote:

I was transferred to work in the radio station. When the Wuhan Officers Division set up a ground-to-air liaison class, they got me to undertake the training, since I was close by. This was a real opportunity and would boost my prospects for promotion, so I was happy to go. The training lasted four weeks.

Leaders often came to give speeches. Wang Jingwei spoke about scorched-earth resistance; Feng Yuxiang spoke about boosting troop morale; Bai Chongxi gave updates about the situation in Taierzhuang and Yudong; Chiang Kai-shek talked about promoting morality and rehabilitating the revolutionary spirit, etc.[11] Chiang also spoke about the Three People's Principles. He even came to roll call once. The trainees came from various units, including some from the [Communist] New Fourth Army. After graduation everyone returned to their original units. The training left me with the following impressions. (1) The regiment had great facilities and an air of grandeur, most of the staff were officers, and most of my classmates were high-ranking officers. (2) While the Anti-Japanese War raged on, our supreme leader took the time to speak to us. I felt honored and grateful. (3) That there were students from the New Fourth Army showed that we were truly united. (4) Studying alongside classmates of a higher rank motivated me to do better. (5) Chiang spoke at length about propriety, justice, honesty, and honor. Seeing such a great leader advocate morality impressed me. The training further reinforced my orthodox ideas.

But I never stopped pursuing personal interests. After the restructuring of the tax police, my income fell by a fifth. At that very moment my old classmate Chen, a commander in the 60th Army's communications battalion, asked me to serve under him as a radio platoon leader. There was a shortage of communications staff, so the pay was good and there were bonuses. I quit my post without seeking permission, and changed my name to Luo Liang to avoid getting caught. Although I wasn't promoted to commander, my conditions were much improved. So I was content for the time being.

In 1939, we headed for Jiangxi, where I was captured and nearly killed. I was forced to do hard labor. I was taken to Hankou by a Japanese and another man called Min. We lived with someone called Chen (a Hankou resident who had been captured and was serving the Japanese as an advisor). All I could think about was escape. I borrowed 30 yuan from a relative who worked for a bank and fled to X in January 1940.

The 60th Army had been reorganized into the First Army Group. I reported on my capture and escape, and was commended and assigned to the Communications Battalion. The Yunnan Army had started organizing a Kuomintang branch. As I was using a different name, I joined again. When the Company Commander resigned, I temporarily replaced him. I was unhappy about the lack of promotion opportunities. A former officer of the Tax Police, Zhao, had become director of the Salt Department, which offered a comfortable lifestyle, so I became a clerk and technician in it.

How could Luo have left the army for the salt industry and become unemployed twice within such a short time? According to him, he was unhappy with the status quo, "having suffered poverty and developed a snobbish attitude under the old society, my sole concern was personal gain and the welfare of my family. I thought only about climbing the ladder and making money."[12] He wrote:

In the winter of 1941, I was transferred to X Town. Zhao had been sacked as the result of an investigation, a fatal blow to my career. I started focusing on financial gain. I quit my job and set up a store in partnership with a colleague. We were amateurs, and had limited capital. Faced with rapid inflation and a slow turnover, we had to shut down. In late 1942, after my wife's transfer, we relocated to X.

In April 1944, Zhang Ronglai set up a transit station and I was appointed as a manager. I operated a small street stall with my wife (she had resigned from the radio station), and we were able to make ends meet. However, the area was remote and communication with the outside world was difficult, so I led a rural life and carried a heavy mental burden. I longed for the war to end.

When the Japanese surrendered, I thought I could finally live a peaceful life, and I made plans to return home. The station closed and I was once again unemployed. Ling from the branch office told me there was a chance of my being reinstated by the head office, so I asked a friend to apply on my behalf. My application was approved in 1946, and I was assigned work as an operator.

After the war, prices skyrocketed and businesses turned to speculation. The station head, Liu, discussed this with me during casual chats. We saw it as a way to make easy money. I earmarked Wu, a former colleague in the tax police, as a potential business partner. In May, Wu and I put our plan into action. But the venture was unworkable—there were too many beneficiaries and not enough funds. We feared our scheme would get us into trouble, so we quit while we were ahead.

In 1948, while I was working at the radio station, commodity prices began fluctuating wildly and interest on loans was high—sometimes doubling in just a few days. Again, I started daydreaming about making a fortune.

During the big fire in C City, equipment was destroyed. The Salt Bureau sent an engineer to buy new equipment, and we over-reported the price and kept the difference. Liu had some vacuum tubes that had not been listed as assets, so we sold them. I got 55,000 yuan from that sale. All these incidents show that I was self-centered and individualistic.[13]

Luo talked about his troubled thoughts after Liberation:

The chief operator of the radio station warned me against engaging in random conversations, which could become the subject of investigation. I believed him. I was already under a suspicion because of the September fire and feared losing my job. Later, the army took over the Salt Bureau. They spoke gently and sincerely, and reassured us that everyone would stay in their positions. This eased my concern. I told Comrade Liu, who took over managing the bureau, about how the Kuomintang had once been popular but was now seen as incompetent and corrupt, and had lost the people's trust and been overthrown by the Communist Party. I added that if the Communists did not do their job properly, they too would one day be overthrown. He said: 'That won't happen. The Communist Party has a system of criticism and self-criticism.' I understood what he was saying, but only vaguely.

By lunar new year, inflation was out of control. Since Liberation I had received no salary (just one hundred catties of rice). I was riddled with anxiety. What would Liberation mean for us poor civil servants? The Communists won the war, but could they succeed on the economic front?

In December 1949, the Salt Bureau was restructured. The Organization wanted me to manage the bureau's internal affairs. I was happy with that. However, less than a month after my transfer, I was assigned to X Province. There were more than twenty levels for technicians and it would be hard to climb to the top, so I commented that things were not what they used to be. I was worried I would receive less pay.

These developments all contributed to my behavior, and I left a bad impression. Representative Sun sought me out for a talk. But despite advice, I remained suspicious. Whenever something happened against my personal wishes, I began suspecting the Organization. I resented the Organization, but did not dare say so. This later led to a series of mistakes.[14]

Luo spent the first half of 1951 confessing his past, while under review by the Organization. However, he did not earn the management's trust. The school made an appraisal clearly not in his favor. Luo "did not take learning seriously, and was always joking"; "he had a strong personality and was subjective"; "he did too little self-study, and his comments in class missed the point." "This student has a chequered history, and has failed to own up to political problems. He can be assigned to a regular workplace, and subjected to ongoing review and scrutiny."[15]

A "SUSPECTED SPY"

When one regime overthrows another by force, a crucial last step in the transition is the purging of the old regime and the creation of a new society to support the new government. Land reform and Zhenfan were effective tools, but tens of millions of people at all levels retained connections to the old regime. The cadres from the rural areas who took over running the cities had to employ large numbers of such people to implement their policies. Part of the cadres' job was to scrutinize such people, and to get rid of the most dangerous elements and control the less dangerous ones. This task was indispensable yet almost impossible.

These old employees came with an intricate web of relationships—family members, relatives, friends, colleagues, teachers, students, and so on. It would be a mammoth task to get to the bottom of the political history of each of them. During major crackdowns, it was easy to identify "dangerous" elements, such as secret agents, leaders of reactionary parties, and those with blood on their hands. The "less dangerous" elements (those who had joined reactionary organizations but had no blood on their hands, and who had not become spies or leaders) made up a big part of most work units, and had the potential to become an opposition. As someone in the second category, Luo was suspect.

Was Luo a spy? Did he have blood on his hands? These questions arose from Luo's own confessions. He had said: "In 1948, the security section regularly sent Yang to carry out inspections and make reports. We became acquainted. Through him, I met Yu, who was in charge of financial news at the radio station. I now know that Yang has turned himself in as an ex-military spy, but I don't know about Yu's background. We were casual acquaintances."

The security section asked X City Public Security Bureau to help find Yang: "Luo Guozheng, a radio operator, has a complicated history. In 1931, he underwent ten months' technical training by the 4th Division. In 1936, he received ten months' training by the Tax Police General Corps. In 1938, he received four months' training at a ground-to-air liaison course. He has been exposed as having joined the Kuomintang. We request your assistance."[16] However, this lead was a dead end. The Public Security Bureau replied: "Yang surrendered at two separate locations, his current whereabouts are unknown."[17] Luo had also mentioned other names, but few could be located. The testimony of those that were found was not worth following up. One former colleague mentioned only "everyday matters." The report was dismissed as immaterial.[18]

He X also featured in Luo's confession. However, the local public security office said that according to He, "Luo did not have much to do with him. They merely knew of each other, they had no interaction."[19] The security section did not give up, but wrote once again asking He whether Luo was a spy. He's attitude changed drastically, and he provided new evidence in stark contrast to what he had previously said. He claimed that "when Luo engaged in conversations with people he had a military air," "they had a relationship with the 6th District of the bandit army, and communicated by telegram." "When Luo worked for the fake army, he was issued with a special work permit," so "he must have been connected to its intelligence operatives."[20]

By 1952, Luo had been designated as a "spy suspect." In the summer of 1953, the authorities investigated the personnel of key departments in the postal and telegram services, which included Luo. He's new testimony reinforced the security section's assessment of Luo. They submitted a report:

> Luo has had a long history of working for the reactionary army, and has performed many reactionary tasks. After Liberation, he was transferred to this department. In 1953, with the help of He X, it was discovered that Luo might have once belonged to a special-service organization. He has performed poorly during his time in this department (his wife also has a dubious background). Decision pending.[21]

This assessment was not endorsed by the Party committee. The Communications Department urgently needed technical staff. Many had problem pasts, some even worse than Luo's. The leadership did not see Luo as a serious problem. In response to the security section's request that Luo be listed as a key review object, the secretary said: "We will speak with Luo, and get him to write detailed materials. A decision will be made once the material has been obtained." The Party committee expressed similar views, and added: "Take care when speaking with him directly to avoid raising any suspicion on his part."[22]

The newly formed team therefore acted with greater caution. After reading Luo's file and speaking with him, they were also of the opinion that his case was not serious. They thought his problems lay mainly in his failure to explain two issues: (1) "He has a complicated history, and it seemed odd that he several times enrolled for training. He has not sufficiently explained the nature of this training." (2) "His relationship with the spy sent by the police department in 1948 raises questions. He has not said what tasks he was given or named persons."

As for He's second testimony, the team's view differed from the security section's. They pointed out that He's statements contradicted each other, and were not credible.

Luo's wife was a bigger problem. She had joined the Kuomintang and worked for the fake Institute of International Affairs, and was no ordinary woman. How did she come to join the fake Institute? What was its nature, personnel, and research? Under what circumstances did she leave? Luo had not dealt with any of these questions.[23]

UNDER INVESTIGATION

After Luo's transfer, he felt that his status had improved. He was happy to be nearer home, though he was worried that he might be ostracized in an unfamiliar workplace. For a while, he displayed some negativity. He thought that as a newcomer his income would be meager, so he acted indifferently during salary appraisal. When assigned as a Level 8 technician, he thought he had been undervalued. However, when he realized that he was not being discriminated against, his attitude became more positive.

Luo mastered both the mechanics and the operational side of his job. He knew how to install and maintain machinery, and he was an expert in radio transmission. He had years of experience. Because of his military training, he approached work "tirelessly and with a strong sense of responsibility."[24] Colleagues agreed that he was "responsible," "collaborative," and "had a good attitude."[25] So despite a recommendation that he be "reassigned pending probation and ongoing evaluation," he continued (because of the staff shortage) to do classified radio work.

By June 1953 Luo was getting past the age for shift work, so he was sent to be a teacher. A year later, the Communications Department established its own training course and assigned him as an instructor.

By then, some of Luo's problems had started to surface. Before 1949, he had changed jobs almost yearly, seeking promotion and money. After Liberation, he could no longer job-hop. He could only complain and vent his dissatisfaction. When he was transferred from the prosperous region south of the Yangtze to the northwest (where the diet was mainly coarse grain) to teach, he had a hard time adjusting. However, he had no choice but to follow the arrangements made by the Organization. He started making cynical remarks, losing his temper, and getting into fights.

Many of the teaching staff were technicians from eastern and southern China. Everyone saw the secondment as temporary: none had families with them. So they spent their spare time in one another's company. A common topic of discussion and complaint was the canteen. They also struggled professionally. Coming from technical backgrounds, they had no teaching experience. Their dissatisfaction led to conflicts with the cadres.[26] Because of his outspokenness, Luo stood out among the teaching staff. His peers commented: "He works enthusiastically for the masses. He was a canteen committee member. He often came up with suggestions to improve the quality of meals."

Equally, Luo's clashes with the leadership led to hostile comments: "Lacks organizational awareness, unable to follow the leadership's decisions. Exhibits the style of a liberal, often makes cynical comments and slanders people."[27]

Luo offended others easily, and knew it. He wrote that he was "fiery and too hot to handle." He "offended people unintentionally." His colleagues described him as "too subjective," "insufficiently modest," "often speaks without thinking."[28] Even his instructor, who had only known him briefly, identified this problem: "Luo is hardworking and responsible, displays enthusiasm, gets on well enough with others, and is able to approach classmates. However, he speaks without regard for the consequences. He does not know how to be discreet. He likes to show off, and often brings up his achievements, afraid they might be overlooked. He is subjective. He is not very forthcoming. Rather than expressing his views boldly, he discusses things behind people's backs."[29]

What mattered was that the Communications Department valued Luo's technical skills. So despite his complicated past and the investigation, Luo retained his post handling classified information and his cadre status.

A SUFAN TARGET

In 1955, personnel with problems became key targets under Sufan. The team in the Communications Department listed Luo as a target, and set out to investigate him. Its report raised the following "points of suspicion":

(1) Between 1931 and 1938 he on three occasions received training in telecommunications technology. If all three sessions related to telecommunications

technology, why was repeated training necessary? His account of the ground-to-air liaison training was inconsistent. Perhaps he concealed his true position or his having joined a special-service organization. The training course might have been for spies.

(2) He participated in inspecting residence permits. His team arrested anyone without a permit or suspected of having links to the revolution. They arrested hundreds. He claimed that most were released, but several dozen remained in custody and were sent to divisional headquarters. Some might have been killed. He fought against the people, oppressed and exploited them, and persisted even after he had been released by the Red Army. He was loyal to the reactionary cause and hated the people and the Red Army.

(3) In 1948, the garrison headquarters sent Yang to conduct surveillance and complete a monthly report. Luo claims that Yang was a casual acquaintance. This is unlikely to be true. This individual may have colluded with Yang. If he had been an ordinary employee, Yang would not have sought information from him. Luo was reporting as one spy to another. He is said to have had dealings with the fake Sixth War Zone. He received telegrams from them. The X highway was an important route for the bandit army, which had granted Luo a special work permit. He is suspected of having been an intelligence worker.

(4) He says he is not particularly close to Qi Huisheng (his brother-in-law, now in Taiwan). This is also inaccurate. In 1947, Qi entrusted Luo with a revolver and a gun license, which Luo handed to Qi's uncle. Why did Luo's brother-in-law own a revolver and flee to Taiwan? That he asked Luo to deliver the gun shows they colluded. After the September fire, Luo wrote to borrow money from Qi. This shows that they had a close relationship.[30]

In July 1955, the security section began searching for Luo's relatives, former colleagues, classmates, and anyone who might help "clarify Luo's reactionary past and criminal activities."[31] They questioned more than forty people in thirteen provinces. They concluded:

> According to Luo's brother, a bank worker, and Wang of the provincial Post Office (formerly Luo's colleague at the radio station), the fake Tax Police Regiment was established in spring 1936. Luo was station director. In the summer, he was trained in military strategy and telecommunications. The Tax Police Regiment was a paramilitary body. It fought the Communist Party in the southwest. In Jiangsu and Henan, it fought the Japanese, but it also fought the New Fourth Army. There were secret agents in the Tax Police Regiment, most of them high-ranking. Luo's name does not appear on the list, so he was probably not a member of the intelligence organization.

Three issues remained: "(1) Luo confessed to having twice joined the Kuomintang, but the investigation has failed to corroborate this. (2) He was said to have participated in ground-to-air liaison training, but there are no other leads on this. (3) The political circumstances of his brothers-in-law Qi Huichun and Qi Huisheng—one in Hong Kong, the other in Taiwan—are unclear."[32]

The investigation came to a temporary end. The five-person team decided "not to pursue the matter any further for the time being."[33]

A MUDDLED REVIEW

In November 1958, Luo again encountered two major problems. The first related to his wife, Qi Huijun, who had following Liberation registered herself as having been a student at the Kuomintang's Institute of International Affairs. This resulted in her becoming a review target during Sufan. She attended a "study group," and was identified as a spy who had "joined the Kuomintang, carried out anti-Communist propaganda, and talked about how to resist the Japanese and exterminate the Communist Party." She was given a "counter-revolutionary" hat.[34]

That was when Luo's second problem arose. A former military colleague, Hu, working for a construction company in another province, confessed during his own unit's Sufan campaign that he had worked for Luo and that Luo had been a spy with a possible blood debt. The report contained little detail: "We served together more than ten years ago. He was commander of the 2nd Company of the Special Services Battalion in the 23rd Army Group. He imprisoned a Communist called Zhang, who went crazy. He imprisoned another Communist called Hu, who escaped and was recaptured. They wanted Hu to repent and imprisoned him for another year. He was sent to X. I heard that he was executed on the way."[35]

This revelation was a blow to Luo. In his previous confessions, he had never mentioned the 23rd Army Group. According to him, his highest military position was deputy company commander. Nor had he said anything about capturing Communists, let alone having possibly killed one. Hu's revelation cast doubt about Luo's confessions. Fortunately, Luo's work unit was inundated with work as a result of the Great Leap Forward, so he was left alone for the time being.

In 1959, Luo was assigned to work in a bus station, suggesting he had again become a serious suspect, and that his problems had merely been suspended.

During rectification in 1960, the security section of the Municipal Public Transport Bureau began a fresh review of Luo. The reviewers concluded that "his problems have mostly been verified, though some require further investigation," and that "we have not yet uncovered any major political problems." However, they found from Hu's material that Luo had concealed his history as a special services company commander and his having "imprisoned two of our undercover Party members," leading to the death of one. They decided to visit Hu and gather further information.[36]

In January 1961, Hu was interviewed at his local police station. Hu wrote down what he knew about Luo:

In 1939, I joined the Special Services Battalion of the 23rd Army Group. Its role was to protect and escort military leaders. Luo Guozheng was a godson of the Corps

Commander. One day in 1944, I was due to go gambling, but we sat around and gossiped instead. At one point we talked about how in 1942 a Sichuanese called Hu had been locked up as a Communist, and another Communist called Zhang had been locked up by 4th Company. They were told to repent. Zhang repented, but he went crazy and was sent back to Sichuan. Hu refused to repent. He was locked up for more than a year, and executed on his way to Shangrao. I wasn't involved in escorting Hu, so I don't know the details. The commander was Luo Guozheng. He would have known about it. When I first joined the 23rd Army Group, Luo was a platoon commander. He later became commander. In 1945, the army went through a restructure. Luo was assigned to Zhejiang and I was assigned to Anhui. I don't know what happened to him after that.[37]

Hu named a fellow soldier called Zeng, who had served under Luo in the 2nd Company and knew of the jailing and execution of the Communist Hu. The investigators tried to locate Zeng to corroborate Hu's statement, but found he had been sentenced to three years' imprisonment and died. They pored over Zeng's confessions, but found no mention of Luo.[38]

The investigators did not give up. They re-examined the files and tried to track down anyone who might know something about Luo's work between 1941 and 1946.[39]

They located some ex-soldiers who had served in the Special Services Battalion. They confirmed that Luo had commanded the 2nd Company.[40] However, records from the Salt Bureau showed that the previous investigation into Luo's activities between 1941 and 1946 had not missed anything.

When confronted, Luo denied having served as a company commander and rebutted everything that Hu said about him. He wrote statements about his activities between 1940 and 1946 and cited evidence. For example, in 1941 he had married; he had his first child in 1942; the whole family had followed his wife to Pengshui in 1943; in 1946, they had returned to C City. All this was supported by witnesses.[41]

The security section again interviewed Hu, and showed him a photo of Luo. It turned out the whole thing had been a mix-up. Hu was unable to identify the person in the photo. When the investigator asked him if it was Luo, he shook his head. He said: "Luo was younger, and his face was rounder and more expressive. He was tall and chubby. He had no other distinguishing features, and did not have any family with him at the time." He said Luo had no military understanding, and only managed to become a company commander thanks to his background. He was the godson of the Army Commander, and his brother had previously commanded the same Special Services Battalion.[42] So Hu and the others were referring to a different Luo. Since their names were identical, the public security authorities had mixed them up.

BECOMING A TARGET ONCE AGAIN

Though this case of mistaken identity was cleared up, it did not help Luo's situation. He was already a key control subject, and he was "mobilized to work in the countryside."[43] He lost his cadre status, and could no longer take care of his family. Luo continued to see himself as a cadre, and was increasingly resentful.

In his second year at the farm, the province was devastated by famine. The food supply to the cities was intermittent. Even farm workers like Luo went hungry. Luo suffered from edema as a result of malnutrition. His mother had just passed away, and his wife was "laboring under surveillance" and had no income. Luo had to maintain a family of five on 60 yuan a month. He resorted to petty theft.[44]

According to the cadres, his thieving got out of control. Sent to buy seeds from the nearby commune, he withheld some, and planned to take them home to plant them in his yard. He was found out. In March, he again stole and was again found out. In May, he stole two spoonfuls of oil, and was criticized. In July, he sneaked into the melon fields at night to steal melons, and was discovered and criticized. In August, when eggplants went missing, everyone suspected Luo. On another occasion, a colleague found Luo eating someone else's noodles in the middle of the night.

Food theft was common at the time, but few went as far as Luo. Despite warnings, he continued to steal, and never acknowledged his mistakes. When told to make a self-criticism, he promised to change, but he justified his actions on grounds of hunger.[45]

The farm leaders knew about Luo's problems at home, so they never punished him. However, they resented his "cynical comments." Luo had strong political views, and regularly expressed them. Some examples:

> I heard the Party secretary say 'some canteens are still rationing their meals, this contravenes Party policy.' The secretary told everyone to eat as much as they want, but within two months rations were cut to 2–3 *liang* of grain a day.
>
> We consume less oil now than we wiped off the table before Liberation. We have nothing to feed our livestock. Even the rats and mice are starving.
>
> Prosperity and comfort breed lust; starvation and poverty lead to theft. Talk about good class background, the peasants are of a good class background but how has that helped? How come they are still stealing? Commune members who don't steal are a minority. Everyone is stealing, it's out of control.
>
> The Great Leap Forward is a problem. Many factories have stopped operating, public money has been squandered. It's at the cost of the people.
>
> The Party has repeatedly spoken about the advantages of the people's communes, especially the economy of scale. So why does it now want to reduce them? Now they want individual households to cater for themselves and work their own plots. Many communes have dissolved their nurseries.[46]

Faced with these negative comments, Luo's team leaders had to make their view clear. When filling out Luo's "fake-military and police personnel registration form," they said that "he behaves badly and is resentful." They requested that he be classified as part of the "social base of enemy forces," and that the leadership "take appropriate action and publicly educate" him as a repeat offender.[47] The request was approved. Luo was demoted, publicly criticized for his negative comments, and made a "key control subject."[48]

Luo continued to work hard, so there was little else the leadership could do. He had many times requested a transfer closer to home, so that he could care for his family. The farm leadership finally supported his request.

In 1962, Luo was transferred to a farm near the city. His old farm told his new farm: "His performance has been average, but his ideology and moral quality are abhorrent. His history is complicated. He was a reactionary military officer. After Liberation, he complained about Party policy. He makes sarcastic remarks and spreads discord. He has frequently requested a transfer to your farm, because of his family. We hope you will keep up his covert monitoring (he is a key control subject) and report monthly to the security section."[49]

UNEXPECTED FORTUNE AND DISASTER

Luo was grateful for the consideration shown to him, so he arrived at his new workplace with a more positive attitude. He made fewer cynical comments and tried harder to get close to the Organization. He did not stop stealing and making comments altogether, but the leadership judged him much more positively.

A report in 1963 said:

Since arriving, Luo has followed instructions and pointed out his own weaknesses. When working in the company of others he is diligent, though he sometimes gets sloppy when working alone. In the fields he likes to stop and chat and to gossip about colleagues behind their backs. He is old, so he is attached to old ways of thinking. He sees things through the lens of the old society, and speaks harshly. Once when we were surveying the land, he said we were 'even stricter than the landlords.' Faced with life's difficulties, he complains and likes to joke. After education, his performance has improved.[50]

The report was prepared for the security authorities, which were investigating Luo's social connections after a routine check showed that he was corresponding with a relative overseas.

The report addressed the issue of Luo's overseas correspondent:

Luo mentioned that his brother-in-law had written to him from Japan, and he showed us the letter. The sender was Qi Huisheng. The letter conveyed general greetings. There was one page in total, containing a couple hundred characters. Luo wrote back in early April and received a further letter from Qi, addressed to his home. The letter mentioned that Qi had been away on business, which was why it had taken him so long to reply. It was again a short letter, no more than two hundred characters. The letter paper was white. Both letters contained a lot of blank spaces (one third or more).

Neither letter suggested anything untoward. Before showing me the second letter, Luo said: 'My wife's brother said he knew things have been tough the last few years in China, and he would try to send some food.' Luo said he thought money would be better, and that 'the brother had probably heard about the three years of disaster overseas.' When I read the letter, there was no mention of sending food.[51]

The report by the security section demonstrated a greater level of political alertness:

> This employee has a complicated history and social connections. He worked for the fake army's radio station, and climbed the ranks. He fought against the people and captured revolutionaries. He was caught by our Red Army, but did not change his ways. He was highly regarded by the reactionaries. He was sent for training on three occasions, and twice joined the fake Kuomintang. He has performed poorly since Liberation, and is dissatisfied with the Organization. He is in contact with his brothers-in-law in Japan and Hong Kong. The latter has sent money and parcels, which should be monitored for any political connection. This employee seems questionable politically.[52]

Though not aware of the authorities' secret investigation, he had disclosed his brother-in-law's letter, which shows that he knew of its potential sensitivity. Luo stressed that his family was struggling financially and the letters were mainly for his wife, who had insisted on asking her brother for money and things. Once the brothers-in-law started sending money and parcels, the family's life improved. However, Luo became complacent. He was no longer discreet about these relationships, and started to show off.

A year later, Luo was transferred back to the Public Transport Bureau. The security section told the Public Security Bureau that he lived quite well, and often ate fish and meat. He was generous to others, as he "receives overseas remittances, ranging from tens of yuan to 100 yuan. The remittances are sent by his brothers-in-law. He gets parcels too. He has received a pair of old leather shoes, some Japanese fabric, a shirt, some old clothes, two jars of lard, and a jar of sugar."

The report said that Luo used his remittances to get cigarettes, flour, and sticky rice, which he shared with his colleagues, so "he gets on well with people." The school at a local factory had sent him "a banner of recognition."[53] The team monitoring Luo reported that he had become a bit corrupt. He had spent more than 2000 yuan on a Swiss Sandoz watch—equal to three years' salary.

With Luo splurging on an imported watch, the security bureau decided to "conduct a comprehensive investigation" of his political history and social connections. Informants were deployed to "monitor Luo's daily activities." The report explained:

In January 1963 we intercepted a letter to Luo from Qi Huisheng in Japan, seeking to establish contact and asking about old acquaintances. We found this to be suspicious, and conducted a preliminary investigation.

Main social connections: Elder brother-in-law Qi Huichun, of the fake Bank of China. Detained [by the Party] after Liberation, fled to Hong Kong to escape corruption charges. Unclear what became of him. Second brother-in-law Qi Huisheng worked as a radio operator for the fake airline company, etc. After the Liberation of S City he fled to Taiwan. His nephew is a technician. He once wore a rightist hat.

Suspicions arising from Luo's overseas contacts: Qi Huisheng in Taiwan was not in contact with Luo until January 1963, when he wrote to him out of the blue. Luo asked Qi to send some "old clothes." Qi sent large amounts of money, food, and clothing, and asked for photos. Luo also wrote to Qi Huichun in Kowloon. Not long after, someone called X popped up in Hong Kong, claiming to be a friend of Qi Huichun's, who asked him to give Luo 30 U.S. dollars. The handwriting on the money order was that of Wang X, a spy at the bandit Ministry of Defense.

Luo's wife Qi Huijun was a spy, and he has suspicious links overseas. He often asked for 'old clothes.' The bandit Kuomintang's spy in Hong Kong, Wang X, remitted to Luo. Luo should be a key target of investigation.[54]

The unit listed points for investigation: Qi Huichun's and Qi Huisheng's role before Liberation; the activities of the Kuomintang's military intelligence organizations in Japan and Hong Kong, and their methods of communication with mainland China; information about Wang X, the person in Hong Kong who wrote to Luo; and information about relatives or friends of the families with overseas links.[55]

THE CULTURAL REVOLUTION STARTS

Once the investigation got underway,[56] Luo was transferred from the bus station to the Transport Bureau's printing plant. He had already undergone several reviews, so it was unlikely that anything new would be uncovered. People connected with Luo had already been interviewed, and there was a mountain of material. His brothers-in-law were out of reach. Luo's correspondence with them had been monitored for two years, and was not suspicious. Another report noted that the "spy Wang" who had sent the remittances might not be a spy after all.[57]

But then the Cultural Revolution started. The struggle to "sweep away monsters and demons" hit people throughout society. Red Guards raided one house after another. With Luo's background in the fake army, and his wife an ex-spy with a hat, they were inevitably targets. Luo's wife was paraded round the streets.

Luo attracted criticism and scorn at work. More than two hundred big-character posters exposing him went up. The posters were gathered into a document and submitted to the Cultural Revolution office: "As the Cultural Revolution advances, the fighting spirit of our employees soars. With their revolutionary big-character posters, they sweep away monsters and demons and have ousted Luo Guozheng, who opposes socialism."

The document summed up the criticisms: (1) attacking the Party's policies; (2) attacking the Three Red Banners; (3) fabricating rumors to confuse the public and undermine Party authority; (4) inciting the masses to oppose the Party; (5) stirring up trouble, alienating the masses, and sabotaging production; (6) reminiscing about the old society, promoting the bourgeois way of life, and fantasizing about peaceful evolution from socialism back to capitalism; and (7) sabotaging the Cultural Revolution.[58]

During the Cultural Revolution, everything was scrutinized through the lens of class struggle. But the campaigns targeting problem elements in the grassroots did not last long. By the time the Party Committee came to dealing with Luo and others, it was about to meet its own downfall. Mao launched the Cultural Revolution to target not the grassroots but leading "capitalist roaders." The Central Committee stressed the need to "beware of people who accuse the revolutionary masses of being counter-revolutionaries."[59] This changed the direction of the movement.

Workplaces everywhere started attacking people in power. In Luo's workplace, even the security section, which Luo dreaded, became a target. Luo started believing that he was a victim of bureaucracy and capitalist reaction and entitled to rebel.

Ever since 1949, high-ups had been pointing the finger at those below, and Luo had always trodden with caution. Even during the 1957 rectification movement, when the authorities solicited public criticism, he had refrained from saying anything negative. In June 1965, the transport authorities launched the Four Cleanups. The leadership came to the factory to mobilize the workers and demanded that they boldly express their opinions about their leaders and write big-character posters. Luo warned colleagues that "if you write big-character posters, you will be punished later. I came very close to being punished in 1952, 1953, and 1957. Luckily, I saved myself by writing only about trivial issues."[60]

This time, however, Luo was overcome with excitement and took an active part. He visited workplaces across the city and joined in struggle meetings. He mingled with rebel organizations. He even took the lead in exposing and criticizing leaders of the Public Transport Bureau and the Communications Department at mass rallies.

However, he used political speeches to air his private grievances, sometimes saying the wrong thing and offending the crowd. At a meeting to criticize factory head X, he said: "In the past, I was only deputy company commander, why did you say I was company commander?" "You said my history stank, well my history smells better than yours! Did you know that when I was deputy commander the Kuomintang and the Communists were cooperating?" He said: "You specialize in persecuting people, using secret-service tactics." But he got carried away: "It's the Communists who persecute people the most." As soon as he said it, he realized he'd gone too far. But before he could correct himself, he was forced to leave the meeting.[61]

Luo joined in the activities of the rebel faction, but no one wanted him. The factory head admitted it had been wrong to criticize him in big-character posters and undertook to restore his cadre status. Luo realized that the source of his problem lay with the factory leaders. If they rehabilitated him, he would be on solid grounds.[62]

In January 1967, the rebel faction declared their intention to seize power. Luo went to the former factory head demanding rehabilitation. The factory head later complained:

> Luo demanded rehabilitation on four occasions.[63] He had been a fake company commander. He incited others with historical problems to seek rehabilitation. They came to my dormitory and made a scene. They said 'tonight we are not holding a criticism meeting, we are holding a rehabilitation meeting. We want an immediate answer.' We said you need to take the matter to the East-is-Red Combat Battalion. We're not the ones who criticized you. In February, Luo incited X to come to our dormitory and demand rehabilitation. X said: 'The sooner this is over, the better. I only ask that mine and Luo's problems are resolved.' We said that according to the Ministry of Public Security, not everyone should be rehabilitated, and if we didn't followed policy, the revolutionary masses would blame us. The third time, X ordered us to rehabilitate them that night, but we said no.[64]

Luo had misread the situation. It did not occur to him that his actions contravened the "Six Provisions of Public Security," which forbade the black five categories from joining revolutionary organizations or forming their own organizations.

Even the rebel organizations disagreed with Luo. By 1967, the movement was dying down. Key departments were under army control, and military representatives were sent to factories and schools to prevent "power seizures."

In May 1968, the Central Committee started "cleaning up the class ranks." Class aliens and problem elements became a target. The Public Transport Bureau came under army control, and Luo and his friends could no longer demand rehabilitation. The former factory head led the revolutionary team. Luo became a focus.

An army representative listed more than sixty of Luo's "reactionary comments" and asked witnesses "to prepare supporting materials. Time, place, people present, and circumstances. Special attention must be paid to 'original words.' Each instance must be substantiated by multiple witnesses, collated in a single document signed by all."[65]

In October 1968, the Military Committee of the Public Transport Bureau asked the Party committee "to arrest and institute proceedings against Luo."[66] The new leadership in the print shop submitted a report titled "The wicked facts about the Kuomintang scum Luo Guozheng" and requested that Luo be "dealt with severely, to realize the dictatorship of the proletariat."[67]

In November, Luo and other counter-revolutionaries and bad elements were hauled before a struggle rally in the sports stadium and denounced.[68] Public security officers arrested Luo on the spot and threw him off the stage.

FRUITLESS INTERROGATIONS

Luo went on trial six months later. He had already spent six months in detention, and was not nervous at all when the trial began. As soon as he was given the chance to speak, he admitted his crimes: "I fought against the Red Army in the past. I inspected residence permits in Jiangxi, where I arrested and beat up civilians. Before Liberation, I colluded with dishonest traders and sold confidential information. During the Cultural Revolution, I violated the Six Provisions by participating in activities."[69]

Luo was also interrogated as a spy and traitor. He denied these allegations. The interrogator focused on Luo's reactionary remarks. Luo addressed them one by one, accepting that some were wrong and reactionary.[70]

After the fifth interrogation, the interrogators had still not obtained the results they hoped for, and were starting to get impatient:

Q: I'm warning you, Luo Guozheng! You have addressed some issues, but you either repeat what you said before or confess things already exposed by the masses. There are still many questions. Think carefully, choose your path.

A: I don't think I've hidden anything. I have explained all my problems. It's been almost twenty years since Liberation, the Organization had not asked me further questions. I have an insufficient understanding of the past.

Q: Not asking further questions doesn't mean everything has been resolved.

A: I don't have a history of participating in any other organization apart from the Kuomintang.

Q: What do you mean, "participating"?

A: I did not formally register. I never participated in any Kuomintang spy organization. I was in contact with people, but I didn't know their identities.

Q: Does not "formally registering" mean not joining?

A: I never participated in any hidden revolutionary organization.

Q: What do you mean by "hidden revolutionary organization"?

A: I never participated in any hidden counter-revolutionary organization.

Q: How did you say it the first time?

A: I left out a word. I left out the word "counter."

Q: Why did you leave out a crucial word?

A: I was speaking too quickly.

Q: Do you have a brain?

A: Yes, I do.

Q: Why did you speak so quickly?

A: It shows I have a reactionary mentality. I am from the old society.

Q: Of course it shows your reactionary mentality. Why did you deny it earlier?

A: Because I was afraid it would add to my punishment. As soon as I said it I wanted to correct it, but I was worried I'd get punished even more.

Q: Can anyone testify that you didn't join any other counter-revolutionary organization?

A: All my former colleagues at the Salt Bureau could testify.

Q: But some colleagues testified you did!

A: If they want to attack me, what can I do?

Q: So people want to attack you?

A: That's their business.

Q: I'm warning you! Not having participated in activities or gone through a formal process does not mean that you never joined. The facts remain that you concealed your identity. You refuse to explain, that's fine, we have other facts to determine your case. We attach great weight to evidence. Taking your statement is simply to assess your attitude to your crime. Do you understand?

A: I understand.

Q: If you understand, why don't you provide the facts?

A: I'm confident that the investigation will provide a clear account of my past.

Q: The investigation is a matter for the government. It has been done already. It's a matter for you whether you confess!

A: I can't lie to win the government's forgiveness. I can't just make things up.

Q: Are you trying to imply that the government is forcing you to make things up? Are you saying that we are not seeking the truth?

A: I have confidence in the government. I never participated in any spy organization. These were just claims by a few people. Just because they accuse me of having joined spy organizations doesn't mean I did.

Q: What does it take for you to plead guilty?

A: Let them specify the names of the organizations, let them say what meetings I attended. It's not enough to claim that I joined spy organizations. For example, to join the Kuomintang you needed an introduction; even going for a job in a shop requires someone to introduce you.

Q: So only attending meetings and participating in activities qualify as having joined? How many meetings did you attend while a member of the Kuomintang? What kind of counter-revolutionary activities did you carry out?

A: Once a week we'd have to go to regular memorial meetings.

Q: That further proves that you are a loyal pawn of the Kuomintang.

A: I admit that I was a loyal pawn of the Kuomintang.[71]

A second round of interrogations started in August. In them, Luo maintained that he had "thoroughly explained" all his historical problems. The interrogators turned nasty: "You have been deliberately unforthcoming. You persist in your reactionary stance, in your wish to oppose the people to the end. Down you go, then!"[72]

By then, the focus was on Luo having been a special agent. His former colleague X said he had been a member of the Salt Bureau security group, and the Public

Security Bureau believed him.[73] This group was "a large group of secret agents established under Zhongtong."[74] But there were no witnesses to corroborate X's statement.

"VICIOUS ATTACK" CONFIRMED

Just as the Public Security Bureau's pre-trial investigation seemed to be going nowhere, things suddenly turned around. In January 1970, the Central Committee launched its "One Thing to Attack and Three Things to Oppose" campaign. A month later, a fellow inmate of Luo's, Prisoner 411, told the "government" (i.e., the guards) that Luo had been spreading reactionary remarks in the detention center. He had questioned government policies and criticized Chairman Mao:

> The Cultural Revolution has been going on for two years, but cannot be wrapped up. The army can't be unified. To resolve these conflicts, they issue slogans about liberating Taiwan, to divert the people's attention.
>
> The economy was able to recover after the Great Leap Forward thanks to Liu Shaoqi, who motivated the farmers. A power struggle is going on in the Central Committee. Liu Shaoqi has stepped down, but his people won't submit. Chairman Mao is propped up by Lin Biao. There will be chaos.
>
> Chairman Mao is in his seventies, how much longer can he live? Once he goes, Lin Biao will take over, but he has limited experience and is held in low regard by the others, so he won't last long. It's obvious.
>
> China's problems lie mainly with the peasants. The forces of production cannot keep up with the relations of production. After the introduction of agricultural cooperatives, the people's communes were established too soon. They were unable to motivate people or stimulate production. The peasants only enjoyed a brief period of prosperity after land reform. Once the cooperatives and communes were introduced, things went downhill.
>
> After Liberation, we had one movement after another: Land reform, Zhenfan, the Three Antis, the Five Antis, Sufan, the Anti-Rightist movement, the New Three Antis, the Four Clean-Ups and now the Cultural Revolution. The number of people who have been punished must be higher than 5 percent. It must be in the millions. This city alone has twenty-five prisons and labor reform farms.[75]

During the Cultural Revolution, it was unforgivable to say such things (and especially to criticize Mao). Luo was bound to be "struck hard." The detention center launched an investigation that led to more accusations.

Luo had said: "Things have gone from bad to worse since Liberation." "Every day the papers report bumper harvests, but people are going hungry. The people are starving, while resources are being sent to aid others." "Nowadays the news is censored. There's no real news, just fabrication and what they want us to see. I have learned a trick: believe the opposite. If they say something is good, it must be bad."[76]

In October 1971, Luo admitted making these remarks. He said he had made them under the incitement of a fellow inmate who had said he would build a "base" in the mountains and move his family there. Luo had always dreamed of "a quiet and peaceful life." He and this inmate (and a third) got on well. He got carried away.[77]

Once it had been proved that Luo had "viciously attacked" Chairman Mao, his sentencing and punishment were a formality:

> The offender served in the fake army. In September 1939, he was captured by the Japanese and became a Japanese informant. He received 30 Japanese yen. He joined in the criminal activity of permit inspection on behalf of the Japanese.[78] He joined the Kuomintang twice. After Liberation he maintained a reactionary stance. During political movements he slandered the Party's policies and madly opposed Mao Zedong Thought. During his detention, he viciously attacked our great leader, displayed hostility toward our Party and the socialist order, and praised the traitor Liu Shaoqi. His crimes are countless. We recommend that he be designated an active counter-revolutionary, given a hat, and sent to the bureau's farm for monitoring and reform.[79]

CASE RESOLVED BY DEATH

In December 1971, Luo was sent to the countryside for monitoring and reform. The other inmates were also sent. Luo escaped a prison sentence, largely owing to his overseas connections.

For many years, Luo had been a key review subject. The Public Security Bureau had hoped to find out about Kuomintang agents in Hong Kong and Taiwan through Luo's overseas connections. If Luo had been sentenced to prison, this potential lead would have been cut off. Luo's offences were verbal and he was well past retirement age, so the authorities decided it was enough to give him a hat and send to the countryside. He would be allowed to visit home regularly, and it would be easy to monitor him.

The Public Security Bureau continued to suspect Luo of being a spy, and his eventual rehabilitation did not change its perception. A comparison of the bureau's 1979 report with its 1973 report shows few changes.[80] Periodic monitoring reports show that the bureau read Luo's overseas correspondence and knew about the activities of his relatives.[81] However, they never discovered any evidence of espionage.

After his rehabilitation in 1979, Luo retired from the factory and started enjoying his retirement, but not for long. Six months later, he fell ill and died. The Public Security Bureau submitted a report requesting that the investigation be terminated: "Key investigation subject Luo Guozheng (a retired worker) died in May. The basis of his investigation was that his brother-in-law Qi Huisheng, who fled to

Taiwan, contacted him from Japan in 1963 and sent money. The handwriting matched that of Wang X of the bandit Ministry of Defense, which raised suspicions. Our investigation yielded nothing. In view of Luo's death, and the fact that his wife Qi Huijun does not come under our jurisdiction, we recommend the termination of Luo's status as a key review subject."[82]

But it no longer mattered whether they thought Luo was innocent or not. Any lingering suspicion was buried with him.

CHRONOLOGY

1937–1945	Anti-Japanese War.
1946–1949	Civil War.
October 1949	Mao founds the People's Republic of China.
1950	China enters the Korean War.
1950–1952	Zhenfan (a campaign to suppress counter-revolutionaries).
1953	China starts its First Five-Year Plan.
1955–1956	Sufan (a campaign to purge hidden counter-revolutionaries).
1957	Mao starts the Hundred Flowers campaign.
1957	The Anti-Rightist campaign starts.
1958	The Great Leap Forward starts.
1959–1962	Millions die in a famine.
1966–1969	The Cultural Revolution (narrowly conceived).
1966–1976	The Cultural Revolution (broadly conceived).
1972	President Nixon visits China.
October 1976	Mao dies.
1978	Reforms and Open-Door Policy.
1979	Special Economic Zones are created.
1980	Deng Xiaoping becomes China's premier.

GLOSSARY

Administrative reform	An arbitrary system of administrative detention without judicial review.
Anti-Rightist campaign (1957–59)	A campaign to purge alleged "rightists" in the wake of the Hundred Flowers campaign.
Back door	To "go through the back door" is to take advantage for private purposes of gaps or loopholes in the bureaucratic system.
Bad element	Initially, a general reference to all corrupt, degenerate, and opportunistic individuals, but later to those whose actions were vile, whose thoughts were impure, and who harmed the Party's work.
Bandits	Either simply robbers or outlaws operating in gangs, or an insult directed by the Nationalists at the Communists and vice versa.
Black material	Politically impure and incriminating documents.
Brigade	A unit in the People's Commune system.
Public Security Bureau	The police and security authority.
Cadre	A public official holding a responsible or managerial position in the Party or government.
Central Committee	The political body that comprises the top leaders of the Communist Party.

Chiang Kai-shek (1887–1975)	Generalissimo Chiang was leader of the Republic of China between 1928 and 1975, first in mainland China and then in exile in Taiwan.
Collective ownership	The system whereby rural land was owned collectively by the peasants.
Commune	The highest administrative level in rural areas from 1958 to 1983.
Contradictions among the people	"The contradictions between ourselves and the enemy are antagonistic contradictions. Within the ranks of the people, the contradictions [. . .] are non-antagonistic" (Mao Zedong, 1957).
County (*xian*)	An administrative level below that of a province.
Cultural Revolution	Launched in 1966 by Mao, avowedly to purge remnants of capitalism and re-impose Mao Zedong Thought as the ruling ideology, but also as part of a power struggle. Its end is dated to either 1969 or 1976.
External investigation	An investigation in which the investigators go outside the workplace or unit.
"Fake"	An adjective applied by Nationalists to Communists, and vice versa, to signal the illegitimacy of an army, government, etc.
File (*dang'an*)	A dossier recording the attitudes and activities of a (usually urban) individual throughout his or her adult life—a major part of the authorities' apparatus of control.
Five Antis (*wufan*) (1952)	A reform movement aimed chiefly at capitalists.
Five black categories	Landlords, rich peasants, counter-revolutionaries, bad elements, and rightists.
Five-person team or committee	A decision-making structure (often not formally established) at central, provincial, municipal and county level, made up of core members of a given body.
Four categories	Landlords, rich peasants, counter-revolutionaries, and bad elements.
Four Clean-Ups (1962–66)	Also known as the Socialist Education movement, aimed at "cleaning up" politics, the economy, organization, and ideology.
"Gang of Four"	A group of Mao's supporters in the last years of his rule, formed by his wife Jiang Qing and her associates Wang Hongwen, Yao Wenyuan, and Zhang Chunqiao.
Great Leap Forward (1958–61)	Mao's crash drive to transform China into a socialist society through rapid industrialization and collectivization. Led to a famine in which millions died.

Green Gang	A secret society and criminal organization prominent in Shanghai and elsewhere before 1949.
Guo Moruo (1892–1978)	A Marxist, Mao-sycophant, and writer.
Historical crimes	Crimes committed before October 1949.
Hu Feng (1902–85)	A writer and literary theorist active in left-wing circles before 1949, arrested as a counter-revolutionary in 1955 and jailed until 1979.
Hundred Flowers campaign (1956–57)	The Communist Party encouraged people to express their criticisms of the government, then cracked down on those who did.
Internal investigation	An investigation conducted within the workplace or unit, without consulting external witnesses or documents.
Juntong	Until 1946, Chiang Kai-shek's National Bureau of Investigation and Statistics (Military Commission), often criticized as a secret police.
Kuomintang	The party that ruled China under Chiang Kai-shek from 1927 to 1948 and then moved to Taiwan.
Land reform	The Beijing government published a Land Reform Law in June 1950 that redistributed land to the peasants.
Lin Biao (1907–71)	A Communist leader and general, and Mao Zedong's anointed successor until his death in a suspicious plane crash in 1971.
Liu Shaoqi (1898–1969)	Groomed as Mao's successor until the Cultural Revolution, when he was purged. Died under harsh treatment in 1969.
Mao Zedong (1893–1976)	A Communist revolutionary who in 1949 founded the People's Republic of China, which he ruled until his death.
Mass line	Mao Zedong's political, organizational, and leadership method, comprising three stages: consult the masses, interpret their suggestions within a Marxist-Leninist ideological framework, and realize the resulting policies.
Mu	A unit of land measurement commonly reckoned at 0.165 acres.
New Fourth Army	Established in 1937 as part of Chiang Kai-shek's National Revolutionary Army, but in fact controlled by Communists.
Opening up	The economic reforms inaugurated by Deng Xiaoping in 1978.
Organization, the	The Communist Party, at its various levels.

Ownership by the whole people	Collective assets were owned collectively by the community, whereas state assets were owned by "the whole people."
People's Republic of China	Founded in Beijing in October 1949.
Plane of principle and the two-line struggle	the level to which issues of politics and philosophy should be raised as part of the struggle in the Party between Marxism and erroneous ideas.
Province	The highest level administrative division.
Rectification movement (1957)	Another name for the Anti-Rightist campaign that brutally ended the Hundred Flowers campaign.
Re-education through labor (*laojiao*)	A system of administrative detention, typically of one to three years, and of subjection to political education.
Reference News (*Cankao ziliao*)	A daily newspaper that selects articles from the world's press and translates them into Chinese.
Reform through labor	A term in the criminal justice system (*laogai*) to refer to penal labour. *Laogai* differed from *laojiao*, re-education through labor, an administrative detention system applied to non-criminals.
Reforms	The economic reforms by Deng Xiaoping starting in 1978.
Republic of China	Established in 1912; lasted until 1949, when its leaders fled to Taiwan after the Kuomintang's defeat in the Civil War.
Revolutionary committee	Set up to wield power in the Cultural Revolution, comprising representatives of the "people," the army, and the Party.
Rightist	The Anti-Rightist campaign (1957–59) aimed to purge "rightists," who in reality included socialist and liberal critics of the government.
Secret societies	Members swore oaths and had family-style ties to one another. Often associated with crime and dissent and, after 1949, with reaction activity.
Sects	Folk-religious organisations and movements defined after 1949 as evil cults.
Small group or team	A group put together for a particular purpose (e.g., to organize work or study or perform a given task).
Socialist Education movement	A movement launched in 1963 to remove "reactionaries" from the bureaucracy and the Party. See also Four Clean-Ups.
Struggle (*douzheng*)	Often used as a transitive verb; to subject a person to political persecution, often violent, when the "masses" are expected to show loyalty to the Party and hostility toward "class enemies" or bad elements.

Sufan (1955–56)	A political campaign to "purge (*su*) hidden counter-revolutionary elements (*fan*)" in the Party, the bureaucracy, and the army.
Sun Yat-sen (1866–1925)	Recognized by Nationalists and Communists alike as the founding father of the Republic of China.
Three Antis (*sanfan*) (1951)	A reform movement aimed chiefly at corrupt Communists, former Kuomintang members, and bureaucrats.
Three Hard Years	The famine of 1959–61, which killed tens of millions.
Three Selfs	A Nationalist movement in the 1930s and 1940s emphasizing self-government, self-defense, and self-sufficiency.
Wang Jingwei (1883–1944)	A Nationalist politician who, later in his career, became a Japanese puppet.
Wang Shiwei (1907–47)	Author of "Wild Lily" (1942), an essay supportive but critical of the Communist Party. It led to his eventual execution.
War criminal	The Communists classed Kuomintang leaders "responsible for launching the counter-revolutionary war" as war criminals.
Yan Xishan (1883–1960)	A Chinese warlord who served in the government of the Republic of China.
Youth Corps (1938–47)	The Kuomintang Youth Corps with a fascist flavour.
Youth League	The Communist Youth, founded in 1920, recruits youngsters aged fourteen to twenty-eight and is organized on the same lines as the Party.
Yuan	In the 1960s, one U.S. dollar bought 2.5 yuan. Ten yuan bought 44 kg. of rice or 3.3 m. of cloth. An average wage in the late 1960s was about 36 yuan.
Zhenfan (1950–52)	A political campaign to "suppress (*zhen*) counter-revolutionary elements (*fan*)."
Zhongtong	The Kuomintang's intelligence service.

NOTES

TRANSLATORS' INTRODUCTION

1. Karl Marx, "Sieg der Kontrerevolution zu Wien," *Neue Rheinische Zeitung* 136 (1848).

2. The story is told in Gregor Benton, *Mountain Fires: The Red Army's Three-Year War in South China, 1934–1938* (Berkeley, CA: University of California Press, 1992).

3. Shao-Chuan Leng, "The Role of Law in the People's Republic of China as Reflecting Mao Tse-Tung's Influence," *Journal of Criminal Law and Criminology* 68, no. 3 (1977): 357.

4. Patricia E. Griffin, *The Chinese Communist Treatment of Counterrevolutionaries, 1924–1949* (Princeton: Princeton University Press), 1976, 39–40..

5. Hua-yu Li, "The Political Stalinization of China: The Establishment of One-Party Constitutionalism, 1948–1954," *Journal of Cold War Studies* 3, no. 2 (Spring 2001): 31.

6. Lung-sheng Tao, "Criminal Law of Communist China," *Cornell Law Review* 52, no. 43 (1966): 53.

7. Thomas P. Bernstein, "The Complexities of Learning from the Soviet Union," in *China Learns from the Soviet Union, 1949–Present,* ed. Thomas P. Bernstein and Hua-Yu Li, (Lanham: Lexington Books, 2011), 8–9.

8. Julia Strauss, "Communist Revolution and Political Terror," in *The Oxford Handbook of the History of Communism,* ed. Stephen A. Smith (Oxford: Oxford University Press, 2014), 366.

9. Li Ruojian, "Cong shuzui dao tizui: Si lei fenzi jieceng chubu yanjiu" ("From atonement to scapegoat: A preliminary study of the four categories class"), *Kaifang shidai* ("Open times") 5 (2006), np, http://www.opentimes.cn/html/Abstract/882.html.

10. Teng P'ing (Deng Ping), "Lawbreaking Elements among the People Definitely Cannot All Be Treated as Objects of Dictatorship," in *The Criminal Process in the People's Republic of China, 1949–1963: An Introduction,* ed. Jerome Alan Cohen (Cambridge, MA: Harvard University Press, 1968), 91–93.

11. Ibid.

12. Yang Kuisong, "How a 'Bad Element' Was Made: The Discovery, Accusation, and Punishment of Zang Qiren," in *Maoism at the Grassroots: Everyday Life in China's Era of High Socialism,* ed. Jeremy Brown and Matthew D. Johnson (Cambridge, MA: Harvard University Press, 2015), 19–50.

13. There seems to have been no exact equivalent to China's categories and elements in the Soviet Union or Eastern Europe, where the focus was more exclusively on the elimination of classes rather than on their containment, shaping, and possible reform. Malcolm Thompson, in a personal communication, suggests "subkulak" as a sort of equivalent. "Subkulak" is defined by Slavoj Žižek "as a peasant who, although too poor to be considered a kulak proper, nonetheless shared the kulak 'counterrevolutionary' attitude," a term (Žižek is quoting Robert Conquest) "without any real social content even by Stalinist standards" (*Less Than Nothing: Hegel and the Shadow of Dialectical Materialism* [London: Verso, 2012], 73). Puck Engman, also in a personal communication, points to distinctions in the treatment of different sorts of black elements across time and space in China. Landlords, for example, were deprived of political rights under the 1954 Constitution, whereas other black elements were not necessarily so deprived. In that sense, landlords in China corresponded directly to Stalin's *lishentsy.* Perhaps the nearest equivalents were "anti-social, parasitical elements" (initially, beggars, tramps, and prostitutes) and *lishentsy* ("deprived," often translated as "disenfranchised"). "Anti-social, parasitical elements" were treated administratively, by removal from cities, but under a 1951 law they could be sentenced to five years' exile. In 1957, a revised law included among them people in the informal economy and those unwilling to work or who liked to hang around foreigners (Sheila Fitzpatrick, "Social Parasites: How Tramps, Idle Youth, and Busy Entrepreneurs Impeded the Soviet March to Communism," *Cahiers du monde russe* 47, nos 1–2: 377). As for *lishentsy,* most gained their status as outcasts because of "past or present economic behavior" or lifestyle and ideology. Although in the Soviet Union bad-class members and their descendants were in many cases unable to earn trust and were regarded as "unreliable," outcasts could also be reinstated if they performed socially useful labor and demonstrated their loyalty to the state (Golfo Alexopoulos, *Stalin's Outcasts: Aliens, Citizens, and the Soviet State, 1926–1936* (Ithaca, NY: Cornell University Press, 2003), 11–14). In these several senses, China's categories and elements had a Soviet counterpart, though there seems to be no evidence that the former were directly based on the latter.

14. Griffin, *The Chinese Communist Treatment of Counterrevolutionaries,* 109–35, 149.

15. James D. Seymour and Richard Anderson, *New Ghosts, Old Ghosts: Prisons and Labor Reform Camps in China* (Armonk, NY: M. E. Sharpe, 1999), 18–21.

16. Aminda M. Smith, *Thought Reform and China's Dangerous Classes: Reeducation, Resistance, and the People* (Lanham, MD: Rowman and Littlefield, 2013), 1–9.

17. Li, "Cong shuzui dao tizui," np.

18. Ibid.

19. Harry Wu, "Classicide in Communist China," *Comparative Civilizations Review* 67, no. 67 (2012): 103.

20. Li, "Cong shuzui dao tizui," np.

21. Ibid.

22. Julia Strauss, personal communication, December 22, 2018.

23. Yang Kuisong, *Bianyuan ren jishi* ("Stories of marginal persons") (Guangzhou, China: Guangdong renmin chuban she, 2016), 343–52.

24. Ibid., 358–66.

25. Lucie Cheng, "Women and Class Analysis in the Chinese Land Revolution," *Berkeley Journal of Gender, Law and Justice* 4, no. 1 (1988): 67.

CHAPTER ONE. RETURNING TO THE PEOPLE'S ROAD

1. Zhou Enlai, "Rénmín zhèngxié gòngtóng gānglǐng cǎo'àn de tèdiǎn" ("Special features of the draft common program of the CPPCC"), September 22, 1949, in Zhōngyāng wénxiàn yánjiūshì, ed., *Jiànguó yǐlái zhòngyào wénxiàn xuǎnbiān* ("Selected important documents since the founding of the Republic"), vol. 1 (Beijing: Zhōngyāng wénxiàn chūbǎn shè, 1991), 17.

2. Li Ruojian, "Cóng shúzuì dào tìzuì—sì lèi fènzi jiēcéng chūtàn" ("From atonement to scapegoating—a preliminary exploration of the social strata of the four categories"), *Kāifàng shídài* ("Open times") 5 (2006), np, http://www.opentimes.cn/html/Abstract/882.html.

3. "Gànbù jiǎnlì kǎpiàn" ("Cadre biography"), May 20, 1950, Liao Xuechang file. It is not possible to cite page locations in this file.

4. "Gànbù cáiliào dēngjì biǎo" ("Cadre registration form"), June 1951, Liao Xuechang file.

5. "Zìzhuàn" ("Autobiography"), June 30, 1951, Liao Xuechang file.

6. See "Zhōngyāng shí rén xiǎozǔ guānyú fǎngémìng fènzi hé qítā huài fènzi de jiěshì jí chǔlǐ de zhèngzhì jièxiàn de zànxíng guīdìng" ("Interim provisions of the Central Committee's ten-person panel on the political limits and handling of counter-revolutionaries and other bad elements"), March 10, 1956. It said that "core elements of the reactionary Party refers to anyone who, since the start of the Liberation War in 1946, had served on a Kuomintang district committee or above or as team leader or deputy leader of the Youth Corps, as well as core elements at an equivalent level in other reactionary organisations (including the Youth Party, the Social-Democratic Party, Yan Xishan's Comrades' Association, and so forth).

7. "Gànbù jiàndìng biǎo" ("Cadre appraisal form"), June 27, 1952, Liao Xuechang file.

8. "Gànbù lǚlì biǎo" ("Cadre personal record"), May 18, 1955, Liao Xuechang file.

9. "Liào Xuéchāng lìshǐ shěnchá jìlù" ("Record of Liao Xuechang's historical review"), August 1955, Liao Xuechang file.

10. "Bǔchōng cáiliào" ("Supplementary materials"), August 9 and 26 and September 1 and 3, 1955; "Tǎnbái jiāodài gèrén lìshǐ jí zhèngzhì wèntí" ("Personal confessions and political problems"), September 3, 1955, Liao Xuechang file.

11. "Liào Xuéchāng de lìshǐ wèntí" ("Historical problems relating to Liao Xuechang"), September 14, 1955, Liao Xuechang file.

12. "Diàochá rén Yú Yǒngshēng guānyú Liào Xuéchāng lìshǐ wèntí de wàichū diàochá bàogào" ("Investigator Yu Yongsheng's report on Liao Xuechang's historical problems"), September 18, 1955, Liao Xuechang file.

13. "Guānyú Liào Xuéchāng de qíngkuàng" ("On the situation of Liao Xuechang"), September 1955, Liao Xuechang file.

14. In a supplementary confession dated October 18, Liao explained that this was not true. Thinking back, he remembered that that the evidence against the suspect had been insufficient, and the person had been released.

15. "Bǔchōng tǎnbái cáiliào" ("Supplementary confession materials"), October 11, 12, and 13, 1955, Liao Xuechang file.

16. "Bǔchōng cáiliào" ("Supplementary materials"), October 18, 1955, Liao Xuechang file.

17. "Dàibǔ bàogào shū" ("Arrest report"), November 20, 1955, Liao Xuechang file.

18. "Liào Xuéchāng zhuān'àn bàogào" ("Liao Xuechang special-case report"), November 1955, Liao Xuechang file.

19. "Shěnxùn Liào Xuéchāng bǐlù" ("Liao Xuechang trial transcript"), December 3, 1955, Liao Xuechang file.

20. "Liào Xuéchāng dìng'àn bàogào cǎogǎo" ("Liao Xuechang's final draft report"), December 1955, Liao Xuechang file.

21. "Bǔchōng cáiliào" ("Supplementary materials"), December 1955, Liao Xuechang file.

22. "Liào Xuéchāng ànjiàn bàogào shū" ("Liao Xuechang's final report"), December 1955, Liao Xuechang file.

23. "Bǔchōng cáiliào" ("Supplementary materials"), January 21, 1956, Liao Xuechang file.

24. "Shēnqǐng fùyì shū" ("Application for reconsideration"), February 2, 1956, Liao Xuechang file.

25. "Zhōngyāng shí rén xiǎozǔ guānyú fǎngémìng fènzi hé qítā huài fènzi de jiěshì jí chǔlǐ de zhèngcè jièxiàn de zànxíng guīdìng (cǎo'àn)" ("Interim provisions for interpreting and handling policy boundaries regarding counter-revolutionaries and other bad elements issued by the Central Committee's Ten-Member Group [Draft]"), December 1955.

26. "Gànbù zhěngfēng zǒngjié jí yòu hóng yòu zhuān guīhuà" ("Cadre rectification and the red and expert programme"), September 15, 1958, Liao Xuechang file.

27. "Gànbù zhěngfēng zǒngjié jí yòuhóng-yòuzhuān guīhuà" ("Cadre rectification and the red and expert plan"), September 15, 1958, Liao Xuechang file.

28. "Gànbù zhěngfēng zǒngjié jí yòuhóng-yòuzhuān guīhuà" ("Cadre rectification and the red and expert plan"), September 15, 1958, Liao Xuechang file.

29. "Gànbù láodòng jiàndìng biǎo" ("Cadres' labor assessment table"), October 20, 1959, Liao Xuechang file.

30. On March 22, 1963, the "Sì lèi fènzi shěnpī biǎo" ("Four categories examination and approval form") in the Liao Xuechang file noted that he was put under control for one year, but on February 22, 1978, it said two years.

31. On August 9, 1957, the State Council formally adopted a regulation requiring that counter-revolutionaries placed under control should only be entitled to "the equivalent wage," in accordance with the principle of equal pay for equal work. In actual fact, this meant the basic minimum.

32. "Sì lèi fènzi shěnpī biǎo" ("Four categories examination and approval form"), March 22, 1963, Liao Xuechang file.

33. "X jiǎnjǔ cáiliào" ("X prosecution materials"), May 10, 1963, Liao Xuechang file.

34. "X fǎnyìng Liào Xuéchāng qíngkuàng" ("X reflects on Liao Xuechang"), December 31, 1964, Liao Xuechang file.

35. "X jiēfā cáiliào" ("X exposure"), June 27, 1965, Liao Xuechang file.

36. "X jiǎnjǔ Liào Xuéchāng gè xiàng wèntí cáiliào" ("X reports on Liao Xuechang and the problem of materials"), June 25, 1965, Liao Xuechang file.

37. "Sì lèi fènzi shěnpī biǎo" ("Four categories examination and approval form"), March 22, 1963, Liao Xuechang file. According to the February 22, 1978 "Four categories examination and approval form," Liao was not only still under surveillance but was wearing a "counter-revolutionary hat."

38. "Sì lèi fènzi shěnpī biǎo" ("Four categories examination and approval form"), July 24, 1965, Liao Xuechang file.

39. Ibid.

40. "Gǎizào sīxiǎng lìgōng jìhuà" ("Plan for transformation of thinking and the rendering of meritorious service"), July 21, 1965, Liao Xuechang file.

41. Ibid.

42. "Bǔchōng cáiliào" (Supplementary materials), July 19, 1965, Liao Xuechang file.

43. By then they were known as the black five elements (landlords, rich peasants, counter-revolutionaries, bad elements, and rightists).

44. "Sì yuèfèn sīxiǎng huìbào" ("April report"), May 1, 1975, Liao Xuechang file.

45. Ibid. See also "Liù yuèfèn sīxiǎng huìbào" ("June thought report"), June 30, 1975, Liao Xuechang file.

46. "Shíyī yuèfèn sīxiǎng huìbào" ("November report"), December 5, 1976, Liao Xuechang file.

47. "Yuán yuèfèn sīxiǎng huìbào" ("January thought report"), January 31, 1975, Liao Xuechang file.

48. "Sān yuèfèn sīxiǎng huìbào" ("March thought report"), March 31, 1975, and "Wǔ yuèfèn sīxiǎng huìbào" ("May thought report"), May 31, 1975, Liao Xuechang file.

49. "Wǔ yuèfèn sīxiǎng huìbào" ("May thought report"), May 31, 1975, Liao Xuechang file.

50. "1975 Nián sīxiǎng gǎizào huìbào" ("1975 report on thought reform"), December 10, 1975, Liao Xuechang file.

51. "Èr yuèfèn sīxiǎng huìbào" ("February thought report"), February 28, 1975, Liao Xuechang file.

52. "Jiǔ yuèfèn sīxiǎng huìbào" ("September thought report"), September 28, 1975, Liao Xuechang file.

53. "Shí'èr yuè sīxiǎng huìbào" ("December thought report"), January 5, 1975, Liao Xuechang file.

54. "1976 nián sīxiǎng gǎizào guīhuà" ("1976 ideological reform plan"), January 5, 1976, Liao Xuechang file.

55. Ibid.

56. "Bā yuè sīxiǎng gǎizào huìbào" ("August ideological transformation report"), August 25, 1977, Liao Xuechang file.

57. See Rénmín rìbào ("People's Daily"), January 29, 1979.

58. "Jiǔ yuèfèn sīxiǎng huìbào" ("September report"), September 28, 1975, Liao Xuechang file.

CHAPTER TWO. THE CONSEQUENCES OF CONCEALING HISTORY

1. "Zhōngyāng shí rén xiǎozǔ guānyú fǎn gémìng fènzi hé qítā huài fènzi de jiěshì jí chǔlǐ de zhèngzhì jièxiàn de zànhíng guīdìng" ("The interim provisions of the 10-member group of the Central Committee regarding the political dividing lines for interpreting and handling counter-revolutionaries and other bad elements"), March 10, 1956, Shanghai Archives, J163/4/167/13–16.

2. Mao Zedong, "Guānyú zhèngquè chǔlǐ rénmín nèibù máodùn de wèntí" ("On the correct handling of contradictions among the people"), February 27, 1957, in Mao Zedong, *Máo Zédōng xuǎnjí* ("Selected works of Mao Zedong)," Beijing: Renmin chuban she, 1977), 5:366.

3. After the "rightists" made their appearance, there was often mention of "five elements."

4. "Lǚlì kǎpiàn" ("Personal record"), date unknown, Li Lesheng file 1, 12.

5. "Tǎnbái dēngjì cáiliào" ("Register of confession materials"), July 1958, Li Lesheng file 1, 14.

6. "Lǚlì dēngjì biǎo" ("Personal history form"), 1958 (?), Li Lesheng file 1, 89.

7. "Gànbù dēngjì biǎo" ("Cadre registration form"), January 5, 1953, Li Lesheng file 1, 18; "Zhígōng dēngjì biǎo" ("Staff registration form"), January 24, 1957, Li Lesheng file 1, 27.

8. "Gànbù dēngjì biǎo" ("Cadre registration form"), January 5, 1953, Li Lesheng file 1, 27.

9. "Bàogào shū" ("Report"), May 3, 1953, Li Lesheng file 1, 27.

10. "Tǎnbái shū" ("Confession"), September 23, 1956, Li Lesheng file 1, 28.

11. Ibid.

12. Ibid.

13. "Tǎnbái dēngjì cáiliào" ("Confession materials"), July 1958, Li Lesheng file 1, 14.

14. "Jiǎnjǔ Lǐ Lèshēng" ("Report on Li Lesheng"), August 24, 1959, Li Lesheng file 1, 15.

15. "Diàochá zhèngmíng cáiliào jièshào xìn" fù "diàochá xiànsuǒ" ("Investigation testimony," with, as an appendix, "Investigation leads"), December 20 and 22, 1960, Li Lesheng file 2.

16. "Diàochá xiànsuǒ biǎo" ("List of leads in the investigation"), 1960, Li Lesheng file 1, 94.

17. "Jì X qíngkuàng jièshào" ("Introduction to the situation of Ji X"), December 17, 1960, Li Lesheng file 1, 58.

18. "Wáng X diàochá bàogào" ("Wang X's investigation report"), February 1, 1961, Li Lesheng file 1, 59–60.

19. "Luò X zhèngmíng Lǐ Lèshēng de cáiliào" ("Luo X's testimony regarding Li Lesheng"), April 6, 1961, August 2, Li Lesheng file 1, 70–71.

20. "Zhāng X duì Lǐ Lèshēng de diàochá bàogào" ("Zhang X's investigation report regarding Li Lesheng"), August 2, 1961, Li Lesheng file 1, 91.

21. "Chá X bǐ shù" ("Handwritten materials regarding X"), September 23, 1961, Li Lesheng file 1, 66.

22. "Zhōnggòng Y shìwěi gōngyè xìtǒng shěn-gàn bàngōngshì zhì Xīnjiāng Chábùchá ěr Xíbó zìzhì xiàn rénmín jiǎncháyuàn hán" ("Letter from the cadre review office of the industrial complex of the CCP's Y Municipality committee to the Xinjiang Chabuchar Xibo Autonomous County People's Procuratorate"), August 5, 1961, and February 16, 1962;

"Xīnjiāng Chábùchár Xíbó zìzhì xiàn rénmín jiǎncháyuàn zhì Zhōnggòng Y shìwěi gōngyè xìtǒng shěn gàn bàngōngshì hán" ("Letter from the Xinjiang Chabuchar Sibo Autonomous County People's Procuratorate to the cadre review office of the industrial complex of the CCP's Y Municipality committee"), October 19, 1961, and April 25, 1962, Li Lesheng file 1, 73 and 79–80.

23. "Wǒ hé Chén X de guānxì wèntí" ("The relationship between me and Chen X"), April 26, 1968, Li Lesheng file 2.

24. "Wǒ de sīxiǎng rènshí" ("My thinking and understanding"), April 26, 1968, Li Lesheng file 2.

25. "Wǒ hé Chén X de guānxì wèntí" ("The relationship between me and Chen X"), April 26 and 28, 1968, Li Lesheng file 2.

26. "Zìwǒ jiǎnchá" ("Self-examination"), May 1, 1968, Li Lesheng file 2.

27. "Xiàng quán chǎng gémìng zhígōng jiǎnchá" ("Self-criticism addressed to the factory's revolutionary workers"), June 2, 1968, Li Lesheng file 2.

28. "Guānyú wǒ táopǎo shí de sīxiǎng qíngkuàng" ("On my thinking at the time of my escape"), June 3, 1968, Li Lesheng file 2.

29. "Jiēfā Chén X gǎo zīběn zhǔyì fùbì" ("Exposing Chen X's restoration of capitalism"); "Zài wénhuà dà gémìng zhòng hé Chén jiēchù" ("My contacts with Chen X in the Cultural Revolution"); "Wǒ hé Chén guānxì wèntí" ("My relationship with Chen X"), June 9, 1968, Li Lesheng file 2.

30. "Zìwǒ jiǎnchá" ("Self-examination"), June 12, 1968, Li Lesheng file 2.

31. "Zìwǒ jiǎnchá" ("Self-examination"), June 17, 1968, Li Lesheng file 2.

32. "Jiāng X bǐlù" ("Jiang X transcript"), September 16, 1968, Li Lesheng file 2.

33. "Gèrén lìshǐ jiāodài" ("Personal confession"), December 25, 1968, Li Lesheng file 2.

34. "Yǒuguān Lǐ Lèshēng de qíngkuàng jiāodài" ("On Li Lesheng's confession"), November 5, 1968, Li Lesheng file 2.

35. "Guānyú wǒ lìshǐ wèntí de jiāodài" ("On my confession regarding historical questions"), November 25, 1968, Li Lesheng file 2.

36. "Bǔchōng cáiliào" ("Supplementary materials"), December 4, 1968, Li Lesheng file 2.

37. "Gèrén lìshǐ jiāodài" ("Personal confession"), December 25, 1968, Li Lesheng file 2.

38. "Zhāng X guānyú wěi S xiàn Nánchí qū sānmín zhǔyì qīngnián tuán gàikuàng" ("Zhang X on the fake S County Nanchi District's Three People's Youth Corps"), January 18, 1969; "Lóu X guānyú wěi Nánchí qū qīngnián zhàndì fúwù duì qíngkuàng" ("Lou X on the fake Nanchi District's Youth Field-Service Team"), January 19, 1969; "Luò X zhèngmíng cáiliào" ("Luo X's evidence"), January 17, 1969, Li Lesheng file 3; Xú X, "Guānyú Lǐ Lèshēng wèntí de dáfù" ("Reply on the Li Lesheng question"), February 3, 1969, Li Lesheng file 2.

39. This movement was based on three documents issued on January 31 and February 5, 1970, titled "Directive on the fight against counterrevolutionary sabotage," "Directive opposing corruption, theft, and speculation," and "Against extravagance and waste." The movement stressed the need to "strike hard," so a large number of people were killed, locked up, or put under control during it.

40. "Zìwǒ jiāodài" ("Confession"), June 17, 1970, Li Lesheng file 3.

41. "Guānyú shōutīng dítái guǎngbò de jiāodài" ("On listening to broadcasts of the enemy and from Taiwan"), August 7, 1970, Li Lesheng file 3.

42. "Qíngkuàng shuōmíng" ("Explanation of the situation"), September 21, 1970, Li Lesheng file 1, 42–43.

43. "Bǔchōng shuōmíng" ("Supplementary notes"), December 4, 1968, Li Lesheng file 2.

44. "Lǐ Lèshēng zhì shì qīnggōngyè jú zhuān'àn zǔ ("Li Lesheng to the Municipal Light Industry Bureau's special team"), January 22, 1972, Li Lesheng file 1, 46.

45. "Tǎnbái shū" ("Confession"), June 23, 1970, Li Lesheng file 2.

46. At the rally in early September, Li was accused of having sex with children as young as twelve or thirteen. He later denied this. See "Jiāodài cáiliào" ("Confession materials"), October 7, 1970, Li Lesheng file 1, 40.

47. "Wǒ zài shēnghuó zuòfēng shàng de fànzuì shìshí xìtǒng jiāodài" ("Systematic confession of crimes connected with my lifestyle"), September 10, 1970, Li Lesheng file 2.

48. "Wǒ fàn yánzhòng zuìxíng de gēnyuán" ("The root causes of my serious crimes"), September 16, 1970, Li Lesheng file 1, 29–39.

49. "Sīxiǎng huìbào" ("Thought report"), October 3, 1971, Li Lesheng file 1, 61.

50. "Lǐ Lèshēng zhì shì qīnggōngyè jú zhuān'àn zǔ" ("Li Lesheng to the Municipal Light Industry Bureau's special team"), January 22, 1972, Li Lesheng file 1, 46.

51. "Guānyú Lǐ Lèshēng wèntí de shěnchá jiélùn hé chǔlǐ yìjiàn" ("Views and conclusions on the investigation and handling of the Li Lesheng question"), April 14, 1972, Li Lesheng file 1, 54–55.

52. "Zuìgāo rénmín fǎyuàn guānyú chéngnián rénjiān zìyuàn jījiān shìfǒu fànzuì wèntí de pīfù" ("The Supreme People's Court on whether or not adult consensual sodomy is a crime"), March 19, 1957. See www.chinabaike.com/law/zhishi/yf/1421055.html.

53. See "Bùgào" ("Notice"), January 21, 1977, Li Lesheng file 1, 3.

54. "Guānyú Lǐ Lèshēng wèntí chǔlǐ yìjiàn de qǐngshì bàogào" ("Report on the handling of the Li Lesheng question"), August 1976, Li Lesheng file 1, 4–5.

55. "Sīxiǎng huìbào" ("Thought report"), January 25, 1977, Li Lesheng file 1, 26.

56. Ibid.

57. "Bùgào" ("Notice"), January 21, 1977, Li Lesheng file 1, 3.

58. "N shì zhōngjí rénmín fǎyuàn xíngshì pànjuéshū (77) fǎxíng zì dì 55 hào" ("N Municipality Intermediate People's Court Criminal Judgment [77], Criminal Justice Court no. 55"), April 21, 1977, Li Lesheng file 1, 1.

CHAPTER THREE. THE IRREMOVABLE HAT

1. "N shì jūnshì guǎnzhì wěiyuánhuì guānyú bānbù 'N shì Jiǎng yánfěi tèwù rényuán shēnqǐng huǐguò dēngjì shíshī bànfǎ' de bùgào" ("N Municipality Military Control Commission notice on the promulgation of 'N Municipality's Chiang-Yan bandit special agents' application for repentance registration'"), 1949, in N Municipality Archives, eds., *Jiěfàng N shì* ("The Liberation of N Municipality") (Beijing: Zhōngguó dǎng'àn chūbǎn shè, 2009), 249.

2. "N shì jūnshì guǎnzhì wěiyuánhuì guānyú Jiǎng-Yán jūn tèwù fènzǐ xū lǚxíng dēngjì shǒuxù de bùgào" ("N Municipality Military Control Commission's notice on the Chiang-Yan armies' special agents' registration procedures"), May 19, 1949, in Ibid., 237; and Gu Feng, "N shì jiěfàng chūqí jǐngbèi zhì'ān gōngzuò zhuījì" ("N Municipality's police security work record in the early Liberation period"), *X wénshǐ zīliào* 4 (cumulative no. 106) (1996).

3. "N shì jūnshì guǎnzhì wěiyuánhuì guānyú Jiǎng-Yán jūn tèwù fènzi xū lǔxíng dēngjì shǒuxù de bùgào" ("N Municipality Military Control Commission's notice on the Chiang-Yan armies' special agents' registration procedures"), May 19, 1949, in *Jiěfàng N shì*, 250.

4. "N shì jūnshì guǎnzhì wěiyuánhuì bānbù 'fǎndòng dǎngtuán huì rényuán lǔxíng dēngjì shíshī bànfǎ' de bùgào" ("Notice promulgated by N Municipality Military Control Commission regarding 'implementation of the registration of members of the reactionary Party and Youth Corps'"), December 10, 1949, in *Jiěfàng N shì*, 248–49.

5. According to the then Minister of Public Security Luo Ruiqing, in the early years of the PRC, nearly one million backbone elements belonging to the counter-revolutionary Party registered for education and were released, as well as about five million reactionary elements and nearly one million reactionary officers. See Luo Ruiqing, "Jìnyībù jiāqiáng rénmín gōng'ān gōngzuò wéi bǎozhàng guójiā shèhuì zhǔyì jiànshè hé shèhuì zhǔyì gǎizào de shùnlì shíshī ér dòuzhēng—zài dì liù cì quánguó gōng'ān huìyì shàng de bàogào" ("Struggle to further strengthen People's Public Security work to protect and ensure the smooth implementation of the nation's socialist construction and socialist reform—report to the Sixth National Public Security Conference"), May 17, 1954, Hebei archives, 2/2/286/30.

6. "Fǎndòng dǎngtuán huì rényuán huǐguò shū" ("Repentance by reactionary Party members"), December 29, 1949, N Municipality staff hospital security section, Fang Liren file 1, 255. The following text is taken from the original record. Names of people and places have been obscured.

7. Ibid., 253.

8. "Gōng'ān dì yī fēnjú dì sān pàichūsuǒ guǎnnèi fǎndòng dǎngtuán huì fùzé rén dēngjì biǎo" ("Third police station of the first branch of Public Security in charge of the registration of leading members of the reactionary Party, Youth Corps, and associations"), January 11, 1950, Fang Liren file 1, 254.

9. "Tèzhǒng hùkǒu diàochá biǎo (dǎng huì xìngzhì 130 hào)" ("Special household survey form, parties and associations [no. 130]"), January 1951, Fang Liren file 1, 251.

10. Fang Liren, "Fàng bāofú, jiē gàizi cáiliào—tiānzhǔ jiào xùnliàn bān" ("Putting down the burden, removing the cover—Catholic training class"), March 5, 1966, Fang Liren file 1, 1–2.

11. Fang Liren, "Wǒ de jiǎnchá" ("My inspection"), June 15, 1965, Fang Liren file 1, 47.

12. Ibid.

13. Fang Liren, "Fàng bāofu, jiē gàizi cáiliào—tiānzhǔjiào xùnliàn bān" ("Putting down the burden, removing the cover—Catholic training class"), March 5, 1966, Fang Liren file 1, 3.

14. "N shì shì gōng'ān jú dì yī fēnjú tèzhǒng rénkǒu qiānyí tōngbào shū" ("Circular issued by the first branch of N Municipality's Public Security Bureau regarding special population movement"), December 14, 1951, Fang Liren file 1, 250.

15. "N shì rénmín zhèngfǔ gōng'ān jú zhì zhígōng yīyuàn gōnghán" ("Official letter from N Municipality People's Government Public Security Bureau to the Workers' Hospital"), January 8, 1954; "N shì rénmín zhèngfǔ gōng'ān jú xiànsuǒ cáiliào jièshào shū" ("Introduction by N Municipality People's Government Public Security Bureau to leads"), January 9, 1954, Fang Liren file 1, 249, 252.

16. "N zhígōng yīyuàn gōnghán" ("N Workers' Hospital letter"), January 23, 1954, Fang Liren file 1, 248.

17. Fang Liren, "Wǒ de jiǎnchá" ("My inspection"), June 15, 1965, Fang Liren file 1, 48.

18. "Shěn gàn zìzhuàn"("Cadre's personal autobiography"), June 1951; "Gànbù dēngjì biǎo" ("Cadre registration form"), October 1953, Fang Liren file 1, 258–63.

19. "Fāng Lìrén zǒng jiē cáiliào" ("Fang Liren summary materials"), November 1953, Fang Liren file 1, 265–66.

20. Bǎowèi kē (Security section), "Duì bèichá duìxiàng Fāng Lìrén de cáiliào zhěnglǐ" ("Materials relating to Fang Liren, object for future reference"), May 26, 1955, Fang Liren file 1, 241–47.

21. "Zhuān'àn dēngjì biǎo" ("Special case registration form"), December 5, 1955, Fang Liren file 2, 112–13.

22. "Zhōnggòng N shì zhígōng yīyuàn dǎngwěi wǔ rén xiǎozǔ guānyú Fāng Lìrén lì'àn cáiliào bàogào" ("The CCP's N Municipality Workers' Hospital Party Committee's five-person team's report on Fang Liren"), August 8, 1956, Fang Liren file 2, 495–99.

23. "Zhōnggòng wèishēng jú wěiyuánhuì wǔ rén xiǎozǔ guānyú duì Fāng Lìrén chénglì sù fǎn zhuān'àn de qíngshì bàogào" ("Report of the five-person team of the CCP's Hygiene Committee on the establishment of a counter-revolutionary suppression case against Fang Liren"), November 28, 1956, Fang Liren file 2, 101–5.

24. "X huìbào zài chūnjié fàngjià qíjiān guānyú liǎojiě Fāng Lìrénzhī qíngkuàng" ("X report during the Spring Festival holiday on understanding Fang Liren's situation"), 1957, Fang Liren file 2, 320–22.

25. "Zhōnggòng wèishēng jú wěiyuánhuì wǔ rén xiǎozǔ guānyú duì Fāng Lìrén chénglì sù fǎn zhuān'àn de qíngshì bàogào" ("Report of the five-person team of the CCP's Hygiene Committee on the institution of a counter-revolutionary suppression case against Fang Liren"), November 28, 1956, Fang Liren file 2, 101–5.

26. "Wǔ rén xiǎozǔ duì Fāng Lìrén zhōng tǒng qiánfú tèwù xiányí àn jìnxíng zhuān'àn dòuzhēng de xiǎojié bàogào" ("Summary report by the five-person team of the struggle in the case concerning the suspicion that Fang Liren was a hidden member of the Kuomintang spy organization"), February 6, 1957, Fang Liren file 2, 72–84.

27. "Zhōnggòng N shì zhígōng yīyuàn wěiyuánhuì wǔ rén xiǎozǔ zhuān'àn zhǐdǎo zǔ duì fǎngémìng fènzi Fāng Lìrén sù fǎn zhuān'àn shěnchá jié'àn qíngshì bàogào" ("Report of the special review by the five-person steering group of the CCP's N Municipality Workers' Hospital Committee on the counter-revolutionary element Fang Liren"), June 20, 1957, Fang Liren file 2, 500–5.

28. Fang Liren, "Wǒ de jiǎnchá" ("My investigation"), June 15, 1965, Fang Liren file 1, 46.

29. "Zhōnggòng N shì zhígōng yīyuàn wěiyuánhuì wǔ rén xiǎozǔ zhuān'àn zhǐdǎo zǔ duì fǎngémìng fènzi Fāng Lìrén sù fǎn zhuān'àn shěnchá jié'àn qíngshì bàogào" ("Report of the special review by the five-person steering group of the CCP's N Municipality Workers' Hospital Committee on the counter-revolutionary element Fang Liren"), June 20, 1957, Fang Liren file 2, 500–5.

30. "Wǔ rén xiǎozǔ sù fǎn wèntí shěnchá chǔlǐ jiélùn" ("Conclusion of the five-person group concerning the review on how to deal with the question of the suppression of counter-revolutionaries"), July 22, 1957, Fang Liren file 2, 566–67.

31. "Shìwěi zhuān'àn zǔ tóngyì Fāng Lìrén zhuān'àn jié'àn de pīfù" ("Municipal Party Committee's special team agrees to close the Fang Liren case"), July 4, 1957, Fang Liren file 2, 41.

32. "Zhōnggòng N shì shìwěi wǔ rén xiǎozǔ sù fǎn wèntí shěnchá chǔlǐ jiélùn" ("The conclusion of the five-person team of the CCP's N Municipality Committee concerning the suppression of counter-revolutionaries"), September 25, 1957, Fang Liren file 2, 240.

33. "Fāng Lìrén zhì zhōnggòng X shěng wěi luòshí zhèngcè bàngōngshì xìn" ("Fang Liren's letter to the CCP's X Provincial Committee's policy-implementing office"), April 10, 1978, Fang Liren file 1, 179.

34. "Fāng Lìrén sù fǎn wèntí shěnchá chǔlǐ jiélùn" ("Conclusion in the Fang Liren case of the review of the problem of the suppression of counter-revolutionaries"), October 19, 1957; "Fāng Lìrén sù fǎn wèntí shěnchá jié'àn cáiliào" ("Materials relating to the Fang Liren case and the review of the problem of the suppression of counter-revolutionaries"), December 19, 1957, Fang Liren file 2, 21–26.

35. "Zhōnggòng N shì shìwěi wǔ rén xiǎozǔ zhì zhōnggòng zhígōng yīyuàn wǔ rén xiǎozǔ hán" ("Letter from the CCP's N Municipality Committee's five-person team to the five-person team of the CCP's Workers' Hospital"), March 25, 1958, Fang Liren file 2, 511.

36. "Zhōnggòng zhígōng yīyuàn wǔ rén xiǎozǔ guānyú Fāng Lìrén sù fǎn yǐhòu biǎoxiàn fǎndòng chóngxīn shěnchá jié'àn cáiliào" ("Materials of the five-person team of the CCP's Workers' Hospital relating to the closure of the case concerning Fang Liren's reactionary behaviour after the suppression of counter-revolutionaries"), October 5, 1958, Fang Liren file 2, 2–3.

37. Ibid., 9.

38. "Zhōnggòng wèishēng jú wǔ rén xiǎozǔ guānyú Fāng Lìrén sù fǎn wèntí shěnchá jié'àn cáiliào" ("Materials relating to the closure of the case by the five-person team of the CCP's Hygiene Bureau regarding Fang Liren's counter-revolutionary problems"), October 19, 1958; "Zhōnggòng wèishēng jú wǔ rén xiǎozǔ guānyú Fāng Lìrén sù fǎn wèntí shěnchá chǔlǐ jiélùn" ("Conclusions on the handling by the five-person team of the CCP's Hygiene Bureau of the case regarding Fang Liren's counter-revolutionary problems"), October 19, 1958 , Fang Liren file 2, 24–25.

39. "Zhōnggòng N shì zhígōng yīyuàn dǎngwěi guānyú Fāng Lìrén tóngzhì shēnsù de chǔlǐ bàogào" ("Report by the Party Committee of N Municipality Workers' Hospital on the handling of Comrade Fang Liren's appeal"), December 24, 1979, Fang Liren file 2, 534–35.

40. "Máo Zédōng zài bādà èr cì huìyì shàng de jiǎnghuà (zhāiyào)" ("Mao Zedong's speech at the Second Session of the Eighth National Congress of the CCP [Summary]"), May 8, 1958, in Máo Zédōng sīxiǎng wànsuì ("Long live Mao Zedong Thought"), 72; "Máo zédōng zài bādà èr cì huìyì shàng de jiǎnghuà" ("Mao Zedong's speech at the Second Session of the Eighth National Congress of the CCP"), May 20, 1958, in Máo Zédōng sīxiǎng wànsuì ("Long live Mao Zedong Thought"), 82.

41. The "Three Guarantees and One Guarantor" system was for controlling the five elements. The "Three Guarantees" were the Party organizations, the public security section, and the mass control and correction group, which "guaranteed" the reform of the control object; the "One Guarantor" was the person to be controlled, who had to guarantee his or her own reform. "Dual-guarantee" supervision referred to the implementation of this organizational approach by means of a specialist team that at all times supervised the object of disciplinary control.

42. "Zìwǒ gǎizào guīhuà" ("Self-reform plan"), October 22, 1960, Fang Liren file 1, 139–40.

43. "1960 niándù sīxiǎng gǎizào zǒngjié" ("Summary of ideological reform in 1960"), February 27, 1961, Fang Liren file 1, 126–43.

44. "Wǔ lèi fènzi píngshěn jiàndìng biǎo" ("Identification form for the five elements"), July 1959, Fang Liren file 1, 228–29.

45. "Zhōngyī kē duì Fāng Lìrén 1959 nián gǎizào zǒngjié" ("The Chinese medicine section on Fang Liren's 1959 reform summary"), December 1959, Fang Liren file 2, 300–1.

46. "Wǔ lèi fènzi píngshěn jiàndìng biǎo" ("Appraisal form for the five elements"), December 22, 1959, Fang Liren file 2, 286.

47. "Wǔ lèi fènzi jì píngshěn jiàndìng biǎo" ("Appraisal form for the five elements"), March 28, 1960, Fang Liren file 2, 291.

48. "Fāng Lìrén jìnlái sīxiǎng gōngzuò gè fāngmiàn de qíngkuàng bàogào" ("Report on various aspects of Fang Liren's recent ideological work"), April 29, 1960, Fang Liren file 1, 95–96.

49. This policy, regarding counter-revolutionaries and bad elements as determined by the various units, required that "a minority should be sentenced to labor reform; some should sentenced to control or dismissal, and gathered together by the state for labor and education; the rest should, as far as possible, be sent to the rural areas to engage in productive labor, receive supervision, and undergo reform." See "Zhōnggòng zhōngyāng pīzhǔn zhōngyāng shí rén xiǎozǔ guānyú gèshěng shì wǔ rén xiǎozǔ fùzé rén huìyì de bàogào hé guānyú chǔlǐ nèibù liúyòng de fǎngmìng fènzi hé huài fènzi de ruògān zhèngcè guīdìng liǎng gè wénjiàn" ("The CCP Central Committee approves the report of the Central Committee's ten-person group regarding the report of the five-person group from the various provinces and municipalities and two documents regarding some policies on the internal retention of counter-revolutionaries and bad elements"), December 10, 1957, Shanghai Municipal Archives, J163/4/167/17–19.

50. "Zhígōng yīyuàn dǎngwěi chéngbào wèishēng jú dǎngwěi hán" ("Report submitted by the Party committee of the Workers' Hospital to the Hygiene Bureau's Party committee"), November 18, 1960, Fang Liren file 1, 92.

51. "Duì fǎn huài fènzi píngshěn chǔlǐ pī hé biǎo" ("On the review form concerning counter-revolutionaries and bad elements"), January 4, 1961, supplementary report, Fang Liren file 2, 235–36.

52. Fang Liren, "Fàng bāofú, jiē gàizi cáiliào—Tiānzhǔ jiào xùnliàn bān" ("Putting down the burden, removing the cover—Catholic training class"), March 5, 1966, Fang Liren file 1, 6–7.

53. This refers to the removal of the "rightist" tag, so that politically people were once again treated as normal citizens and recovered rights removed as a result of the "rightist" designation.

54. "Ménzhěn zhībù guānyú duì qǔxiāo lìshǐ fǎngémìng fènzi Fāng Lìrén de jiāndū gǎizào chǔfèn de yìjiàn" ("The out-patient branch on the removal of the supervision and reform of the historical counter-revolutionary Fang Liren"), March 13, 1962, Fang Liren file 2, 305–7.

55. "Yīyuàn bǎowèi kē wèi Fāng Lìrén zhāi diào fǎngémìng fènzi màozi de yìjiàn bàogào" ("Report by the Hospital Security Division removing Fang Liren's counter-revolutionary hat"), March 13, 1962, Fang Liren file 1, 35.

56. Ibid.

57. See "Máo Zédōng zài zhōngyāng gōngzuò huìyì gè zhōngyāng jú huìbào shí de chāhuà" ("Mao Zedong's interjection at the working conference of the various Central Committee bureaus"), December 27, 1960.

58. "Máo Zédōng zài bā jiè shí zhōng quánhuì shàng de jiǎnghuà" ("Mao Zedong's Speech at the Eighth Plenary Session of the Eighth Central Committee"), September 24, 1962, *Máo Zédōng sīxiǎng wànsuì* ("Long live Mao Zedong thought"), (5), 34–35.

59. "Píngshěn chǔlǐ pīshěn biǎo" ("Review and criticism of examination and appraisal form"), January 1963, Fang Liren file 2, 278; "Yīyuàn bǎowèi kē wèi gěi Fāng Lìrén zhāi diào fǎngémìng fènzi màozi de yìjiàn bàogào" ("Report by the Hospital Security Division on removing Fang Liren's counter-revolutionary hat"), March 13, 1963, Fang Liren file 2, 254–55.

60. "Gōng'ān jú dì èr chù zhì zhígōng yīyuàn bǎowèi chù hán" ("Second department of the Public Security Bureau to the security section of the Workers' Hospital"), December 30, 1963, Fang Liren file 2, 256.

61. "Zhōnggòng zhōngyāng guānyú nóngcūn shèhuì zhǔyì jiàoyù yùndòng zhōng yīxiē jùtǐ zhèngcè de guīdìng (xiūzhèng cǎo'àn)" ("Regulations of the Central Committee of the CCP on some specific policies in the Campaign for Socialist Rural Education" [revised draft]), September 10, 1964, in "Zhōnggòng dǎng shǐ cānkǎo zīliào" ("Reference materials for CCP history") 24, 486–500.

62. Fang Liren, "Wǒ de jiǎnchá" ("My investigation"), June 16, 1965, Fang Liren file 1, 45–73.

63. "Duì fǎngémìng fènzi Fāng Lìrén píngshěn dàhuì yuánshǐ jìlù" ("On the original record of the review conference of the counter-revolutionary Fang Liren"), June 21, 1965, Fang Liren file 2, 269–74.

64. "Nèikē sì qīng xiǎozǔ duì Fāng Lìrén de píngshěn cáiliào" ("Review materials from the clinic's Four Clean-Ups group regarding Fang Liren"), June 22, 1965, Fang Liren file 1, 43–44.

65. Ibid., 44.

66. "Zhōnggòng zhígōng yīyuàn gōngzuò duì wěiyuánhuì guānyú gěi Fāng Lìrén zhāi diào fǎngémìng fènzi màozi de píngshěn yìjiàn" ("The opinion of the CCP's work committee of the Workers' Hospital on removing Fang Liren's counter-revolutionary hat"), July 8, 1965, Fang Liren file 1, 55–57.

67. Ibid., 57–58.

68. "Zhōnggòng zhígōng yīyuàn gōngzuò duì wěiyuánhuì, dǎng wěiyuánhuì duì fǎngémìng fènzi Fāng Lìrén zhāi mào de yìjiàn bàogào" ("CCP Workers' Hospital work committee team on removing the hat of the counter-revolutionary Fang Liren "), July 8, 1965, Fang Liren file 1, 150.

69. "Zhōnggòng zhígōng yīyuàn gōngzuò duì wěiyuánhuì, dǎng wěiyuánhuì duì fǎngémìng gōngzǐ Fāng Lìrén zhāi mào de yìjiàn bàogào, 1965 nián 7 yuè 8 rì, Fāng Lìrén dǎng'àn dì 1 cè, dì 149 yè" ("Report of the CCP's working committee and the Party committee of the Workers' Hospital on the removal of the hat of the counter-revolutionary feudal prince Fang Liren)," July 8, 1965, Fang Liren file 1, 149.

70. "Chéngshì shè jiào yùndòng ànjiàn chǔlǐ pīshì biǎo" ("Instructions on handling cases in the Municipality's Socialist Education Movement"), October 6, 1965, Fang Liren file 1, 41.

71. "Fāng Lìrén zhì shì wèishēng jú xìnfǎng bàngōngshì shēnsù hán" ("Fang Liren's letter of appeal to the Municipal Health Bureau"), October 13, 1974, Fang Liren file 1, 151–52.

72. "Guānyú bèi qiǎnsòng rényuán Fāng Lìrén wèntí de fùchá bàogào" ("A re-examination of the review of Fang Liren's case"), September 29, 1973, Fang Liren file 1, 39.

73. "Guānyú zài wénhuà dàgémìng zhòng bèi yí sòng hòu fǎn jīng rényuán de chǔlǐ bànfǎ" ("On the handling of persons sent back to Beijing in the Cultural Revolution"), March 18, 1967. See "Jìyì" ("Recollections"), 93.

74. "Fāng Lìrén zhì zhōnggòng S shěng wěi luòshí zhèngcè bàngōngshì de xìn" ("Letter from Fang Liren to the CCP Provincial Committee's Policy Implementation Office"), May 14, 1978, Fang Liren file 1, 173–74.

75. "N shì zhígōng yīyuàn dǎngwěi guānyú bèi qiǎnsòng rényuán Fāng Lìrén wèntí de fùchá bàogào" ("N Municipality Workers' Hospital's re-examination of Fang Liren's case"), May 24, 1978, Fang Liren file 1, 32–34.

76. "Xīguān dàduì dǎng zhībù, gé wěi huì zhèngmíng cáiliào" ("Xiguan Brigade's Party branch and Revolutionary Committee validate the material"), June 23, 1978, Fang Liren file 2, 524.

77. "Fāng Cànrán gěi N shì shìwěi xìnfǎng bàngōngshì de shēnsù xìn" ("Fang Canran's letter of appeal to the N Municipality committee's letters and visits office"), July 9, 1978, Fang Liren file 1, 158–62.

78. "Fāng Lìrén zhì yīyuàn dǎngwěi xìn" ("Fang Liren's letter to the hospital's Party committee"), September 22, 1978, Fang Liren file 1, 167–68.

79. "Zhōnggòng N shì shìwěi gōngjiāo zhèngzhì bù duì Fāng Lìrén wèntí de chǔlǐ pīfù" ("Reply from the Political-Work Department of Industry and Communications of the CCP's N Municipality Committee regarding Fang Liren"), November 28, 1978, Fang Liren file 2, 195, 166.

80. "Guānyú dìzhǔ, fùnóng fènzi zhāi mào wèntí hé de fù zǐnǚ chéngfèn wèntí de juédìng" ("Resolution on the question of the children of landlords and rich peasant elements wearing hats"), January 11, 1979, in Zhōngyāng wénxiàn yánjiū shì, eds., *Sān zhōng quánhuì yǐlái zhòngyào wénxiàn huìbiān* ("Important documents since the Third Plenary Session") (Beijing: Renmin chuban she, 1982), 76; "Gōng'ān bù guānyú guànchè luòshí zhōnggòng zhōngyāng [1979] 5 hào wénjiàn de tōngzhī" ("Ministry of Public Security on the implementation of the Central Committee of the CCP's [1979] No 5 Notice"), January 23, 1979; "Sì lèi fènzi zhāi mào wèntí cáiliào huìbiān" ("Collection of materials on the removal of hats from the four categories"), in H shěng gé wěi huì gōng'ān jú, eds., February 1979, 4–6; "Shíshìqiúshì de jiějué hǎo sì lèi fènzi zhāi mào wèntí—gōng'ān bùzhǎng Zhào Cāngbì dá Rénmín rìbào jìzhě wèn" ("Solving the problem of the removal of hats from the four categories pragmatically—Public Security Minister Zhao Cangbai talks with a journalist from *People's Daily*"); "Shìyìng qíngkuàng biànhuà de yī xiàng zhòngdà juécè" ("A major decision to adapt to change"), *People's Daily*, January 30, 1979.

CHAPTER FOUR. THE PRICE OF "REACTION"

1. Translators' note: On the Three Selfs Lectures, see https://read01.com/oDmAGN.html.

2. "Sù fǎn tǎnbái yùndòng zìwǒ jiǎnchá" ("Self-investigation during Sufan"), August 22, 1955, Mu Guoxuan file, 210–11, 214.

3. "Lìshǐ zìzhuàn jí sīxiǎng biànhuà qíngkuàng" ("Historical autobiography and ideological changes"), October 7, 1955, Mu Guoxuan file, 217–29.

4. "Fǎnxǐng cáiliào" ("Reflective materials"), October 14, 1955, Mu Guoxuan file, 199.

5. "Mù Guóxuān gěi X kēzhǎng de xìn" ("Mu Guoxuan's letter to section head X"), May 23, 1953, Mu Guoxuan file, 126.

6. "Mù Guóxuān gěi X fù zhǔxí de xìn" ("Mu Guoxuan's letter to Deputy Chairman X"), May 6, 1953, Mu Guoxuan file, 58.

7. "Mù Guóxuān gěi X tīngzhǎng, X kēzhǎng de xìn" ("Mu Guoxuan's letter to director x and section chief x"), June 6, 1953, Mu Guoxuan file, 59.

8. "Mù Guóxuān gěi X tīngzhǎng, X kēzhǎng de xìn" ("Mu Guoxuan's letter to director x and section chief x"), July 9, 1953, Mu Guoxuan file, 60.

9. "Mù Guóxuān zōnghé cáiliào" ("Mu Guoxuan's comprehensive materials"), October 1955, Mu Guoxuan file, 50.

10. "Fǎnxǐng cáiliào" ("Reflective materials"), October 14, 1955, Mu Guoxuan file, 199.

11. "Sù fǎn tǎnbái yùndòng zìwǒ jiǎnchá" ("Self-investigation during the movement for suppressing counter-revolutionaries and making self-criticism"), August 22, 1955, Mu Guoxuan file, 210.

12. "Fǎnxǐng cáiliào" ("Reflective materials"), October 14, 1955, Mu Guoxuan file, 42.

13. Ibid., 214.

14. "Xiǎo jítuán de jiāodài" ("Small clique confession"), October 27, 1955, Mu Guoxuan file, 33–5.

15. "Mù Guóxuān cáiliào" ("Mu Guoxuan materials"), August 21, 1955, Mu Guoxuan file, 189–90.

16. "Sù fǎn tǎnbái yùndòng zìwǒ jiǎnchá" ("Self-confession during the movement for suppressing counter-revolutionaries and making self-criticism"), August 22, 1955, Mu Guoxuan file, 210–1.

17. In December 1936, they arrested Chiang Kai-shek, in league with the Communists.

18. "Sù fǎn tǎnbái yùndòng zìwǒ jiǎnchá" ("Self-confession during the movement for suppressing counter-revolutionaries and making a self-investigation"), August 22, 1955, Mu Guoxuan file, 214–5.

19. "Fǎnxǐng cáiliào" ("Reflective materials"), October 14, 1955, Mu Guoxuan file, 196.

20. Qīng fǎn bàngōngshì, eds, "Shénme rén de rìjì?" ("Whose diary?"), August 31, 1955, Mu Guoxuan file, 138.

21. Ibid., 149–50

22. Duke Wen of Jin (c. 697–28 B.C.E.), a monarch in the Spring and Autumn period.

23. Qīng fǎn bàngōngshì, eds, "Shénme rén de rìjì?" ("Whose diary?"), August 31, 1955, Mu Guoxuan file, 144–46.

24. Zhang Yi (d. 309 B.C.E.) was a famous diplomat in the Warring States period.

25. Beria (1899–1953), the former Soviet interior minister and a driving force behind the great purge, was dismissed and executed after the death of Stalin.

26. Qīng fǎn bàngōng shì, eds, "Shénme rén de rìjì?" ("Whose diary?"), August 31, 1955, Mu Guoxuan file, 146–48.

27. "Guānyú Hú Fēng fǎngémìng jítuán de dì sān pī cáiliào biānzhě àn" ("Editor's note on the Hu Feng counter-revolutionary clique's third batch of materials"), People's Daily, June 10, 1955, first edition.

28. "Fǎngémìng fènzi Mù Guóxuān cáiliào" ("Materials on the counter-revolutionary element Mu Guoxuan"), August 31, 1955, Mu Guoxuan file, 57.

29. "Qīng fǎn bàngōngshì tōnggào" ("Notice from the office for purging counter-revolutionaries"), August 30, 1955, Mu Guoxuan file, 151.

30. "Fǎnxǐng cáiliào" ("Reflective materials"), October 14, 1955, Mu Guoxuan file, 37.

31. Ibid., 130.

32. Ibid., 131.

33. Ibid., 138–39, 199.

34. "Zōnghé cáiliào" ("Comprehensive materials"), October 1955, Mu Guoxuan file, 44–53.

35. Ibid., 44–45, 47.

36. "Xùnwèn bǐlù" ("Interrogation record"), November 7, 1955, Mu Guoxuan file, 203–8.

37. "Mù Guóxuān diàochá cáiliào tígāng" ("Outline of the Mu Guoxuan survey materials"), November 8, 1955, Mu Guoxuan file, 102–3.

38. By that time, the purge office had already been renamed the office for the suppression of counter-revolutionaries.

39. "Mù Guóxuān gěi yuàn dǎngwěi sù fǎn bàngōngshì de shēnqǐng jiànyì" ("Mu Guoxuan's proposal to the hospital office for suppressing counter-revolutionaries"), March 30, 1956, Mu Guoxuan file, 81.

40. "Zhuān'àn zǔ diàochá yìjiàn" ("The opinion of the special team after its investigation"), 1956, Mu Guoxuan file, 8–9.

41. "Guānyú duì jiējí díduì fènzi Mù Guóxuān de chǔlǐ yìjiàn (gǎo)" ("Views [draft] on the treatment of the enemy-class element Mu Guoxuan"), May 1956, Mu Guoxuan file, 83–86.

42. "Guānyú duì jiējí díduì fènzi Mù Guóxuān de chǔlǐ jiélùn" ("Conclusions on the treatment of the enemy-class element Mu Guoxuan"), June 1, 1956, Mu Guoxuan file, 344–45.

43. "X xiàn rénmín fǎyuàn xíngshì pànjué" ("X County People's Court Criminal Judgment"), March 20, 1957; "Liáoyǎng yuàn guānyú jiāng fǎngémìng fènzi Mù Guóxuān chúmíng de bàogào" ("Report by the sanatorium on the striking from the lists of the counter-revolutionary Mu Guoxuan"), March 26, 1957, Mu Guoxuan file, 349–51, 326.

44. "Guānyú gěi xíng mǎn shìfàng xiànxíng fǎngémìng fènzi Mù Guóxuān dài huí fǎngémìng fènzi màozi tíngzhǐ shìyòng sòng yuánjí jiāndū láodòng de chǔfèn bàogào" ("Report on the released current counter-revolutionary element Mu Guoxuan, wearing a counter-revolutionary hat, and the cessation of probation and his return to his original place of labour supervision"), February 10, 1960, "Mu Guoxuan file", 329–31.

45. "Pàichūsuǒ zhùxiāo kǎ" ("Cancellation of card by police station"), April 29, 1960, Mu Guoxuan file, 236.

46. "Mù Guóxuān wèntí de fùchá bàogào" ("Report on the review of the Mu Guoxuan problem"), March 20, 1979, Mu Guoxuan file, 352–53.

47. Ibid., 353.

48. "Guānyú Mù Guóxuān wèntí de diàochá qíngkuàng" ("On the Mu Guoxuan investigation"), May 6, 1982, Mu Guoxuan file, 354.

49. "Mù Guóxuān yǒuguān gèrén lìshǐ wèntí de shēnsù" ("Mu Guoxuan's appeal regarding his personal historical problems"), 1981, Mu Guoxuan file, 362–68.

50. "Guānyú Mù Guóxuān wèntí de diàochá qíngkuàng" ("On the Mu Guoxuan investigation"), May 6, 1982, Mu Guoxuan file, 355.

51. "X zhì X xiàn wèishēng jú hán" ("Letter from X to X county health bureau"), August 6, 1983, Mu Guoxuan file, 356.

52. "X zhì X xiàn wèishēng jú hán" ("Letter from X to X county health bureau"), August 4, 1983, Mu Guoxuan file, 357.

53. "Guānyú Mù Guóxuān wèntí de fùchá bàogào" ("Report on the review of the Mu Guoxuan question"), June 6, 1984, Mu Guoxuan file, 312–14.

54. "X xiàn rénmín fǎyuàn xíngshì pànjuéshū" ("X County People's Court Criminal Judgment"), March 20, 1985, Mu Guoxuan file, 408.

55. "Guānyú Mù Guóxuān shànhòu chǔlǐ de qǐngshì bàogào" ("Report on the aftermath of the handling of Mu Guoxuan"), May 15, 1985, "Mu Guoxuan file", 391.

56. "Guānyú gěi Mù Guóxuān bǔ shēng yī jí gōngzī de qǐngshì bàogào jí pīfù" ("Report on the approval of a wage increment for Mu Guoxuan"), January 1987, Mu Guoxuan file, 245–46.

CHAPTER FIVE. THE "FALL" OF A BRANCH SECRETARY OF THE COMMUNIST YOUTH LEAGUE

1. "X kuàng zhì zhōngnán wū kuàngjú, A shì yǒusè jīnshǔ gōngyè xuéxiào hán" ("Letter from X mine to the Central South Tungsten Minerals Bureau and the A Municipality non-ferrous metal school"), October 29, 1957, Chi Weirong file; "A shì yào yòng bōlí chǎng dǎng'àn·bǎowèi dǎng'àn·tānwū lèi" ("A Municipality Medicinal Glassware Factory file, security section file, corruption category"), cumulative no. 2, file no. 15, np, Chi Weirong file. Because all documents are from this file, from now on I only cite "Chi Weirong file" and no longer indicate the original source. It is not possible to cite page locations in this file.

2. "Dài X zhèngshí cáiliào" ("Dai X testimony"), August 2, 1966; "Gāo X zhèngshí cáiliào" ("Gao X's testimony"), July 13, 1966, Chi Weirong file.

3. "Wáng X zhèngshí cáiliào" ("Wang X's testimony"), July 12, 1966, Chi Weirong file.

4. "Dòu X zhèngshí cáiliào" (Dou X's testimony"), July 11, 1966, Chi Weirong file.

5. A shì yào yòng bōlí chǎng gòngqīngtuán zǒng zhī wěiyuánhuì, "Duì Chí Wèiróng tuán jì chǔfèn de bàogào" ("A Municipality Medicinal Glassware Factory, Communist Youth League, 'Report on the disciplining of League secretary Chi Weirong'"), September 27, 1959, Chi Weirong file.

6. "Chí Wèiróng de fǎndòng yánxíng" ("Chi Weirong's reactionary words and deeds"), July 6, 1966, Chi Weirong file.

7. "Zhī X zhèngshí cáiliào" ("Zhi X's testimony"), July 12, 1966, Chi Weirong file.

8. "Nà X zhèngshí cáiliào" ("Na X's testimony"), July 14, 1966, Chi Weirong file.

9. According to the factory, Chi Weirong stole food stamps worth 240 pounds or so of grain. See "Zhōnggòng A shì huàgōng bōlí chǎng zǒng zhī wěiyuánhuì duì Chí Wèiróng tānwū wèntí de jiélùn yìjiàn" ("Verdict of A Municipality's general branch committee of the Communist Party in the chemical glassware factory regarding Chi Weirong's corruption"), August 31, 1961, Chi Weirong file.

10. "Gāo X zhèngshí cáiliào" ("Gao X's testimony"), July 20, 1966, Chi Weirong file.

11. "Chí Wèiróng de tānwū zōnghé cáiliào" ("Materials regarding Chi Weirong's corruption"), August 13, 1961; "Wú X zhèngshí cáiliào" ("Wu X's testimony"), July 6, 1966, Chi Weirong file.

12. "Fú Xiùméi zhèngshí cáiliào" ("Fu Xiumei's testimony"), August 11, 1966, Chi Wei-rong file.

13. "Chí Wèiróng jiāodài cáiliào" ("Chi Weirong's confession)", n.d., Chi Weirong file.

14. "Zhōnggòng A shì huàgōng bōlí chǎng zhībù guānyú duì tānwū dàoqiè fènzi—Chí Wèiróng wèizuì qiántáo de bàogào" ("Report by A Municipality Chemical Glassware Factory Party branch on corrupt and thieving elements and Chi Weirong's absconding"), October 19, 1960, Chi Weirong file.

15. "A shì huàgōng bōlí chǎng bǎowèi gǔ guānyú jūbǔ tānwū fènzi Chí Wèiróng wèizuì qiántáo de bàogào" ("Report by the A Municipality Chemical Glassware Factory's security section on the arrest of the corrupt element Chi Weirong and his absconding"), November 9, 1960, Chi Weirong file.

16. "Zhōnggòng A shì huàgōng bōlí chǎng zǒng zhī wěiyuánhuì duì Chí Wèiróng tānwū wèntí de jiélùn yìjiàn" ("Verdict of A Municipality chemical glassware factory's general Party branch on Chi Weirong's corruption"), August 31, 1961, Chi Weirong file.

17. "Chāolù X tǎnbái dēngjì biǎo" ("Transcript of X's confession form"), July 28, 1966, Chi Weirong file.

18. "Yin X jiēfā cáiliào" ("Yin X's denunciation"), June 18, 1966, May 28, 1970, Chi Wei-rong file.

19. "Yǐn Míngdé jiēfā cáiliào" ("Yin Mingde's denunciation"), June 18, 1966, May 28, 1970, Chi Weirong file.

20. Ibid.; also see "A shì yào yòng bōlí chǎng bǎowèi gǔ duì liúmáng dàoqiè fènzi Chí Wèiróng de zònghé cáiliào" ("Material from A Municipality Medicinal Glassware Factory's security section on the hoodlum element Chi Weirong"), March 11, 1963, Chi Weirong file.

21. "A shì yào yòng bōlí chǎng xíng xián fènzi dēngjì" ("A Municipality medical glass-ware factory registration of criminal suspect"), April 13, 1962, Chi Weirong file.

22. An officer in the transceiver room said that Chi Weirong and others left by the main gate, and Yin Mingde recalled that Chi climbed over the factory wall to get out. "Wēn X zhèngshí cáiliào" ("Wen X's testimony"), February 24, 1963; "Yǐn Míngdé zhèngshí cáiliào" ("Yin Mingde's testimony"), July 19, 1966, Chi Weirong file.

23. "Wēn X zhèngshí cáiliào" ("Wen X's testimony"), February 23, 1963; "Yú X zhèngshí cáiliào" (Yu X's testimony"), March 11, 1963; "A shì yào yòng bōlí chǎng láodòng jiàoyǎng duìxiàng dēngjì biǎo" ("Registration by A Municipality's Medical Glassware Factory of an object for labor rehabilitation"), March 12, 1963, Chi Weirong file.

24. "A shì yào yòng bōlí chǎng bǎowèi gǔ duì liúmáng dàoqiè fènzi Chí Wèiróng de zònghé cáiliào" ("Material from A Municipality medical glassware factory's security section on the hoodlum element Chi Weirong," April 11, 1963, Chi Weirong file.

25. "Chē X zhèngshí cáiliào" ("Che X's testimony"), July 7, 1966, Chi Weirong file.

26. "X chéngrèn shū" ("X's admission"), May 18, 1965; "E shěng E xiàn X shìchǎng guǎnlǐ suǒ xúnwèn bǐlù" ("X market management inquiry record, E County, E Province"), May 18, 1965, Chi Weirong file.

27. "E shěng E xiàn X shìchǎng guǎnlǐ suǒ shìchǎng wéifǎ xíngwéi chǔlǐ shū" ("X market management's dealing with illegal acts, E County, E Province"), June 20, 1965, Chi Weirong file.

28. "Chí Wèiróng jiāodài cáiliào" ("Chi Weirong's confession materials"), 1966, Chi Weirong file.

29. "Gāo X zhèngshí cáiliào" ("Gao X's testimony"), July 13, 1966; "Zhāng X zhèngshí cáiliào" ("Zhang X's testimony"), July 9, 1966, Chi Weirong file.

30. "Yīn X jiēfā cáiliào" ("Yin X's exposé"), July 19, 1966, December 1, 1968, May 28, 1970; "Wáng X zhèngshí cáiliào" ("Wang X's testimony"), July 12, 1966, Chi Weirong file.

31. "Chí Wēiróng de fǎndòng yánxíng" ("Chi Weirong's reactionary words and deeds"), July 6, 1966, Chi Weirong file.

32. Wu Yanjin's oral testimony, edited by Zhong Yi, in *Sìshísān nián wàng zhōng yóu jì* ("Forty-three years of hope") (Zhōngguó wénhuà chuánbò chūbǎn shè, 2009), 175n1; see http://www.wyzxsx.com/article/class14/201001/124989.html.

33. "Chí Wēiróng dàzì bào chāolù" ("Copy of Chi Weirong's wall poster"), December 1, 1966, Chi Weirong file.

34. "Yīyào A shì fēn gōngsī gōngzuò duì yào yòng bōlí chǎng gōngzuò fēnduì duì fǎn dǎng fǎn shèhuì zhǔyì fènzi chí wèi róng de zònghé cáiliào" ("Materials on the anti-Party, anti-socialist element Chi Weirong collected by the work team of the medical glassware factory in A Municipality branch of the pharmaceutical company"), July 29, 1966.

35. "A shì yào yòng bōlí chǎng gōngzuò fēnduì pīdòu duìxiàng shěnpī chéng bàobiǎo" ("Record of the sub-work team of the A Municipality medical glassware factory approving the interrogation and criticism of the object"), July 30, 1966, Chi Weirong file.

36. "Wáng X zhèngshí cáiliào" ("Wang X's testimony"), March 11, 1963; "Gāo X zhèngshí cáiliào" ("Gao X's testimony"), August 3, 1966, Chi Weirong file.

37. "Lǐ X zhèngshí cáiliào" ("Li X's testimony"), July 20, 1966, Chi Weirong file.

38. "Yīn X zhèngshí cáiliào" ("Yin X's testimony"), August 18, 1966, Chi Weirong file.

39. "Lǐ X zhèngshí cáiliào" ("Li X's testimony"), July 1966, Chi Weirong file.

40. "Yáng X zhèngshí cáiliào" ("Yang X's testimony"), July 8, 1966, Chi Weirong file.

41. "Wáng X zhèngshí cáiliào" ("Wang X's testimony"), August 6, 1966; "Xú X zhèngshí cáiliào" ("Xu X's testimony"), July 9, 1966, Chi Weirong file.

42. "Yīn X zhèngshí cáiliào" ("Yin X's testimony"), June 18, 1966, Chi Weirong file.

43. "X kuàng zhì zhōngnán wū kuàng jú, A shì yǒusè jīnshǔ gōngyè xuéxiào hán" ("Letter from X mine to the non-ferrous metal industry college"), October 29, 1957, Chi Weirong file.

44. "Chí Wēiróng huǐguò shū" ("Chi Weirong's repentance statement"), August 1966, Chi Weirong file.

45. "Chí Wēiróng rènzuì shū" ("Chi Weirong's confession statement"), August 13, 1966, Chi Weirong file.

46. "Chí Wēiróng rènzuì shū bǔchōng jiāodài" ("Chi Weirong's supplementary confession"), August 15, 1966, Chi Weirong file.

47. "Chí Wēiróng jiāodài cáiliào" ("Chi Weirong's confession material"), late August 1966, Chi Weirong file.

48. "Zhōngguó yīyào gōngyè gōngsī A shì fēn gōngsī sì qīng gōngzuò duì A shì yào yòng bōlí chǎng fēnduì, A shì yào yòng bōlí chǎng zǒng zhī wěiyuánhuì duì sīxiǎng fǎndòng fènzi Chí Wēiróng chǔlǐ bàogào, 1966 nián 10 yuè 19 rì" ("Report by the A Municipality Four Clean-Ups sub-work team in the A Municipality branch of the Chinese pharmaceutical industry company branch and the general committee of the medical glassware factory on the reactionary thinking of Chi Weirong"), October 19, 1966, Chi Weirong file.

49. "Chí Wēiróng shēnsù cáiliào" ("Chi Weirong's appeal material", October 19, 1966, Chi Weirong file.

50. "Chí Wèiróng dàzì bào chāolù" ("Copy of Chi Weirong's wall poster"), December 15, 1966, Chi Weirong file.

51. See "Yǐn X zhèngshí cáiliào" ("Yin X's testimony"), December 1, 1968, and May 28, 1970; "Mǎ X zhèngshí cáiliào" ("Ma X's testimony"), May 30, 1970, Chi Weirong file.

CHAPTER SIX. WEIGHTY FILES

1. "Shàng Hàowén zhì Mǎ zhèngwěi xìn" ("Letter from Shang Haowen to Commissioner Ma"), May 4, 1980, Shang Haowen file, 154–55.

2. "Guānyú shēnqǐng chèxiāo dǎng'àn cáiliào de bàogào" ("Report on application for removal of material from file"), December 6, 1979, Shang Haowen file, 156–58.

3. Ibid., 156, 158.

4. Yue Fei (1103–42) was a Song Dynasty general, famous for his loyalty. Qin Hui betrayed him.

5. Zou Rong (1885–1905) was a Chinese nationalist revolutionary under the Manchus.

6. "Dòuzhēng xiǎozǔ zhěnglǐ zhī cáiliào" ("Materials for the small group's struggle"), September 12, 1955; "Shàng Hàowén sù fǎn jiélùn fùjiàn" ("Annex to the verdict on the struggle to eliminate the counter-revolutionary Shang Haowen"), June 1956, Shang Haowen file, 71–72, 81–82, 86, 148–49.

7. "Chūshěn páiduì dēngjì biǎo" ("Registration form for first trial"), February 12, 1955, Shang Haowen file, 7–8.

8. "Sōují zīliào" ("Collected materials"), September 1, 1955; "Dòuzhēng xiǎozǔ zhěnglǐ zhī cáiliào" ("Materials for the small struggle group"), September 12, 1955, Shang Haowen file, 33, 76–77.

9. "Wàichū diàochá fāng'àn" ("External investigation scheme"), February 24, 1955, Shang Haowen file, 9–10.

10. "Zhōnggòng zhōngyāng guānyú shěnchá gànbù de juédìng" ("CCP Central Committee decision on cadre review"), November 1953, in Zhōngguó rénmín jiěfàngjūn zhèngzhì bǎowèi bù, eds., Sù fǎn yùndòng wénjiàn xuǎn ("Selected documents on the movement to eliminate counter-revolutionaries") (1959), 1–2.

11. "Zhōnggòng zhōngyāng guānyú kāizhǎn dòuzhēng sùqīng àncáng de fǎngémìng fènzi de zhǐshì" ("Directive by the CCP Central Committee on the struggle to clear out hidden counter-revolutionary elements"), July 1, 1955, in Ibid., 8–16.

12. Ibid., 12–15.

13. "Dì yī cì shūmiàn jiāodài cáiliào" ("First written confession"), September 30, 1955, Shang Haowen file, 99–100.

14. "Sù fǎn yùndòng xiǎozǔ huì jìlù" ("Record of the small-group meeting in the Sufan Movement"), August 30, 1955, Shang Haowen file, 21–22.

15. "Yǒuguān Shàng Hàowén xiànshí huódòng de jiǎnjǔ cáiliào" ("Report on the activities of Shang Haowen"), August 1 and September 1 and 23, 1954, Shang Haowen file, 28–36, 95–6.

16. "X zhì bùduì shǒuzhǎng tóngzhì de xìn" ("Letter from X to the senior officer"), August 30, 1955, Shang Haowen file, 156–57.

17. Guo Moruo (1892–1978) was a writer and famous as a sycophant of Mao.

18. "Sù fǎn yùndòng xiǎozǔ huì jìlù" ("Record of the small-group meeting in the Sufan Movement"), August 23 and 30, 1955, Shang Haowen file, 14–17, 20.

19. Ibid., 17–19.

20. Ibid., 18–20.

21. "Sù fǎn yùndòng xiǎozǔ huì jìlù" ("Record of the small-group meeting in the Sufan Movement"), September 5, 1955, Shang Haowen file, 41, 60.

22. "Sù fǎn yùndòng xiǎozǔ huì jìlù" ("Record of the small-group meeting in the Sufan Movement"), August 30–1 and September 3, 1955, Shang Haowen file, 22–24, 40.

23. "Sù fǎn yùndòng xiǎozǔ huì jìlù" ("Record of the small-group meeting in the Sufan Movement"), August 31, 1955, Shang Haowen file, 24–26.

24. "Sù fǎn yùndòng xiǎozǔ huì jìlù" ("Record of the small-group meeting in the Sufan Movement"), 1955, Shang Haowen file, 93–94.

25. "Huìyì jìnzhǎn qíngkuàng huìbào huì jìlù" ("Report on the progress of the meeting"), September 3, 1955, Shang Haowen file, 36.

26. "Sù fǎn yùndòng xiǎozǔ huì jìlù" ("Record of the small-group meeting in the Sufan Movement"), September 4, 1955, Shang Haowen file, 49–61.

27. "Dòuzhēng xiǎozǔ zhěnglǐ zhī cáiliào" ("Materials on the regulation of the struggle group"), September 12, 1955, Shang Haowen file, 67–87.

28. "Dòuzhēng xiǎozǔ huì jìlù" ("Record of struggle-group meeting"), September 13, 1955, Shang Haowen file, 88–91.

29. "Dì yī cì shūmiàn jiāodài cáiliào" ("First confession"), September 30, 1955, Shang Haowen file, 97–102.

30. Ibid., 103–13.

31. "Dòuzhēng xiǎozǔ huìyì jìlù" ("Record of struggle-group meeting"), October 3 and 4, 1955, Shang Haowen file, 62–63.

32. "Dòuzhēng xiǎozǔ huìyì jìlù" ("Record of struggle-group meeting"), October 5, 1955, Shang Haowen file, 63–64.

33. "Dì yī cì chuánxùn kǒugòng cáiliào" ("Confession at the first interrogation"), November 17, 1955, Shang Haowen file, 116–20.

34. "Dì èr cì chuánxùn kǒugòng cáiliào" ("Confession at the second interrogation"), December 1, 1955, Shang Haowen file, 117–29.

35. "Dì sān cì chuánxùn kǒugòng cáiliào" ("Confession at the third interrogation"), December 3, 1955, Shang Haowen file, 130–3.

36. "Shěnchá gànbù jiélùn" " ("Conclusions of cadres' review"), June 19, 1956, Shang Haowen file, 137–39.

37. "Shěnchá gànbù jiélùn" ("Conclusions of cadres' review"), June 20, 1956, Shang Haowen file, 140–41.

38. "Tuánwěi guānyú Shàng Hàowén tuán jì chǔfèn wèntí de juédìng" ("Youth League committee resolution on the disciplining of Shang Haowen"), June 20, 1956, Shang Haowen file, 136–37.

39. "Xiǎozǔ jiàndìng yìjiàn" ("Small-group appraisal"), November 24, 1960, Shang Haowen file, 152.

40. "Duì Shàng Hàowén tóngzhì sù fǎn jiélùn de fùchá juédìng" ("Resolution on the reconsideration of the conclusion against Comrade Shang Haowen in the Movement to Eliminate Counter-Revolutionaries"), June 30, 1980, Shang Haowen file, 161.

CHAPTER SEVEN. "NON-POLITICAL DETENTION"

1. "C shì gànbù xuéxiào bàomíng dēngjì biǎo" ("C Municipality cadre school registration form"), July 21, 1950, Che Shaowen file. It is not possible to cite page locations in this file.

2. "Kǒushì yìjiàn biǎo" ("Views on the oral test"), July 21, 1951, Che Shaowen file.

3. "Sīxiǎng jiǎnchá" ("Ideology check"), December 20, 1950, Che Shaowen file.

4. "Zìzhuàn" ("Autobiography"), September 1951, Che Shaowen file.

5. "Wèndá juàn" ("Question and answer paper"), September 1951, Che Shaowen file.

6. "Zhèngzhì kè kǎojuàn" ("Politics examination paper"), October 1951, Che Shaowen file.

7. "Dì èr dānyuán xuéxí xīndé" ("Second unit learning experience"), November 1951, Che Shaowen file.

8. "Sīxiǎng jiǎnchá" ("Ideology check"), December 20, 1951, Che Shaowen file.

9. "Jiàndìng shū"("Appraisal"), December 20, 1951, Che Shaowen file.

10. "Chē Shàowén biǎoxiàn jìlù" ("Che Shaowen's performance record"), September 1951, Che Shaowen file.

11. "Dānyuán xiǎojié biǎo" ("Unit summary"), October 1951, Che Shaowen file.

12. "Gè dānyuán biǎoxiàn zhāiyào" ("Summary of performance for each unit"), December 1951, Che Shaowen file.

13. "C shì gànbù xuéxiào gōnghán" ("C Municipality cadre school letter"), December 3, 1951, Che Shaowen file.

14. "Diàochá jiǎn biǎo 1, 2, 3, 4" ("Surveys 1, 2, 3, and 4"), November 1951, Che Shaowen file.

15. "Sīxiǎng jiǎnchá 1, 2" ("Ideological examinations 1 and 2"), November and December 1951, Che Shaowen file.

16. "Sīxiǎng zǒngjié" ("Ideological summary"), December 20, 1951, Che Shaowen file.

17. "Jiàndìng shū" ("Appraisal"), December 20, 1951, Che Shaowen file.

18. "Zōnghé fēnxī yìjiàn" ("Comprehensive analysis of opinions"), December 1951, Che Shaowen file.

19. "Diàochá jiǎn biǎo 2, 4" ("Surveys 2 and 4"), December 14, 1951, Che Shaowen file.

20. "Diàochá jiǎn biǎo 1, 3" ("Surveys 1 and 3"), December 27 and 29, 1951, Che Shaowen file.

21. "Zōnghé fēnxī yìjiàn" ("Comprehensive analysis of opinions"), December 1951, Che Shaowen file.

22. "Shěnchá biǎo" ("Review"), February 1952, Che Shaowen file.

23. "Biānwài rényuán chǔlǐ dēngjì biǎo" ("Registration of irregular staff"), July 1952, Che Shaowen file.

24. "Sān fǎn xuéxí sīxiǎng zǒngjié" ("Ideological summary of the Three Antis study movement"), June 9, 1952, Che Shaowen file.

25. "Gànbù jiǎnlì biǎo" ("Cadre biographical notes"), June 9, 1952, Che Shaowen file.

26. "Shěnchá biǎo" ("Review form"), 1952, Che Shaowen file.

27. "Biānwài rényuán chǔlǐ dēngjì biǎo" ("Registration of irregular staff"), July 19, 1952, Che Shaowen file.

28. "Dìfāng jīguān gōngzuò rényuán shēnqǐng tuìzhí dēngjì biǎo" ("Local authorities' application for discharge"), July 24, 1952, Che Shaowen file.

29. "Rénshì cáiliào zhāilù kǎ" ("Excerpts from personnel material"), 1957, Che Shaowen file.

30. "Tǔchǎn gōngsī sān fǎn yùndòng tǎnbái jiāodài biǎo" ("Local produce companies confessions during the Three Antis movement"), September 1, 1960, Che Shaowen file.

31. "Dān X zhèngmíng cáiliào" ("Dan X's evidence"), April 24, 1957, Che Shaowen file.

32. "Dù X zhèngmíng cáiliào" ("Du X's evidence"), April 26, 1957, Che Shaowen file.

33. "Wú X zhèngmíng cáiliào" ("Wu X's evidence"), April 25, 1957, Che Shaowen file.

34. "Guānyú Chē Shàowén de huáiyí wèntí diàochá yìjiàn" ("Views on the investigation of suspicious questions regarding Che Shaowen"), May 6, 1957, Che Shaowen file.

35. Ibid.

36. "Gèrén jiāodài dēngjì biǎo" ("Registration of personal confessions"), March 29, 1957, May 2, Che Shaowen file.

37. "Guānyú Chē Shàowén de huáiyí wèntí diàochá yìjiàn" ("Views on the investigation of suspicious questions regarding Che Shaowen"), May 6, 1957, Che Shaowen file.

38. "Bì X, Dān X, Hán X, Li X, Wú X zhèngmíng cáiliào" ("Bi X's, Dan X's, Han X's, Li X's, and Wu X's evidence"), May 1, 14, 18, and 26, 1958, Che Shaowen file.

39. "Guānyú qǔxiāo Chē Shàowén tóngzhì hànjiān xiányí wèntí de shěnchá bàogào" ("Report on the review rescinding the suspicion of treason regarding Comrade Che Shaowen"), June 23, 1958, Che Shaowen file.

40. Ibid.

41. Che Shaowen's performance in this regard was consistently affirmed. See the various assessments in the file.

42. "Rìjì zhāilù" ("Diary"), March 2, 1963; "Zhěngfēng sīxiǎng zǒngjié" ("Summary of ideological rectification"), September 9, 1958, Che Shaowen file.

43. Ibid.

44. "Zhōnggòng zhōngyāng guānyú zài nóngcūn zhōng kāizhǎn 'sān fǎn' yùndòng de zhǐshì" ("The CPC Central Committee on the implementation of the Three Antis movement in rural areas"), May 15, 1960, in Jiànguó yǐlái zhòngyào wénxiàn xuǎnbiān, ("Important documents since the founding of the People's Republic"), 13:380.

45. "Zhū X jiǎnjǔ cáiliào" ("Zhu X's report"), June 30, 1960, Che Shaowen file.

46. "Chē Shàowén de diàochá cáiliào" ("Che Shaowen survey materials"), August 1, 3, 13, and 14, 1960; "X shāngchǎng Xú X, Chén X, Wáng X, shípǐn shāngdiàn tóng X jiǎnjǔ cáiliào" ("X market's Xu X's, Chen X's, and Wang X's and the food store's Tong X's reports"), August 14 and 15, 1960, Che Shaowen file.

47. "Wáng X jiǎnjǔ cáiliào" ("Wang X's report"), August 4, 1960, Che Shaowen file.

48. "Liú X, Liáng X, Wèi X, Zhū X, Tián X, Hé X, Zhèng X jiǎnjǔ cáiliào" ("Liu X's, Liang X's, Wei X's, Zhu X's, Tian X's, He X's, and Zheng X's reports"), August 20, 22, 25, 28, 29, and 31, 1960, Che Shaowen file.

49. "Tǎnbái jiāodài" ("Confession"), August 19, 1960, Che Shaowen file.

50. "Tǎnbái jiāodài" ("Confession"), August 20, 1960, Che Shaowen file.

51. "Tǎnbái jiāodài" ("Confession"), August 21, 1960, Che Shaowen file.

52. "Tǎnbái jiāodài" ("Confession"), August 22, 1960, Che Shaowen file.

53. "Tǎnbái jiāodài" ("Confession"), August 23, 1960, Che Shaowen file.

54. "Tǎnbái jiāodài" ("Confession"), August 26 and 27, 1960, Che Shaowen file.

55. "Tǎnbái jiāodài" ("Confession"), September 2, 1960, Che Shaowen file.

56. "Duì Chē Shàowén yánzhòng wéifǎ luànjì, tānwū shòuhuì, zàochéng guójiā cáichǎn zhòng dà sǔnshī wèntí de chǔlǐ bàogào" ("Report on Che Shaowen's serious violations of the law, corruption, and bribery, resulting in significant loss of state property"), September 8, 1960, Che Shaowen file.

57. "Sān fǎn ànjiàn dìng'àn chǔlǐ nèibù shěnpī biǎo" ("Final internal approval of the resolution of the Three Antis case"), September 10, 1960, Che Shaowen file.

58. "Chē Shàowén de bǔchōng cáiliào" ("Che Shaowen supplementary material"), September 22, 1960, Che Shaowen file.

59. "Guānyú diàochá Chē Shàowén yǒu dàomài shāngpǐn xiányí de bàogào" ("Report on the investigation of Che Shaoxing's being suspected of reselling goods at a profit"), September 24, 1960, Che Shaowen file.

60. "Chē Shàowén tānwū cáiliào duìzhào biǎo" ("Comparative table regarding Che Shaowen's corruption"), September 23, 1960, Che Shaowen file.

61. "Duì Chē Shàowén yánzhòng wéifǎ luànjì, tānwū shòuhuì, zàochéng guójiā cáichǎn zhòng dà sǔnshī wèntí de chǔlǐ bàogào" ("Report on Che Shaowen's serious violations of the law, corruption, and bribery, resulting in significant loss of state property"), September 8, 1960, Che Shaowen file.

62. "Guānyú duì wéifǎ luàn jì fènzi Chē Shàowén chǔlǐ de shěnchá yìjiàn" ("On the review of the lawless and undisciplined element Che Shaowen"), October 18, 1960, Che Shaowen file.

63. "Láodòng jiàoyǎng juédìng shū" ("Decision on re-education through labor"), December 19, 1960, Che Shaowen file.

64. "Zhōnggòng zhōngyāng guānyú chèdǐ sùqīng àncáng de fǎngémìng fènzi de zhǐshì" ("Central Committee directive on the complete elimination of hidden counter-revolutionary elements"), August 25, 1955, in Zhōngguó rénmín jiěfàngjūn zǒng zhèngzhì bù bǎowèi bù, eds, Sù fǎn yùndòng wénjiàn xuǎnbiān ("Selected documents on the movement to eliminate counter-revolutionaries") (1959), 26.

65. "Lù Dìngyī tóngzhì zài gèshěng, shì, zhōngyāng zhíshǔ jīguān, zhōngyāng guójiā jīguān hé jūnshì xìtǒng wǔ rén xiǎozǔ fùzé rén huìyì shàng de zǒngjié" ("Comrade Lu Dingyi's summary at the meeting of leaders of five-person groups at the level of provincial organs, municipal organs, state central organs, and the military system"), January 1956; "Luō Ruìqīng zài gèshěng, shìwěi wǔ rén xiǎozǔ fùzé rén huìyì shàng de zǒngjié fā yán" ("Luo Ruiqing's speech at the meeting of leaders of five-person groups in the provincial and municipal committees"), July 5, 1956, Shaanxi province archives, 123/40/15/78–7.

66. "Láodòng jiàoyǎng fènzi dìngqí chéng pī biǎo" ("Regular approval form for re-education-through-labor elements"), September 30, 1961, Che Shaowen file.

67. "Láodòng jiàoyǎng rényuán bǎowàijiùyī zhíxíng chéng pī biǎo" ("Approval form for release on medical bail of personnel undergoing re-education through labor"), July 1962, Che Shaowen file.

68. Ibid.

69. "Sīxiǎng qíngkuàng huìbào" ("Ideological report"), April 16, 1963, Che Shaowen file.

70. "Láodòng jiàoyǎng fènzi bǎowàijiùyī zhíxíng diàochá biǎo" ("Investigation of release on medical bail of personnel undergoing re-education through labor"), April 1963, Che Shaowen file.

71. "Jiāndū bàogào" ("Supervision report"), April 25, 1963, Che Shaowen file.

72. "Chē Shàowén qíngkuàng bàogào" ("Report on Che Shaowen"), April 25, 1963, Che Shaowen file.

73. "Láodòng jiàoyǎng fènzi bǎowàijiùyī zhíxíng diàochá biǎo" ("Investigation of release on medical bail of personnel undergoing re-education through labor"), April 1960, Che Shaowen file.

74. "Bàogào" ("Report"), July 17, 1963, Che Shaowen file.

75. "Huìbào" ("Report"), August 20, 1963, Che Shaowen file.

76. "Bàogào" ("Report"), September 14, 1963, Che Shaowen file.

77. "X nóngchǎng zhì C shì chéng dōngqū gōng'ānjú X pàichūsuǒ gōnghán" ("Letter from X farm to C Municipality Chengdong District Public Security Bureau's X police station"), September 21, 1964, Che Shaowen file.

78. "X pàichūsuǒ zhì X nóngchǎng hán" ("Letter from X police station to X farm"), November 4, 1964, Che Shaowen file.

79. "Láodòng jiàoyǎng fènzi dìngqí chéng pī biǎo" ("Regular approval form for re-education-through-labor elements"), July 5, 1964, Che Shaowen file.

CHAPTER EIGHT. THE CURSE OF THE "OVERSEAS CONNECTION"

1. "Guānyú Luó Guózhèng tóngzhì de fùchá jiélùn" ("Conclusion regarding Comrade Luo Guozheng's review"), August 5, 1979, Luo Guozheng file 1. It is not possible to cite page locations in these files.

2. "Jiāotōng tīng bǎowèi kē guānyú Luō Guózhèng dài shàng xiànxíng fǎngémìng fènzi màozi liè wéi sìlèi fènzi jiāo qúnzhòng jiāndū gǎizào de fùchá bàogào" ("Report by the security section of the Department of Communications regarding Luo Guozheng's wearing a current counter-revolutionary hat and being ranked as a member of the four categories and handed over for mass re-education and reform"), August 1, 1979, Luo Guozheng file 1.

3. Ibid.

4. "Zhíyuán dēngjì biǎo" ("Staff registration form"), February 2, 1950, and July 14, 1950; "Luó Guózhèng zìzhuàn" ("Luo Guozheng's autobiography"), May 12, 1950, Luo Guozheng file 1.

5. "Zhíyuán dēngjì biǎo" ("Staff registration form"), February 2, 1950, Luo Guozheng file 1.

6. "Tǎnbái bàogào" ("Confession report"), March 24, 1951, Luo Guozheng file 1.

7. "Sīxiǎng zǒngjié" ("Ideological summary"), June 1951, Luo Guozheng file 1.

8. "Wǒ zài wěi dì sì shī diànxùn xùnliàn bān de qíngxíng" ("My time with the fake Fourth Division's telecommunications training course"), 1951, Luo Guozheng file 1.

9. Ibid.

10. "Wǒ zài Wǔhàn jūnguān lù kōng liánluò bān de qíngxíng" ("My time with the Wuhan military officers' army and airforce liaison class"), 1951, Luo Guozheng file 1.

11. Wang, Feng, Bai, and Chiang: Nationalist leaders.

12. "Gànbù jiǎnlì biǎo" ("Cadre biographies"), June 14, 1952, Luo Guozheng file 1.

13. "Xuéyuán jiàndìng shū" ("Student appraisals"), July 1, 1951, Luo Guozheng file 1.

14. Ibid.

15. "Jiāotōng bù X jiāotōng fēnxiào xuéyuán jiàndìng shū" ("Appraisal by the X communications school of the Ministry of Communications"), July 1, 1951, Luo Guozheng file 1.

16. "Jiāotōng tīng bǎowèi kē zhì C shì gōng'ān jú hán" ("Letter from the security section of the Department of Communications to the Public Security Bureau in C Municipality"), October 10, 1951, Luo Guozheng file 1.

17. "C shì rénmín zhèngfǔ gōng'ān jú dì yī chù yí wén dān" ("Unclassified document from the first office of the Public Security Bureau of the C Municipality People's Government"), December 12, 1951, Luo Guozheng file 1.

18. "X yóudiànjú Zhōnggòng zhībù wěiyuánhuì de shuōmíng" ("Declaration by X Post Office's CCP branch committee"), January 17, 1932; "X shěng rénmín zhèngfǔ gōng'ān tīng cáiliào huífù dān" ("Response to the material provided by the security office of X Provincial People's Government"), February 12, 1953, Luo Guozheng file 1.

19. "Hé X zhèngcí" ("He X's testimony"), February 21, 1953; "X shì rénmín zhèngfǔ gōng'ān jú shuǐshàng fēnjú zhì X jiāotōng tīng bǎowèi kē hán" ("Letter from the waterborne section of the Public Security Bureau to the security section of the Ministry of Communications," March 12, 1953, Luo Guozheng file 1.

20. "Hé X zhèngcí" ("He X's testimony"), March 15, 1953, Luo Guozheng file 1.

21. "X jiāotōng tīng bǎowèi kē gōnghán" ("Letter from the security office of the X Communications Department"), August 31, 1953, Luo Guozheng file 2.

22. "Duì Luó Guózhèng cáiliào de pīshì" ("Memo regarding the Luo Guozheng materials"), November 1, 1953, Luo Guozheng file 2.

23. "Luó Guózhèng cáiliào" ("Luo Guozheng materials"), July 1953, Luo Guozheng file 1.

24. "Zhíyuán dēngjì biǎo" ("Staff registration form"), February 2, 1950, Luo Guozheng file 1.

25. "Diàoxun xuéyuán dēngjì biǎo" ("Trainee registration form"), January 11, 1951, Luo Guozheng file 1.

26. "X, X, X, X guānyú Luó Guózhèng zài wǒ xiào gōngzuò shí de qíngkuàng" ("X, X, X, and X on Luo Guozheng's work in our school"), March 29 and 30 and August 26, 1956, Luo Guozheng file 1.

27. "X diànxìn xuéxiào gànbù jiàndìng biǎo" ("Cadre appraisal at X telecommunications school"), April 1954, Luo Guozheng file 1.

28. "Zhíyuán dēngjì biǎo" ("Staff registration form"), February 2, 1950; "Diào xun xuéyuán dēngjì biǎo" ("Trainee registration form"), January 11, 1951; "Sīxiǎng zǒngjié" ("Ideological summary"), June 1951, Luo Guozheng file 1.

29. "Diànxùn rényuán lǚlì biǎo" ("Personal details of telecommunications personnel"), December 5, 1954, Luo Guozheng file 1.

30. "Luó Guózhèng chūbù zīliào" ("Preliminary information regarding Luo Guozheng"), July 1955, Luo Guozheng file 1.

31. This can be found in various statements made against Luo Guozheng in Luo Guozheng file 2.

32. "Luó Guózhèng zhèngzhì lìshǐ shěnchá bàogào" ("Report on Luo Guozheng's political history"), May 31, 1956, Luo Guozheng file 2.

33. See "Diàochá duìxiàng Luó Guózhèng de wèntí" ("On the subject of investigation Luo Guozheng"), December 20, 1960, Luo Guozheng file 3.

34. "Chāo Qí Huìjūn dǎng'àn cáiliào" ("Material copied from Qi Huijun's file"), March 10, 1964, Luo Guozheng file 6.

35. "Jiǎnjǔ cáiliào dēngjì biǎo" ("Form for registering materials"), November 16, 1958, Luo Guozheng file 1.

36. "Zhěngfēng yùndòng rényuán shěnchá dēngjì biǎo" ("Registration form for personnel reviews during the rectification movement"), October 12, 1960; "Diàochá duìxiàng Luó Guózhèng de wèntí" ("On the subject of investigation Luo Guozheng"), December 20, 1960, Luo Guozheng file 2.

37. "Duì Luó Guózhèng de cáiliào" ("Materials on Luo Guozheng"), February 1, 1961, Luo Guozheng file 3.

38. "Zēng X dǎng'àn zhāilù" ("Excerpt from Zeng X's file"), February 12, 1961, Luo Guozheng file 3.

39. "Luó Guózhèng de bǔchōng diàochá tígāng" ("Outline for Luo Guozheng's supplementary investigation"), March 17, 1961, Luo Guozheng file 3.

40. "Duì Luó Guózhèng de diàochá cáiliào" ("On the materials concerning the investigation of Luo Guozheng"), March 20, 1961, Luo Guozheng file 3.

41. "Guānyú Hú X jiāodài 42–46 nián wǒ rènguò mǒu bù tèwù yíng èr lián liánzhǎng wèntí" ("On Hu X's confession that he served in 1942–46 as company commander in a special-agent battalion"), March 28, 1961, Luo Guozheng file 1.

42. "Guānyú Luó Guózhèng de qíngkuàng" ("On Luo Guozheng's situation"), April 14, 1961; "Guānyú Luó Guózhèng dì èr ci tánhuà" ("On Luo Guozheng's second conversation"), April 14, 1961, Luo Guozheng file 3.

43. "Zhěngfēng yùndòng rényuán shěnchá dēngjì biǎo" ("Registration form regarding personnel review during the rectification movement"), October 12, 1960, Luo Guozheng file 2.

44. "X zhì Zhāng chǎngzhǎng xìn" ("X's letter to farm head Zhang"), October 20, 1960, Luo Guozheng file 3.

45. "Luō Guózhèng jiǎnchá" ("Luo Guozheng investigation"), May 26, 1961, Luo Guozheng file 1.

46. "Guānyú Luó Guózhèng zài nóngchǎng yīguàn tōudào jí yīxiē cuòwù yánlùn" ("On Luo Guozheng's embezzlement and some erroneous remarks at the farm"), August 11, 1961, Luo Guozheng file 3.

47. "Wěi jūn jǐng xiàn rényuán dēngjì biǎo" ("Fake military police officers' registration form"), May 26, 1961, Luo Guozheng file 3.

48. "Wěi jūn jǐng xiàn rényuán dēngjì biǎo" ("Fake military police officers' registration form"), July 13, 1961, Luo Guozheng file 3.

49. "X zhì Zhāng chǎngzhǎng xìn" ("X's letter to farm head Zhang"), October 20, 1960, Luo Guo Zheng file 3.

50. "Guānyú Luó Guózhèng de xiànshí biǎoxiàn" ("On Luo Guozheng's current performance"), May 2, 1963, Luo Guozheng file 3.

51. Ibid.

52. "Guānyú Luó Guózhèng de zhèngzhì lìshǐ hé xiànshí biǎoxiàn cáiliào" ("On Luo Guozheng's political history and current performance"), March 4, 1964, Luo Guozheng file 6.

53. "Guānyú Luó Guózhèng de yǒuguān qíngkuàng" ("About Luo Guozheng's situation"), February 29, 1964, Luo Guozheng file 3.

54. "Guānyú jiāng Luó Guózhèng liè wéi zhòngdiǎn diàoyán duìxiàng de bàogào" ("Report on making Luo Guozheng a key target of research"), March 25, 1965, Luo Guozheng file 6.

55. "Guānyú gōu lián xiányí xiànsuǒ Luó Guózhèng de cáiliào" ("On clues leading to suspicions about Luo Guozheng"), July 16, 1965, Luo Guozhen file.

56. "Guānyú duì Luó Guózhèng de zhèngzhì lìshǐ diàochá tígāng" ("Outline regarding the investigation into Luo Guozheng's political history"), May 25, 1965, Luo Guozheng file 6.

57. "Xiānggǎng Wáng X de qíngkuàng" ("On Hong Kong Wang X's situation"), May 25, 1965, Luo Guozheng file 6

58. "Guānyú jiē pī Luó Guózhèng dàzìbào nèiróng huìbào" ("Report on the contents of the big-character poster exposing and criticising Luo Guozheng"), July 23, 1966, Luo Guozheng file 4.

59. Ibid.

60. "Luó Guózhèng jìnkuàng" ("Luo Guozheng current situation"), May 17, 1965, Luo Guozheng file 6.

61. "Guānyú Luó Guózhèng de yánxíng" ("On Luo Guozheng's words and deeds"), March 18, 1967, and "Luó Guózhèng de qíngkuàng" ("Luo Guozheng's situation"), 1967, Luo Guozheng file 4; "Yùshěn jìlù 4" ("Pre-trial record 4"), May 7, 1969 and "Yùshěn jìlù 6" ("Pre-trial record 6"), May 23, 1969, Luo Guozheng supplementary file 2.

62. "Yùshěn jìlù 6" ("Pre-trial record 6"), May 23, 1969, Luo Guozheng supplementary file 2.

63. Actually, three times.

64. "Guānyú Luó Guózhèng zài wénhuà dàgémìng zhōng jìnxíng pòhuài huódòng de shìshí" ("The facts concerning Luo Guozheng's carrying out sabotage in the Cultural Revolution"), March 30, 1967; "Jiēfā cáiliào" ("Exposing materials"), October 20, 1968, Luo Guozheng file 4.

65. "Duì Luó Guózhèng rúxià fǎndòng lùndiǎn xū xiěchéng zhèngmíng cáiliào" ("The following reactionary arguments of Luo Guozheng need to be written up as evidence"), 1968, Luo Guozheng file 4.

66. "Dàibǔ ànjiàn chéng pī biǎo" ("Arrest approval form"), October 5, 1968, Luo Guozheng supplementary file 1.

67. "Guānyú Guómíndǎng cánzhā yúniè Luó Guózhèng de zuìè shìshí" ("The evil facts about the Kuomintang remnant Luo Guozheng"), November 9, 1968, Luo Guozheng file 4.

68. "Fènnù jiēfā pīpàn fǎngémìng fènzi Luó Guózhèng de tāotiān zuìxíng" ("Angry criticism of the counter-revolutionary Luo Guozheng's heinous crimes"), November 20, 1968, Luo Guozheng file 4.

69. "Yùshěn jìlù 1" ("Pre-trial record 1"), April 30, 1969, Luo Guozheng supplementary file 2.

70. "Yùshěn jìlù 4" ("Pre-trial record 4"), May 7, 1969, Luo Guozheng supplementary file 2.

71. "Yùshěn jìlù 5" ("Pre-trial record 5"), May 21, 1969, Luo Guozheng supplementary file 2.

72. "Yùshěn jìlù" ("Pre-trial record"), September 1, 1969, Luo Guozheng supplementary file 2.

73. "X jiāodài cáiliào" ("X's confession"), April 7, 1961, Luo Guozheng file 3.

74. "Wěi yán wù xìtǒng de 'bǎowèi xiǎozǔ' gàikuàng" ("Regarding the fake salt system's 'security group'"), January 15, 1969, Luo Guozheng file 5.

75. "Guānyú Luó Guózhèng zài dì èr kānshǒusuǒ 53 jiān fáng de fǎndòng yánlùn" ("Luo Guozheng's reactionary utterances in cell 53 in the second detention center"), March 2, 1970, Luo Guozheng file 5.

76. "Guānyú Luó Guózhèng fàngdú qíngkuàng" ("Regarding Luo Guozheng's spreading poisonous ideas"), March 30, 1970; "X bàogào" ("X's report"), November 12, 1971, Luo Guozheng file 5.

77. "Xúnwèn bǐlù" ("Interrogation transcript"), October 22, 1971, Luo Guozheng file 5.

78. Regarding Luo Guozheng's escape after his capture in 1939, the trial officers in September 1969 found that his previous confession had concealed various facts, and that he had worked for the Japanese before his escape. He was therefore a traitor. See "Guānyú Luó Guózhèng zài yījiǔsānjiǔ nián jiǔ yuè shíliù rì zhì yījiǔsānjiǔ nián shí'èr yuè sānshí rì zhè duàn zhèngzhì lìshǐ de qíngkuàng diàochá bàogào" ("Report on the investigation into the political history of Luo Guozheng between September 16, 1939, and December 30, 1939"), September 27, 1969, Luo Guozheng file 1.

79. "Duì Luó Guózhèng chǔlǐ yìjiàn" ("Views on how to deal with Luo Guozheng"), September 24, 1971, Luo Guozheng supplementary file 1.

80. "Diàoyán duìxiàng shěnpī biǎo" ("Approval form regarding the object of investigation"), November 1, 1973, and June 9, 1979, Luo Guozheng file 1.

81. "Qíngkuàng huìbào biǎo" ("Response form"), March 14, 1979, Luo Guozheng file 1.

82. "Guānyú chèxiāo zhòngdiǎn diàoyán duìxiàng Luó Guózhèng de yìjiàn" ("On the revocation of the decision on the key research object Luo Guozheng"), November 10, 1980, Luo Guozheng file 1.

INDEX

acupuncture, 85, 88, 97, 100–101, 102, 103–4, 105, 110

administrative control. *See* control and supervision

"alien elements," 24, 162, 231

Anti-Japanese War, 3, 7; Che Shaowen's experiences during, 185–87, 188, 189, 190–93, 195, 196, 197; Luo Guozheng's experiences during, 212, 214–15, 216–18, 223; Mu Guoxuan's experiences during, 115–17, 121–22. *See also* Japanese occupation

anti-rightist campaign, 38, 61–62, 64, 197, 242. *See also* rectification movements; rightists

August 31 Rebels, 64, 65, 66–71

backbone reactionaries, 5, 6, 79, 81, 163, 253n5; Liao Xuechang as, 29, 31, 35, 37, 38, 41, 50

back-door procurement, 73, 106, 107, 198–99, 201, 239

bad elements: common and counter-revolutionary, 5, 6–7, 53; definition of, 6, 53, 239; hats worn by, 5, 7, 75; hooligans as, 6, 71; one of four categories, 54, 240; policies directed against, 7, 53–54; reform of, 7; term used by Kuomintang and CCP, 6–7, 53; women as, 10. *See also* counter-revolutionaries; four categories; hats

bad timing, 1, 11

Bai Chongxi, 217

Banbu Bridge Detention Center, 17–18

bandits, 7, 81, 239; Communist, 32, 127; as counter-revolutionaries, 10, 63; Japanese, 87, 116; Kuomintang, 41, 79, 92, 93, 171, 220, 223, 229, 236

beatings, 16–17, 19, 65, 77, 151, 154, 187; of fathers by sons, 117; under the Kuomintang, 215, 232; of maids, 115; of sons by fathers, 166, 168, 169

beggars, 8, 115, 246n13

Beijing, 19, 109, 138–39

Beijing Artillery Bureau, 15

Beria (Stalin's interior minister), 125, 259n25

big-character posters, 60, 61, 62, 64, 68, 229–30. *See also* wall posters

black elements, 246n13, 249n43. *See also* bad elements; five black categories

black material, 147, 155, 239

bureaucracy, 12, 167, 239; capitalist, 23–24, 185; couplet satirizing, 146; criticism of, 55, 60, 61, 119, 198, 230; prison, 8; reactionaries in, 242

bureaucratic landlords, 113, 121, 123, 125

Bureau of Commerce and Industry, 194

cadres, 1, 9, 159, 179, 197; defined, 239; personal history form, 25, 57, 114. *See also* cadre school

cadre school: attended by author, 16, 21; Che Shaowen and, 182–85, 188; evaluation of political awareness and historical problems, 184, 188, 189; Mu Guoxuan and, 117–18, 121, 123, 127, 129, 134

collective ownership, 156, 240

communes, 226, 234, 240

Communist Manifesto, 48

Communist Youth League, 54, 55, 56–57, 136, 137, 243; Shang Haowen and, 164, 177, 178, 179

comrades' society (Kuomintang), 115, 117, 123, 127, 130

Confucianism, 116, 124, 173, 177

Constitution of 1954, 246n13

contradictions: between the enemy and the people, 74, 132, 133; among the people, 40, 76, 78, 208, 240

control and supervision, 5, 6, 7, 74; dual-guarantee supervision, 255n41; key control subjects, 226, 227; objects of, 9, 41, 43, 51, 52, 69, 74, 76, 98, 108, 131, 141, 168, 251n39; wages under, 41, 248n31

corruption: business and, 11, 196; campaigns against, 69–70, 139, 141; Che Shaowen and, 199–200; targeted in Three Antis, 198

counter-revolutionaries: active and historical, 5–6; bandits as, 10, 63; campaigns against, 4–5, 37–38, 162; categories of, 5, 163; under control, 5, 6, 43, 108, 248n31, 251n39; "counter-revolutionary social base," 10; definition of, 5–6; distinguished from other bad elements, 5, 6–7, 53; hats of, 7, 11, 24–25, 41, 52, 100, 104, 107, 131–32, 208, 224; Hu Feng as, 29, 120, 125, 162, 163, 164, 177, 241; internal retention policy, 101, 256n49; landlords as, 10; number of, 9; office for suppression of (purge office), 123, 125, 126, 127, 129, 260n38; the old lag at Banbu Bridge Detention Center, 1, 15–21; as one of four categories, 54, 240; political and economic, 3; radio broadcasts, 70, 73, 75; regulations for handling, 5–6, 20, 38; seeking refuge in Taiwan, 19, 20; in the Soviet Union and Eastern Europe, 2, 246n13; treatment of, 3, 7, 47; voices of, 1; women as, 9–10. *See also* Fang Liren; five black categories; Liao Xuechang; Luo Guozheng; Mu Guoxuan; Sufan; Zhenfan

courts, 2, 8, 19, 117, 134; "fake," 31; sentencing by, 36, 78, 114, 131, 133; Supreme Court, 37, 75; vindication of Hu Feng, 132. *See also* trials

crimes: of bad elements, 6, 53–54; of Che Shaowen, 201–2; of Chi Weirong, 142, 143–44, 147, 151–55; counter-revolutionary, 5, 6, 18, 19, 20, 37, 47, 208; criminal cases, 3–4; of Fang Liren, 92, 93, 94, 96–97, 103–4, 105, 106, 107, 108; "heinous," 1, 20, 25, 27, 37, 59, 74, 77, 131, 151, 172; historical, 33–34, 94, 103, 107, 108, 127,

130, 241; of Li Lesheng, 59, 62, 63, 69, 70, 71, 72, 73–75, 77–78; of Liao Xuechang, 29, 30, 31, 32, 33–35, 36, 37, 38, 47, 51; of Luo Guozheng, 208, 223, 232–33, 235; of Mu Guoxuan, 127, 128, 130–31; thought, 1; war, 4, 24, 25, 243. *See also* theft

criticism and self-criticism, 219. *See also* mass criticism; *and under* Che Shaowen; Li Lesheng; Mu Guoxuan

cronyism, 176, 177

Cultural Revolution: campaigns and movements of, 4, 69, 71, 75, 155, 210, 234, 251n39; categories and elements during, 5, 45, 108, 181; Che Shaowen and, 181, 207; Chi Weirong and, 147–48, 153, 155; and class struggle, 230; dates of, 240; as factional struggle, 210, 231, 240; Fang Liren and, 108–9; Li Lesheng and, 64–65; Luo Guozheng and, 208, 209–10, 229–35; purifying class ranks, 75, 231; Red Guards and Rebels in, 64, 65, 66; rustication, 181; saying the wrong things during, 211; wall posters, 147, 229–30

Dai Li, 31

Dalian, 128

dancing, 138, 142, 143, 144, 149

"dangerous classes," 8. *See also* beggars; prostitutes

declassed elements, 7

Deng Ping, 6

Deng Rong, Branch Secretary, 60, 61, 62, 74

Deng Xiaoping, 241, 242. *See also* reform and opening up

diaries, 113–14, 154, 157–58. *See also under* Chi Weirong; Mu Guoxuan; Shang Haowen

doctors, 11–12, 119, 121, 126, 131. *See also* Fan Liren

Dong Biwu, 37

dual-guarantee supervision, 255n41. *See also* Three Guarantees and One Guarantor

electoral system, 122

"elements," 5, 7, 20, 246n13. *See also* bad elements

Engman, Puck, 246n13

escape attempts, 19, 65, 135, 139, 140, 217

espionage, 11, 212, 220, 235. *See also* secret agents

ethnic minorities, 38, 39

"evil hegemons and local bullies," 9

executions, 4, 5, 7, 10, 94, 96, 168, 171, 179, 187, 190, 224–25; of Beria, 259n25; of Wang Shiwei, 243. *See also* killing

external investigations, 29, 62–63, 67, 69, 129–30, 162, 293, 208, 240

element, 219–20; overseas connections of, 11, 227–29, 235; punishment of, 210; review finding and rehabilitation of 1979, 208–9, 210, 211, 235; sent to the countryside, 226–27, 235; and the Sufan movement, 222–23, 224; suspected as spy and traitor, 220–21, 223–24, 229, 232–34, 235, 273n28; used name Luo Liang, 215, 217; wife of, 212, 221, 224, 228, 229, 236; work history, 212, 213–15, 217–18, 221–22, 224

Luo Ruiqing, 253n5

Manchus, 160
manual labor: Li Lesheng and, 74, 76; Liao Xuechang and, 24, 38–40; Mu Guoxuan and, 114, 131; of prisoners, 8; re-education through, 241; reform through, 8, 12, 17, 76, 108–9, 181, 201–3, 207, 242; Shang Haowen and, 178
Mao Benqing, 67, 69
Mao Zedong, 2, 3, 53, 241; criticism of, 234; and the Cultural Revolution, 211; death of, 18; emphasis on class struggle, 41, 104; on peasants, 158–59, 175; preface to *Materials Relating to the Hu Feng Counter-Revolutionary Clique,* 29; Shang Haowen on, in his diary, 158; writings of, 51, 65, 99, 165
Mao Zedong Thought, 73, 209
"marginal man" (Lewin), 13
Marxism, 5, 8, 173, 179
mass criticism, 41, 72, 148–49, 151, 162–63
mass line, 3, 159, 167, 241
mass trials, 3, 4, 8
Materials Relating to the Hu Feng Counter-Revolutionary Clique, 29
medical parole, 203–7
Mencius, 21–22
merchants, 11, 125, 161, 198; as friends of Fang Liren, 81, 83, 84, 89; Che Shaowen as, 11, 182, 186, 190–91, 197, 198, 200
migrants, 144
Military Control Commission, 74, 79; "Measures for the handling of persons returned to Beijing," 109; repentance registration required of Kuomintang agents, 79–80, 92
Ministry of Public Security, 111, 231, 253n5, 255n41. *See also* Public Security Bureaus
Mongolia, 128
Mu Guoxuan: appeals lodged by, 114, 132–33; attended cadre school then dodged assignment, 117–18, 121, 123, 127, 129, 134; attitude toward Communist Party, 115, 117, 118, 122, 123–25; case review in 1984, 134; confessions and self-criticisms, 120, 121–22, 128–29; criminal activities of, 127–28; diary of, 113–14, 122–27, 130, 132, 133–34; failed probation after sentence, 131–32, 133; family and background, 113, 115, 121; hat of, 131–32; historical autobiographies, 114–18; historical crimes, 127, 130; investigation and interrogation of, 126–31; materials on, 114–15; medical study and work assignment, 118–20; as reactionary and counter-revolutionary element, 113–14, 118, 123, 126; reactionary attitude of, 113–14, 120–22, 124, 130–31; rehabilitation of, 114; request for transfer, 119–20, 121; sentenced to control and manual labor, 114, 131; status as cadre, 114; and the Sufan movement, 113, 114, 118, 120–22, 123, 125, 131, 132, 133; suicide attempt, 126, 131; support for Chiang Kai-shek and the Kuomintang, 115–17, 118, 120, 122, 124, 126–27, 128–29; wrote reactionary slogans, 128–29, 130, 132; and the Zhenfan movement, 128–29, 130, 134
Mukden Incident, 186

Nanjing Massacre, 184
National Revolutionary Comrades' Association, 79
natural rights theory (Rousseau), 172, 177
Neo-Confucianism, 124
New Democracy Youth League, 54
New Fourth Army, 191, 192, 196, 217, 223, 241
"New Life schools," 8
news censorship, 234
newspapers, 122, 125, 146, 175
Nimu Cooperative, 41, 43–44, 45
"nine black categories," 5
19th Route Army, 214
Niu, Director, 60, 64
North China Military General Hospital, 97
novels, 59, 183; pornographic, 72, 73
Number One Detention Center (Banbu Bridge Detention Center), 17–18

objects of dictatorship, 6, 46, 47, 50, 148
Office for the Suppression of Counter-revolutionaries, 260n38. *See also* purge office
"one thing to attack and three things to oppose," 69, 71, 75, 155, 210, 234, 251n39
on-the-spot education, 71, 72
opening up, 21, 50, 132, 156, 241

Soviet Union (continued)
   186–87; Ma Guoxuan's views on, 128, 130;
   radio broadcasts, 70; revisionism of, 66;
   and the Second World War, 122, 125; Shang
   Haowen on, in his diary, 159
spies, 220. See also secret agents
Spring Festival, 48, 49, 93–94, 143, 144
Stalin, Joseph, 3, 4
Stoelzner (German instructor), 216
Strauss, Julia, 4, 10
"striking hard," 20, 41, 234, 251n39
struggle (douzheng), 7, 242; meetings, 4, 19, 38,
   45, 64, 66–67, 95, 117, 121, 132, 151, 165–68, 174,
   230; mass criticism and, 162; small-group, 8,
   33, 93, 126, 177, 179; two-line, 73, 115, 131, 242.
   See also class struggle
study classes, 69, 71, 72
Sufan movement (1955–56), 5, 34, 243; Che
   Shaowen and, 195; compared with Zhenfan,
   57; directive of July 1, 1955, 29; Dong Biwu on
   spirit of, 37; Fang Liren and, 91–92, 94, 95,
   97, 101; "Interim Provisions for Interpreting
   and Handling Policy Boundaries Regarding Counter-Revolutionaries and Other
   Bad Elements," 38; Li Lesheng and, 57; Liao
   Xuechang and, 24, 28–32, 34, 36–37, 39; Luo
   Guozheng and, 222–23, 224; mass criticism
   and struggle procedures, 162–63; Mu Guoxuan and, 113, 114, 118, 120–22, 123, 125, 131, 132,
   133; Qi Huijun and, 224; Shang Haowen and,
   157, 158, 161, 162, 179; targets of, 222
Sun Yat-sen, 115, 165, 216, 243
supplementary confession, 30, 37, 44, 65, 68, 94
sworn brotherhoods, 58, 59, 62, 63, 67–69, 74

Taiwan: flight to, 63, 187, 189, 193, 223, 229, 242;
   items from, 149; Kuomintang agents in, 235;
   Ma Guoxuan's stand on, 128; radio broadcasts from, 19, 70, 120, 128, 146; relatives in,
   223, 229, 235–36; slogans about liberating, 234
Tang Xixian, 136
Tao, Lung-sheng, 3–4
Tax Police (Kuomintang), 213, 217, 218, 220, 223
theft: by Chi Weirong, 142–44, 148, 149, 151, 152,
   153, 154–55; food, 153, 226; by the old lag, 1,
   16–19, 20
Thompson, Malcolm, 246n13
thought crimes, 1
thought reform, 5, 7–8, 44
thought reports, 45–46, 48, 49, 50, 72, 74, 77,
   206

Three Antis (sanfan): 1951, 5, 28, 243, 193–94;
   1960, 139, 140–41, 198
three categories, 5. See also four categories
Three Guarantees and One Guarantor, 98–99,
   255n41
Three Hard Years, 102, 106, 142, 243
Three People's Principles, 87, 217
Three People's Youth Corps, 79. See also
   Kuomintang: Youth Corps
Three Red Banners, 230
Three Selfs, 85–88, 115, 117, 127, 130, 243
Tian'anmen Incident of 1976, 16, 19, 21
trade unions, 55, 60, 61–62, 70, 95
traitors, 11, 116, 185, 189; as bad elements, 5, 6, 53;
   Che Shaowen as, 192–93, 195–97; Liu Shaoqi
   as, 235; Luo Guozheng as, 220–21, 223–24,
   229, 232–34, 235, 273n28; "national," 3. See
   also secret agents
trials, 3, 4, 8, 12, 33, 41, 77, 90, 232
two-line struggle, 73, 115, 131, 242. See also plane
   of principle

unemployment, 48, 194–95, 203
United States: imperialists, 2, 75, 183, 185, 186;
   praise of, 128, 147, 148, 154, 187; Sino-US
   training classes, 34; war against, in Korea, 119

vagrants, 8
Vietnam, 4
Voice of America, 70, 130

wall posters, 125, 142, 147, 154, 155. See also big-
   character posters
Wang Anshi, 165
Wang Heting, 144–45
Wang Hongcai, 149
Wang Hongfa, 149
Wang Jingwei, 116, 217, 243
Wang Shiwei, 161
Wang Wenguang, 216
war crimes, 4, 24, 25, 243
Wei Lihuang, 128
Wen, Duke of Jin, 124, 259n22
Whampoa Military Academy, 120, 131, 210
women as counter-revolutionaries, 9–10
working class: Kuomintang remnants, 23, 77; as
   leadership of revolution, 158, 167, 170, 175,
   176, 179, 184–85; meager incomes of, 149–50;
   as part of the people, 23, 24; purifying the
   ranks of, 98. See also factory workers
work points, 18, 145

Founded in 1893,
UNIVERSITY OF CALIFORNIA PRESS
publishes bold, progressive books and journals
on topics in the arts, humanities, social sciences,
and natural sciences—with a focus on social
justice issues—that inspire thought and action
among readers worldwide.

The UC PRESS FOUNDATION
raises funds to uphold the press's vital role
as an independent, nonprofit publisher, and
receives philanthropic support from a wide
range of individuals and institutions—and from
committed readers like you. To learn more, visit
ucpress.edu/supportus.